Impurity of Blood

Impurity of Blood

Defining Race in Spain, 1870–1930

JOSHUA GOODE

Louisiana State University Press ✶ Baton Rouge

Published by Louisiana State University Press
Copyright © 2009 by Louisiana State University Press
All rights reserved
Manufactured in the United States of America
First printing

Designer: Barbara Neely Bourgoyne
Typeface: Quadraat
Printer and binder: Thomson-Shore, Inc.

Library of Congress Cataloging-in-Publication Data
Goode, Joshua, 1969–
  Impurity of blood : defining race in Spain, 1870–1930 / Joshua Goode.
    p. cm.
  Includes bibliographical references and index.
  ISBN 978-0-8071-3516-7 (cloth : alk. paper) 1. Ethnology—Spain—History. 2.
Anthropology—Spain—History. 3. Race—Social aspects—Spain—History. 4. Spain—Race
relations—History. I. Title.

  DP52.G684 2009
  305.800946—dc22

                                                            2009021199

The paper in this book meets the guidelines for permanence and durability of the Committee
on Production Guidelines for Book Longevity of the Council on Library Resources. ∞

To Karina

Contents

Acknowledgments

This project began, presumably like many others, with a brief conversation between student and graduate advisor. In my case, because my advisor did not work on Spanish history, I worried particularly about speaking in terms broad enough to be interesting. I offered a nervous recitation of the idea, waited through an anxious moment of silence, and finally received for my efforts an interested upturned eye. The nervousness proved to be good training for explaining a topic in Spanish history to an audience most often not particularly interested in Spanish history. My efforts to keep people's attention from drifting out the window, whether successful or not, have led to the accumulation of many debts and much gratitude owed to a long list of people and institutions that have aided in the completion of this work.

The formulation of this topic and my effort to ground it in a comparative way owes much to the mentoring of Peter Baldwin at the University of California, Los Angeles. It was his upturned eye that gave me a sense of the potential of the topic. He continues to be a cheerful, patient, and reliable mentor and friend. Carolyn Boyd at the University of California, Irvine, has also been a constant source of aid, saving me from any number of blunders of thought and writing throughout many years. Her friendship and guidance, especially as this project transitioned from dissertation to book, never wavered and always proved essential. It has never failed to amaze me that James Amelang, of the Universidad Autónoma de Madrid, working well outside his own time period, has seemed to know more about this project than its author. I cannot measure his immense help or friendship. Others colleagues and friends have provided generous and seemingly unbounded time, patience, and debate, including Courtney Booker, Sandie Holguín, Stephen Jacobsen, Geoff Jensen, Karen Lang, C. Brian Morris, David N. Myers, Pamela Radcliff, Chris Schmidt-Nowara, Douglas Smith, Marla Stone, Eric Storm, Enric Ucelay Da

Cal, and Robert Wohl. My colleagues in the History Department at Occidental College always treated me and this project like one of their own. Any positive contribution I make in this work owes much to the input of all of these people. Even though it goes without saying, any errors in the text are mine alone.

Given the understudied nature of the Spanish sciences and the vagaries of the concept of race, my work on this topic benefited from the help of many skilled people in finding appropriate archives or the existence of unpublished sources. Deserving special mention is Patricia Zahnisser at the Commission for Educational Exchange between the United States of America and Spain, which administers the Fulbright in Spain. She helped me contact numerous archives, large and small, a service so important when at first these archives were reluctant to open their doors. Once at the archives, I was aided by many generous archivists, especially Rosana del Andrés of the Ministerio de Interior in Madrid. Dr. Miguel Grimau of the Facultad de Medicina and Dr. Miguel Botella of the Anthropology Department, both of the Universidad de Granada, gave me generous access to and advice on handling Federico Olóriz's papers. Dr. José Martínez Pérez did the same for materials at the Instituto de Historia de la Medicina at the Universidad Complutense in Madrid. Also at the Complutense, Juan Carlos Suárez and his staff at the Biblioteca-Hemeroteca of the Facultad de Medicina gave me exceptional access to the library. In the Basque country, Dr. Francisco Etxeberria Gabilondo at the Universidad del País Vasco has provided me with constant help and invaluable materials relating to the life of Telésforo de Aranzadi. Manuel Armijo Valenzuela and his excellent staff, Ignacio and Asunción, at the Real Academia Nacional de Medicina were exceedingly generous with finding resources materials, catalogued and uncatalogued, in their archive. Also deserving special mention are the staffs at a variety of other libraries and archives, namely: the Real Academia de Historia; the Casa-Museo Unamuno at the Universidad de Salamanca; the Hemeroteca Municipal in Madrid; the Archivo General Militar in Segovia; the Servicio Histórico Militar in Madrid; the library of the Museo Nacional de Etnología in Madrid. Dietrich Briesemeister, the former director, and the staff at the Ibero-Amerikanisches Institut in Berlin also were generous in providing me a home for research and camaraderie while in Germany. On this continent, I am grateful to John de la Fontaine and the staff at Occidental College's library, who cheerfully and quickly answered many questions, large and small. I also would like to thank the staff at the College of Physicians in Philadelphia for use of some materials on Spanish doctors unavailable elsewhere.

The following institutions supplied financial support that allowed me to perform archival research in Spain and enjoy unfettered time to produce this work. The Graduate Division and the History Department at UCLA both provided important grants, a Chancellor's Dissertation Grant and an ICFOG, respectively, to complete research and writing. The Commission for Educational Exchange between the United States of America and Spain administered the Fulbright Fellowship that allowed me to perform research in Spain. The Del Amo Endowment at UCLA also provided essential assistance for this purpose. Finally, the Program for Cultural Cooperation between Spain's Ministry of Culture and U.S. Universities Research Grant allowed me to revisit archives and find new materials in Spain important for the development of this book.

Back in the United States, the criticisms, suggestions, and ideas of participants at conferences where I have presented portions of this work have sharpened arguments and clarified ideas. I especially appreciate the invitation from José Álvarez Junco to present parts of my work to the Iberian Study Group of the Center for European Studies at Harvard University. Thanks go to David Ringrose and Pamela Radcliffe of the University of California, San Diego, for the opportunity to present works in progress to the Southwestern Spanish History Consortium at UCSD. Also, participants in the UCLA European History Colloquium helped me expand the focus of this work and place it in a wider historical context. Lastly, I want to express my deep appreciation to the many discussants and participants at the annual meetings of the Society of Spanish and Portuguese Historical Studies, where many portions of this work have been presented over the years.

Some colleagues and friends who have read and commented on many different versions of this work deserve to be singled out. The best part of the personal camaraderie and intellectual debate shared in graduate school has been that it has remained long after. Thanks to Rachel Bindman, Ethan Kleinberg, David McBride, Tom Millar, Charles Romney, Gavriel Rosenfeld, Adam Rubin, and Eugene Sheppard. Alisa Plant, Lee Sioles, and the staff at the Louisiana State University Press deserve special thanks for shepherding this work through its various stages. I would like to thank Susan Murray, who provided extraordinarily precise and meticulous copyediting that improved this manuscript immensely.

There are a few people to whom I owe the greatest debt. First are my parents, Paul and Judith Goode, who have helped guide me and my work through the years. My mother, an anthropologist with a long history of training graduate students, performed dual duty as parent and informal academic adviser, reading my work and commenting on it, all with far more than a mother's eye or interest, and she worked on weekends, too. Gratitude also is too small a word to describe what I feel for those who have slept under the same roof as I have while I worked on this project. The excitement that my children, Milo and Anabel, have had for the appearance of Daddy's book, even if their interest in its subject is yet to be determined, has provided all of the impetus I needed to complete it. Most important, though, has been the patience, love, and companionship that my wife, Karina Sterman, has given me through the years. She knew me first as someone working on his dissertation, married me anyway, and now persists in making me feel like I do something worthwhile. For those not so little things, I dedicate this book to her.

Impurity of Blood

1. The Racial Alloy

The Meanings and Uses of Racial Identity in Late-Nineteenth- and Early-Twentieth-Century Spain

A Jewish church? . . . [I]t could mean many things! Synagogues, mosques, and
churches passed into and out of many hands. Jews, Moors, Christians were all
here, and the contact with Spain purified them.

—from *Raza*, screenplay by Francisco Franco, 1941

Franco's screenplay *Raza* remains famous today mostly as a curiosity, a mediocre film written by a dictator not normally associated with literary pursuits.[1] Almost always overlooked in the discussion of the film is the
meaning of the title Franco chose: *Raza* (Race). What could a Spanish dictator
who had courted the Nazis allies in the Spanish Civil War mean by the word
"race"? Franco's racial ideals certainly appeared to have little to do with the
kind of pure lineage that obsessed the Nazis.[2] Indeed, his idea of race—that
of a National Catholic state as the happy meeting ground of many different
peoples willingly blended together—differed from most European conceptions of race in this period.[3] Franco believed that racial strength was based
on mixture and hybridity—the fusion of peoples. In fact, the notion of the
Spanish race he proposed was, in a sense, counterintuitive, particularly at
this moment in European history. Racial strength, in Franco's view, emanated
from bringing races together, not the domination of one pure race over all
mixed ones. Yet, even given the distinctiveness of this formulation, historians
have directed very little attention toward Spanish notions of race in the first
half of the twentieth century.

The actual explanation for this historical neglect of racial thought in
Spain is wide-ranging and begins first with the effort to deny that Spain ever
possessed an idea of race akin to those of its European counterparts. Some

scholars have assumed that for a few obvious reasons, racial identities simply failed to develop in Spain. On the one hand, Spain's multiethnic past would undermine any defense of Spanish racial purity. The backwardness of Spain's scientific disciplines in the nineteenth and early twentieth centuries also would have seemed to forestall any attempt to formulate scientific theories of the Spanish race. Others have claimed that the missionary spirit within traditional Spanish Catholicism clashed with the idea of an immutable racial identity that denied any possibility of conversion or change. The reality of Spain's experience with racial ideas—the existence of scientific inquiry into the makeup of the Spanish race, the use of this knowledge in the establishment of social policy, and the later shifts in the meanings ascribed to this racial identity—belies these explanations.

Despite historical and religious limitations, Spanish racial theorists did exist in the late nineteenth and early twentieth centuries, when race and racial sciences were most in vogue in the rest of Europe. Spaniards devised their own racial identities using scientifically substantiated racial ideas. Even more interesting is that these theorists confronted head-on the apparent limitations of Spain's history and actually used them as the defining characteristics of la raza española. In the late nineteenth and early twentieth centuries, racial theorists forged an identity whose main buttress was Spain's history of multiethnic contact. Racial strength was rooted in the proficiency of the Spanish race to fuse the different groups that had coexisted on the Iberian Peninsula. Even more, as the quotation from Franco's Raza suggests, Spanish racial ideas assumed that Spaniards and their various component parts were made all the stronger for the mixture. Thus, the task of the Spanish sciences was to trace the history of racial fusion: to study both the separate elements of the Spanish composition and the factors already existent in Spain that had nurtured their positive qualities and expunged the negative ones.

This study shows that, although Franco's Raza was written within the historical context of the Civil War's aftermath, the basic framework of the ideas he expressed in that work was rooted in earlier grappling with Spanish racial identity in the late nineteenth and early twentieth centuries. In fact, it is the actual historical ubiquity of racial language and the constantly shifting meanings of this racial discourse throughout the nineteenth and early twentieth centuries that make such a study important.[4] Even the most cursory glance through early-twentieth-century periodical literature will uncover specific references to the discrete and unique Spanish raza. A more focused search would reveal the variety of often competing political ideologies that shared language touting Spain's unique racial identity. Yet, shared language did not necessarily imply shared goals, and the political implications of this racial identity varied quite broadly across the ideological spectrum.

Still, the inclusion of Spain in this historiography would surprise most historians of race. For too long, historians of Europe have focused on race through the lens of the Nazi regime, forming an implicit and often explicit comparison between any manifestation of racial language and the Nazi genocide performed in the name of a supposed racial purity. Spanish racial ideas have been dismissed because they seemed to have had a different basis— a celebration of racial hybridity that could not then be considered "racial thought" because it did not conform to the idea of racial purity espoused by the Nazi German model. This reliance on a false comparison is of course quite common in European history. As in the debates about the model Bourgeois Revolution or Industrial Revolution, historians tend to identify one nation as emblematic or original in its experience of the phenomenon and then assess the validity or authenticity of the phenomenon elsewhere in terms of the experience of that nation.[5] More than just a historical habit, however, this tendency to compare national experiences often hides an intentional effort to advance clear political purposes. On the one hand, ascribing to opposing political groups the taint of racial ideology always resonates with the specter of genocide that lurks behind any contemporary claim of racism in Europe. This tendency is most pronounced today in discussions dealing with the nettlesome issues of immigration, citizenship, and the rise of right-wing extremism in postwar Europe.[6] On the other hand, such comparisons can serve the exculpatory mission of denying one nation's flirtation with racial politics or ethnic ideas as naturally akin to the Nazis, i.e., as potentially genocidal.

Spaniards, for instance, have gone to great lengths to deny any similarity between Iberian racial thought and its northern European counterparts. A common boast, for example, among members of the Spanish fascist party, the Falange Española Tradicionalista, even before the Civil War and repeated long after World War II, was that Spanish fascism had always remained free of racial or racist ideas. The fascist party founder, José Antonio Primo de Rivera, who died in the first months of the Civil War, is reputed never to have made racist comments in any of his writings.[7] Dionisio Ridruejo, the poet and early member of the Falange Española, best summed up the Falangist disavowal of racist ideas in the late 1970s: "Spanish fascism differentiated itself from Nazism by having no racist policies which would, in a country as racially mixed and as Catholic as Spain, have been nonsense."[8] Or, as the writer and later Falangist propagandist Ernesto Giménez Caballero wrote in 1932: "Hitlerism is acquiring renewed vigor because of its myth of blood purity. . . . If Spain one day decides to institute a Fiesta de la Raza, it will be precisely in the opposite sense of the German idea. We deny the purity of our race, admitting that the foundation of our genius is the fusion of races."[9]

Yet, such constant comparisons with Nazi horrors and barbarity have truncated the actual purposes of the historical study of racial thought. One should not study race simply to keep tabs on those areas on the potential slippery slope to genocide. Race's ubiquity as a topic in almost every modern national context demonstrates that it is a concept far more widely attractive and multipurposed. Extremely flexible in its meaning, race has been the most dangerous idea of the nineteenth and twentieth centuries. This is not because racists have always used used the term coherently and systematically—even the Nazis, after all, were wildly inconsistent in their racial definitions and practices.[10] The danger of race is that it has functioned more as a worldview than as an idea; it has been used as a method of structuring society according to a supposedly natural order of difference and hierarchy that includes some in the racial fold and excludes many others.

It has been the modern state that has advanced these views of a racially structured society, most often in service of nationalism. European nationalist movements after the French Revolution functioned as the great equalizer, placing all those living within the national territory on an equal footing as English, French, Spaniard, Italian, German, Pole, Dane, and so on. Social and economic class would not matter; all citizens would be equal based on their rights as humans. Yet, defining inclusion in the nation was also invariably a process of exclusion.[11] Nationalists of the nineteenth century, even actively nonracist ones like Johann Gottfried von Herder, worked very hard to define not only who belonged but, by default, who did not. Behaviors, attitude, language, dress, and appearance all played roles in assessing who was of the nation and who was not. This kind of cultural nationalism worked together with the rise of Romanticism, which sought to explore the passionate, irrational side of humanity, not just the rational side promoted by the Enlightenment, to fashion the ethnic nation. A state defined by ethnicity saw itself as a spiritual entity, with its citizenship partaking of an inborn collective soul and possessed of an uncontrollable, indelible personal drive to act, think, and feel in a particular way. Even more important, this belonging was natural, transmitted down through the ages so that people were connected inimitably to their forebears. By the end of the nineteenth century, bureaucracies, state functionaries, and nationalist ideologues began to define both internal populations and colonized ones according to a rigid set of such natural differences, not merely by phenotype, like skin color, but also by other characteristics all considered inherited and indelible. Racial thought demonstrated that even where obvious physical differences in appearance did not exist, they could easily be created. Thus, the agents of the state, especially in the late nineteenth and early twentieth centuries—the newly minted legions of anthropologists, census takers, biologists, sociologists, and even prison officials—worked especially hard to show that racial differences were real and identifiable only through expert scientific detection, not just visual observation.

Yet, the historical debates about race in Europe have usually veered off into disagreements about the content of the racial idea presented in various contexts. What, in fact, does race mean in France, Germany, or England? Is "race" merely a charged political term, different from more comfortable or easily pinned-down locutions like "ethnicity," "nationality," or even "class"? Are these all equally ambiguous identities, as Etienne Balibar and Immanuel Wallerstein have said, or is race the "hardest and most exclusive form of identity," as Eric Weitz has argued?[12] Again, if race is better understood as a process, as a mode of thought, a system of (il)logic, rather than a fixed and clear idea, then a study of race in modern Spain demonstrates that racial thought can exist regardless of the content of the racial ideal. What Spain's manifest notion of racial fusion proves is that the structure of racial thought—the logical connections between ideas and social deployment of these ideas—is a constant in the formation of racial ideas, regardless of the definition. Hence, the danger of race is not just the potential slippery slope toward genocide as in Nazi German society but also its malleability, its tendency to fit into any historical milieu and be defined in manifold, often even contradictory ways. Inserting Spanish racial notions into this debate proves that definitions matter far less than historical context and that the purposes to which racial thought is put show how and when racial logic operates and even when it can ultimately become deadly. What has become clear in the study of race in the United States and Latin America has not necessarily arrived in European historiography: that racial identity at its core is historical, "partial, unstable, contextual and fragmentary."[13]

Some recent histories of race in usually unstudied areas of Europe suggest an opening of the race concept in a way that welcomes this recognition of instability and drive for contextualization. Recent works on the Soviet Union have demonstrated how the Soviet ideal of a single-class society actually relied upon racial, national, and ethnic characteristics to structure and order Stalin's Soviet Union. Others have argued that because Stalinist policies were not clearly articulated as racial programs, it is wrong to label them as racist. Some have countered that many states have practiced "racism without the concept" of race.[14] Such states defined difference based on immutable characteristics that were passed down over time, and used them to disenfranchise, expel, or move around entire populations in different historical moments. Yet, even amid this debate, the explicit comparison with Nazi Germany remains an element of this newfound reinterpretation. As one historian has written, the Soviets were like the Nazis, that in deporting national groups or in killing Kulaks—or Jews, for that matter—the Soviets "raised the specter of Nazi-style policies."[15]

Perhaps the most important addition these works have made is their assumption that race and racism do not have to meet a litmus test that promotes purely biological transmission of traits to be considered racism. Cultural attributes as well as biological markers can coexist as telling characteristics of racial identity in the racist's imagination. This view of race happens to conform to how scholars of U.S. race and racism have already treated the definitions of race and racial thought that dominated in the United States in the late nineteenth and twentieth centuries. Yet, what scholars of race in the United States have called "racialism" has rarely been discussed in the European context. In an attempt to understand the legal definitions of race in miscegenation cases in the United States, Peggy Pascoe noted a strong recourse to cultural and behavioral attributes when physical or biological definitions about race proved to be too unreliable and unstable in defining identity. Rather than dismissing the idea of race or the assumption of its biological reality, courts, judges, and juries worked with a wider, more implicit definition of race, which included imagined differences, such as behavior and language, as equally compelling indicators of racial identity. Peggy Pascoe used the term "racialism" rather than "racism" to describe this use of "amorphous ideas" about identity. For racial thinkers, especially in the late nineteenth and early twentieth centuries, "the important point was not that biology determined culture"—a distinction only "dimly perceived" in any case—"but that race, understood as an indivisible essence that included not only biology but also culture, morality, and intelligence, was a compellingly significant factor in history and society."[16] W.E.B. Dubois noted even earlier in the twentieth century that groups thought of as races were knit together in the racialist's eye by far more than physical characteristics; race, he wrote, is most "clearly defined to the eye of the Historian and Sociologist."[17] Even a Spanish eugenicist in the midst of the Spanish Civil War seemed to signal a desire to complicate the race concept when he called for the new Francoist state to pursue "racial but not racist politics."[18] It is clear that racial thought has long included an assumption that biology and culture are intricately, if not always visibly, linked.

As a result, by using this litmus test of Nazi genocide, historians of race in Europe have generally made the concept of race too rigid and hermetic.[19] The concept of race defined by this wider notion of racialism has clearly implanted itself in different parts of the world even when its manifest or operative meaning has varied widely. As a result, scholars of race have also focused on the function of ideas—the discursive practice of race—rather than on meaning alone.[20] Laura Otis has signaled this more expansive approach in her work *Organic Memory*, which explores the penetration of notions of heredity into psychology, biology, medicine, literature, and philology, fields that all helped impel racial thinking in the sciences. In her reading, notions of difference as a product of inherited, transmissible characteristics formed the basis of all racial thought. She also shows that the preoccupation with racial identity was gladly seen among a wide host of nineteenth-century scientists and writers who viewed race as composed of far more than the accumulation of physical characteristics. Memories, cultures, behaviors, thoughts, attitudes—the building blocks of racial thought—all had to be transmitted across the generations in some sort of material, biological way, even if the mechanism of their transmission remained mysterious and unproven; for most racial thinkers, "heredity played a powerful role in determining character."[21] Only the presumption of biological difference amid more obvious cultural, behavioral, and national differences served as the driving force of racial theories. As Pío Baroja, a Spanish writer who was trained as a doctor, wrote in 1904: "At bottom, although physiology cannot appreciate it with exactitude, we have retinas, bronchial passageways, stomachs, livers and skin different from those of a German, an Englishman, or a Russian and we cannot feel the way they do."[22] Racial theorists were always more comfortable knowing that difference existed and was permanent and immutable even if the biological facts could not be appreciated with "exactitude." Neil Macmaster has recently concluded that all racial thought of the nineteenth and early twentieth centuries was "fundamentally an expression of cultural attitudes that were recoded through the methodologies and discourse of 'objective' and empirical research . . . in this sense all racism was cultural."[23]

Understanding race with this more expansive definition does not deny there were variations in its definition or in the kinds of social attitudes and policies that racial thought tended to underwrite. In fact, the definition of race varied because of the distinct historical contexts in which it unfolded. Some contexts proved more resistant to the kinds of scientific knowledge that turned prejudice into racist certainties and actions. In Spain, for example, the actual validity of science was a basic epistemological question that formed alongside the debate about the meaning of race. The flexibility of racial explanation in Spain allowed the concept to develop among a wide array of thinkers, intellectuals, scientists, and laypeople who differed over the basic hermeneutic value of Enlightenment reason and science versus religious and Romantic explanations of national identity. The language of race was much used and rarely rejected out of hand in Spain. And, despite the uniqueness of Spain's intellectual tradition, race still accrued power over time as both a scientific and cultural explanation for Spain's social problems. Hence, the formulation of race was unique; but its deployment in the context of European experiences of race was not.

Again, this conclusion will run counter to the usual understanding of race and how it worked in different regions of Europe. Southern Europeans, for example, have long noticed the differences that have existed in their notions of race compared to those of their northern counterparts. Italy and other southern European countries have long distinguished themselves as nonracial states, as areas where intellectual tradition and culture deny the development of race as a mode of thought or racism as a viable social practice.[24] These denials of racism again are in comparison only to Nazi policy, the legacy in many ways of the embarrassment of wartime alliances between southern European countries and the Nazis. If, as this study articulates, a more pliant and open definition of racism is taking shape, then the long-standing bifurcated view of a racist northern Europe and an open, tolerant southern Europe appears false, the product of an older political agenda distancing the latter from the taint of wartime alliance. New and more interesting questions emerge as a result: How do various racial traditions produce distinct or similar, severe or placid, murderous or merely reformist racial policies? Are these traditions even determinative? Or are actual historical events the most decisive factors? Did the peculiarities of German history produce the racism of Nazi Germany? Was the contradiction posed by the passage of Italy's fascist racial laws of 1938 and the refusal to send Italian Jews to death camps the product of particular historical circumstances rather than a supposedly timeless intellectual tradition? How did Spain, the nation of blood purity laws of the medieval world, produce the supposedly open and tolerant notion of the nation as a racial melting pot in the nineteenth and twentieth centuries? Even more interesting, how did this reliance on the melting pot produce systems of exclusion, the classification of populations into hierarchies of strength and weakness, and a view of dissident political and regional groups within the national state as racial others?

By adding Spain to the equation, this book expands our understanding of racial thought in Europe in the late nineteenth and early twentieth centuries. Theorists averring racial mixture designed methods to shape and promote racial health and treat racial diseases, just as those espousing racial purity created such programs elsewhere. Spanish history proves that approaching the topic of race from the manner in which the idea was expressed and applied rather than from historiographical comparison with a supposed teleological end point makes far more complex and accurate our contemporary understanding of race, especially given its continued hold and importance in Europe and elsewhere.

Denying the Racism of Raza in Modern Spanish Historiography

The rejection of racial language or the denial of its influence in recent Spanish history is usually entangled with a desire to claim Spanish exceptionality. On one level, claims for exceptionality, especially in this case to describe the absence of a dangerous concept like race, have been a cornerstone of Spanish nationalism. Ironically, in fact, the Spanish claim for freedom from racial thought is perhaps one of the only successful and unifying themes in the complex and largely unsuccessful story of Spanish nationalism in the nineteenth and early twentieth centuries. If Spanish nationalism has proven weak because of internal regional differences and an enfeebled central state, race as a nationalist tool has played a far more illuminating role in demonstrating the political, ideological, and even cultural alliances, possible connections, and shared discourse across the Spanish political spectrum.[25] In fact, the assertion of race as a fusionary process in a discourse of natural law and science proved to be common across the political spectrum in Spain. Conservative, liberal, regional separatist, and Spanish nationalist alike all used the new scientific language of racial fusion to demonstrate that Spanish nationhood should be defined in a multitude of images. While the idea of fusion was shared, the mechanisms of fusion differed. How and why groups fused became the locus of ideological contest and ultimately the basis for the setting of social policy to defend racial health. Claims of racial purity did emerge in Spain but were often asserted in reaction to the otherwise overwhelming acceptance of mixture. Even the claims of Basque separatists like Sabino Arana de Goiri who commonly asserted the purity of the Basque race in the late nineteenth and early twentieth centuries were counterbalanced by others who envisioned the Basque as a fused element of the Spanish race. These latter Basque racial thinkers could assert Basque racial difference as a part of the larger racial fusionary process that had taken place throughout the rest of Spain. Basques were different but still part of the Spanish race, the components of which were at one time different.[26]

Yet, given this ubiquity of race, the denial of even the presence of racial thought in Spain has enjoyed a long half-life in twentieth- and twenty-first-century Spain. In fact, a common political purpose can be identified in this denial. Active disavowal of racial ideas in Spain seems to have begun in the 1930s, as noted above, at the moment when political actors elsewhere were first beginning to confront these ideas. Yet, both present-day historians and political ideologues of the past have attempted to differentiate whatever racial theories they did discern in Spain from those of their German cousins, and obviously, as a result, to distance Spanish racial ideas from the murderous implementation of Nazi racial thought. Although some historians have been more forthright in acknowledging the actual presence of racial ideas in Spain, most have neglected any rigorous analysis of the actual meanings or potential uses of racial ideas. In addition, historians, like earlier Falangists, have confined their search to the appearance of racial ideas in the 1930s and 1940s, when racial notions were the main purview of the Francoist forces. As a result, historians have left an equally uncontextualized, ahistorical portrait of what actually constituted the Spanish *raza*. For example, while attempting to explain Franco's choice of the word "raza" as the title for his screenplay, the historian Stanley Payne noted that the word "race" had a "strong patriotic-cultural (rather than *merely* bioethnic) connotation in Spanish."[27] In other words, Spanish racial ideas were unlike their European, specifically Nazi German, counterparts. On another occasion, Payne reiterated Ridruejo's earlier comment by suggesting that the supposed absence of racial ideas is due to the obvious "stupidity" of their expression in a country as racially mixed as Spain.[28] Thus, if racial ideas existed, they were voiced only by a few historically naive people who lacked an awareness either of the impossibility of racial ideas in Spain or, as Payne later concluded in regard to Franco's screenplay, that these people were somehow oblivious to the more accurate biological meanings of the term as everyone else understood it.

The issue, however, is not merely the illogic of racial notions in a country where obvious differences in physical appearance did not exist. If race is a social construction, then far more important is the study of how, given this illogic or lack of physical differences, racial ideas actually did form, were elaborated upon, and changed over time.[29] This book demonstrates that racial language similar to that used by Francoists existed long before the 1930s. In fact, these concepts long preceded the Francoists and in some cases emerged from groups and people who represented political sentiments quite different from those of Spanish conservatives and fascists mentioned above. Race was a prismatic category—an idea through which myriad political, social, and cultural attitudes and positions were reflected.[30]

Spain as the First Racial State

The irony of modern Spain's absence from historical studies of race is that most recent studies of race in European history usually point to the Iberian Peninsula as the first center of racial thought and even racial policies. Spanish historians have noted that as a result of their initial contact with Arab and North African populations in the Middle Ages and with indigenous populations in the Western Hemisphere after 1492, Spaniards actually were the first to ascribe perceived differences in appearance and aptitude to race, long before the Enlightenment classification systems that more specifically identified these supposed subgroups of humanity. Jorge Cañizares Esquerra recently noted that while such ideas of difference appeared in Spanish colonial settings in the early modern period, they did not seem to influence later-nineteenth- and twentieth-century ideas.[31] James Sweet has pointed historians exactly in the opposite direction, asserting that medieval Spanish ideas on slavery were racial in essence, borrowed from Muslim antecedents, and served as the underpinnings of racist ideas that justified U.S. slavery.[32] Others have argued that the contact with populations in the Americas helped Spaniards formulate more open and tolerant racial ideas based either on the absorption of different characteristics via the ecumenical mission of Catholic conversion or via older Greek philosophic concepts of natural slavery that presented people who were perceived to be uncultured savages as potentially redeemable.[33]

Race also appeared as an important but unnamed character in a series of twentieth-century historical debates in Spain. One of the first historians' debates about the makeup and nature of treating difference, real or imagined, in a European society began in Spain soon after World War II. These debates examined the fifteenth-century statutes of blood purity (*estatutos de limpieza de sangre*), the Inquisition, and the expulsion of the Jews in 1492. A unique form of *Historikerstreit*, or historians' debate, that unfolded in the 1950s and was in its own way tinged by the Holocaust, focused on the similarities between medieval policy toward Jews in Spain—the compulsory wearing of yellow stars, the "proto-scientific" language of blood purity, and the notion of lasting racial identity based on lineage—and the extermination of Jews during the Third Reich.[34] These studies have all, in one way or another, explored the generalized view that *convivencia* (coexistence) of groups predominated in the peninsula until it was disrupted either by the social pressure of assimilation in the fourteenth century or the national consolidation and expansion of empire in the fifteenth.[35] This view asserted that racial, or at least "proto-racialist," ideas emerged to keep track of older populations that were "disappearing" or assimilating into the "Spanish" population, like Jews who were converting to Christianity, and to impose a new kind of cultural and religious orthodoxy after the unification of the country under the throne of Ferdinand and Isabella in 1469.[36] These historical phenomena of the medieval era have been used to show that Spanish history provided the first example of ethnic, national, and religious differences becoming "racialized," made immutable and transmittable, in any context and at any moment. Even more, Spanish experiences with race have testified to the fact that race is a function of the modern state with its complex bureaucracies and concern for social order and control over large populations. Later Spanish history will also prove that race or ethnicity can be defined against this state policy: the Basque efforts to define their own pure race can be viewed as the story of resistance to centralizing state policies.[37]

The question of connections between the racial thought of the nineteenth and twentieth centuries with that of fifteen and sixteenth centuries is illuminating not because it indicates a national or ahistorical trajectory of thought, as if the ideas were connected over time in some Spanish replication of the canard that Nazi behavior was redolent of a clear and unbroken cultural heritage that stretched from "Luther to Hitler."[38] Rather, showing the use of race in a historical context proves that the idea itself is quite malleable and multiform. Some recent work in Spain in fact has rejected this "from Isabella to Franco" approach, laying claim to the historicity of dealing with difference in Spain. In one important study of relations between minorities and dominant groups in Spain in the medieval period, David Niremberg consciously avoids comparison with twentieth-century expressions of hatred.[39] Niremberg's approach is compelling because he portrays Spanish ideas about difference as the product of specific historical contexts. Hatred and the notions of difference used to structure it did not form an ageless pall draped over the entire course of Spanish history. Instead, race and divisiveness are seen as tools used in different moments arising out of a number of causative factors to structure social relations and define social roles.[40] Historical comparison over time might elicit compelling arguments, tautological as they might be, to explain different national traditions. The trick is to explain how these national traditions themselves are fungible and open to alteration over time. Thus, a good history of racial ideas considers the social world these racial ideas inhabited and, in addition, the racial "others" against which the racial ideal was defined.

While one must be careful in drawing comparisons between the fifteenth century and more recent eras, so too must one carefully consider the role of Spanish imperial history in the seventeenth, eighteenth, and nineteenth centuries in forging Spanish racial thought of the late nineteenth and early twentieth centuries. The language and celebration of racial mixture in the Spanish colonies must be considered in terms of the colonial context from which they emerged. Spain's racial theorists of the late nineteenth and early twentieth centuries, for example, were products of a liberal Spain hoping to forge a naturalistic and scientific sense of unity in a Spain increasingly seen as fractured by region, class, and political ideology. The Spanish used different racial rhetoric on the peninsula than in the overseas colonies, where obvious physical differences in appearance did exist and conditioned the unfolding of racial ideas. Historians have rightly focused on pinpointing what function the "continuum of racial categories"—the infamous categories that specified shades of skin color, and other physical characteristics into dozens of racial types—had in defining and maintaining the colonial enterprise in all of its complexity and variation throughout Latin America.[41]

In the Iberian Peninsula itself, the social needs for racial ideas were different. Clearly the ethnic mix of Spain did not warrant a racial classification system so reliant on physical differences in appearance. In fact, by the late nineteenth century, the colonial concern with racial ordering of populations rooted in mixture, or mestizaje, appears to be surprisingly absent from Spanish discussions. After Spain lost its last overseas colonies in 1898, the distance between peninsular and colonial discourse on race seems to have grown only wider. The colonies, especially after 1898, became mere symbols of the process of racial fusion, bringing many groups together to form one race. Spanish colonialists in North Africa did not rely on the same rhetoric of racial fusion. Interestingly, the return of Spanish intellectuals' attention to Latin America in the 1920s in concepts like *Hispanidad*, *Hispanismo*, and *Latinidad* emerged in the language of racial fusion but was much more consciously divested of the specific racialist, biological language with which race had been discussed earlier. In some sense, this transitional discourse tied together older scientific notions with the more avowedly nonscientific discussions of race that emerged in the 1930s and 1940s that was really an attempt to distinguish Spain from its wartime allies in Germany and Italy.[42]

Thus, viewing Spanish notions of race as they changed over time proves the well-established point that racial formations are contingent on historical circumstance and that the process of racial formations can take place regardless of its intellectual or ideological basis.[43] Inserting Spain into the new historiographical framework of race makes more comprehensive the new trends that already are appearing in this historiography. George Frederickson has recently and quite rightly stressed that race can be defined apart from notions of purity, presenting in a recent work two kinds of racism, one of exclusion, and one of inclusion, concepts he borrows from the French sociologist Pierre-Andre Taguieff. One might say that the Spanish version, the idea of fusion, is a racism of inclusion, "incorporating groups on the basis of a rigid hierarchy justified by a belief in permanent, unbridgeable differences between associated groups."[44] Yet, Spanish notions of race prove that a simple bifurcation of inclusive or exclusive racial thought is unnecessary. Modern Spanish racial thought rooted in fusion was in a sense inclusive, while the purposes to which it was put always led to divisive sense of ethnic isolation. There is nothing benign or surprising in the Spanish notion of fusion or its social use or deployment. Inclusive racism does not preempt the creation of crude racist practices. Someone or some group is always left out.

The same observation has already been made in the history of racial thought in Latin American countries. Similarities between Latin American and Spanish language of race rest not only in the content of racial ideals but also in terms of the role that these racial ideals play in expressing nationalist claims of uniqueness and strength. The Latin American interest in mixture, or *mestizaje*, has long been considered one of the reasons for Latin America's great freedom from racism. From Vasconcelos's *Raza cósmica* (1912) even to Carlos Fuentes's *Buried Mirror* (1992), many nations in Latin America have supported the notion of the mixture of many peoples as the cornerstone of a new national identity, opposed to European and U.S. notions so dependent on ethnicity and skin color as the basis of civil rights and liberties. Nationalist movements especially of the late nineteenth century, often working against colonizing presences to the north or across the Atlantic, took advantage of "cross-racial alliances" bred by what Giberto Freyre argues was Spain's original experience with *convivencia* in Iberia and their transport of that openness to the Latin American colonies. This cross-racial alliance helped forge united, often multiethnic military, fronts against colonizing powers.[45] Ironically, Freyre has argued that this openness was age-old, rooted in medieval Spain's tolerance of miscegenation between Arab, Jew, and Christian.[46] This supposed uniqueness of Latin American conceptions of race, especially in comparison to the U.S. "one-drop" rule and European notions of race, has served as the explanatory mechanism for understanding the development of different slave systems in Latin American and the United States.[47]

Whether openness and tolerance is timeless, this Latin American sense of *mestizaje* has undergone an important revision recently that complicates the view of mixture as the great antiracist ideology. Recent historians and anthropologists, among them Ada Ferrer, Alejandra Bronfman, and Peter Wade, have demonstrated that the notions of mixture in the nationalist imaginary of many Latin American countries have served the ultimate purpose of denying or obliterating certain segments of the population from any particular public or social role in the nation.[48] One historian has noted that, even in the United States, a hybrid notion of race at the turn of the twentieth century actually led to the intensification of racial categories and ever-finer differentiation of supposedly separate racial groups.[49] Spain belongs in this historiography to show that racial ideas based on inclusion are no different in their practice from notions based on exclusion.

Racial Thought in Nineteenth- and Twentieth-Century Spain

The context of Spain between 1875 and the Spanish Civil War produced racial ideas focused on national unity, either emphasizing or deemphasizing regional differences (depending upon the outlook of the racial thinker) and also on the quelling of class unrest and dramatic political fractionalization. This study analyzes how the scientific field of anthropology provided a new kind of racial analysis to explain the reasons for Spanish disunity and offer views of Spanish unity. Two factors most shaped the development of the scientific disciplines, especially anthropology, which provided the portrait of racial identity in the late nineteenth and early twentieth centuries. The first was the political and intellectual shifts surrounding Spain's liberal 1868 Revolution that gave rise to the disciplinary formation of many of Spain's human sciences and, in particular, anthropology.[50] The republican and liberal politics of many scientific pioneers in Spain produced racial analyses that served to substantiate or verify the political changes taking place during this revolutionary era. The consolidation of these political changes in the Restoration of the Bourbon monarchy in 1875 and its negotiated pact of alternating political power between Liberal and Conservative parties led to concomitant shifts in the goals of these sciences.[51]

The study of race varied along with these political changes. In part, the variety of racial ideas was due to the number of different political visions espoused by the figures most responsible for formalizing the disciplines aligned with racial studies: anthropology, sociology, history, medicine, and criminology. Some figures who had supported the radical republican politics of the revolutionary period and the First Republic sought new definitions of the Spanish race, its makeup, and its capabilities after the Republic collapsed in 1875. Others continued to present a view of Spanish racial fusion as supportive of more radical republican politics. Both, however, offered portraits of the Spanish race that were fundamentally more supportive of the liberal status quo; the factors that produced the positive elements of racial fusion denied the legitimacy of revolutionary workers' parties, regional separatism, and other threats to a liberal social order by identifying them as racially degenerate or unhealthful. This work documents how race came to play important roles in the disciplinary formation of anthropology just at the moment when the social sciences were working to establish themselves as important and relevant fields for social and political reform. This confluence of disciplinary formation and racial study gave race a more influential role in the promotion of social reforms and public policy than is usually presumed.

This evolution from scientific development to social application was not always direct or easily traceable.[52] Yet, the fundamental structure of this movement was not difficult to assess.[53] Intellectuals and scientists with positions in universities or at private education institutions presented their ideas to students and also within private intellectual clubs like the Athenaeums of Madrid and of Barcelona. In those cities, newspapers and other more specialized press would publish the content of these lectures and thus begin the diffusion of ideas to a larger audience.[54] As a result, the scientific discussion of race enjoyed a much larger hearing from a wider cross-section of the Spanish intellectual and political community than is usually thought to have existed.[55] In addition, positions of leadership in academic clubs and private institutions allowed a certain setting of the agenda that increasingly included discussions of the Spanish racial makeup from the 1870s through the 1920s. Some of Spain's most prominent anthropologists and racial theorists served in these positions. As a result, this work devotes close attention to tracing the actual positions these scientists came to occupy. This study also follows the changing status these scientists enjoyed in their professional careers and in the view of their importance in Spanish society in solving seemingly intractable problems.

The flow of ideas, in this case about race, from the university into governmental policy was not static, established in one moment and then fixed for subsequent decades. Given the instability and constant changes in governments that marked the Restoration, the long tenure of many of the proponents of racially based social policy in government ministries and advisory commissions was surprising. This longevity can be explained partly by the nature of the racial ideas these thinkers presented. The theme of racial fusion formulated within anthropology did not contradict the ideological framework of either the Left or the Right. In fact, most elites agreed that Spain represented some type of racial fusion. The mechanisms that were thought to have brought these groups together, however, did vary depending on political outlook and ideology. Race was malleable but it always reflected a belief in mixture.

This book begins with two introductory chapters. Chapter 2 provides a history of the racial thought in Spain from the medieval era through the first two-thirds of the nineteenth century. This historical background places the early formation of the Spanish state and the contentious history of the fifteenth-century blood purity laws in relation to later discussions of race that occupy the rest of the book. This chapter pays particular attention to the historical lineage of racial thought in Spain and also foreshadows the unique shifts within racial thought as Spaniards began to borrow racial theories from outside Spain in the nineteenth century, when racial thought was particularly ascendant throughout Europe.

Chapter 3, which begins part 1, examines the development of anthropology in the context of the political struggles that defined Spain's Restoration government, which followed a brief republican experiment in Spanish politics. Liberal scientists who served as politicians in the First Republic (1873–74) were thrown into the opposition with the return of the constitutional monarchy in 1875. They responded to the defeat by developing new scientific disciplines through which they hoped to remake Spanish society and politics. Race was the motor force of this effort. Working within Spain's most important universities in Madrid, Salamanca, and Granada, these scientists hoped that a new, empirically verified vision of Spain as an ethnic nation rather than a spiritual or religious community would help bring about a new republican order. Chapter 4 focuses more generally on the role that racial fusion played in the consolidation of the study of anthropology between 1890 and 1910. This chapter examines in particular the absorption of these anthropological debates into nonscientific intellectual and cultural discussion in Spain. Here the historical context of Spain's defeat in 1898 and the consequent debate about Spain's decay and the need for "regeneration" shaped the development of both a scientific concept of race and the popular conception of the Spanish nation. Chapter 5 explores how anthropological debates about race fueled calls for the Spanish state to use the racial sciences to solve Spanish national problems. This new discussion led to divisions among Spanish social scientists about the meaning of Spain's racial fusion. These divisions soon were reflected in the political appropriation of anthropological discourse of race to support the liberal, conservative, anarchist, and fascist ideas that were in play at the approach of the Civil War period.

Part 2 of this book considers how the idea of racial fusion penetrated more applied social sciences, like criminology, in early-twentieth-century Spain. This section takes advantage of the potential not only to uncover the theoretical changes in describing the Spanish race that unfolded in Spanish scientific and intellectual debate, but also how these ideas were appropriated by state functionaries and applied within Spanish society in a prophylactic effort to heal the country and its population. Chapter 6 examines the military appropriation of race after the 1898 defeat by the United States in the Spanish-American War. Instead of examining the structural and strategic failures of the Spanish military in 1898, the military analyzed the losses as the product of improper recruitment that disturbed the delicate process of Spanish racial fusion. Chapter 7 explores the infusion of anthropological concepts of identity and behavior into legal definitions of crime and the predictability of criminal behavior among Spaniards. Looking especially at the period between 1890 and 1917, this chapter considers how Spain's unique racial fusion informed the definition of criminal responsibility and of the kinds of criminals that existed in Spain. The seepage of political and social ideologies into the definition of improper racial fusion forms the backbone of these chapters.

Chapter 8 follows these themes in a much more specific biographical context. This section analyzes in particular the work of Ángel Pulido y Fernández, a figure whose career in a sense mimicked the trajectory of racial thought presented throughout this study. Pulido began as an early and influential Spanish anthropologist who turned his attention to social applications of scientific ideas as he moved into governmental positions, including the director of public health. His ideas relating to race and racial fusion appeared throughout his political career, especially after he became a permanent member of the Spanish Senate, when he began an effort for which he remains famous today to repatriate Jews of Spanish origin, the Sephardim, to Spain. This biographical approach is important because the general anthropological vision of racial fusion lay behind the myriad public programs Pulido sponsored. In addition, the elements of the racial fusion that he defined as beneficial or dangerous— the groups that kept Spain together or were splitting it apart—changed over time and mimicked the political changes with Spanish liberalism from the 1860s through the 1920s. This last chapter functions as a synthetic case study to reinforce the argument made throughout this work—that racial fusion had both an inclusive and exclusive component—and to refute the exculpatory and quite common refrain that Spanish racial ideas were devoid of negative or potentially divisive consequences because they were rooted in fusion. The epilogue considers the lingering influence of racial thought in contemporary Spain.

2. Finding a Science in the Mystery of Race in Spain

In 1971, the historian of Spain and Latin America Frederick Pike offered the then standard summation of the meaning of raza, a view that had been held for the previous one hundred years: "A fundamental characteristic of Spaniards has always been the unassailable conviction that there are fundamental characteristics of the Spanish people. . . . And it has never mattered in the least whether there is scientific evidence to support the view that there are basic character traits of the Spanish people or of any national group. Spaniards tend to be convinced that there are things science knows not of and that one of these is the existence of a character, a nature . . . a raza."[1] Pike implied that the Spanish notion of race remained stuck in the Romantic era, ignoring the value of science and celebrating instead the mysteries of the intangible but nevertheless meaningful components of racial identity, like culture, behavior, values, etc.[2] Missing in Pike's assessment is an acknowledgment that this conception of the Spanish race, like all racial definitions, was not without ideological components or a historical context. The notion of a raza, culturally determined or not, connoted a historical link, a unity of people over time. Yet Pike ignored the idea that the term itself might be imbued with political or ideological connotations that were dependent on historical contexts.

In reality, the term raza has a complicated historical lineage that requires further analysis. Though the term traces its lineage to the twelfth century, its ideological meaning in the nineteenth century crystallized around the idea of Spain's legacy as a conqueror, empire builder, and unifier of different peoples.[3] This idea of the Spanish race as a conqueror was often the tool of historians, writers, philologists, and ideologues of the nineteenth and twentieth centuries hoping to align the political and imperial history of Spain with the Catholic Church as the great unifying forces of the Spanish past. It was to this end that, in 1918, the Spanish King Alfonso XIII initiated—through royal decree and with the support of conservative prime minister Antonio Maura—the Fiesta de la Raza, to be celebrated on October 12, a day laden with religious, political, and national symbolism. October 12 commemorated Columbus's first landfall in the Western Hemisphere and also was the day of the appearance of the Virgin Mary to Saint James, the patron saint of Spain. La Virgen del Pilar is considered the patron saint of the Hispanic peoples, and, in a sense, of Spain and its empire. Thus, the idea of race connoted both the ecumenical mission of the Catholic Church and the conquering spirit of the Spanish state. The Spanish race was fundamentally a religious entity, united by common religious principles and values. Its ecumenical generosity, reflected in its willingness to convert all peoples to Spanish Catholicism and thus to Spanish identity, made it capable of absorbing vast numbers of people.[4] Recently, however, historians have begun to reexamine the meanings of *raza* over a much wider swath of time, long before the nineteenth century. Even in this reexamination, the older meanings of *raza* are viewed in connection with their more modern incarnations. Whether *raza* had a Romantic quality or a Catholic ecumenical one, the term over the past five centuries has also carried an ethnic connotation, making human difference a product of the natural world, and assuming traits shared across time and generations.

The Use of Raza before the Nineteenth Century: To Include or to Exclude

In many ways, the idea of *raza* was linked to a number of linguistic tools that defined inclusion and exclusion prior to the nineteenth century. For example, early responses to the contact with the indigenous populations of the Western Hemisphere relied on the idea that Spanish identity was something attainable, via conversion or via linguistic appropriation, i.e., learning to speak Spanish.[5] Yet, such ecumenical notions about Spanish identity in the New World were often matched by an equally divisive language of exclusion within the Spanish peninsula. The 1492 act of expelling Jews from the Iberian Peninsula utilized a separatist discourse that worked in close proximity to the rhetoric that supported the potential inclusion of the colonized populations.[6] Thus, the actual history of the term is far more complicated as it intermingled with many other ideas over Spain's complicated history of human contact, conquest, and imperial retrenchment over the past five hundred years. One could even argue that Spanish notions of identity relied on an ethnic component for longer than many other European nations because of the ostensible old age of the Spanish state.

Avoiding, for the moment, the long, acrimonious debate about the fifteenth-century blood purity statutes and the existence of "modern" racism in medieval Spain, it is important to consider the linguistic and social methods of exclusion and inclusion in operation in medieval and early modern Spain. An official effort to define and compose a religiously and politically uniform population arguably occurred earlier in Spain than elsewhere. Spaniards began to entertain notions of being Spaniards, of belonging to a historically discrete entity (rather than to separate kingdoms) at the end of the fifteenth century with the Catholic Kings' unification of the disparate crowns in 1469. The Spanish monarchy set about fostering this separate identity while both the state and the church sought to incorporate broad and diverse populations. The result was the development of a language of difference and inclusion intended to define who fit into—and who lived outside of—the walls of this new political entity.[7]

Race was one term that helped frame the contours of inclusion and exclusion. Certainly, it is difficult to know the precise meaning that raza has had in popular usage. Yet, its continuous appearance in literature and law clearly suggests that the term contained the working presumptions of racial thought. A scan of the dictionary definitions of raza over the past centuries bears out both the actual ethnic meanings of the word and the contradictory inclusive and exclusive connotations it carried. From its first publication in 1726 through the 1940s, the Royal Academy's dictionary defined raza as a positive term relating to the distinct breeds of bulls or horses that were produced through animal husbandry. The dictionary also consistently noted that raza had a negative connotation when it referred to human groups, relating to membership in a caste, group, or lineage within a larger ethnic community. Between 1726 and 1843, the dictionary applied this negative connotation to Jews, noting their position as a nonassimilable group preferring separate identity rather than a larger group identity. In 1884, the dictionary also began offering a biological meaning for raza, noting that for "scientists the term connotes specific membership within one division of the human species."[8] Interestingly, this biological connotation still appears in present-day versions of the dictionary, as does the negative connotation of raza meaning divided identities and loyalties. In these dictionary definitions, there is a clear association between the natural world of animal breeding, differences within a species, and the basis of human difference.[9]

Other words also mixed behavior and temperament with descent and reproduction. In fact, most surprising is not that words related to race and historical group identities existed, but rather how many words with at least contemporary racial connotations existed. *Casta* (caste), *estirpe* (stock or ancestry), and *linaje* (lineage) all shared a tendency to view the world of human differences, both in appearance and in behavior, as a product of the natural world rather than as a socially constructed concept. Used interchangeably, these terms implied a clear link between the natural world of reproduction, shared descent, and temperament.[10] Different peoples shared distinct cultures, breeding, and behaviors born of shared characteristics passed down through the generations. These terms also referred to clear class distinctions in the feudal world—the lineage of aristocracy, for example, or the *estirpe* of a particular family—that moved them beyond mere linguistic usages into the realm of defense of social hierarchies. All of these concepts helped legitimize social policies and religious definitions that tied land ownership, occupations, and, later, expulsion to one's lineage or associated one's character with one's descent.[11]

At the same time, the locutions that appeared in the fifteenth century imply that an equally strong effort to forge communal identities with positive connotations also existed. These same tools that implied difference also forged an ethnic community of shared history, traits, and lineage over time. Only recently have historians begun to study these terms of communal identity as shared ideas, not mutually exclusive or contradictory, but rather containing different emphases and meanings depending on their literary, philosophical, or ideological purposes. Hence, *linaje* implied both a positive and negative historical link. In 1438, defending the exclusion of *conversos* (Spanish Jews who converted to Christianity) from holding offices in Toledo, Alfonso Martínez de Toledo discussed the permanence of character based on descent: "you will see every day in the places where you live, that the good man of good *raça* always returns to his origins, whereas the miserable man, of bad *raça* or lineage, no matter how powerful or how rich, will always return to the villainy from which he descends."[12] Popular sensibilities do not have to have biological rigor or even a longing for biological rigor behind them. Also, one should not assume that these terms possessed rigid or fixed meanings in popular usage. As David Niremberg has written: "there is no doubt that this language was saturated, then as now, with resonance to what contemporaries held to be "common sense' knowledge of the reproductive systems of the natural world."[13] The most important issue is not to measure these locutions in terms of modern cognates or of whether they possessed a modern biological sensibility but rather to examine how they were used, and how medieval actors assumed that behavior and comportment were rooted in distinct lineages and lines of descent.

Overall, the complexity of Spanish locutions that seemed to naturalize group identities should be viewed through the lenses of inclusion and exclusion or, in other words, their social purpose. As Yosef Yerushalmi has suggested, the social pressures of assimilation in the medieval world often served as the trigger for what one might call racial thinking, or the creation of permanent immutable and transmissible characteristics among separate groups *within* one society.[14] He linked Nazi Germany and medieval Spain as two societies that flirted with racial thought when already well-entrenched populations—in both cases Jews—began to assimilate or "disappear" into society. For Yerushalmi, Nazi antisemitism and Spain's blood purity statutes of the fifteenth century both emerged from societies that saw a loosening of proscriptions against certain populations, especially Jews, who began to participate actively and openly in society, owning land and serving in political, economic, or cultural roles. Christiane Stallaert has expressed the same point but in the inverse. Blood purity became a mode of defining allegiance to the monarchy, not solely a means of viciously excluding the Jew. For her, the blood purity statutes reflect the "assimilationist ferocity" of the monarchy of the Catholic Kings.[15] The emphasis resided in forcing people into, rather than defining them out of, the social body.

Assuming that collective identities require both a positive definition of the self and a negative definition of the other is leading to an energetic and complex grappling with these historical ideas in Spain. In particular, the discussion of the inheritability and transmission of the positive qualities of Spanishness that typified the medieval era to the present has begun to draw some scholarly attention. Recently, one historian has shown that the *castizo* tradition in Spain had always carried with it at least traces of what present-day sociologists would call an ethnic identity.[16] *Casticismo* asserted an implicit, discrete set of religious, behavioral, cultural, and even biological characteristics that endured even during intermixture with other peoples over the centuries. This new interest in the multiple, ethnic, meanings of *casticismo* has linked the notions of identity common in the nineteenth century with notions expressed earlier. In fact, based on this brief overview, one can argue that later-nineteenth-century invocations of race replete with naturalist discourse of difference were not novel but rather bound to a linguistic habit familiar to the Iberian Peninsula. Populations and social contexts changed, and the need to turn some people into "others" shifted over time. The issue remains not whether medieval and early modern Spaniards were "racist" but rather how and when the tendency to naturalize difference and link one's character to one's genealogy was deployed.

Answering this question does not represent an anachronistic wish to see the present in the past, as some have asserted, but rather to see similarities in historical methods of defining difference. As David Niremberg and others have pointed out, when Sebastian de Covarrubias in his 1611 Spanish dictionary linked descent with character in his definition of *raza*, he also implied that identity was not always easy to see. *Raza*, he wrote, referred to "the breed of thoroughbred horses, which are branded with an iron so that they can be known."[17] He continued that race also defined human differences, negative differences: "race in [human] lineages is understood pejoratively as having some Moorish or Jewish race."[18] In this definition, like those in the dictionary of the Royal Academy, race connoted breeding, descent, and difference. In the end, it is clear that Spanish concerns with national identity, religious orthodoxy, and colonial administration fostered an energetic focus on contours and limits of identity. This focus usually presumed that human differences were natural, genealogical, and shared.[19]

Whether these differences could be overcome was another important question that altered over time. The answer depended on the historical moment. Spanish celebrations of mixture certainly existed in the early modern era. But then, as later, the issue was what values, behaviors, and physical attributes distinguished people from each other. The only clear historical pattern that emerged in Spain during the medieval and early modern period was that, whether defining difference in the colonies or in the peninsula, the idea of *raza* seems to have alternated between exclusion and inclusion in a way that bespoke an overall tendency to grade populations in terms of their relation to an always shifting definition of the *castizo*, *lo español*, of an organic unity that was Spain.[20]

The Use of Raza in the Nineteenth Century

The complexity of ideas related to internal and external difference continued to function into the nineteenth century. What changed in this period was the rise of nationalism and increasingly intricate methods of defining human difference and similarities. In the nineteenth century, the fields of inquiry into this ethnic quality of communal identity exploded and made far more complex the discussion of national pasts. In Spain, this Romantic exploration of the nation developed in conjunction with a number of regionalist movements that also defined their own enduring nationhood, often at odds with the more centralizing versions of Spanish nationalism. Compounding this process was a weak central state that in the end had a difficult time corralling the various versions of nineteenth-century Romantic nationalism into a cohesive national vision. Spanish struggles to frame a unified usable past in the late nineteenth century coincided exactly with the moment of European nationalist ascendancy.[21] Again, context determined whether the main thrust of the notion of raza would be inclusive or exclusive.

By the nineteenth century, the splintering of the Spanish empire in the 1820s had in fact triggered a new connotation for raza. Peninsular Spaniards, in attempt to maintain some sense of hegemony over former colonies throughout Central and South America, began to assert that Spain's greatest contribution to the Western Hemisphere was an enduring cultural legacy, the product of the development and spread of Western, and especially Catholic, civilization in their colonies.[22] Thus, the assertion of a Spanish raza came to reflect less a substantive political or national identity, and more a series of ideas, a temperament that united generations within the Spanish-speaking world (itself a locution of the nineteenth century) in response to colonial losses.[23] Though this idea of a Spanish legacy relied on the notion of some kind of transmission of characteristics to successive generations, most theorists who developed the idea of the Spanish raza were less concerned about the actual mechanism of this transmission than they were in defining the attributes that were to be inherited. In fact, many who asserted the notion of the Spanish raza consciously avoided using the term with any of the physical, anthropological, or biological connotations that the term "race" was beginning to acquire in the first half of the nineteenth century.[24] The Spaniards were a race defined in Herder's sense of having a unique and distinct temperament, genius, culture, etc., expressed in a fixed character, without the concomitant physical and political expressions of this genius in consistent facial angles or particular state formations.[25]

But also this idea of race was appearing during a period of European imperial expansion. Spain, of course, was losing its empire. As a result, this imperial failing came to condition Spanish racial thought in important ways well into the late nineteenth and early twentieth centuries. Race appeared not as a method of defining the difference between conquered and conqueror but rather as a way of explaining the moribund condition of Spain. Racial discussions pinpointed the causes of this decline, tying them not just to historical forces but also to the natural forces of human congress and mixture in the Spanish past. What followed is best described as a process of internal colonialism where anthropologists and their political emissaries diagnosed and prescribed treatments for problems supposedly inherent or ingrained in the peninsular population.[26] The tensions between the incorporation of what was thought of as universal scientific methods and the employment of them to define Spanish uniqueness has to do with both the level of development of the sciences in Spain of the 1870s and the position of science in Spanish society, i.e., the political and social context in which this development took place. On one level, developing slightly later than many of their European counterparts gave most modern Spanish scientific fields the benefit of defining professional and theoretical debates not at the nascent level of a new science, but rather within a climate of already sharply defined intellectual and ideological positions that had emerged elsewhere in Europe. In addition, many of the early formulators of Spanish science—influenced by European models and engaged in what they called the "Europeanization" of Spain—transported to Spain the debates then raging in European sciences.[27]

Thus, the nature of these debates and how they were imported into Spain helped demarcate how Spanish anthropologists investigated race in the late nineteenth century. At the same time, this notion of Europeanization also plays a part in determining the interests of those arguing the contrary position, against the importation of European sciences or the consultation with foreign sources as the basis of Spanish regeneration. Conservative and Catholic traditionalists, while not rejecting the need for scientific education and training in Spain (a common stance among the *europeanistas*), attempted to overcome these positions by finding a science rooted within Spanish tradition and history.[28] Santos Juliá has discussed the contradictory nature of this group of intellectuals who protested "for and against everything" at the end of the nineteenth century in order to regenerate Spain with the newest techniques, and who, at the same time, saw the return to the "*pueblo*" as a means to find the enduring qualities of Spain and its region.[29]

A case in point is the famous approach to studying history that Miguel de Unamuno devised in the 1890s, known as intrahistory (*intrahistoria*). Unamuno rejected earlier philosophical idealism that sought out the transcendent values and idylls of the national past and instead hoped for a systematic observation of the daily life of the masses to glean a sense of enduring qualities of Spanishness, or *casticismo*. This empiricism would uncover the basic components of the organic memories of the *castizo* Spaniard, the essential Spaniard, which traveled through the centuries, linking people across time through the "stratified layers" of their existence.[30] Despite his later rejection of positivism, Unamuno clearly saw intrahistory as an epistemological welcoming of scientific modes of understanding the past, even if the results would elicit profoundly Spanish qualities. Only the ancient Spaniards as representative of an ancient nation possessed these stratified layers. Nations younger than Spain would not necessarily elicit much from *intrahistoria*.[31]

This view of the nation as comprised of spirits, traditions, and history, combined with the modern biological assumption that elements of identity are passed down physically through the millennia, remained a constant leitmotif among Spanish intellectuals of the late nineteenth and early twentieth centuries. Unamuno's friend and later collaborator José Ortega y Gasset once wrote that he wanted to create a "postmodern world" that could link together the universal forces of modernity and the backward-looking faith in national traditions and culture: "The essential note of this new sensibility is the decision to never forget that spiritual functions, or culture, are also biological functions."[32] Unamuno, Ortega and others demonstrated that by the end of the nineteenth century, Pike's notion that Spaniards were ambivalent about the value of science was anachronistic. As Unamuno and others would demonstrate, ambivalence toward science was counteracted by an appreciation of the particular lessons it provided. Some historians have even begun to name this particular Spanish view of the past as a kind of organic determinism latent in the notions of nationalism of the Spanish Right.[33] This view of Spanish decline, so important in the Spanish conservative and fascist circles later in the 1930s and 1940s, began at the end of the nineteenth century among a wide range of thinkers whom the historian Santos Juliá has called the "publicists" of Spain's decline. These figures sought new scientific methods from European sociology and archaeology, all tinged with social Darwinist ideas, from which they could elicit the pathways for Spanish regeneration.[34] Far more than presenting "organicist metaphors," these thinkers lived in an era when social problems were viewed as natural phenomena and thus, their treatment would be through "biological relief."[35]

Thus, even when many Spanish thinkers opposed scientific theories of race, they also comfortably and actively advanced many of the common themes of late-nineteenth-century nationalism and Romanticism that contributed to and imbued racial thinking elsewhere in Europe. To have collective identities, components of this identity must linger through time and be transmitted. As a result, both positivists and reactionaries in Spain worked to uncover the mechanism or mechanisms to explain inheritance. As the biologist turned historian Laura Otis, once wrote, "thoughts of heredity invite thoughts about race."[36] Race proved an attractive term to explain this inherent quality, whether represented in physical or cultural terms. That it was transmitted, that it lingered through time, and that it was unique to Spain—the "blood bond," as the Spanish writer Emilia Pardo Bazán called it—gave these ruminations a racial tone.[37] The later ambivalence toward scientific race in the 1920s and 1930s that Pike described was not matched in this earlier period. In the formative 1880s and 1890s, a far more unified discursive pool seemed to exist around the idea of race as the basis of Spanish identity. The Restoration was not merely a period of political retrenchment and a search for stability after the failures of the First Republic but also of energetic examination of national pathologies that gave rise to these failures. Anthropologists participated quite actively in this debate. The scientific imagination and the awareness of the worlds that science uncovered marked late-nineteenth-century intellectual life in Spain as much as they did elsewhere.[38]

As some scholars have recently shown, the idea that the historical problems besetting Spain came from within led to a number of new forms of regional and national analysis of Spanish history. Among more centralizing nationalists in Spain, the promotion of casticismo and an enduring Spanishness helped relate problems in Spain to historically problematic populations within Spain. Ghosts of Spain's racial past were resurrected, with antisemitism reappearing to explain Spain's endemic problems despite the absence of any real Jewish population at the turn of the twentieth century.[39] Oddly, a new philo-Semitism also emerged to counter this ethnic myth. The glories of Spanish Jewish culture became one of many historical myths that motivated Spaniards to define the essential characteristics of the Spanish and trace the mechanism of their transmission through time.[40] Because of this story of decay and isolation, Spain was left in the odd position of locating and treating its problems from the inside out. Spain's problematic nineteenth century, defined by civil wars, political and military insurrections, and an endemic regional problem, led most racial thinkers to be more concerned with the enemy within than the enemy without far earlier than the early national socialist movements in France or Italy, for example.[41]

The seeming backwardness of Spain in the nineteenth century elicited a few other ideas about race. By the 1860s and 1870s, a group of intellectuals and politicians debated a new form of Spanish identity, their membership in the Latin race, or the *raza latina*. Responding partly to the racial superiority arguments emerging from France, Germany, and England—and to the attendant arguments about the apparent degeneration of Spain and Italy—Spanish, Italian, and French intellectuals began to discuss the racial, cultural, and historical affinities that united the Latin race and distinguished it from its Nordic, Teutonic, and Anglo-Saxon counterparts in the north.[42] The Latin race was supposedly afflicted with the same weaknesses that had characterized their Roman forebears, most important among them racial intermixing. These ideas, first popularized by Arthur de Gobineau, proliferated later with what was thought to be the scientific substantiation of the dangers of race mixing, most notably by Georges Vacher de Lapouge in the 1880s; these notions then spread among many others, including Richard Wagner, who gave them further currency.[43]

Reacting against these claims, racial theorists presented the Latin race as a compendium of the qualities of their Roman forebears. The qualities that were stressed were often quite different and mutually contradictory. Some argued, for example, that Latin countries were indeed in decline, but that the source of their regeneration lay in particular forms of modernization and in understanding the value of racial mixing.[44] Others argued that biological race mixing was irrelevant to regeneration, and that unity in economic trade, colonial ambitions, and even cultural output would offer a buffer against the encroachment of English and German power. Others were less motivated by such material and political concerns. They envisioned the Latin race rooted in a Roman greatness that began with Constantine. According to these thinkers, what differentiated the southern European descendants from their northern European counterparts was Catholicism. Catholicism, as opposed to German Protestantism, was fundamental for one group of theorists often associated with monarchical and traditionalist positions, but also occasionally tied to liberal, pro-science, and Enlightenment forces. Often these dueling forces coexisted, united by the common enemy of the German or Anglo-Saxon races. One clear statement of this coexistence was offered in the journal *La Raza Latina* that was published throughout the 1870s. The participants formed a wide coalition of liberal, monarchist, and republican forces in France and Spain. Leon Gambetta, later a prime minister in the Third Republic, served as a French editor of the journal, while the head of the Conservative Party and architect of the Restoration government in Spain, Cánovas de Castillo, served as a Spanish advisor. In equal opposition to German Protestantism and English materialism, the journal defined the struggle between nations, coming on the heels of the Franco-Prussian War, and the end of Spain's First Republic, in the Romantic terms of differing racial spirits battling in Europe for power:

> Through history, there has always appeared in the world a colossus, a force that has destroyed the equilibrium of nations. In turn, these nations, obeying the necessary relationships that the natural order provides, have always formed a coalition to fight this threat. Today, the Teutonic Empire presents itself as that force with its immense material strength and with the ability to absorb, as the French have had occasion to observe. In response, in Europe, or in Latin Europe, a virtue of that law to which we have earlier referred has been born. The desire to join together in the interests of our Race, and supporting ourselves with Catholicism, has produced a league of nations to oppose the currents of mere force and ambition that German Race has demonstrated.[45]

These versions of defining racial differences in Europe or in the world were certainly not unique to Spain. In fact, the roster of thinkers involved in defining the components of a Latin race was quite long and emerged from a variety of contexts.[46] Republicans, anticlericals, liberals, monarchists, and Catholic traditionalists all had differing ideas as to what composed the Latin race. Yet, implicit in all of this discussion of the Latin race was the idea that each component of it, whether Italian, Spaniard, or French, had its own identifying traits. The rise of Darwinian evolutionary theory and the attendant development of Social Darwinism and Spencerian notions of national competition expanded the search for these traits into the natural sciences.[47]

While these transitions from literary and philological discussions of race to those rooted in natural science have been avidly studied in Germany and in France, an analysis of them in Spain has yet to be done. Spanish scientists captured both the science and the mystery of race in the nineteenth and early twentieth centuries.[48] Ironically, Spain's past status as the leading light of European civilization in the medieval and early modern era complicated the sense among Spanish scientists that their native science was inherently backward. In fact, the desire to resurrect past traditions to revitalize Spanish science imputed far more nationalist bravado and confidence into Spanish science. There was an assumption that Spanish scientists belonged among European elites of science and only the political context held Spain back. Even more, Spanish scientists attempted to mesh modern science with what they considered to be Spanish traditions that were at one time quite advanced and, even more, once guided other European scientific development.

What has been missing in Spanish historiography and even in the historiography of many southern European countries is the view that the scientific exploration of race actually informed larger debates about Spanish social problems, colonial concerns, and the definition of the nation. The new social sciences, with anthropology at the head, were formative centers of this new discussion of race. The history of the disciplinary formation of these new sciences in Spain clearly demonstrates a slow development compared to European counterparts. However, this delay was never so long that Spanish scientists were incapable of participating in the most up-to-date scientific debates raging across Europe. In addition, many individual Spanish scientists, especially within anthropology, biology and other human sciences, worked at the highest level of European scientific development. Anthropology in particular represented one of the fields where, although the discipline advanced slowly, individual scientists participated and were important members of the international scientific community.

Despite having long roots in the fifteenth and sixteenth centuries, the discipline of modern anthropology formed in Spain in the 1860s and 1870s, separated from its European contemporaries by only a few years. The first anthropological society in Spain was formed in 1865, six years after its French counterpart, two years after the British and Russian societies, and at roughly the same time as its equivalents in Berlin, Vienna, Florence, and the United States.[49] Spain's first anthropological museum opened in 1875 at the same time as most of its European counterparts.[50] While these institutions formed in Madrid, their regional affiliates in Granada, Barcelona, and Seville all followed in close order.[51] The Free Institute of Education (ILE, Institución Libre de Enseñanza) was offering courses in anthropology as early as 1878, and in 1892, the first chair of anthropology was established at the Central University of Madrid.[52] Yet, the question of how these Spanish centers absorbed and developed European scientific ideas remains to be studied. Important and telling in this development is the study of racial identity in Spain precisely because the scientific probing of race expressed both the nationalistic and universalist interests of these scientists. For example, to define the contours of their racial identity, Spanish scientists attempted to employ European methods of identifying races. Yet, it is clear that their view of the Spanish nation and how they wanted to define it conditioned their scientific observations.

Within a decade of its formation, Spanish anthropology was marked by ideological debates similar to those that had occurred in Europe. Certain anthropologists envisioned the Spanish race composed of elements that highlighted Spain's history of imperial conquest in the Western Hemisphere, a common feature of conservative and Catholic traditionalist rhetoric.[53] Others focused solely on physical characteristics as the definitive elements of the Spanish race, ignoring behavioral or cultural traits as too contingent and unscientific for racial categorization. Still, despite their different explanatory models, most racial thinkers relied on the idea that Spanish uniqueness rested on its supposed history of racial mixture. Because this idea conformed to already existing ideas of fusion as the cause of Spain's past imperial success, the reliance on racial mix also made scientific analysis of race acceptable to a broader range of Spanish thinkers than might otherwise have been the case. Instead of an image of conservative Catholic traditionalists holding steadfast against the incursion of any scientific analysis for understanding what constituted the Spaniard, the general reliance on the theme of racial fusion provided an idea amenable to many groups. Republican oppositional figures, engaged in anthropological study of the Spanish race, sought to break with the idea of Catholicism and its power to convert disparate groups as the sole uniting force of Spaniards. Instead, they presented this racial fusion in purely physical terms. Others brought the two approaches together, seeing Spanish racial fusion as the physical by-product of cultural or religious openness to the blending of disparate groups and people.

External political and social events also helped shape the nature of anthropological debates of race. The liberal Revolution of 1868 and the six-year period of official secular education in Spain aided the formation of a vigorous scientific examination of race that relied on the latest lessons from European racial sciences. Later social, cultural, and political conflict, culminating in the loss of the last remnants of the Spanish empire in 1898, was accompanied by a long-running discourse of decay and degeneration that anthropological study was designed to confront. As in other European countries, Spanish anthropologists calibrated their definitions of race and racial strength or health to older nationalistic notions of Spanish greatness, to present a scientific understanding of Spain's potential racial strength amidst cultural, political, colonial and economic decline. Racial debates in Spanish anthropology provided a scientific skein of understanding and the promise of solving lingering concerns over Spain's historical decline and its unique position as crossroads of Europe and Africa.

The idea of the Spanish *raza* and how it appeared in the burgeoning Spanish science of anthropology of the late nineteenth century is the subject of the next chapter. The ideas about race detailed above existed in Spain and influenced the anthropological exploration of race that emerged in the late nineteenth century. Clearly the idea of race mixture existed prior to the emergence of Spanish anthropology. Yet, anthropologists in Spain attempted to demonstrate that the power of admixtures actually superseded those of racial purity and attempted to assert, using a variety of scientific approaches, that the Spanish people were a racial alloy, a fusion of many others, and all the stronger for the mixture.

1 | Defining Race

3. Race and the Emergence of Physical Anthropology
The Predominant Head, 1875–1894

The scientific inquiry into race began in the late 1860s and exploded in the years between 1870 and 1900. In Spain, as in its European counterparts, the racial sciences began against the backdrop of liberal optimism that science might solve many of the intractable social problems brought on by modernization and industrialization. Even amidst the political ferment in Spain in the late nineteenth and early twentieth centuries, racial thought actually knit together a wide-ranging and ecumenical assemblage of political thinkers and ideological positions. The liberal and republican view of race, yoked to the liberal and republican scientists who first explored the supposed racial composition of Spain, survived these scientists' political exile after the Restoration of the Spanish monarchy because of how well their ideas conformed to a shared sense that the Spanish past was the product of fusion and mixture. Disagreements formed over the question of how the Spanish race had come together. This focus on mechanism allowed different political thinkers to identify a wide range of culprits behind Spanish disunity. Fusion, in the end, was the constant that tied all interpretations together.

Spanish anthropology began to evolve in a context of official state support followed by the almost immediate withdrawal of state funding. As a result, while anthropology continued to evolve, it did so only with its most important practitioners performing day jobs in other disciplines.[1] The result was a tremendous amount of work for the dozens of Spanish anthropologists attempting to devise what their field would comprise: a comprehensive understanding of all human behavior, physical makeup, and uniqueness among animal species through the study of psychology, biology, sociology, morphology, linguistics, art history, anatomy, geology, botany, archaeology, among other academic fields.[2] Perhaps unsurprisingly, the research agenda of Spain's first anthropological society numbered over fifty pages. The synthetic nature of early anthropological analysis meant that in most European societies, different figures handled different subfields, with conflict arising over methodology and interpretive frameworks. In Spain, there was far more coherence and less division among the various figures involved in anthropological analysis because there were fewer people engaged in a much larger range of research objectives.

Still, two primary modes of analyzing human variation existed in Spanish anthropology. Anthropology in Spain, as in most European countries, had its roots in two separate and older scientific fields, medicine and ethnology. Medical practitioners interested in anthropology tended to have an inductive perspective; they looked first at the individual to glean evidence about the group. They saw anatomy as the warehouse not only of individual health but also of the history of a people. Anthropology studied individuals, according to one early Spanish anthropologist, because we are all "collections of individuals, not isolated men."[3] These figures were drawn to physical anthropology that worked to measure differences between races. Politically, this group gravitated to Spain's republican political circles of the 1870s, which were ascendant during the period of the First Republic and in exile afterward.

The other field of anthropology emerged from the amateur world of ethnography, which involved the charting not just of physical differences but also of cultural and behavioral traits. Like their medical brethren, this group saw human difference as part of a panoply of forces, culture, and behaviors that determined the level of "civilization." In Spain, individual ethnographers enjoyed the most state support. Some found work in the government-funded Museum of Natural History (Museo de Historia Natural) in Madrid, where the pursuit of a more comprehensive comparison of peoples directly aided state projects, especially in maintaining Spain's colonial missions in the nineteenth century. While Spain had not been particularly successful performing scientific explorations in and around their overseas possessions, these missions were still important to military and civilian planners hoping to better understand colonized peoples.[4] These lessons also were meant to serve a popular political purpose, expressing the imperial power of the Spanish state to the population through exhibitions that usually began in Madrid's Retiro Park and then traveled to other cities. Among the largest was the Exposition of the Philippines in 1887, in which people could travel in dugout canoes around the Retiro's large lake. An exposition in 1897 of members of the Ashanti tribe featured human zoos in which Madrileños could observe people living in their transported villages. A similar exhibition of Inuit people took place in 1900.[5] Most of the ethnographers in the Museum of Natural History were not drawn to the same kinds of revolutionary politics that attracted their physical anthropology colleagues. Instead, the ethnographers were far more interested in verifying the older traditions of *casticismo*, of portraying through popular exhibition and museum work the historical connection between Catholicism and imperialism in the Spanish state. Noteworthy, however, was the agreement between these two different groups on the issue of racial mixture. This chapter begins with a discussion of the beginnings of physical anthropology among the doctors.

Measuring Skulls for Spain's Progress: Political Context and the Arrival of Physical Anthropology

The period of Spain's first republican government, though quite short-lived, helped solidify the foundations of Spain's scientific disciplines, especially in the university. Known as the Generation of 1868, or the Generation of the Learned (Generación de los Sabios), a group of republican and liberal doctors, lawyers, scientists, and historians during the First Republic (1873–74) and the six-year period of nonmonarchical parliamentary democracy in Spain (1868–74) had allowed Spanish sciences for the first time to develop free from governmental or church control.[6] University positions were created; scientific societies were established; and professional organizations modeled on European counterparts were formed. In addition, these new organizations introduced many of the latest developments of European science into Spain. However, once the Republic failed in 1874 and the monarchy was restored, many of those involved in these activities found themselves exiled once again from their university chairs and their societies cut off from government support. As a result, many of the Spanish sciences developing in this period depended upon private money for their continued evolution, whether to create postgraduate education, laboratories, or teaching positions.[7] Yet, the new Restoration government proved less hostile to scientific inquiry than it was to the state support of these endeavors. As Paul Broca, the French anthropologist, wrote in a letter to a Spanish colleague: Spanish scientists now found themselves "free to think, but . . . authorized to stay silent."[8] Still, even without the same kinds of institutional and official support, the contacts gleaned from university positions both in Spain and abroad, and, even more importantly, the implantation of an intellectual culture more open to scientific lessons, especially in the liberal press of the era, many of Spain's early anthropologists helped perpetuate Spanish sciences at a level at least intellectually commensurate with European sciences.

Anthropology, in fact, represented one of the firmest centers of scientific expansion during the Restoration. In part because of the personal wealth of its early practitioners and also because it was a science in vogue elsewhere in Europe, anthropology in Spain became the model of how scientific expansion unfolded during the Restoration. Spain's first institutionalizer of anthropological investigation in Spain, Pedro González de Velasco, developed the discipline largely through his unique ability to fund a free institution, an effort that included paying the salaries of teachers and the expenses of building and maintaining a research facility.[9] Velasco's wealth grew out of his medical practice and, in particular, the international fame he garnered from skillful and often daredevil techniques in surgery.[10] Velasco's interest in anthropology developed precisely from this confluence of training inside Spain and his professional contacts outside Spain. Comparative anatomy, which had generally been a practical element of medical education in Spain, was the core area of study for anthropologists in Europe. Thus, Velasco's contact with European doctors quickly evolved into a fascination with the new field of anthropology.[11] He corresponded with such renowned anthropologists as Paul Broca in France, whom he had befriended in Paris, Ernst Haeckel in Germany, Karl Vogt in England, and George Wood in the United States.[12] Like them, Velasco saw comparative anatomy as the best means of distinguishing not just between individuals but also between races. Velasco's contact with Paul Broca, who at the time was the president of the Société d'Anthropologie, turned many Spaniards' attention to physical anthropology. This friendship helped give early Spanish anthropology, especially within Velasco's Anthropology Society (Sociedad de Antropología), a decidedly French cast.

In these early years, however, the Spanish field did not engage in the contentious and fractious debates that plagued French society. Ethnographers and physical anthropologists in France had already fought out the issues of what was the most valuable and effective means of defining human difference.[13] Broca's choice of physical characteristics as the means by which to identify races and to predict the quality of these races made the debate about culture versus physical roots rather more moot in Spain than it had been in other societies in Europe. The tension that defined the Spanish Anthropology Society had to do with identifying the origins of humanity, the other great subject of disagreement in European anthropology. Velasco brought this debate back with him to Spain from France. In a sense, it was logical that this more philosophical fight about human origins occupied Spaniards more than did debates involving evidence and the interpretation of it because, in general, they had fewer skulls and far less infrastructure to work with. The human origins debate, with its epistemological overtones about religion versus science, also proved more accessible to those who did not have the medical training required to engage in the increasingly minute and complex measurements that came to define physical anthropology. The debates oscillated between monogenism, which posited an original race from which all subsequent races had emerged through population movements and intermixture of people, and polygenism, which argued that a variety of "pure" races had existed during the early period of human life that had remained relatively stable over the generations despite subsequent intermixing. Broca was an importnat defender of the polygenist position, arguing that certain races, or "species of men," could not successfully interbreed.[14]

Despite its use to promote racist hierarchies, polygenism also buttressed claims of tolerance and racial equality. Broca's ideas, for example, did not have the pessimism of polygenism's most famous advocate, Arthur de Gobineau. Gobineau argued that intermixture was inevitable. Humans, he wrote, are expansionist by nature and must conquer others. While the weaker races were elevated by this contact, the strongest would always degenerate and ultimately disappear. Broca, on the other hand, supported what he called "polygenic transformism," which allowed for some alteration of the original pure species through contact with others.[15] He stressed the ways in which interbreeding lifted up the weaker races and thus focused on the positive elements of intermixture rather than the ultimate decline of all races. The difference reflected political differences between the two thinkers. While Gobineau's ideas expressed the pessimism of a conservative who wanted ultimately to undo the egalitarian spirit of the French Revolution and contemporary republicanism, Broca's more liberal leanings prompted him to emphasize the potential improvement of the weak by explaining their ostensible inability to progress.[16] Clearly, this monogenist/polygenist debate had a social and political dimension that allowed racial debate throughout Europe to transcend scientific argument and engender the kinds of racial hierarchies that underscored European racism of the late nineteenth century.[17] Ultimately, how Spaniards came to celebrate racial fusion was the product of how they

connected European ideas about origins and racial types with their own particular national scientific context. Velasco's incorporation of French anthropology was a key example of how an ecumenical approach to defining the
Spanish nation based on the idea of biological mixture came to develop.

Sharing Broca's medical background, Velasco felt most comfortable assuming that human difference was a measurable aspect of a human being's
physical attributes. Through this analysis, anthropologists would uncover
the vestiges of the pure races that survived in the shapes of heads and the
angles of the face. Monogenists in Spain followed Armand de Quatrefages'
arguments at the Société d'Anthropologie. Although a personal friend of
Broca, Quatrefages was Broca's staunchest intellectual opponent in the Société. Their fight had an odd impact in Spain. For one, Broca and Quatrefages' conflict did not emerge in France until well after Velasco's institute had
closed in 1882, shortly after his death.[18] The result was that Spanish anthropology began during the First Republic with a decidedly polygenist, physical
cast. But when the Republic ended, and anthropology fell more directly under
the strictures of the Restoration government, physical anthropologists were
shunted into other disciplines, and Spain's monogenists ultimately refash-
ioned, but did not wholly overturn, their predecessors' work.[19] The two approaches never entirely cancelled each other out, and their conclusions both
ultimately relied on racial fusion.

Velasco, Polygenism, and Physical Anthropology

The polygenist position was in one sense the logical choice for anthropologists trained in medicine like Paul Broca and Velasco. Extrapolating from observations of individuals, polygenists tended to assume that they were analyzing whole populations.[20] But others were skeptical. As one Spanish doctor
and monogenist, José de Letamendi, wrote about the work of Velasco and
his assistant Ángel Pulido: they were "very smart and determined but often
confused the organ for the organism."[21] The nexus of this fight was really a
matter of how one hoped to apply anthropology in particular national settings. Could one extrapolate from individuals the identity of the entire race?
How did one deduce general national conditions from individual measurements? Like most scientific debates, this one emerged from disagreements
over interpretation; how one drew conclusions from the data presented. Here
racial prejudice seeped into the conclusions of the scientists. Despite the supposedly biological basis, the clearest and most irrefutable evidence of racial

strength still remained political domination and economic power. Understanding which nations had mixed eugenically from these ancient races, and which had failed, would allow for clearer understanding of the progress and value of nations past, present, and future. For example, Broca argued that anthropology would provide lessons for French colonial missions, offering a prior understanding of which groups were compatible with, or potentially capable of, European civilization.[22]

The context of Spanish racial study was quite different. Ironically, Spain had initiated ethnographic expeditions for the purposes of scientific progress and imperial control much earlier in the nineteenth century than most European countries. Their failure and the increasing weakness of Spain's empire left Spanish anthropology with a different set of explanatory missions. Velasco, for example, did not infuse such imperial concerns in his own anthropology. He was far more concerned with political matters more relevant to the Spanish home population. For Velasco and the Anthropological Society, scientific analysis of the Spanish race was the key component in the modernization and progress of a nation. Anthropologists would be working for the improvement of Spain through better understanding of Spaniards.

Other differences in context were important in differentiating Spain from its European counterparts. Whereas Broca felt supported in his labors by the Third Republic—his only fear, in fact, was of government spies stealing his research—Velasco had to work in opposition to an unsupportive state.[23] Writing to Broca in 1865, Velasco bemoaned the absence of governmental support, questioning whether scientific endeavor would ever be allowed to lift Spain from its doldrums.[24] For Velasco, the backwardness of Spanish science was due to the political backwardness and immaturity of the modern Spanish state. Yet, his own success and international stature led him to conclude that Spain's failures were not the product of an ethnic or racial incapacity. In fact, Velasco argued that the proclamation of the First Republic in 1873 signaled the inherently civilized nature of the Spaniard, not only because of the lack of bloodshed in its creation, but also the immediate support given to scientific inquiry.[25]

During the First Republic (1873–74), the minister of development appointed Pedro González de Velasco, his old friend, as director of anatomical studies at the Central University of Madrid. There Velasco began to accrue skeletal collections and other anatomical tools that he took with him to his private museum when he lost his university position in 1874. This collection became the start of Spain's first anthropological museum.[26] He also used the opportunity to develop another anthropological society to follow his short-lived first effort in 1867. The earlier society had put itself in the difficult position of identifying its mission as defining racial groups and, more specifically, the Spaniard, even though it lacked a collection of skulls with which to perform such an anthropological study. Of the six areas of research outlined in the inaugural session's minutes, three included the classification of human races and the "discussion of their origin." One specifically delineated the goal of seeking and defining the "aboriginal races of the Spanish peninsula, the Balearic Islands and the Canary Islands and their crossings with each other."[27] Politics intervened in this program, however, with the Revolution of 1868. Velasco's attention was briefly drawn away from his institute when he was appointed Madrid's civil governor. These events preempted the further development of the Anthropology Society.

After the end of the republican experiment, Velasco founded the Free School and Laboratory of Anthropology in 1875. The relative stability of the Restoration in its first years helped the Free School and Laboratory become the leading force in the formation of the modern discipline of anthropology in Spain. Because of Spain's lack of graduate education, the tuition cost of attending medical schools at the university, and the removal of certain scientific courses taught there, a number of the exiled professors started their own institutions to provide Spain with "free education." For these institutional leaders, the "free" in their institutions' titles meant that they were free of government control over curriculum and faculty, free for the students to attend, free of church control over curriculum, and free to perform experiments that were not allowed in official centers.[28] The emphasis on practical training provided centers for young doctors and scientists already holding university degrees to practice in their sciences, to hone abilities that helped them attract clients, and to experiment, all of which had been extremely difficult outside the context of the university.[29] In addition, these institutes made efforts to establish contacts between Spanish scientists and European scientific institutions, whose journals were unavailable in Spanish universities because of political or scientific disputes. In one of its first meetings, Velasco's institute established relations and journal subscriptions with more than fifteen anthropology, geography, and science academies in Germany, Italy, France, Austria, Russia, England, and the United States.[30] The institute also initially published its own two journals, the Revista de Antropología (1874), the organ of the Sociedad de Antropología, and the Anfiteatro Anatómico Español. The two merged into the Revista de Antropología in 1875.

For Velasco, these journals became mouthpieces for his institutes and his school, for the spread of anthropological ideas, and for republican political propaganda. The journals' first issues, published just as the Republic was formed, made clear that Spanish renewal would have to be predicated upon the scientific diagnosis of social ills. These journals were portraits of a European liberal mind-set that saw the purpose of scientific inquiry as the improvement of the individual and the social organism. As Velasco wrote in the first edition of the *Anfiteatro*, all science is "medicine for the nation," and all anthropologists should do is merely "elevate *la medicina patria* to such heights that everyone in the world can see it; we want to make the rest of the world understand that Spain is right when we place ourselves among the nations marching at the forefront of progress."[31] The rest of the journal in these first years was devoted to detailing how social reforms could be based on a scientific understanding of the functioning of "social organisms."[32] For Velasco, this study was essential precisely because other nations had already begun the study and were leaving Spain behind: "Even if we continue at this pace, people and nations do not realize in one day all of the changes that are necessary to raise themselves to states of relative perfection. The Anthropology Society believes that the time has arrived to renew its public and private work, especially if the *patria* does not want to suffer from the lack of indispensable knowledge, to live outside the scientific moment that nourishes the center of European culture."[33]

Underscoring this apparent backwardness, Velasco filled the society's curriculum with the largest possible number of scientific fields. The professors and students who attended the first academic year (1875–76) in the institute and free school included a wide range of doctors, psychiatrists, specialists in legal or forensic medicine, and geologists, all from a variety of ideological and philosophical backgrounds. Among this student body were the leading lights of Spanish science of the late nineteenth century: Juan Vilanova Piera, the first translator of Darwin into Spanish; Luís Simarro, a doctor, psychiatrist, and, later, student of Charcot in Paris; and Ángel Pulido, a doctor, psychiatrist, and, later, the director of public health of Spain and a senator in the Cortes.[34] Yet, the mission of the institute was primarily the acquisition of anthropological knowledge about Spain. For Velasco and Pulido, the society's first secretary, anthropology provided the basic portrait of human origins and was the root of all other sciences. Anthropology was the first human science and thus contained a wealth of analysis in its purview: "particular description of races and their determination; the study of their differences and similarities all in relation to their physical constitution, their social and intellectual state; the investigation of their actual affinities, of their appearance in the past and the present, of their historical significance, and of their probable lineage, and of their respective position among the variety of human races."[35]

Yet, because of the influence of French anthropology and specifically of Broca, Velasco coordinated the goals of the Anthropology Society with those of his anatomical institute. Broca's mission to define racial categories and to designate "normal" and pathological structures for different groups based on the measurement of physical characteristics appealed to Velasco's medical interests and anatomical knowledge.[36] In his opening address for the anthropological and anatomical societies in 1875, Velasco identified anatomy and the charting of human difference as the best guarantors of national health: "Vast, vast science, as vast in the life of man as it is precarious in some corners of the world, so vast that if we only decipher a small amount of the mystery written into the book of life, we will have clues to . . . the composition and existence of superior-organized beings . . . the cement of classification, the light of physiology, the torchlight of hygiene, the illustration of pathology, that is Anatomy, the firm and secure base that supports the colossal edifice of Hippocratic science."[37]

For anthropology to provide a holistic portrait of a race, however, physical measurements alone were known to be insufficient. Again following Broca, Velasco included morphology in the curriculum at the institute. Morphology provided a more comprehensive portrait for Velasco because it measured not only individual body parts but also the physical shapes of the body in relation to each other. For Velasco and his students, body shape and the relations of body parts to each other betrayed physical, intellectual, and emotional characteristics of the organism. The classification of this internal organization of the body was the ultimate goal of anthropology. As Velasco mentioned in a speech at the opening of the anthropological museum in 1875 with King Alfonso XII and various government ministers in attendance, the key to anthropological understanding rested in the measurement of the human body: "If through the prism of experimentation and analysis, your anatomical lessons seem unintelligible, then you must find and use morphology . . . [and if] you want to understand the depths of the human body? Then resort to anthropometry, the tool of morphology."[38] Velasco wanted anthropology to be as comprehensive as possible in defining not only individual racial histories but also social histories. In his speech in front of "official Spain," Velasco stressed that the goal of the Anthropology Society was nothing short of defining the Spaniard, using the science of anthropology to identify physical characteristics as the primary measure of difference.[39] Anthropologists had to shake off their traditional role as passive "observers of men," like earlier ethnographers had been.[40] Indeed, the Anthropology Society and Free School would take further steps to define the Spaniard by not confining itself to mere physical measurement.

Instead, they would apply these measurements to a more formal diagnosis of the cultural, intellectual, and social potentials of the Spaniard. Anthropology would study physical qualities, yet it would also provide insight into the underlying cultural and intellectual capabilities that these physical characteristics revealed. In the inaugural address of the school year in 1875—again to the members of the society, as well as to the king and representatives of the Ministries of Education and Development (Fomento)—Velasco's secretary, Ángel Pulido, argued that Spain's lack of involvement in the earlier development of nineteenth-century anthropology in one sense helped the country to avoid the pitfalls of other European sciences.[41] While noting that nationalist concerns had often clouded the conclusions of other European scientists in the early nineteenth century, Pulido suggested that Spain would be able to engage in anthropological study when less corruptible forms of scientific endeavor were available. Least corruptible was the craniological analysis of the population. Pulido followed Velasco's claims for the value of morphology, writing that one of the benefits of craniological study was that one could trace through analysis of the physical makeup of people many psychic and cultural elements of their behavior. Pulido traced a line of anthropological thought from Blumenbach to Broca that saw the head as the area of the body where all factors governing identity, behavior, and intellectual and racial characteristics were embedded: "If [the study of the head] had not reached the level of such preponderant importance, if it had not arisen almost immediately . . . to dominate and finalize the slender end of the human construction, then one could be more or less transiently faithful to its content and shape. But the skull is a more sublime and mysterious organ where the psychic faculties are developed, which governs all of the different levels of development, and which points to the predictable destinies of different beings."[42]

For Pulido, Velasco, and the other members of the Anthropology Society and the Free School, the only element that Spain lacked to bring about this scientific renaissance was the corps of scientists to perform the experiments. Arguing against a broader assumption that Spaniards somehow lacked the scientific wherewithal to conduct experiments, the members of the Anthropology Society noted that their mere presence signaled Spain's capacity for science. Spain merely lacked the army of scientists necessary to do the experimentation.[43] The final argument for establishing the training center for anthropology was clearly nationalistic. Recognizing anthropology as the new science of nationalism, these figures argued that only homegrown anthropologists could adequately classify their nation. If Spaniards did not define themselves, others would do it for them. The implication was clear: others would define Spaniards improperly: "ethnological study in this country, as painful for me as it is to confess it, remains mostly unknown (for the sake of national pride, at least it is not completely abandoned), much to the disappointment of foreign countries, who need our data, and who as a result find it necessary to try to do their own studies of Spain, to fill in the gaps."[44]

The image of Spaniards presented in most European anthropology required an initial overhaul by Spanish anthropologists. European interest in Spain had fixated only on the inexplicable anthropological oddities the peninsula contained, like the Basques. For some, Spain was the prime example of racial decay. For example, one of the few instances in which Gobineau mentioned Spain in his racial history was in presenting the Basques, the only group in the Iberian Peninsula to resist Arab conquest, as an example of racial isolation and decay rather than purity.[45] Indeed, this interest in the Basques troubled those Spanish anthropologists who had helped other Europeans study Spain. Once Velasco began to study the physical components of the Spanish head, the legacy of European influence on his own scientific interpretation troubled him. The main source of materials that the museum had was a series of skulls culled from a Basque village in the 1860s. Velasco had sent measurements of these skulls to Broca, who used them as the basis for his conclusion that Spain was in a process of racial decay.

Velasco interpreted them differently. For the Spanish anthropologist, the evidence of intermixture embedded in these skulls was clear. For Velasco, the Basque region was the proving ground of racial intermixture through the ages, proof of the lasting imprint of many different racial groupings fused together that made up the contemporary Spaniard. These two hundred skulls were not analyzed to find an ancient and foundational race. Instead, Velasco hoped to uncover in them the peculiar process of Spanish racial fusion.[46] Oddly, he turned to one of the great voices of Aryan supremacy to make his claims. Velasco used Karl Vogt's racial categories not to hunt down the essence of a pure past race embedded in the Spanish crania as Vogt had done, but rather to find the telltale signs of the many different European head types fused together in the Spanish skull. Proof of fusion was the goal, not proof of purity. For example, the dolichocephalic group, the most longheaded, was then associated with intelligence and high levels of civilization. According to Vogt, Germans generally predominated in this group.[47] The brachycephalic group was the more round-headed, or short-headed, and was considered the least developed emotionally or intellectually of the peoples of the world. Spaniards and Italians most clearly comprised the brachycephalics. One last group was created because their measurements did not neatly fit into either category. They were the mesocephalics, who lived in border regions between northern and southern Europe. Velasco hoped to uncover all of these attributes fused together in the Spanish head.[48]

Velasco let his student Ángel Pulido perform the first analysis of the skulls. The measurements proved inconclusive. Undeterred, Pulido saw the failure as a call for more research. He wrote that the various shapes and sizes of the skulls represented every "step between brachy- and dolichocephalic" and that, without further analysis, it was not possible to develop a subtype among these skulls to define as Spanish.[49] As a result, he would normally be unwilling to include Spaniards as a discrete type in his general cephalic ranking of various races.[50] But Pulido was undaunted in his assumption that a Spanish racial subtype existed. He wrote that the lack of clarity owed more to the lack of adequate study of the Spanish head. He was confident that further measurement would bear out the assumption of Spanish uniqueness. He concluded from these measurements that the first indications showed that indeed the Spanish head was different in the range of possible head shapes. What significance that fact held was a matter of increasing debate in Spain.

Before further analysis of the skulls and the accumulation of more evidence were possible, Velasco died in 1882, and the society and anatomical institute went into decline.[51] It was a pattern typical in the mid- and late nineteenth century that demonstrated the tenuous development of the Spanish sciences, especially the reliance on wealthy patrons and individual scientists. A small community of scientists flourished briefly in one institutional setting only to disband as their institution lost funding or individual interests turned to other matters. Ángel Pulido, for example, returned to private medical practice and served as a city councilor in Madrid, all the while maintaining a career as a journalist, editing an important medical newspaper, El Siglo Médico, and acting as coeditor of the newspaper El Liberal.[52] It was a similar trajectory to those followed by other faculty in Velasco's Free School. Luís Simarro traveled to Paris to work with the pantheon of French medical professionals of the late nineteenth century, including Jean Martin Charcot, the head of the Salpetrière Hospital, Jean Paul Ranvier, Ernst Renan, and the embryologist Matis Duval.[53] Simarro returned a few years later in 1885 and began publishing and lecturing on the anthropology and anatomy research being performed in the laboratories of these scientists and also on the experimental psychology then being practiced.[54] Others took positions in universities in an era of expansion of the professorial ranks and relative openness in the early years of the Restoration.[55]

In Spain, the death of institutions did not necessarily prefigure the death of all anthropological study. Certainly the effort to define the Spanish race through the measurement of skulls slowed from its early peak in Velasco's society. Yet the causes were not just the result of a lack of interest or large-scale resistance from governmental sectors. The greatest impediment that Velasco and his brethren faced in performing physical measurements was their popular image as ghouls scouring the Spanish countryside for fresh cadavers to measure. As testimony to his devotion to scientific experiment, Velasco found solace after the death of his teenage daughter in the fact that he could use her bones for research.[56] Velasco's reputation for a few years after his death seemed determined by his behavior toward his daughter's remains. The Spanish press ran fantastically macabre stories of Velasco bringing his daughter's cadaver to the opera or to restaurants. Novelists used the sensationalized image of Velasco in a number of stories reminiscent of the work of Edgar Allen Poe.[57] But it was the larger shifts in anthropological study, not the popular sense of anthropology as perverse or unnatural, that influenced the development of Spanish anthropology. A more important factor was a broader crisis within the European study of physical anthropology. This crisis led to the overall questioning of the idea of racial purity throughout Europe, a fact usually ignored in European historiography of race. Anthropologists abandoned purity as the ultimate goal of anthropological analysis, and it was this tradition that formed the basis of much of European racial sciences over the next half century.[58] Spanish reliance on mixture then was just a part of a questioning throughout Europe of the idea of racial purity. Yet, questioning racial purity did not militate against the idea of racial competition in Spain nor between European nations more broadly.

Federico Olóriz and the Discovery of a "Spanish Racial Type"

Interest in physical anthropology continued after Velasco's death. But Pulido's pessimistic comments about the two hundred skulls in the Anthropology Society's collection did anticipate a crisis that occurred in both French and Spanish physical anthropology. Despite the multitude of measurements they collected, physical anthropologists failed to uncover obvious and consistent characteristics that clearly identified European racial groups. Broca in particular grew frustrated with the fact that so many skull measurements seemed only to provide a compendium of different groups defined by increasing shades of grey defining. None proved wholly representative of any one race.[59] As a result, anthropologists in the 1880s began to question whether they could directly measure the original purity of different races solely through physical measurements of individual body parts.

But rather than abandon physical measurements, some anthropologists responded with a positivist desire to increase the number of measurements and then compare large groups of data. Such an approach would allow anthropologists, and especially the polygenists associated with Broca in France, to ignore the statistical confusion created by too many conflicting physical measurements. Instead, they could search for averages and proportions among these physical measurements to define present-day races. They began to use averages of multiple measures, or indices, which produced a single number rather than multiple fractions. One could not see race so much as elicit it from increasingly sophisticated measurements. Among these indices, the cephalic index provided the clearest racial typology. Paul Topinard, Broca's disciple and successor as director of the Société de l'Anthropologie, was the key figure in this reformulation.[60] And, again, Spanish physical anthropologists would follow their French colleagues and expand their own racial analysis to include complex indices of racial characteristics. If an index was technically more complex, it also seemed scientifically more revealing. An index of measures unmasked the traces of racial mixtures in the past, and demonstrated mixture as a new racial paradigm to oppose the model of racial purity.

This approach also placed far more emphasis on data collection, on gathering as many possible measurements of groups already thought of as races, to ferret out the definitive averages that proved the presumed racial identification. For Topinard, this endeavor was a way to avoid the racist efforts of other anthropologists to prove superiority of one group over another based on notions of purity. No races remained pure, Topinard wrote in 1879, and the search for racial types was the only possible method for finding the composite races that made up each racial type. Perhaps in a dig at his German colleagues, Topinard blamed the ideal of racial purity on the philological and archaeological view that European civilization was rooted solely in ancient Greece.[61] Such a view, he wrote, was not anthropological enough for it failed to acknowledge the long history of intermixture between Europeans and others. Anthropologists, too, had erroneously defined races based on a physical appearance of beauty that was not real, measurable, or empirical. He called this veneration of beauty "a disastrous Grecian gift to anthropology."[62]

Topinard's most avid follower in Spain was also the most prolific anthropological measurer of the Spanish population, Federico Olóriz y Aguilera. Olóriz was trained as a doctor in the Medical Faculty of the University of Granada, which was then under the directorship of Antonio Martínez Molina, an early follower of Darwin in Spain, and also a close friend of Velasco.[63] In fact, Olóriz was able to attend some of Velasco's anatomy and physical anthropology classes in Madrid during his time in medical school because of a recommendation from Martínez Molina.[64] Such connections quickly elevated Olóriz's standing among medical anatomists. Upon graduation from the medical faculty in 1875, Olóriz became a teaching assistant in anatomy classes, and attempted to publish the anatomical lessons of Martínez Molina.[65] In 1878, he also edited the second edition of Julián Calleja's 1869 anatomy text that was exclusively used in Spanish medical faculties.[66] Two years later, he followed Martínez Molina to the Central University in Madrid to act as an assistant when Molina became the chair of the anatomy department.[67] In 1883, Olóriz took over Martínez Molina's chair at the university and immediately began to fuse his own anthropological interest with the traditional anatomical study done in Spain's leading university.[68] In the chair of anatomy, Olóriz worked to acquire the collections from Velasco's anthropological museum that were left to gather dust in Velasco's offices after his death.[69] In 1887, the Spanish government purchased Velasco's building and its contents and sent his collection to the rival Museum of Natural History in Madrid a few months later.[70] Olóriz was given access to its contents, again probably on the recommendation of Martínez Molina. Following Velasco's own trajectory, Olóriz became interested in morphology, or the study of the functions of and relationships between organs and skeletal elements.

Once again, Spanish anthropology benefitted from its late development. The popularity of Ernst Haeckel's ideas among a broad swath of European scientists had begun to spread into Spain. Spaniards joined others who saw within Haeckel's notion of ontogeny recapitulating phylogeny—that is, that the individual's development mimicked the historical development of the entire species—the possible existence of a divine plan expressed through biological evolution. Haeckel had removed some of the chaos and unpredictability of Darwin's universe. Development was ordered, reflecting all of God's creation in each individual specimen. Although many of Spain's early anthropologists may have been anticlerical republicans, they were not antireligious. Discovering a scientific basis for divine order was for many, in fact, an exciting prospect. As a result, Haeckel's appeal in Spain was wide; he was, in fact, the first honorary member of Velasco's free Anthropology Society. He enjoyed personal contacts with Francisco María Tubino, the vice secretary of the society. Luís Simarro also maintained close ties to Haeckel's Monist League in Germany.[71]

Following Haeckel, Olóriz was drawn to the possibility that larger human differences might be related to potential differences in the development of bodily structures and their uses.[72] This process was always more relational and conjectural than the more positivist reliance on physical measurement alone. But, Olóriz sought to reconcile seemingly contradictory approaches, combining the more idealist Haeckelian approach—which presumed a unity of the individual with the species—with those of his positivist brethren in France. Olóriz hoped one could actually measure this unity within one species and then express whatever differences existed between races through the comparison of indices. As a disciple of Topinard, Olóriz believed he could deploy morphologies as more accurate measures of identifying the minute differences between racial types. Only in the study of relationships between physical structures might one derive the racial origins of different groups.[73] After looking at the skulls from Velasco's Anthropology Society institute, Olóriz knew that to perform the proper morphological analysis, he would need to collect more specimens. He noted, as Pulido had written earlier, that the most fundamental problem of anthropological study in Spain was the lack of materials to perform study of the Spanish race. Yet he remained optimistic; Spain would advance with "the enthusiasm that existed ten years ago but has since disappeared. I only hope that we are not dead, but merely sleeping. . . . I have already begun this work in the preliminary collection of pieces, work in which I find the secret of success for all scientific enterprise that relies upon positive data at its base."[74] Olóriz was convinced that the greatest obstacle was only Spanish culture as anthropologists continued to be plagued by their popular image as ghouls collecting cadavers. The generally negative reaction he received to his mere request to perform autopsies was, according to Olóriz, sufficient grounds for pessimism:

There could be so much done in this country if only Spain could acclimate itself to the idea, for example, of an association for autopsies like those that exist north of the Pyrenees. But our customs are less free, our family ties are tighter, and our religious feelings are deeper so that a society of dissection for autopsies, for example, would take a long time to set up here. Even though we have plenty of capable people, it is difficult for us to do anything but lament an almost unanimous feeling of the nation and wound their sensibilities with requests. We must unfortunately respect these feelings and their origins and must combat them slowly and with measure, so that ultimately we can get families to deliver their loved ones to science, rather than to the sepulchre.[75]

The fear of Spanish sensibilities was deep enough for Olóriz that when this article appeared in the wider medical press, Olóriz excised his criticism of Spanish society. In his articles, he counseled Spanish anthropologists to use more caution when approaching family members in hospitals to ask for the bodies of their kin in order to build a large sample of conclusive ethnological data for understanding the Spaniard.[76] In the end, Olóriz decided that culture was at best a flimsy barrier, easily finessed by the wily scientist, whose greater scientific purpose would ultimately overwhelm a backward population with its noble purpose. In 1886, he advised his followers to appeal to the Spanish rationality and fundamental desire for truth and national progress: "In an essentially Catholic country like ours, one should always place some religious symbol on the cadavers that we study so as to respect the beliefs of the aggrieved whose loved ones' remains should be brought to us to serve education, science, and sometimes even judicial investigations."[77]

As it turned out, this kind of prudence was not entirely necessary. While conservative and Catholic critiques did exist in government circles and among popular journals and newspapers, within the scientific community even opponents of the aggressively empirical methods of Olóriz supported such study to be performed in the name of Spanish progress. This phenomenon was another legacy of the ideas of the First Republic. The expansion of scientific study, the growing number of graduates from the university in the sciences, and an increasing openness to scientific study within government ministries allowed many scientists to move into positions within the university and also within the government. Thus, when scientists like Olóriz requested expanded facilities and freedom to perform experiments, often they were granted from within the university in the interests of science, rather than rejected in the name of state or church interests.[78] Thus, by 1889, the longtime critic of positivist and empirical sciences in Spain and an avid attendee at Wagner's circle in Bayreuth,

José de Letamendi, the dean of the Central University of Madrid, allowed Olóriz to expand his studies from measuring the skulls already in his collection, to collecting bodies from the university's hospital for measurement.[79]

With this ability to expand his collection, Olóriz started an anthropological laboratory in the medical faculty at the Central University of Madrid. Yet, because of the ostensible position of the university as a national center and with his laboratory the only one of its kind in a Spanish university, Olóriz devoted himself to national definitions in order to deduce an anthropological composite of the Spanish type.[80] Olóriz argued that the Spanish peninsula was a perfect location to prove Topinard's argument that racial types were the only possible method to locate the vestiges of ancient pure races. Yet, an enlightened Olóriz also saw Spain as essential for all of European anthropology. Because Iberia had been a historical crossroads, Olóriz argued that anthropological study of the Iberian Peninsula as a whole would demonstrate in microcosm the universal process of race mixing and the emergence of racial types.

Olóriz wanted to perform national studies of Spanish crania to show the historical and ethnological roots of the contemporary Spaniard. Science would define the nation, proving that biology and anthropology were at the center of any national weakness, including those of regional separatism and the weakness of Spanish nationalism. The cranium was the treasure map of Spain's problems: "In reality, every Spanish cranium whatever its origin is useful and should be examined attentively. More than knowing the median size of Spanish crania . . . it is more important to know the ethnological differences that give the physiognomic uniqueness to the crania from every region, and that have historically divided our nation."[81] By 1891, Olóriz had received permission to begin measuring Spanish crania throughout the peninsula, focusing specifically on areas where mass measurements could take place. While Olóriz was diligent in his efforts, he had to work harder to prove the scientific relevance of anthropology to a diffident Spanish government. While the German government granted access to its anthropologists, like Rudolf Virchow, to enter schools and military academies to perform their fieldwork as early as the 1860s, Olóriz had to be more creative overcoming official obstacles. For example, Olóriz did not have access to schoolchildren because the church, which controlled most primary education in Spain at the time, refused to allow anthropologists and doctors armed with cranioscopes and charts to enter their buildings. Denied access to schools, Olóriz instead asked the director of public education in Spain for funds to design maps and racial charts that would be distributed to doctors throughout the peninsula.

Doctors would then perform anthropological measurements of their patients and their relatives while they performed general examinations.[82] He also contacted the military, asking that cranial measurements be taken of all incoming soldiers.[83] For Olóriz, these more indirect means of gathering national data still would provide an anthropological definition of the nation.

Based on this research, Olóriz prepared a book-length analysis of the cephalic index, or a comparison of various measures of the head. Again, through averages, racial types would emerge. For Olóriz, the cephalic index was the clearest measure of racial types among a mixed population. Olóriz assumed that the relationship between head size and facial angles, among other measurements provided in the cephalic index, betrayed the racial fingerprints of mixed-race populations. As a result, Olóriz based this study almost entirely on models provided by Topinard and Broca.[84] He experimented with the measure of other physical characteristics, including hair and eye color, only to find them too inconclusive and variable as indicators of racial provenance.[85] In addition, he found only too late that doctors often neglected to provide such details in their surveys. As a result, he decided to put off the study of all other characteristics to a later date, hoping to convince the director of public education to allow him into schools to assess the pigmentation of the young so as to begin lifelong studies of the Spanish population.[86]

The implications of Olóriz's work were not lost on Spain's leading scientific and political thinkers. Among them was Olóriz's childhood friend Santiago Ramón y Cajal. Ramón y Cajal, Spain's first Nobel laureate and the discoverer of the neuron, impelled the younger scientist to help define the Spaniard through comparative anatomy and morphology.[87] By 1892, Olóriz was prepared to present his first findings, based on the study of over 8,368 skulls and skeletons gathered from doctors throughout the country. Presenting his study to a joint meeting of Spanish, Portuguese, and South American geographers and anthropologists, Olóriz argued that studies of the Spanish race were essential for two reasons: (1) to provide future generations with the beginnings of anthropological understanding of ethnological, physiological, and social problems among Spaniards; and, (2) to understand both the differences and similarities between members of the white races of Europe and the Americas. Again, the uniqueness of Spain's complex history of mixture left it at the vanguard; answering Spanish racial questions would help revivify Spain and solve its social and political problems and potentially those of other European races. He concluded, "thus, it is essential that we begin the work now so that after years of difficult labor, perhaps the generation that follows us even more than our own, might create the scientific foundations of Spanish Anthropology and contribute effective solutions to a variety of ethnological, sociological and physiological problems that afflict the individual and collective life of our *patria*."[88] His study not only uncovered the various racial and ethnic strains that had fused to form contemporary Spaniards. In addition, Olóriz was able to construct a vision of contemporary Spain as a particular kind of racial conglomeration, describing how the various racial mixtures had combined to form a new racial type. Assuming that all groups were mixed, that racial purity was a statistical impossibility if not a myth, Olóriz asserted that a long history of stable racial mixture would breed a physically distinct race, with the Spanish race as the best example of mixed stability.

> It is probable that the general roots of the geographical distribution of the [cephalic] index have not changed in Spain since the beginning of the Roman domination of the peninsula. One can thus consider the Spanish among the purest in Europe, since not only because of the affinity or interrelationship of its principal characteristics, but also because of the intimate mixture and advanced fusion that can be shown between them, with great uniformity extending throughout the entire length and width of the national territory.[89]

In fact, not only was the Spanish race Europe's best example of the effects of racial fusion, but also, because Spain was one of the oldest nations in Europe, Olóriz concluded that Spain represented the racial vanguard of Europe. Olóriz noted that superiority and inferiority of races were no longer defined solely by the capacity of the crania or the particular angle of the face. Rather these characteristics would be used only as possible evidence of the quality and amount of racial mixing in the past. Spain's cephalic index, according to Olóriz, placed it exactly at the middle point of the known racial groupings then studied. Since moderation of the index was the result of mixture, then the extremes of large or small capacity would demonstrate less mixture. As a result, Olóriz was willing to dismiss the possibility that a position to either extreme of the cephalic index was a sign of superiority or inferiority. Instead, proximity to the midpoint was the sought-after quality.

European Responses to Olóriz and the Spanish Racial Type

Throughout Europe, Olóriz's colleagues had a largely positive response to his work. But the content of this response reveals both the difference of Spanish racial theories from others and the idea that racial claims, no matter their basis, lent themselves to notions of racial hierarchy and exclusion. Olóriz was clearly ambivalent about associating himself with German claims to Aryan superiority. While still strongly averring Spanish racial mixture, Olóriz also celebrated the fact that Spaniards approximated their German cousins in terms of their superiority. While comparing the overall significance of the average Spanish head shape, Olóriz rejected claims of superiority based solely on size:

> There is no discernible relationship between the cephalic index and the hierarchy or position in which races are organized, either from most inferior to those reputed to be among the most elevated of the human species. The general form of the head and individual or collective aptitudes of different peoples do not correspond in such a way as to presume that knowledge of the first yields knowledge of the second. There is no reason in light of what has been presented here to classify Spain, in terms of its average cephalic index in *such a scaled* hierarchy of races.[90]

Yet, when his research showed that Spaniards were becoming more dolichocephalic (longheaded) over the course of their racial mixing, and as a result, closer to their German cousins in general head proportion, Olóriz concluded that Spaniards were by default approaching the same kind of superiority that Germans possessed.[91]

In a sense, Olóriz was playing a double game, using the German proof of superiority to deny its basis. Mixture produced equally superior results. For, if all races were really conglomerations of many groups, then the Spanish race had proven to be one of the most advanced in its fusion. The Spanish race had betrayed through the measurements of crania a kind of homogeneity in its mixture, a virtual resettling of diverse racial characteristics into a fused collection of ever fewer variations. In fact, the influence of this racial fusion was so strong that it was seen even in the former colonies of Spain's empire, most notably in Spain's former European empire. Olóriz noted that the inhabitants of the Mediterranean islands of Sicily and Corsica, former extensions of the Spanish empire of Charles V and Phillip II, still bore more resemblance statistically to their Spanish neighbors than to their Italian compatriots, suggesting that such territories' reincorporation into the Spanish domain at least made anthropological sense:

> If similarity of the cephalic index, instead of other affinities between peoples, were reason alone for political organization of groups, Spain should reincorporate into its dominions the Mediterranean islands it possessed in other times including the most southern parts of Italy, because in all of these areas, there continues to exist

the same cephalic formations in the proportion to each other that we have among ourselves here in Spain. This is true not solely because of the secular influence of our blood [on Italy], but also because it should be acknowledged that some people emerge from the same roots as others.[92]

Rather than scorn, Olóriz's study actually received a surprising, if now forgotten, amount of international acclaim. Olóriz received the Prix Godard in 1895 from the French Museum of Natural History (Musée d'Histoire Naturelle,) sharing it with the Italian Rodolfo Livi, whose anthropometric study of the Italian military had also received the attention of the Parisian committee.[93] More surprising was the support he received from organizations that disagreed with his assertions. Olóriz received invitations to become an honorary or corresponding member of a variety of European anthropological societies throughout 1895 and 1896, including from Johannes Ranke of the German Anthropological Society in Munich. Olóriz was solicited to review books and also received many requests for copies of the Spanish cephalic index, including from Cesare Lombroso in Bologna and Rudolf Virchow in Berlin.[94]

This international attention also led to some professional disputes with European anthropologists who did not agree with the supposedly salutary effects of racial mixture. Some attacked Olóriz's explanation for the causes of this racial fusion. Olóriz assumed, as did his French mentors, that racial fusions would occur over time, with groups able to propagate and eventually mute the characteristics of their ancestors. In fact, the same German anthropologists whose work Olóriz had mined for his claims of the superiority of mixture were critical of Olóriz's conclusions. Olóriz's old friend Otto Ammon, for example, faulted the Spaniard's assertion of the potential superiority of mixture, but charitably assumed that the conclusions were merely a lapse in thinking, not in methodology. Ammon's own approach, which he called anthroposociology, relied on anthropometry as did Olóriz's. But anthroposociology had as its intellectual undercurrent the writings of Georges Vacher de Lapouge and Arthur de Gobineau that placed Germanic or Teutonic superiority at the zenith of racial development.[95] Mixture with other groups, especially Jews, only dragged down the great Aryan. Spaniards apparently were not racial threats. In fact, Ammon welcomed some Spaniards into the Teutonic hordes if their racial background proved sufficiently interconnected. Overall, Ammon assumed that the coming together of races resulted in their weakening, that racial fusions were fundamentally destructive to pure races. But if racial ties existed long in the past, then some mixture might not prove too weakening. Racial bonds, in other words, could stretch across national boundaries.[96]

Racial theory based either on purity or mixture was clearly quite pliable. Ammon called for further anthroposociological research of possible links between the Iberian Peninsula and northern Europe. Ammon surmised from Olóriz's research that the areas on the peninsula in which German blood mixed with Spanish blood corresponded to areas of Germanic incursions into the peninsula either by Vandals or Goths. These mostly urban settlers then mixed with brachycephalic early Spaniards. Instead of a model of positive fusion, Ammon wrote, most of the dolichocephalic features shown in the Spaniard were lingering vestiges of these Germanic ancestors who died off because of an inability to adapt to the environment on the Spanish steppes. Brachycephalic head shapes dominated in the peninsula because early Spaniards were able to absorb the descendants of dolichocephalic Germans. Yet, it was the Spaniards of German stock who were most successful at propagating themselves while the rural stock—of purer Spanish descent—led to Spanish degeneration. Thus, Ammon did not quibble with Olóriz that Spaniards were a mixed race but with his conclusion that Spaniards had produced a stronger race as a result. Ammon even used Olóriz's research to further his claims of Aryan superiority, arguing that strong Spaniards were of German ancestry and those with less German stock were weaker. He kindly concluded that he was disagreeing only with the Olóriz's interpretation of his findings, not with the findings themselves. The disagreement remained entirely professional with the men continuing their correspondence amicably over the next few years. Ammon often asked Olóriz to translate German works into Spanish, and to provide reviews of German studies to Spanish audiences in scientific journals in Spain.[97]

"Solving the Iniquitous Law of Races": The Positive Response to Olóriz in Spain

Within Spain, Olóriz benefited from an audience already well disposed to the concept of mixture as the base of Spanish identity.[98] Very few of those who reviewed Olóriz's work disagreed with the premise of racial fusion. Most merely critiqued the lack of a clear-cut explanation of how the process unfolded in Spain. The question was never whether there was fusion but rather who was fused together and why. In spite of the overwhelmingly positive reception of the work when Olóriz presented it to the Madrid Athenaeum in 1894, one colleague lamented the absence of any discussion of the social implications and cultural significance that such knowledge of the physical bases of Spanish identity offered.[99] This reaction signaled at least the general sense among liberals and progressives that science was a potential new source for the liberal state's rehabilitation of the nation.

Yet, as in early German experiments with racial thought, philology provided especially fertile ground for the expansion of racial arguments. Both academic and literary elites gravitated to the new scientific language of race and saw it as one more example of an inherited past that verified the kinds of mixture almost all agreed had to have taken place.[100] Most surprising in this appropriation was the generally positive response Olóriz received from conservative and even ultra-Catholic circles within Spain. Despite a far different and antagonistic attitude toward empiricism and, indeed, the Enlightenment as foreign and debilitating forces in Spanish history, many Catholic traditionalists found Olóriz's study valuable as a validation of their view of Spanish history. Even if the basis of Olóriz's argument differed from a Catholic traditionalist's notion of mixture, both shared an implicit agreement that Spain's history was one of fusion. Perhaps because Olóriz did not outline a clear policy agenda growing out of his work, readers less drawn to empiricism did not sense any great difference between their view of Spain's mixed past and that outlined by anthropology. The crux of the disagreement rested on defining the mechanisms for this fusion.

The eminent Catholic historian and philologist Marcelino Menéndez y Pelayo came out in support of Olóriz's work. Menéndez y Pelayo had engaged in a polemic against Spanish positivists in the 1870s and 1880s because they worked in what he felt was an essentially non-Spanish field of inquiry. For Menéndez y Pelayo, Olóriz's study was valuable because it provided a proper Spanish perspective on science. He had argued that Spain's long history of Catholic theocracy had produced a specifically Spanish science from the sixteenth through the nineteenth century, one that unified disparate ideologies, religions, and peoples. The Inquisition represented one of the great tools of this unification. This unification resulted in an elite class, which he called a "race" and at times a "caste" that organized and defended this unity of spirit and culture. They created a special understanding of the world from a Spanish perspective (la ciencia española) and in turn created a common national purpose or identity. The Inquisition, for example, exemplified Spanish science by demonstrating the need to unify the intellectual and political life of Spain: "I comprehend, applaud, and bless the Inquisition as a formula for unified thought that determined and governed national life through the centuries, as the daughter of the genuine spirit of the Spanish people."[101] Menéndez y Pelayo maintained a long polemic with Spanish positivists, arguing that history proved that there was science particular to the Iberian Peninsula, and that positivism, with its reverence of universal categories of reason and empirical knowledge, conflicted with this indigenous scientific tradition and Spain's Catholic orthodoxy. Interestingly, however, Menéndez y Pelayo's notion of orthodoxy did not deny influences from a variety of groups that coexisted on the peninsula. He often argued that Catholic orthodoxy in Spain had been produced by figures like the Roman philosopher Seneca and Jewish philosophers like Averroes and Maimonides. The influences of these diverse thinkers, Menéndez y Pelayo argued, had been absorbed (españolizadas) into Spanish culture.[102]

With these ideas in mind, Menéndez y Pelayo did not criticize Olóriz's anthropological conclusions despite their empirical basis. For Menéndez y Pelayo, Olóriz's study both demonstrated that Spain had indeed brought together a variety of different ideas and portrayed the Spanish as a unified racial group. The mechanism for this unification of races remained opened to further study, which Menéndez y Pelayo provided in his La historia de los heterodoxos españoles, first published between 1880 and 1882. In the second edition, published after the appearance of Olóriz's book, Menéndez y Pelayo included a long section on the anthropology of Spain. He paid special attention to Olóriz's study, calling it "fundamental" and "admirable." He lauded Olóriz's study for showing the racial roots of the Spaniard, portraying in a biological form what he himself was attempting to show in the history of Spanish Catholicism. Menéndez y Pelayo carefully argued to his presumably resistant audience the value that such scientific endeavor had: "Th[is] digression through geographical anthropology might seem excessively long and impertinent to some, when we are supposedly only discussing religious history. But, how is it possible to consider any aspect of our history, much less our prehistory, without attending to analysis of the physical constitution of man, which in the end is the fundamental element of all of these subjects, and who has left us not only his name in writings but also the relics of his skeleton?"[103]

In subsequent editions of his book, this passage did not reappear. In later editions, especially after his death in 1912, Menéndez y Pelayo's editors included in the discussion of the late-nineteenth- and early-twentieth-century history of Spain a passage arguing that Catholicism alone, and presumably not the biological function of racial fusion, had acted as the glue of Spain's racial past. One passage that remained, however, was Pelayo's ultimate conclusion that Catholicism had "cleansed [Spain] of the iniquitous law of races."[104] Fusion still operated, according to Menéndez y Pelayo, but the catalyzing agent was not organic or natural. Catholicism had been the binding agent of racial groups in the Spanish past; a racially dominant group did not have to survive. This abhorrence for historicist explanations that emanated from European science led many scholars to divest from Menéndez y Pelayo any kind of racial thought.[105] However, his reading of Olóriz proved that distinctions between historical explanations and more biological ones were not so sharply divided in the late nineteenth century. Menéndez y Pelayo could be attracted to scientific determinism as long as it did not directly contravene his view of Catholicism at the center of Spain's historical development. He had only changed the catalyst for this fusion from a biological one to religious one. The following decades of political turmoil and the sharpening of political difference in Spain might account for the excision of these passages for the sake of removing any contradictory (i.e., liberal, progressive) ideas within the works of a person whom one historian has described as the father of Spanish fascism.[106] Clearly, politics might have moved to extremes, but in the late nineteenth century, race and the rhetoric of fusion provided one area of historical agreement across the Spanish political spectrum. Race offered far more possibility for providing a usable past to liberal and Catholic conservative thinkers alike in the late nineteenth century. Racial fusion would help unify nationalist thought.

Olóriz's Professional Failure and the Subsequent Rise of Spanish Anthropology

Olóriz's study not only elevated his position within anthropology but also anthropology's status among the Spanish sciences. In 1896, he was admitted to the Royal Academy of Medicine (Real Academia de Medicina), presenting data on the average size of the Spaniard in his inaugural address. Apparently responding to earlier critics, he suggested ways of applying this anthropological study to fix problems in contemporary Spanish society. This proposal proved timely. Delivering this lecture during the second year of the Spanish-American War, Olóriz argued that monitoring the various racial components of the Spanish population would aid not only in military recruitment but also in judicial and civil administration.[107] Proper recruitment would be based on scientific understanding of the racial groups in each area of Spain. Recruiters would take soldiers from the areas where the racial mixtures produced the best soldiers, ever careful not to take too many and thus deplete the local racial stock.[108]

At the end of the speech, Olóriz also voiced his frustrations with the lack of financial and material support for anthropological sciences. He lamented that his study was based only on 7,300 measurements of Spaniards; while this sample was large by Spanish standards, Olóriz claimed the study provided only a tentative assessment of the Spaniard.[109] Eventually, however, the persistent failure to gain subjects to measure—the same problem that had forced Velasco to measure his own daughter's corpse—afflicted Olóriz. The problem proved so acute that he began to pursue other interests. Pathological cases of abnormal size, or head shapes, increasingly drew his attention, especially because they were often easier to come by in prisons and hospitals than the more ostensibly standard samples of people who would have to consent to the measurements. Olóriz assumed that abnormalities were the result of racial factors. Thus, if he could not study the healthy to define the norm, he decided to work in the inverse direction, defining the abnormal as the means to define the normal.[110] Perhaps the result of serving on government commissions, Olóriz also turned his attention more directly to the social and practical meaning of his anatomical research.[111] In what can be seen as a second career for Olóriz, criminology and the measurement of criminals' skulls became the focus of the last decade of his life. This aspect of his career will be discussed in the next chapter on the second stage of development of Spanish anthropology.

Competition for the new chair in anthropology at the Central University of Madrid also energized Olóriz's interests. Olóriz had been one of the most vocal proponents of such a position throughout the 1880s and early 1890s. Yet, when Olóriz's colleague, the French-trained anthropologist and staunch monogenist Manuel Antón y Ferrándiz of the Museum of Natural History in Madrid, was given the chair in 1893, Olóriz received the final reason to refocus the direction of his anthropological research. He had lost the opportunity to create the next generation of Spanish anthropologists and did not want to continue to work in anthropology as an adjunct of other disciplines. In addition, Olóriz's failure to become the chair of anthropology unfolded at the same moment of larger crisis that confronted physical anthropology. Franz Boas's demonstration of the instability of head shapes among European immigrants after their arrival in New York conflicted with many of the basic assumptions of physical anthropology. As a result, other areas of anthropological analysis, like the study of culture, and the growing sense that physical features were not so telling in the differentiation of races, led Olóriz to pursue other avenues of physical study. In a sense, Olóriz lost out on the official imprimatur of the chair of anthropology because he never offered a clear purpose for his kind of anthropological study. The fact that everyone could agree about the basic fact of Spain's national mixture meant that Olóriz would have had to offer a clearer anthropological portrait of the actual mechanisms of racial fusion. Understanding the mechanisms of racial fusion represented the crux of the racial debate for it was in the process of racial mixture that others gleaned their sense of the social mission of this new science. What were the components of proper fusion? What were the deleterious elements?

Olóriz's anthropological background partially obstructed his ability to see the social applications of his work. His training in medicine and physical anthropology kept him from developing wider anthropological objectives that included ethnology, the comparison of culture and behavior that also formed part of the larger science of natural history. Thus, Manuel Antón y Ferrandiz, Olóriz's rival for the chair of anthropology, who was not trained solely as a physical anthropologist, represented another scientific approach in early Spanish anthropology, an approach more devoted to finding not only the physical bases of Spanish racial fusion, but also the motor force behind it.

Manuel Antón, Monogenism, and Catholicism as the Mechanism of Spanish Racial Fusion

The institutionalization of Spanish anthropology began to crystallize around the debate over how the Spanish race fused. The new chair of Spanish anthropology, Manuel Antón y Ferrándiz, had emerged from another clique within the Spanish sciences, the publicly funded wing, which was far more open to merging Catholicism with scientific thought. The differences in interpretations between Antón's group at the Musem of Natural History and Velasco's physical anthropologists often formed along a hairline, and were more often the product of a different interpretive framework than of vastly contradictory findings. Antón's more favored status, his public position, and his energetic devotion to the study of race would lead to a far wider dispersal of anthropology into mainstream public and scientific debate. The remainder of this chapter explores how the ideas of race and racial mixture were positioned by the turn of the twentieth century to become the locus of public debate about the health and makeup of Spanish society and would end up as fairly unifying concepts amid the factionalization of politics in early-twentieth-century Spain.

Antón began his career in anthropology slightly later than Olóriz even though he was six years older than his Granadine colleague. Classification of species served as the heart of Antón's early career. In 1878, Antón joined the

Museum of Natural History as a zoologist, specializing in the classification of mollusks. He worked under the direction of Lucas de Tormos, who had also been one of the founding members of Velasco's Spanish Anthropology Society.[112] Antón's interest turned to racial classification in early 1883, when he traveled to Spanish Morocco as part of a military ethnological survey of the various populations of the area.[113] Upon his return two months later, Antón requested time away from the museum to attend the lectures of Armand de Quatrefages de Bréau and Charles Verneau at the Société d'Anthropologie in Paris. Spending most of 1883 and 1884 in the French capital, Antón became embroiled in the same debates between polygenists and monogenists then dominating the Parisian society that had interested Velasco. Upon Broca's death in 1880, the Société d'Anthropologie split between followers of Broca's polygenist disciple Paul Topinard, and Broca's great antagonist Quatrefages. Quatrefages had long defended the monogenist position, arguing that no proof existed for the polygenist belief that races had emerged separately and were, thus, unrelated to each other. For this to be true, Quatrefages argued, different races would not be able to procreate effectively. Quatrefages dismissed the polygenist argument as mere speculation with little supporting evidence. Quatrefages aligned with Haeckel and the belief that individual human development duplicated the evolution of the species. Yet, Quatrefages thought Haeckelian monism remained too materialistic—finding proof of the interrelation of species in the measurable qualities of human morphology. For Quatrefages, the development of religion and morality separated humans from the animal kingdom.[114] Not only did people acquire physical characteristics in the same way animals did based upon environmental necessity, but Quatrefages believed that humans had also acquired religious and moral characteristics in a way that would ultimately distinguish humans from animals and place them in their own classificatory kingdom: what he called "la règne humaine."

As a naturalist, Quatrefages believed that both biological and moral factors were needed in the classification of races. As a result, he relied not only on anthropological measurement as a means to identify the races, but also argued that the capacity for religious practice and ethical behavior further differentiated races. For Quatrefages, the "milieu" of the race, its environmental setting, its isolation as a discrete population, and, importantly, what groups crossed with it represented the multiple components of racial differentiation. What also distinguished Quatrefages from his colleagues was that, like his Spanish student Antón y Ferrandiz, he trained first as a zoologist, not a doctor. Quatrefages was trained to study whole populations and not to rely on individual observations of single skeletons or crania as evidence for racial categorization.[115] Like Broca and others within the Société d'Anthropologie, they considered "customs, instincts, industries, kinds of life, geographical distribution in the present and past" all as part of human experience and, most importantly, areas in which to differentiate peoples.[116] As monogenists, Quatrefages and Antón envisioned humanity as one species, unlike their polygenist cousins Topinard and Broca, who saw groups defined by distinct head morphologies as potential members of distinct species.[117] It is important to note that, despite monogenists' claims to view the world in less racist terms than their polygenist compatriots, monogenism proved to offer no less discriminatory or hierarchical views of race. Though believing that all humans were linked via both spiritual and physical characteristics, monogenists still saw differences rooted in varying degrees of ability or desire to civilize in supposedly objective, scientific terms.

When Antón returned to Madrid from his classes at the Société d'Anthropologie, he immediately called for the creation of a chair of anthropology at the Museum of Natural History. The museum, unlike Velasco's earlier society, was a public institution, and granted Antón's request in 1885. No official records of the curriculum, the class lists, or reading materials have appeared in archives. However, Antón's lectures do remain, having been copied down by a student and published in longhand.[118] Other materials survive from the period following the creation of the chair in anthropology at the Central University of Madrid in 1892. The program for his classes on anthropology that Antón offered and the exams from the competition (oposición) for the chair also survive.[119] Also surviving is a large archive of photographs of Moroccans and Europeans that Antón began to collect in 1887 and would use for his "study of the races of Europeans."[120] These photographs were sent to Antón from military officials stationed in Spain's colonies in Morocco and from European anthropologists Antón contacted. Thus, in addition to some of Antón's early research and Olóriz's discussions of the physical bases of the Spanish race, various documents testify to the fundamental role that race played in the development of the contemporary discipline of anthropology in Spain in the late nineteenth century.

In his first lectures, Antón recapitulated Quatrefages' ideas about the unity of races. For example, Antón argued that Darwin's association of species and race was inaccurate. Rather, all of humanity was one species, with races reflecting a grand variety of different kinds of human beings. The ability to procreate created a species; races were the historical formations that then appeared within them: "we understand that race and species are not the same thing, and that our criteria for establishing a species rests upon reproduction. Varieties within a species that can reproduce among themselves easily, if the reproduction takes place over a long period of time, produce races. Only when species become so isolated that they can no longer reproduce among themselves do they become separate species."[121] Assuming that all of humanity was one species, Antón offered racial formation as a purely local phenomenon, contingent on the unfolding of isolated characteristics of human groups. Variation was the product of local events; context shaped racial variation. This focus on local variation allowed for a greater degree of national pride to shape Spanish anthropology. For above all other geographical areas, Spain provided the clearest example of racial formation as the product of local variation. If procreation provided the proof of species formation, then Spanish history represented the clearest example that humanity could clearly procreate and do so healthfully based on the admixture of different groups. Antón wrote that one needed only to look at the Spanish case of colonization of the Western Hemisphere to see both the ease and value of racial mixture. In fact, he often chided other Europeans performing racial studies for ignoring Spanish imperialism as the case study of the positive effects of racial mixture.[122] Antón's historical vision closely aligned with the broadest integrist history of Spain promoted by Catholic traditionalists like Menéndez y Pelayo.[123] Yet, Antón, like Olóriz before him, provided scientific proof of acute intermixture and subsequent superiority. Antón's view of racial formation offered a unified Spain that was not just the product of a strong centralizing Spanish state but also of natural bonds forged by racial mixture. The Iberian Peninsula as the crossroads of Greek, Phoenician, Visigothic, Celtic, and Arab incursion into Europe, all intermixing with the indigenous Iberian populations, provided Spain a privileged vantage point from which to demonstrate the value of mixture. This anthropological lesson provided Spain's imperial missions of the past and the present with one more arrow in the quiver to defend Spanish power through imperial conquest.

Having asserted Spanish supremacy, Antón went on to describe the failures of other European colonial/racial policies. Out of fealty to his French mentors, Antón most ardently attacked Broca's polygenism. Extrapolating from English colonial experience, Broca had written that Tasmanians and the English had to be members of different species since their offspring rarely prospered and, when they did, they were themselves infertile. Antón suggested that Broca misread the historical data. The English simply did not mix with indigenous populations. Unlike their Spanish counterparts, the English isolated their colonized subjects as a matter of colonial administration. Antón even suggested that perhaps because of some racial affinity with the British, the United States did the same with their different populations. Hence, according to Antón, Americans did not create the necessary process of racial mixture. In contrast, the Spanish experience of colonization demonstrated that if the proper ideological—that is, cultural and religious—framework was provided for colonization, imperial power would uplift the lower races and undo, as Menéndez y Pelayo had put it, the iniquitous law of races:

> Spaniards have civilized wherever we have gone. . . . It is true that Spaniards destroyed some idols and some monuments. Yet is also certain that we gave them our laws, our religion and even our blood, which was the most that we could give. And this is something the British have never known how to give. We have even done so in the Philippines where, when we arrived, we found only about one million inhabitants, most of whom were bound in horrible slavery. We gave them a superior culture and improved their lives to the degree that today the population exceeds six million. Thus, the argument of Broca is destroyed.[124]

For Antón, the mixture of races was both a physical and social phenomenon. As a result, he gave a wide reading to the goals and purview of anthropology as a scientific discipline. This complicated formation of race required both specialization and wide reading in a variety of disciplines:

> When we occupy ourselves in the study of human anatomy, apart from the differences between humans and animals, what most interests us is distinguishing between races of man. We call this science anthropometry, which is best studied through craniometry, and it is the great leap forward that represents modern anthropology. It allows us to distinguish with greater and greater precision between the races. But, in addition, anthropology studies another important characteristic: the social character. The study of societies is also one of the most important subjects in which anthropologists can engage. . . . [F]rom the errant tribes of savages of Australia to the most modern societies, there is a series of gradations that we have to study . . . touching upon history, and upon all the distinct sciences of law and society.[125]

One needed to understand not only the ways in which a race formed physically but also, as he called it, ethnologically.[126] It was the latter that Antón believed required the most attention in Spanish anthropology because Spaniards had proven so adept in the past at assimilating different populations. Among these disciplines, Antón stressed in his written proposal for the chair of anthropology that the discipline had to encompass physical anthropology or morphology, comparative sociology, comparative psychology, and ethnology.[127] "Among the spheres of scientific inquiry," he wrote, "anthropology rests on top of the natural sciences and provides the roots for morphology, psychology, philosophy, law, and history."[128]

In this partitioning of anthropology, Antón did not distinguish the Spanish version of the discipline from other countries. Even if the Spanish past was unique, he wrote, each nation should engage in the same kinds of study of intermixture, on even the minutest level, so that the lessons learned of fusion in one country could be shared across national boundaries, and not just among European countries. Invited to give the inaugural address to faculty and students to open the 1895–96 academic year, Antón wrote that for too long European anthropology had been embroiled in the "Aryan debates" between Germans and the rest of Europe regarding the provenance of European civilization. To ignore some of the causative factors in racial fusion, like the central role of religion in facilitating biological intermixture, was to obliterate what made humans unique: the creation of religions and culture.[129] In addition to inveighing against the "myopia" of European anthropologists, he also encouraged the formation of the discipline in colonies throughout the world, including Spain's colonies in North and West Africa.[130] From Antón's position in the Museum of Natural History, in addition to his more powerful position within the university, he began to educate a large contingent of anthropologists in Spain. Between 1896 and 1898, he taught over 190 students in postgraduate classes on the anthropological roots of Spaniards at the Madrid Athenaeum, in addition to organizing Olóriz's lectures on the potential anthropological roots of the physical size of Spaniards in 1896.[131]

But Antón could not merely present the process of racial formation without also defining the unique characteristics of the Spanish race that had formed over the years. Again, the mechanisms of mixture were what differentiated Antón's ideas from others. For Antón, the first question that had to be answered was, Were Spaniards unique among European races? Quatrefages had prodded Antón to pursue this line of inquiry when discoveries of skulls in caves in southern Spain had led anthropologists to speculate that the remains came from a possible third race of ancient humans, the Alhama, named for the region in southeastern Spanish in which they were discovered. Antón set about studying these skulls and comparing them with their closest relatives, the Cro-Magnon and Neanderthal, which at the time were considered separate races of humanity, not an earlier evolutionary stage of humans. There was no denying that these skulls represented forebears of all or some Europeans. He concluded that their proximity to the Cro-Magnon heads was not close enough to classify them as part of this race. Rather, Spaniards were primarily composed of one ancient race, a race hitherto unknown in European anthropology.[132]

Contemporary Social Concerns Creep into the Definition of the Spanish Race

The other element in Antón's pursuit of Spain's racial roots was an analysis of the forces that helped forge the contemporary Spanish race. It was in this inquiry that Antón brought together the various factors that he had argued were crucial to provide a complete anthropological assessment of the Spanish race. Antón used Olóriz's craniometric evidence to demonstrate the physical fact of Spanish racial mixture. In addition, he deployed explanations rooted in history, geology, and religion to discern the formation of the Spanish race. Instead of Olóriz's earlier depiction of the Spanish race as a purely physical phenomenon, Antón attempted to demonstrate that Spain's unique geographical position helped forge a racial identity based on the fusion not only of different racial types, but also of different cultures. Spain's geographical and historical position as crossroads between Europe and Africa became the basis for Spanish racial uniqueness among European nations and the source of its racial strength. Visible both in behaviors and in physical appearance, the uniqueness of the Spanish race again lay in its fusion of different races and temperaments.

For Antón, Spain was the crossroads of two racial incursions, one by a European race, marked by blond hair and longheadedness, or dolichocephaly, which had actually left little ethnic mark on the Spanish populace. The other racial group was of North African descent, what Antón called the libio-ibérico, or Libyan-Iberian, with roots in North Africa, and the siro-árabe, or Syrian-Arab, with roots in the eastern Mediterranean and Asia Minor. The assimilation of these latter groups into the Spanish racial mix provided the basis of the Spanish race. Unlike Olóriz, Antón argued that based on race and comportment, i.e., physiology and culture, Spain's closest racial affinity lay to the south. "The first steps in using the methods of modern anthropology to investigate the races of Spain," Antón wrote, "guide us inexorably to the shores of Morocco."[133] By studying the peoples of North Africa, Antón would also be studying the key component that differentiated the Spaniard. Antón saw Spaniards as Europeans with a dose of something else, an ingredient that made an important difference. Antón's hope was that this study, replete with photographs of both racial types and also examples of their mixtures, would provide a template for understanding not only the races of Morocco but also the present-day social and political divisions of Spain.

In addition to the recognizable physical characteristics of the Libyan-Iberian and the Syrio-Iberian, there were also cultural and behavioral traits that could be discerned. The first, the Libyan-Iberian, which he wrote was the "nucleus" of the racial groups between the Pyrenees and Egypt, was recognizable through their "regular stature," their moderately long heads, their "prominent but not excessive noses." In addition, they were "congenial, frank and resolute, with an independent, egalitarian, democratic and separatist character." The second, the Syrian-Arab, was tall, very longheaded, with a prominent, narrow, and aquiline nose, and with a suspicious, unpredictable, and nervous temperament.[134] Because of the multitude of invasions of Greeks, Visigoths, Arabs, Phoenicians, and Romans, Spain had acquired a mixed bag of physical and temperamental characteristics, becoming not merely a strong European race but an intermediate race, one responsible for the cultural interchange between East and West that marked the development of European civilization. For Antón, Spain represented a new racial grouping, the Mediterranean race.[135] This race, he argued, provided the true racial patrimony of European civilization: "These two racial types are so intermixed and intertwined in almost all the Peninsula that they produced out of this intimate mixture a new race, which one would call Mediterranean, whose most beautiful expression can be found in Roman statuary."[136]

Yet, this view of a Mediterranean race had so far failed to afford Catholicism the crucial role it played in the integrist view of Spanish nationalism. Here, interestingly, Antón argued that Christianity proved to be the galvanizing force that fused the North African, Arab, and Spaniard. What had existed in Northern Africa prior to its incursion into Christian Spain was a fanatic Islam, bereft of reason or civilization. Christianity had becalmed populations who had dwelled too long in the desert. Interestingly, religion was not the fundamental difference; environment was.

> Meditative and dreaming spirit that divined the unity of God, that invented the sensual variety of the Harem, the poetry of David, the knowledge of Solomon on the green hillsides of Jericho, and in the shadows of the trees of Lebanon; but in the desert, the son of Ishmael, in the sun that browned their skin sent into their souls the ardor and delirium of Mohammed with a lazy fanaticism that rejected

the reasoned thought of European civilization and instead sent them into the hysterical and often hypnotic convulsions of their religious fanaticism.[137]

A clear, steadfast awareness of the world became a calling card of southern Europeans. The Mediterranean race, which had tamed religious fanaticism with sober reason, had in the process created a distinct race of people. Racial change was the product not only of physical alteration but also of cultural assimilation.

Certain elements of the Arab incursions in the Iberian Peninsula still had left their mark within Spanish political and social life, however. Though the divisive, warlike elements of the Moroccan races had been pacified in Spain, certain remnants of both the independent nature of the Libyan-Iberians and the war-like behavior of the Syrian-Arabs continued to express themselves in Spain: "It is quite clear that the peninsular populations rose up a grade in their racial fusion because of the influence of Christian civilization; but the *physiology of race* still reveals itself in the nationalist separatism of Portugal and certain regions of Spain. It is still all too clear that the Caliph will occasionally reveal the atavistic daggers in his nature, in the fights in Bejar and Calendario, and among the various fighting and brawling one sees between teenage boys and even young men in the streets of our neighborhoods."[138] This kind of atavistic remainder appeared for the first time in Spain as a way to explain contemporary political issues. Replete with a neo-Lamarckian sense of rapid and permanent acquisition of traits, Spanish anthropology reflected the contemporary concern for regional separatism that remained as an atavism of past fusions. Not all fusion was salutary. Degenerative elements could remain, acquired as they were in different moments of the racial past.

Later anthropologists would pick up this line of argument, applying it not only to regionalist politics but also to trade unionism and a host of other political enemies. This legacy remained one of the most crucial of Antón's racial science. Neo-Lamarckianism and its view of quick and often transitory acquisition of traits actually aided the identification of which element from the racial past was hurting the racial fusion. Spain's African heritage was two-sided in more than a physical sense. Positive elements washed down the historical eddy of racial development as did negative traits. Antón's comments contain the first signs of political arguments being made based on the idea of racial mixtures. While both Olóriz and Antón had followed their French counterparts in denying the possibilities of racial purity, they both also had made cases for the potential benefits of racial mixtures. For Antón, however, it was clear that the racial fusions occasionally left potentially negative legacies. How to deal with these negative legacies, and understanding their origins in the racial past, became elements, throughout this early development of Spanish anthropology, of political and intellectual discussions.

Conclusion

The disciplinary formation of anthropology took place as a result of a gradual opening of Spanish society to scientific endeavor. Partially the legacy of the social and political shift that occurred as a result of the First Republic and the Restoration, the politics implicit in Spanish anthropology did not represent a purely liberal, positivist response to conservative control over education by a traditionalist Catholic Church or an acquiescent government. Instead, the Spanish sciences, including anthropology, found themselves absorbing a variety of perspectives from European sciences. The liberal, indeed republican, sensibilities of early physical anthropologists like Velasco and his disciples from France found their culmination in the studied apolitical positions of Federico Olóriz. Olóriz's faith lay in scientific endeavor, and he addressed political issues only rarely, and almost always in response to the lack of state or popular support for science. Olóriz's friend José Gómez Ocaña recalled in his obituary of Olóriz that the only lasting image he had of the late doctor was of Olóriz "planted there in his house, working with all of his crania, preparations, files, digital impressions, books and statistics, the greater part of every day, and adding to it all his teaching interests, he never had any time, interest or desire for political fights."[139]

Olóriz's study did endure as the standard work of physical anthropology on the Spanish race for the next fifty years. In the 1923 Espasa-Calpe Enciclopedia universal ilustrada's entry on the anthropology of Spain, the author, Manuel Antón, noted that Olóriz's study, later copied and expanded by others, had never been surpassed in the quantity or quality of the measurements and conclusions.[140] The entry even included a variety of charts and maps on Spanish hair color distributions, eye color, height, dental conditions, cephalic indices, and a variety of other physical characteristics, all gleaned from Olóriz's 1894 study.[141] Olóriz's legacy in Spanish anthropology lay in the mass of data that he left behind, not in his ability to form institutions or nourish a vast number of students to carry on his work. Partly because of changes in physical anthropology, and partly because of his later decision to apply his anthropological knowledge to social practice, Olóriz's legacy in anthropology was cut short. As a criminologist, however, his legacy was longer lasting, as will be discussed in chapter 6.

Yet, the legacy of Olóriz's work on the cephalic index survived in better shape precisely because of the message it relayed. That the Spanish people were a mixed race, and was superior in its mixture to other races, coincided with other notions then current in Spanish social, political, and historical discussions. This idea also conformed to the more general legacy of anthropological discussion in Spain. Antón was able to fill in a blank left by Olóriz's discussion. He presented a race unique not only in its physical mixture, but also in its cultural and religious composition. Strengthened by its Catholic legacy, the Spanish race was also a scientific phenomenon for Antón that gave Spanish anthropology an acceptable position as both a Spanish and a European science.[142] In this, Spanish anthropology was not unique. Robert Proctor points out that German anthropology was split between its physical and its more spiritual practitioners in the 1880s and 1890s. For Germany, it was not until the advent of Mendelian genetics after 1900 that the issue of the heritability of both physical and more socially defined characteristics like disease or moral unfitness appeared.

The links that existed between Spanish anthropologists and their French and German counterparts demonstrate that the question of what interpretive framework defined different national explorations of race is not very consequential. Different views of racial origins did not produce fundamentally different applications of racial thought. Neo-Lamarckianism did not defuse the more barbaric possibilities of racial thinking merely by focusing scientists on amelioration of social conditions. In Spain, the question of direction is germane for a variety of political and social practices remained in the future for Spanish sciences. Anarchists, conservatives, liberals, and Catholic traditionalists all promoted eugenic practices based on racial ideologies in the following few decades. What roots they had in anthropology require further analysis. The anthropology that Antón presented became the state-sponsored discipline of anthropology and came to inform Spanish social and political policy. How this took place will be the subject of the next chapter.

4. How Spain Became Invertebrate

Race, Regeneration, and the Expansion of Anthropology,
1894–1917

By the 1890s, Spanish anthropology had gone from the speculative science of a few exiled doctors to one at the cusp of offering political plans and responses to social pressures in Spain. This chapter will consider the particular political and social purposes to which the new anthropological study of racial mixture was put in the period between 1890 and 1920. Specifically, this chapter will focus on the second generation of Spanish anthropologists, disciples mostly of Manuel Antón y Ferrándiz, who continued and expanded upon the study of the Spanish race. Highlighting the fact that this anthropology was to be used for social purposes, Antón once urged his students to remember that even though the influences and methods of anthropology had to be imported into Spain, the focus of Spanish anthropology was to be Spain and the Spanish people.[1]

Anthropologists, in turn, conceived of the Spanish nation in scientific terms, offering a relatively unified portrait of a country made up of disparate elements that had formed over time through a process of racial mixing. This notion was used to justify a wide range of political and social programs; the language of race was malleable enough to serve many interests. Most tellingly, the flexibility of race mixture would appear in the multiple visions of national unity and disunity. Race could promote any number of nuanced portraits of Spain. Spain could be the first great racial melting pot, with diverse ingredients blending together to create the present-day Spanish race. This idea was particularly attractive to Spanish nationalists concerned with regional separatist movements; race fusion had produced national unity. Racial thinkers could also concentrate on the negative components of the mix, calling for the rejection or elimination of negative ingredients. Ultimately, the ideas of racial exclusion and improper mixture would not rest far from each other; melting pots always required the boiling away of original or undesirable traits.

Given that the study of anthropology in Spain was less advanced than in other European countries, the fact that anthropology played such an important role in these discussions of race and the social question was surprising. Spain's educational system did not prepare many postgraduate students, especially those with the necessary background to study race in this anthropological sense.[2] However, with cultural and intellectual institutions, journals, societies, and even café discussions all caught up in debate about the apparent withdrawal of Spain from the world stage, Spain's cultural and historical patrimony came to be the starting point of any discussion of Spanish social issues. With this discussion about patrimony came many components of racial thought. Matters of inheritance, the quality of transmitted traits, and the strength of historical development began to underpin discussions of Spain's social problems. The result was that any social problem could easily be traced to some glitch in Spain's unique racial lineage. In the end, debates about race and the regenerationist climate in Spain soon came to reinforce the growing support for scientific exploration of race. Used to explain Spain's relatively backward position, race also became the focus of social policies that were thought to help modernize the state.

With racial mixture identified as the hallmark of Spain's national strength rather than the source of its enervation, the Spanish relationship with European racial sciences more focused on racial purity would be defined by a careful effort to absorb and reject at the same time: absorb the technique, reject the conclusions. For example, the theories of Arthur de Gobineau and his disciples, like Georges Vacher de Lapouge, were avidly translated from French into Spanish and plumbed in an effort to diagnose Spain's particular racial problems.[3] Yet, very quickly Spanish anthropologists also realized that Spain did not seem even to register in these classic French texts of racial strength and hierarchy. Writing in 1893, Manuel Antón derided his French colleagues for being "more than myopic, [they are] completely blind to all of Spanish science."[4] The sense that Spain was considered an empty space on the European anthropological map encouraged many Spanish anthropologists to try to work their country into these theories and, perhaps, they thought, to rewrite European racial science through their own focus on Spain's unique racial story. This approach gave Spanish racial thought a particularly strong nationalist tilt. The ultimate focus of Spanish racial thought was both to distinguish Spain from other races and also to include Spain in the story of European racial dominance.

Ironically, this defensive focus allowed race to seep into the larger political and social debates of the period in Spain. The message Spanish racial thought presented was particularly attuned to the ears of Spanish intellectuals associated with regenerationism, a discourse devoted to finding solutions to political, social, and economic changes affecting late-nineteenth- and early-twentieth-century Spain. Even the ideas of lesser-known anthropologists eventually found their way into mainstream intellectual discourse through the works of the more famous intellectual cadres known as the Generation of 1898 and the Generation of 1914. If the years between 1868 and 1890 saw a dramatic increase in and coalescence of the practice of Spanish anthropology, the years between 1890 and 1920 saw its consolidation. During this latter period, textbooks on anthropology were written, and courses were designed and taught both in the university and in a variety of private schools. Seminars on the new methods of performing anthropological research were offered in a variety of intellectual centers, including the Madrid and Barcelona Athenaeums, the Free Institute of Education in Madrid, and a variety of regional cities.[5] Governmental agencies and literary clubs also sponsored national studies to provide a fuller portrait of the composition of the Spanish race. In this way, scientific practice expanded outside anthropology classrooms, with the military, for example, performing anthropological analysis of its recruits in an effort to assemble a more effective soldiery from the Spanish population. Lastly, anthropological ideas spread outward into other areas. Social policy, for example, was increasingly influenced by anthropological knowledge, as former anthropologists sought out and received positions in government. This process was not entirely the product of social debate and intellectual culture. Anthropologists, in particular, often had close family ties to some of Spain's leading cultural voices outside the scientific disciplines. These nonscientific relatives would often help disseminate the scientific debate to the larger world. The process was aided by the fact that some of these intellectuals had originally trained in the sciences, often as fellow students of Spain's new generation of anthropologists. Because of family connections and the more general receptivity to anthropological study such connections engendered, these anthropologists ended up talking to a larger audience than their anthropological brethren could have on their own. This chapter will trace that dissemination.

Anthropology and Regenerationism in Spain at the Turn of the Twentieth Century

The consolidation of anthropology as an academic discipline took place in Spain at roughly the same time and certainly at the same pace as in many other European countries. This consolidation occurred first in the important universities, especially those most involved in producing bureaucrats and scientific professionals to staff the new state. Spain's first university chair was established in the Spanish capital, at Madrid's Central University, in 1892. The second chair, at the University of Barcelona, was not created until 1920. This pace was only slightly slower than the development of the profession in Germany. The first chair of anthropology in Germany, held by Johannes Ranke in Munich, was not created until 1886; and the second was created in 1906 in Berlin and held by Felix von Luschan.[6] Despite the similar pace of development, Spanish anthropology was never quite as stable as a profession. Anthropology was never widely taught outside of Spain's urban centers, and most anthropologists were concerned about attaining positions upon completion of their degrees.

This view of Spanish anthropology as both successful in consolidating as a discipline and as influencing governmental policymaking and social thought, while at the same time only slowly developing into a widely taught, nationally recognized, and officially valorized scientific discipline is not necessarily contradictory in the Spanish context between 1880 and 1920. These four decades, dominated by slow but gradual economic development, contentious labor conflict, and political violence, marked Spain's first encounter with social upheaval brought on by political, economic, and cultural modernization.[7] As elsewhere in Europe, these changes were accompanied by active and heated debates about the solutions to the social problems they caused. Historians of Spain have long defined this period around one of its central events, the rapid and humiliating defeat by the United States in the colonial wars in Cuba, Puerto Rico, and the Philippines in 1898. While this event, and the scale of the defeat, sharpened the critiques and perhaps dramatized the extent of Spanish troubles, many of the most famous discussions of sources of the *problema de España* had already been published prior to the war.[8] Most of these works were the legacies, as well, of earlier reformist ideas associated with the First Republic (1873–74), and the responses to its failure. Among these were positivism and Darwinian evolutionary theory, both of which were the products of late-nineteenth-century political defeat and inquiry into the sources of national decline.[9] As a result, the legacy of liberal, empirical science, whose expression in anthropology was the subject of chapter 3, continuously appeared in the works associated with the regenerationist movement.

Known under a variety of guises, the intellectual and political efforts to reform Spain, to diagnose the source of its perceived economic and social lag, and to prescribe adequate solutions included efforts from across the political spectrum. These efforts have been loosely categorized with the use of a nonpartisan—or at least not politically fixed—moniker, "regenerationism," or as the conflict between Europeanizers and Hispanizers.[10] Historians have also tended to attribute these calls for reform to a variety of mostly educated and urban elites often classified under generational headings. The Generation of 1898—whose first political experiences came as children observing the failure of the First Republic in Spain and whose defining moment came with the great trauma of the loss of Spain's overseas empire in 1898— was known for its desire for social and political reform. The Generation of 1914 was closely allied with the Generation of 1898, but is associated with more modernist, youthful reactions against the belief in purely rational modes of discourse held by their elder generational counterparts.[11] This group was connected to and, some have even argued, formed the core of the more general European criticism of positivism and rationality that took place before and after World War I. Spain, in one sense, had a running start at such criticism for its regenerationism was always inflected with more of a sense of national difference than of internationalist modernism. Spain possessed the ingredients for a conservative revolution and a modernist movement at the same time, and sometimes even earlier than its European counterparts.[12]

Still, the development of racial thought in Spain points out one weakness of these generational labels: they usually bind together a group of thinkers whose careers spanned periods far longer than their generational identity would allow.[13] As a result, generational thinking has tended to mute similarities between rival generations. More importantly, partitioning groups in this manner tends to ignore the ideological influences shared across these generations. Lastly, these labels have tended to focus attention on only a small group of writers who share obvious intellectual and biographical characteristics. This focus on a small group has led one historian to call for further study of "the other generation of '98," or the groups of lesser-known writers and thinkers who also made contributions to the turn-of-the-twentieth-century debates and represent a much wider slice of Spain's political and social spectrum at that time.[14] Race as a concept was shared widely across the timeline of these generational groups. Also, the idea of racial fusion attracted any number of diverse thinkers who could, like their anthropological brethren, find an element of the racial mix to accentuate as a positive while critiquing another element of the past racial fusion. Lastly, focusing on race uncovers a range of influences among the regenerationists that has received very little attention: the role of science in its calls for Spanish advancement.

A synchronic focus on an idea rather than on the intellectuals themselves helps reveal how restrictive generational identities are, at least in Spain. Many of the figures associated with the earlier generation were still quite active in the later one. In addition, the ideas that often animated later regenerationist literature—for example, attitudes toward science and the role positivism would play in Spain's regeneration—were acquired in a period that would not necessarily place them with their usual generational cohort. Many historians have noted the abundance of biological and scientific metaphor in regenerationist literature.[15] Others have looked at the role positivism and scientific thought played during certain moments in the careers of a few individual thinkers.[16] Rarely, however, have scholars studying regenerationist literature traced the sources of this scientific thought and the metaphorical use of science in the regenerationist writing of the post-1898 period. Such investigations are, nevertheless, crucial to understanding the perception of Spain's national decline.[17]

With its roots in medicine and ethnography, anthropology provided much of this scientific language. Anthropology even fueled the ideas of intellectuals as they transitioned from positivist science—the focus of their early training—to less rational modes of thought later in their careers. The roster of individuals who would fall into this category include Miguel de Unamuno, Ramiro de Maeztu, José Ortega y Gasset, Pío Baroja, among many others.[18] Anthropology, in fact, helped bring about this transition because, during this period, anthropologists began to move away from the scientific certainties expressed in the measurements of physical anthropology and gradually included the study of culture and social values as determinants of racial identity. Considered in its historical context, Spanish anthropology followed the intellectual currents of the European fin de siècle, and was, as a result, often appropriated by better-known and more influential Spanish intellectuals of the period. More than mere metaphor, anthropological language and ideas in regenerationist writing borrowed from the anthropological debates of the period and demonstrated a far greater penetration of scientific, specifically anthropological, ideas into Spanish intellectual debates. The increasing focus on ethnography as the supposedly new science of cultural and social difference that Spanish anthropology began to pursue after the publication of Federico Olóriz's 1896 cephalic index provided new perspectives for reformers and re-generationist writers. The content of this anthropological exploration of race and the lessons it provided proved pliable enough to be attractive to thinkers from a variety of political and ideological viewpoints. Thus, the role anthro-pology played in attempts to address social and political problems upsets the usually bifurcated portrait of Spanish political and intellectual life in the fin de siècle. Instead of a clear opposition between conservative and liberal visions of Spanish identity, race demonstrated that a far more unified dis-course existed within Spanish political and intellectual life at the turn of the twentieth century. There were many more than two Spains.[19]

Exploring Racial Mixture and the Nation in Spain before 1898

The idea of what social and cultural mixture meant for the Spanish state started to receive the attention of a variety of intellectuals after 1898. How-ever, the issues that motivated these thinkers, such as the general departure of Spain from positions of importance in international affairs, the seemingly backward state of its economic system, and the lack of industrialization out-side a few small areas of the country, had begun to attract attention long be-fore the loss of the colonies in 1898. Reformers like Joaquín Costa had already begun to argue that the Restoration political and economic system was not sustainable because it did not conform to the "general spirit" of the Spanish people. The question of how to define this spirit became an important focus of study for Costa and his colleagues in intellectual and educational centers of the country, especially in the Madrid Athenaeum and the Free Institute of Education (ILE; Institución Libre de Enseñanza) in Madrid.[20]

Anthropology worked in part to define this spirit. Rooted in Spain's ama-teur ethnographic societies of the mid-nineteenth century, folkloric societies had formed to study the cultural practices and institutions of Spain's particu-lar regions throughout Spain in the 1870s and 1880s. Borrowing from the style of ethnographic surveys from other European countries, these societies sent questionnaires to Spain's regions asking for information regarding ritu-als, dances, cuisine, and folk medicines.[21] In addition, the ILE, the influential private school founded by Spanish liberals forced out of their university posi-tions after the First Republic, had begun to distinguish what they called "so-cial anthropology," which meant the drawing together of ethnological data of social practices throughout Spain. Students in the ILE were required to take note of local customs, modes of behavior, and other ethnological data during their excursions outside of Madrid. In addition, all students entering the ILE after 1880 were required to visit Pedro González de Velasco's anthropological museum in Madrid until its closure in 1882.[22]

These efforts to define the Spanish *pueblo* were, in a sense, part of the Spanish cultural wars of the late nineteenth and early twentieth centuries fought over the definition of Spanish nationalism. The language and even the approach of supposedly modern, new, scientific methods of defining the nation infiltrated any number of nationalist literatures of the period, including regionalist ones.[23] And, in a sense, this infiltration from so many voices helped elevate the scientific pursuit of anthropology as a discrete discipline. The organic and empirical approach of the scientific anthropologist soon split with the Romantic approach of the nonprofessional anthropologist. The scientist disapproved of the mystical, Romantic view of Spanish nationhood that linked the people, or a national spirit, with its environment and the supposedly appropriate governmental form to rule over this *pueblo*.

Not surprisingly, anthropologists in the university in Madrid disapproved of the regional practitioners who did not share their sense of professional and methodological rigor. Telésforo de Aranzadi, a student of Manuel Antón, was disappointed that these regional centers considered the definition of race, pueblo, and nation as synonymous. Nonscientists, he thought, were far too cavalier in using these three words interchangeably. Yet, even as Aranzadi faulted nonanthropologists for misusing ethnography, he applauded the tacit signal that rigorous ethnographic study of culture had arrived in Spanish national debates. For example, Joaquín Costa borrowed widely from French and German sources to define the nation. He followed the French thinker Hippolyte Taine to show that a people, or a *pueblo*, was a mixture of environmental conditions, cultural practice, historical lineage, *raza*, and the contemporary political and social situation, *el momento*.[24] Costa also followed the German philological tradition by trying to locate the Spanish *Volksgeist* in popular culture, especially literature and folk songs. As he once wrote, "the poet makes the nation, race, and humanity."[25] The tools he used were not necessarily scientific, yet his goal was to trace the basic structure of race, the transmission over time of characteristics that were essential and, indeed, immutable elements of the nation.

Other, even nonreformist writers appropriated this ethnographic and anthropological discourse of the nation. The mechanisms of this fusion differed, but the idea of racial amalgamation was widely attractive. The Catholic traditionalist Marcelino Menéndez y Pelayo, long before praising Olóriz's work as proof of racial fusion, hewed close to an ethnological position, arguing that links of blood (*estirpe*) and subjection to the same physical and moral identity (*linaje*) bound people together far more than did political and cultural elements. While his overall argument did not depart widely from Catholic traditionalism, the mechanism he saw and his mode of explanation were clearly drawn from scientific works with which he had been familiar. Racial fusion, as opposed to political or social discord, proved attractive to Menéndez Pelayo precisely because it presented a deeper, more unalterable notion of national unity, bound by material conditions, not just spiritual and moral ones: "It is materially impossible (given the laws of transmission and of inheritance and always leaving room for the strength of genius and free will) that thinkers with the same blood, born on the same land, subject to the same physical and moral influences and educated directly one by the other, will not share one and all traits, even though they might fight over different ideas or remain lifelong enemies."[26] The original moment of fusion and the causes of the fusion differed, but the end result was an inheritable, unavoidable, and ineluctable identity that could not merely be washed away by temporal differences in opinion. As Laura Otis pointed out, when figures in the late nineteenth century began to discuss cultural inheritance, the idea of race was never far behind.[27]

By the 1890s, these borrowings of racial fusionary language between scientists and nonscientists moved from the vagaries of a few philological pronouncements to the realm of fieldwork and active ethnological study. In other words, the Romantic assumption that past fusion was the key to understanding Spain evolved into far more empirical study. This symbolized the substantial incursions that material explanations and the natural sciences had made into Spanish intellectual debate. Under Costa's tutelage in the 1890s, the Athenaeum of Madrid began to pursue anthropological study of the Spanish racial composition and ethnological diversity. The goals of the organizers of these studies were two-tiered. The first was to define the variety of cultural practices of the various regions of Spain. In turn, with the clearer understanding of all elements of Spanish culture, these thinkers presumably could prescribe the form of government best suited to Spanish culture.[28] After 1892, Antón and his two most important students, Luís de Hoyos Sáinz and Telésforo de Aranzadi, became responsible for adapting older folkloric studies of the Spanish people to the new methods of ethnology, the comparative studies of human races. First, they introduced the members of the Athenaeum, who were otherwise unschooled in scientific observation and experimentation, to the methods of ethnological fieldwork and anthropological theory in general. As a sign of the dispersion of these ideas, these courses remained some of the most popular and well-attended in the years they were offered.[29]

However, tension did exist between the popular, or nonscientific, discourse of race and the specific, carefully demarcated definitions of *raza*, *pueblo*, and *nación* that Spanish anthropologists like Antón, Hoyos, and Aranzadi defended. Both Antón and Aranzadi argued strenuously that the particular derivation of the Spanish race could ultimately be traceable only through anthropometric analysis of skulls in addition to study of the contemporary Spanish populace. They also thought that over time these racial characteristics produced ethnic or cultural characteristics of the Spanish people that differentiated them from the populations of other countries. The differences emerged in how each thinker defined the galvanizing forces of the Spanish racial blend. In 1895, three years after the publication of the *Lecciones de antropología*, Antón opened the academic year at the Central University in Madrid with an inaugural lecture on the development of the races and nations of Europe. He began with a proper definition of anthropological subject matter that bridged both physical and ethnological concerns: "Because there is no solution to the continuity of the ceaseless labor of Creation, narrated by natural history and by the history of human civilization, one should not confuse the organism of the most perfect of creations, human beings, in their enigmatic unity, and its life force with the indefinite and mysterious spirit whose agitations are the subject of science, art, religion and law."[30]

Antón clearly wanted this address to be an introduction of Spanish anthropology to Spain's larger intellectual community. Antón attacked what he feared had been the strongest influences on Spain's reformist liberal intellectual community, that is, German linguistic and philological traditions of the nineteenth century. Indirectly, Antón was leveling these attacks at his disciple Telésforo de Aranzadi, who was strongly drawn to German ethnographic traditions. This attack signaled the important shift that Spanish anthropology would undergo in the next few decades, with Hoyos and Aranzadi struggling to apply their teacher's lessons even as they sought different, often competing influences to make their case. Antón thought that new historical writing had to be crafted with the tools both of scientific practice and the contributions of already known historical narratives.[31] He forged a vision of Spanish anthropology, largely informed by the Parisian anthropological approaches of his mentor Armand de Quatrefages, but also linked to Spain's unique national formation. For example, he was opposed to French and German efforts to find a pure line of racial descent in the Aryan. The clearest condemnation of Aryanists was that the philology upon which arguments of Aryan supremacy were rooted did not stand up to anthropological analysis. The historical narrative conflicted with scientific knowledge. Most importantly, Antón noted that Aryan purity theories ran counter to archaeological evidence. They were dependent instead solely on the supposed flow of language from India to Europe, as Aryan linguists like the French Adolphe Pictet or the German Friedrich Schlegel asserted.[32]

Antón argued that such reliance on weak scientific foundations allowed nonscientific, usually nationalistic, presentiment to overtake the evidence that should feed scientific theory. He noted that little evidence, other than Schlegel's or Pictet's spurious claims, demonstrated the origins of European races in India: "Certainly by situating in Asia the origin of the Aryans with the origins of art and language, one does not answer the question, but rather makes it more obscure. Yet, what else would one expect to happen when one turns to written and natural history to find the origins of things? And if this obfuscation of history makes the goals of understanding reality more remote, do these histories really represent a step toward the source from which human history sprang?"[33] He also noted that several recent histories had shown that not all linguistic roots rested in the supposed ancient Aryan language of Sanskrit. For Antón, even the roots of language were the results of mixture: "Today's distinct nationalities and peoples of Europe are constituted of an apparent confusion of different races. The precise methods of modern anthropology attempt to describe the various ethnic types with these various and diverse mixtures. These methods uncover the Caucasian and Mongol roots of Europeans who have preserved their purity through the atavistic forces that lie within these intermixtures."[34] Most importantly, Antón's arguments were attempts to buttress his own theories about the unique roots of Spain's racial lineage. According to Antón, the comparative analysis of craniological features revealed that Spain's racial heritage lay as much to the south of the Iberian Peninsula as to the north.[35] By highlighting racial incursions in Spain, and in turn, Europe, from the south, Antón was offering an alternative to German philology that rooted European racial origins in the north of India, later spreading via Teutonic migration into the European continent. In turn, Antón was arguing against the Aryan supremacy theories that this philological tradition had produced.

A particular target of attack was Arthur de Gobineau's 1835–55 *Essai sur l'inégalité des races humaines*. Anton lambasted Gobineau's work as an example of the kind of theoretical arguments that this philology, rather than a more anthropometric and ethnographic rendering of European racial roots, would encourage. Worse, Gobineau left out of his racial history a discussion of Spain's population, an absence consistent with one of the primary arguments made by Spanish anthropologists: Looking only eastward, European anthropologists wrongly ignored the historical invasion and substantial racial fusion that African immigration into Europe had created, at least in Spain. This migration would force a reworking not just of the role of Spain in European history but also of an understanding of the roots of Western civilization. In addition to the north of India, he argued, Africa was also a fountainhead:

> These conclusions force me to the study of constitutions of the populations of Classical Civilizations, and against the supposed excellence of blood purity, supported by Gobineau. This work gives me the data needed to assume that the Egyptian civilization, like the Hellenic, first demonstrated the contact and general intermixture of the Libyan-Iberian races and the Syrian-Arab races. . . . The Great Romans that saturated the world first demonstrated the contact between the Celts who lived in the Po river valley, called Umbrians and Etruscans, and the waves of Libyans who came to dominate the Mediterranean, who called themselves Oscas and Samites.[36]

With this altered portrait of the roots of Western civilization, Antón reconfigured the way in which Europeans should see both the physical and the cultural roots of European races. This new calibration of the racial lens showed that the political and social lives of nations were not the products of their access to Aryan civilization alone, but to both southern and northern European races:

> The influence of race on the character and nature of nations is undeniable. The confident observations of Taylor about the significance of religion in each of the great races of Europe cannot be questioned. Yet, all of the intimate communication between people in Europe has produced in us ethnic differences in law and in politics, that certainly could be tempered and modified by education and cultural changes. For example, aristocracies and hierarchy have made inborn the warrior and conqueror spirit of the Teuto-Scandinavians, the individualism and democratic spirit that lead Libyan-Iberians into revolt and separatism, and the sociability and utilitarian spirit that have produced Empires, Republics and Monarchies in the Celt-Slav races. Certainly, exceptions to these racial spirits exist. More important, however, is understanding the intimate and determinative interpenetrations to which a people is exposed and that modify their ethnic makeup.[37]

Thus, the Lybian-Iberian racial roots of the Spanish population provided a template for Antón with which he could explain the roots of Spanish behaviors.

Ironically, the various interpretations of the Spanish past demonstrated how deeply racial thought at the turn of the twentieth century resonated with far more contemporary discussions of acculturation and assimilation. Antón saw the process of fusion as directed by the guiding force of European cultural and intellectual supremacy. In this view, the potential rhetoric of the melting pot was lost in a contemporary racial assumption of hierarchy. Despite the reconfigured portrait of European races, and the apparent welcoming of Arab and African influence in Europe, Antón did not eschew the basic value of the hierarchy of races that seemed to be forever the companion of racial thinking. In a sense, Antón merely replaced one hierarchy for another. In the attempt to deny the racial and cultural supremacy of Aryan civilization, Antón inserted instead an image of North African incursion into Europe that was equally based on a rigid racial hierarchy. He merely inverted the standard Aryan model by placing the "Libyan-Iberian" race on top. Yet, the mechanisms still mattered. Rather than identifying the southern or African role in Spanish history as foundational or essential, the focus of this analysis was how the Christian or "European" populations ingeniously took the best elements of southern thinking and rejected the worst. Like Gobineau, Antón demonstrated that the acknowledgment of racial mixture did not necessarily indicate a racial openness or welcoming of difference.

This tension most clearly emerged in Antón's 1909 essay on the races and tribes of Morocco. This work, the product of fieldwork in Morocco, attempted to expand this view of the Libyan-Iberian race by offering a firsthand sketch of the original cultures that contributed to the Spanish racial mix. This study was conducted only within the Spanish holdings of Ceuta and Melilla in Morocco, and was intended by Antón to demonstrate the supposed racial links between the populations of Morocco and the Spaniards. The fact that the study only considered inhabitants from Spanish-controlled areas has led some historians to suggest that Antón was working to provide scientific justification for the unpopular military efforts in the region. Spain's Moroccan protectorate had been experiencing a relatively successful colonial insurgency with an attendant loss of Spanish lives.[38] Antón's effort was part of an apparent effort to reach a more ethnographically rooted understanding of the colonial enterprise. He noted that while the Spanish military needed to follow the military model of the French army to impose civilization, the Spanish protectorate was not a primeval wasteland of savages. Antón used his racial thought to prove that ethnological understanding of North Africans would allow a fuller understanding of the contemporary Spanish social setting as well. Indeed, the portrait Antón's study provided demonstrated the tempering effects of Spanish Catholicism on the warlike characters of some of the North African tribes. However, Antón presented the effects as dialectical, moving in both directions. The North African races had left a legacy of democratic individualism on the Spanish peninsula that was still clearly evident in the Spanish racial spirit.[39] Again, this vision of the racial contribution of the Libyan-Iberian race to Spanish racial existence did not depart from a number of other historical interpretations of the Spanish race. The notion that Spain was the European conduit for democracy and for a fundamentally individualistic approach to social theory and organization was the basis of both Joaquín Costa's and Menéndez y Pelayo's images of Spanish history.[40] Antón was no different in arguing that the galvanizing force of Catholicism had knit together disparate racial groups to form the Spanish nation.

The differences between these thinkers and their approaches to Spanish history were often only matters of emphasis. For Antón, the rebelliousness of Spain's regions was a racial characteristic, altered over time only by the gradual modification of the ethnic type through racial fusion. For other writers, religion actually solved what were laws of immutable racial difference. Celebrating the unity of the different racial groups that had populated the Spanish peninsula, Menéndez y Pelayo wrote that Catholicism, and not the unstoppable balm of racial, or anthropological, fusion had united the Spanish population: "Our unity was not created by the iron of conquest or the wisdom of legislators. . . . Prudence and faith rang out in verse from the hammers of the Celtiberians who triumphed over Manichaeism, Oriental Gnosticism, Aryanism of the Barbarians and the African charity."[41] Yet if the scientific basis of arguments for racial fusion differed from the nonscientific approaches of Menéndez y Pelayo and Costa, both relied on the idea that Spain represented a positive and forceful fusion of various characteristics to form a unified whole.

Fusion in the Colonies: Race outside Spain

The continued maintenance of colonies in North Africa became an increasingly important focus of anthropological theories of racial fusion. Certainly, anthropology was the choice of optimists who hoped that a rational understanding of the colonized peoples would make North African colonization a much-needed success after the losses of Spain's overseas colonies in 1898. Fusion was at the basis of Spanish colonial policy, which anthropologists noted had been far more effective and had produced fewer divisive results than the colonial policies of their European counterparts. In fact, the Moroccan protectorate would function as a modern example of the fusionary process that had typified the Spanish past. Anthropologists saw Morocco as a chance to renew the successes of the Spanish racial past in a supposedly primitive setting of interaction between Spaniards and Arabs, Christians and Muslims. On the issue of colonial policy, Antón's disciples reinforced their mentor's assertions. Writing in the second edition of *Lecciones de antropología: Etnología*, Aranzadi claimed that Spaniards had long been more successful in establishing peaceful and more productive colonies because of their willingness to mix with indigenous populations. In turn, this openness allowed colonial rulers to gain knowledge about the indigenous populations' culture, behaviors, and religious practices and thus facilitate the expansion of their colonial control:

> As for physiological criteria, observations today force us to confirm that all crossings and intermixtures between individuals are fertile. Others have countered with the evidence that in Tasmania, a mixed race formed between Anglos and Tasmanians never appeared. But one has to keep in mind the relations that the English have maintained with Tasmanians have been defined by murder without concern for the potential extermination of the colonized people. In contrast, one sees in the Spanish colonies in the Philippines, sextupling the indigenous population. Fecundity increases with the mixture of Hottentot and white. The unions of white with Indians in America are so much more fecund than between Indians that the greater part of the population of Mexico and the Central American populations are mestizo.[42]

For Aranzadi, the knowledge that colonial forces accrued by mixing with native populations was essential in forming effective and productive colonies. He added an important caveat: knowledge of the cultural practices of the native populations was helpful only in the effort to have colonial subjects live peacefully under colonial rule. Of the major colonial powers, Aranzadi noted, Spaniards were the only European colonists who fostered this empathetic colonial rule. As a result, Spaniards came to be expert in adapting indigenous cultures to colonial needs and ultimately in modifying their original culture to form a new mixed one. Aranzadi provided some examples of how Spaniards had adapted their colonial rules to suit the cultural practices and forms of their colonial subjects in order to produce a nonrebellious colonized population:

> The success of improving barbarians and savages depends in great part on the favorable or pernicious influence of the cultural instruction presented to them.

Their rebelliousness is predictable when one presents them with conquest, commerce, slavery, economic revolution. The delicacy of the missionary is important in the assimilation of animism, the cult of the dead, cosmological myths, and any other indigenous beliefs to the new religion, making sure not to use too lightly the names of indigenous Gods, because they so often incite the full weight of superstitions. It is important to offer economic improvement that is appealing to the indigenous populations that seems efficacious and worthwhile to them. Missionaries have to take care not to convert too vigorously the artisan, the businessman, or the plantation owner, but rather to do so slowly using that person's own mysticism, ascetic feeling, and abnegation. It always helps to provide certain medicines that counteract ineffective superstitious remedies. The greatest difficulties in improving the indigenous populations are in overcoming their own slavery and polygamy. Yet it is best to understand that these are examples of their ideas about social organization and attitudes toward sexual appetites.[43]

Fusion inside Spain: Regionalism and the New Catalysts of Racial Fusion around 1898

Fissures did begin to appear between Manuel Antón and his students Luís de Hoyos Sáinz and Telésforo de Aranzadi precisely over the mechanisms of fusion in the colonial context. These fissures would come to demonstrate part of the array of possible views of Spanish nationalism that racial fusion offered. Political values led to vastly different interpretations of how the Spanish race came together and how it was to stay fused. Antón continued throughout the remainder of his career at Central University in Madrid to offer an anthropological verification of conservative visions of Spanish history, a history of racial mixture stabilized and nurtured by conversion to Catholicism. He continued his defense of the formative role that the Libyan-Iberian race played in Spanish development and the important part that Catholicism played in uniting these various races and cultures.[44] Aranzadi and Hoyos, on the other hand, offered alternatives to this interpretation of Spanish racial history.

Oddly enough, these alternatives were the product of applying the successful lessons of Spanish colonization to the interior of Spain. For Spanish anthropologists, the uneven development of the Spanish economy over the centuries had left pockets of the country with the same kind of racial primitivism that had existed in Morocco. Hence, Spanish anthropologists offered a plan of internal colonialism guided by racial fusion. Hoyos and Aranzadi began to argue for the application of colonial structures, government, and institutions, which had been so successful outside of Spain, inside Spain. They wanted to use anthropology as the basis for a kind of internal colonialism, to study the cultural and physical makeup of the populations living in the peninsula and thereby adapt them to the overall mission of Spanish nationalism. Like any colonial project, the trick for Spanish anthropologists was to convince the native populations of the value of absorption, of the clear backwardness of their culture and the intellectual, cultural, and military superiority of the conquering forces.

Yet, regionalism would complicate this colonization, sharpening it for the more nationalistic anthropologists and exemplifying the weaknesses of the Spanish nation for those anthropologists with regionalist sympathies. An example of the latter, the Basque anthropologist Telésforo de Aranzadi argued that Spanish governments had for too long assumed that the subjugation and elimination of regional cultures was commensurate with the goals of Spanish nationalism. This effort to deny regional cultural differences, Aranzadi argued, had paradoxically worked to diminish Spanish national strength. Participation in the incipient world of Basque nationalism seemed to incline Aranzadi toward policies that fostered the coexistence of different races and cultures within nations. For Hoyos, the strength of the Spanish state was paramount both politically and racially for the strong absorption of regionalist groups. The pathway to this fusion was economic and social modernization. The technical lag of Spanish science behind other European countries and the lack of social support limited the impact of any of these anthropological lessons. Hoyos thought that only the development of a strong national culture could support and fund this kind of modernization. Aranzadi's work was increasingly concentrated on the development of social stability via proper understanding of the various racial and cultural elements that undergirded modern nations. Hoyos's work emphasized instead programs of national consolidation focusing on the suppression of regional differences. Both, of course, believed the process of racial mixture was essential in both programs.

Aranzadi issued the first salvo in this growing nationalist contest in the second edition of his *Etnología*. He concluded the volume quoting Antón on the positive effects of racial mixture on national characters. Aranzadi argued against the goal of collapsing racial elements into larger national projects, a process that Antón thought was a natural outgrowth of racial intermixture. Rather, Aranzadi argued for the naturalness of regional difference and variety, dependent as they were on climate, temperament, and racial mix, a common view among ethnographers of the era, especially the Germans. Differences did not necessarily disappear because of the formation of a state, especially when the regional groups remained relatively uncorrupted in their home territories. When state formation was strong and successful, proper political rule encouraged and fostered these regional differences as intrinsic parts of a modern nation. Ethnological knowledge, which provided particular awareness of the cultural differences within a nation, was as important as charting the physical roots that produced a strong nation.

It was essential for Spain's peaceful maintenance of its regional differences that cultural appropriation remained a multivalent process. Lesser racial groups absorbed the lessons of more advanced societies, as in the conversion to Catholicism that helped unify the various Spanish races. In addition, elements of the cultural as well as the physical makeup of the lesser racial groupings were transmitted to the larger society. Thus, knowledge of the racial makeup, of the physical components of Spain, was incomplete unless one understood the roots and derivations of all racial crossings and how they transformed each other over time:

> what the Germans call particularism is not necessarily something that resides in the blood of a nation, especially since it is a word that is used in a thousand ways in internal affairs. . . . Whom government officials call ungovernable are sometimes merely badly governed. There are effects that, more than character, are reactions against rigid uniformity that suffocates and absorbs different peoples and causes suspicion toward the government throughout the population. If the division of labor and differentiation of individuals is propitious for the production of internal cohesion in a society, as long as these divisions are not so rigid as to create a petrified social structure, then the division of labor among pueblos is also beneficial for a society as long the differences between them are not forced to stagnate. . . . The security of civilizations depends on the coexistence of different social entities. Only by guaranteeing this coexistence can one preserve the possibility of future adaptations. The salvation is in the knowledge, estimation, and love of all of the differences within a family, within a nation, and within the human species.[45]

Despite their calls for a greater study into the give-and-take of cultural and racial exchange in Spain, Aranzadi and Hoyos both failed to find a particular power base from which to consolidate their approach to studying anthropology. With Antón in the only chair of anthropology in Spain, both Hoyos and Aranzadi were forced to pursue academic employment in other disciplines, which prevented them from devoting their full attention to anthropological study. Aranzadi, who had been teaching pharmacy at the University of Granada between 1895 and 1899, accepted a professorship in descriptive botany

at the University of Barcelona, where he would remain for the rest of his career.[46] Only in 1920 was he asked to accept the first chair of anthropology at
Barcelona. Hoyos accepted a professorship in physiology in the Andalusian
city of Córdoba. Both disciples of Antón maintained their international professional relations, working as correspondents for German and French anthropological societies.[47] Both also traveled outside of Spain, again to attend
anthropological conferences throughout the next two decades. Still, Aranzadi
and Hoyos remained optimistic about the possibilities of expanding the discipline in Spain, especially through their efforts at building a long bibliography
in Spanish anthropology and in expanding the prestige of the discipline in
professional groups both within and outside of Spain. Writing in 1899 to his
cousin, the Spanish philosopher Miguel de Unamuno, Aranzadi observed
that despite his failure to obtain a lectureship in anthropology—a sign, he
thought, of an intellectual climate not quite ready to accept his ideas—he
remained optimistic about the future: "the oven isn't always ready to bake
muffins, sometimes you have to let it warm up first."[48]

The oven warmed more quickly after the military defeat in 1898. In the
first two decades of the twentieth century, a variety of organizations whose
purpose was to spread the instruction of science appeared in most major cities in Spain. Modeled on a French predecessor of 1872 and an older English
version from the 1830s, Spain's Association for the Advancement of Science
became an important center for the importation of European science into
Spain. With the presentation of scientific studies and with clear recommendations for implementation of this science into public policy, in addition to published minutes and invitations to the press, the association wanted to convey
to a wider audience the beneficial role of science in the amelioration of social
and political problems. Open political fighting was discouraged. Science had
to be seen as valuable to society regardless of the lessons this science would
provide.[49] The specter of defeat in 1898 clearly motivated many of the participants. One commentator at the association's first meeting noted that the
only reason for the loss of the colonies in 1898 was the military's ignorance
of scientific affairs. The presence of generals and their support staff at these
meetings attested to the military's tacit acknowledgement of its own lack of
awareness: "I also want to tell you that the army, far from ignoring science . . .
instead provides a phalanx of officials for its study. The papers presented here
to this Association demonstrate that the Armed Forces represent not only the
safeguard and guarantor of public order and the Honor of the Nation, but
also . . . of the development of scientific inquiry and progress of the nation."[50]

This valorizing of scientific training also dovetailed with most reformers' view that Spain's defeat was tied to the pitiful state of Spanish education. Science would renovate the moribund state of Spanish society. The appearance of new scientific organizations and new courses taught in already existing cultural and intellectual institutions testified at least to the growing awareness of a scientific *weltanschauung* among Spain's intellectual elite.[51] Spanish anthropology was a ubiquitous participant in this development. Despite the lack of institutional study of anthropology in Spain, the discipline itself was attracting more intellectual interest. Miguel de Unamuno, for example, wrote to his cousin Telésforo de Aranzadi asking for literature on ethnology after Aranzadi sent him some of his work from the 1890s. Perhaps the ethnic components of Unamuno's *intrahistoria* reflected the influence of his cousin's work for his letters to Aranzadi reflect the curiosity that Unamuno had about ethnology.[52] He told Aranzadi in one letter that he had aspired to include more of this anthropological background in his lectures and his own philological work.[53]

Anthropologists' influence also spread into other nonprofessional circles. Anthropologists served in important bureaucratic positions that were reshaping Spanish education. In the Madrid Athenaeum, Antón and Hoyos led the Section on Natural History for most of the first two decades of the twentieth century.[54] In the Association for the Advancement of Science, Hoyos and Aranzadi, along with fellow scientists Ángel Pulido and Rafael Salillas, led the organizing committees for the Sciences Section, a category that ranged from physics and chemistry to sociology and anthropology. One of the first products of this enhanced interest in anthropological analysis after 1898 was a national study sponsored by the Madrid Athenaeum. In 1902, Hoyos returned to Madrid from Córdoba to help with the redaction of the study that purported to be the largest ethnographic inquiry into Spanish customs and cultural practices ever performed. In fact, the study remains one of the largest performed in Europe. The information gathered in the study was the source of continued academic study well into the 1960s (before access to the archival materials became far more restrictive in the 1980s, for reasons unknown). In 1966, the art historian George Foster wrote that the study remained one of the most important to have been performed in Europe.[55] The study's authors followed Hoyos's wish that the study uncover the roots of a Spanish national culture rather than merely offer a compendium of local and regional practice. The work affirmed the general anthropological portrait of a multirooted racial populace. Though the study was focused on sending questionnaires to various regions of Spain, these regions were not solely determined by traditional political boundaries. Rather the regions were devised according to the ethnic identities of the populations that Olóriz, Antón, Hoyos, and Aranzadi had delineated in their physical and ethnographic works.[56]

Perhaps not surprisingly, the effort to devise the questions, make copies, and find correspondents in the various regions of Spain exhausted the funding of the project. Thus, even though more than 38,000 profiles were returned from the original mailing of 289 questionnaires, the data languished virtually untouched in the library of the Athenaeum for almost twenty years. On only two occasions were the materials used, both times by Rafael Salillas, Spain's most important criminal anthropologist, for works on folklore in 1906 and 1907. In 1922, Antón had the materials transferred to the Spanish Society of Anthropology, Ethnography and Prehistory (Sociedad Española de Antropología, Etnología y Prehistoria), where Hoyos and Aranzadi began to use them for their own ethnographic studies.[57]

Despite this example of the lackluster use of Spanish anthropological data, a greater incursion of anthropological knowledge about the Spanish race only proliferated in subsequent years. Their inability to find a reliable set of followers to put their ethnographic data to use did not deter Spain's anthropologists from advancing their ideas or their own influence within Spanish circles. In fact, at best, accommodation with the political regimes of the era marked Spanish anthropological attempts to find social applications. Through their own efforts and also due to the increasing hopes of the government to find solutions to the changing Spanish populations and the attendant stresses of modernity, racial thought found a far more attentive audience than is usually presumed. The shift in interest in these anthropologists' work inspired one of Aranzadi's close friends, Dr. Enrique de Areilza, to write to Aranzadi in perhaps a bit of flattery or exaggeration that, from his vantage point in Bilbao, "anthropologists seem to be on their way to controlling all of politics on the peninsula. I suppose Salillas will be a minister when the Republic comes . . . and for you they will reserve something that [your cousin] Unamuno turns down so he can stay cacique of that University [of Salamanca]."[58] With their ideas seemingly implanted everywhere and a sense that their political clout was expanding, anthropologists began to seek applications for their ideas in the nettlesome problems that faced Spain. The next section (Applying Race) deals with the efforts to find applications.

5. Race, Regionalism, and the Colonies Within
Anthropology Confronts Spain's Problems

As anthropologists increasingly became convinced that racial fusion had been the modus operandi of the Spanish past, the challenge increasingly facing them was to identify the proper and improper elements of this fusion. Spain's anthropologists saw the uniqueness of Spanish race as mixture, but how was it mixed? What were the components and how did they vary from region to region? How did they ultimately combine to form a distinct Spanish racial type? Spain's racial problem became a question of both keeping the foreign elements out and also finding and nurturing the supposedly proper components together within Spain. The answer to Spain's racial problems would come to demonstrate the flexibility that racial fusion offered Spanish thinkers. A diverse array of political ideologies would find a racial explanation—a permanent, immutable, transmissible quality—that defined the Spanish past, Spanish nationalism, and, most importantly, the sources of its present-day stability or decay.

In addition to providing a portrait of racial fusion, Spanish anthropology also offered a sheen of scientific objectivity to various political views. Of course, in defining the bad ingredients within the racial mixture, Spanish anthropologists began to demonstrate how personal prejudice could overwhelm their scientific objectivity. Not surprisingly, when Spanish racial theorists sought practical applications for fixing the Spanish racial mix, a variety of social and political prejudices became apparent. These explanations were not affixed to any particular political ideology. The liberalism of Spanish anthropologists like Pedro González de Velasco and Ángel Pulido gave way in their students' generation to a more complicated array of conservative, anarchist, liberal, and republican ideas. Spain's anthropologists demonstrated that the mechanisms of racial mixture placed in the context of social upheavals of urbanization and modernization in Spain led to dramatically different views about the makeup of the Spanish state. The definitions of the improper ingredients proved most various as they related to the question of regionalism and the anthropological explanation for why Spain seemingly struggled with regional divisions and failures to unify. Despite sharing similar anthropological approaches and still often publishing jointly, Antón, Hoyos, and Aranzadi began to disagree in the first two decades of the twentieth century about the basic nature of Spanish fusion. Aranzadi and Hoyos differed about what kind of unified whole, what kind of alloy, existed in the Spanish race.

Aranzadi's increasing interest in defending Basque culture amid the complicated development of Basque regional and separatist movements led him away from purely physical arguments. He began to argue that a Spanish race, defined physically, did not exist, but that races united within the Spanish state did. Aranzadi's interest in Basque culture would ostensibly strain his ability to promote the field of anthropology as an important source of knowledge about the nation. On the other side, Hoyos and Antón argued for a view of the Spanish race as once mixed but now united. Their view was far more top-down, seeing the Spanish fusion as a product of an idealized set of values that helped bring different races together. With Aranzadi ultimately positioned in Barcelona, and Hoyos and Antón in Madrid, the basic thrust of their anthropological views would sharpen the differences in how Spanish racial fusion was defined.

Still Working Together before the War to Define the Spanish Average Type

After their failures to gain positions in private schools in Madrid, Aranzadi and Hoyos both turned to other arenas to perform anthropological analysis.[1] Antón continued to offer classes in anthropology at Madrid's Athenaeum. Hoyos and Aranzadi took over those responsibilities in 1911–12 and again in 1917.[2] These lectures began to stress that anthropological study, both of physical measurements and of ethnological comparisons, could be used to identify not only racial identity but also the social and cultural capability of different people. This anthropological approach revealed the interest Aranzadi and Hoyos had in presenting the importance of anthropological study to untrained audiences. In addition, both Aranzadi and Hoyos were increasingly affected by concerns shaped by their historical context. In the years immediately before World War I, Aranzadi and Hoyos began coordinating the themes of their anthropological work with issues of national conflicts and the internal disarray that seemed to afflict Spain more than other nations.

In their joint work, Aranzadi and Hoyos documented the various racial components of the contemporary Spanish population. In a study they presented throughout Europe—in Paris to the Société d'Anthropologie, in Geneva during the International Congress of Anthropology and Archaeology, and in Granada to the Spanish Association for the Advancement of Science—they remeasured the skulls that Olóriz had used in *Índice Cefálico* of 1894, using an expanded array of indices and measurements. Their goal in this remeasurement was to define both the "unities and constants with Hispanic crania" to compare them both with other "European craniological types and also the diverse peoples that constitute the ethnological integrity of the *patria*."[3] The actual identification of these diverse *pueblos* was not complete, and thus the overall portrait of the Spanish nation was not yet known. To complete the picture, they wrote, anthropologists had first to discern the number and identity of various races that had mixed together to form the contemporary Spanish population.

In the course of their measurement of Spanish skulls in the first decade of the twentieth century, both Aranzadi and Hoyos had difficulty establishing one clear set of measures or even an average that united all of the people on the peninsula. The variations were too great to extrapolate one unified group of people. They concluded that all Spanish regions were made up of a variety of different races and different mixtures. No one area of Spain, they argued, displayed racial purity or even a mixture so slight as to be close to purity. This conclusion distinguished Aranzadi and Hoyos from their predecessor Olóriz. Olóriz had decided both that certain regions of Spain were racially homogeneous because their measurements were uniform, and that the Spanish race was more advanced in its fusion than its European counterparts. Aranzadi and Hoyos argued that conclusions like Olóriz's represented nothing more than speculation because of the small size of the samples tested.[4]

Telésforo de Aranzadi and the Pastoralist's Confusion

Aranzadi had the strongest reaction against Olóriz's conclusions because of the way in which Olóriz and other anthropologists in Spain, Europe, and the United States presented his fellow Basques.[5] Aranzadi found most disappointing the failure to accurately identify the precise uniqueness of the Basque race. Caught between an increasingly virulent Basque nationalist movement, which posited Basque racial and historical distinction from and superiority to the rest of the inhabitants of the Iberian Peninsula, and European anthropologists, who also largely argued that Basques were unique, Aranzadi worked to demonstrate that the complicated historical lineage of Basques was far more marked by mixture with other peoples surrounding the Basque country. Their intermixture was unique, as were all the mixtures throughout the peninsula.[6] Because of Aranzadi's effort to prove the uniqueness of the Basques, he is still considered to be a racial theorist who defended Basque separatism.[7] If one considers what Aranzadi meant by "mixture," however, and the way this notion fit with the broader anthropological framework in which he worked, it becomes clear that this assumption is not entirely accurate. Even in his personal life, Aranzadi had a strained and complicated relationship with the most virulent and racist Basque nationalists like Sabino Arana de Goiri.[8] Aranzadi defied the broad ethnic arguments about Basque uniqueness that were used strategically and inversely by Basque nationalists and Spanish nationalists. Aranzadi fit into a developing narrative of Basque identity that Fernando Molina Aparicio called the "separatist" versus "separated" storylines that projected Basques either as fundamentally different or in need of further education about how to exist within the Spanish nation.[9] Aranzadi wanted to overcome the traditional ethnic stereotyping of the Basque as a problematic people that Jon Juaristi describes as essential to the Spanish Right's nineteenth-century nationalist formulations, while still offering an ethnic understanding of the Basque as fundamentally linked into the Spanish *ethnie*.[10]

Perhaps Aranzadi's most impressive legacy was a faith in empiricism that made him resistant to claims of racial superiority from any particular camp. In an article written in 1915, Aranzadi was still criticizing much of the European anthropological research on the Basques because of the general conclusion it offered that the Basques had at one time in the past exhibited a "characteristic measurement."[11] He wrote that his own research on Basque skulls suggested that the Basques, like others in Spain, were a composite of a variety of groups. Despite the relative homogeneity of certain regions, the Basque, for example, one could not argue that purity or even a "characteristic measurement" existed. Mixture, he argued, was an ongoing and far more complicated process than even Spain's first physical anthropologists had concluded. Aranzadi asserted that the only method to track the ongoing process of *mestizaje*, or mixture, was through constant accumulation of ever more precise physical measurement.[12]

This concern for accurate anthropological depictions of the Basques gradually reoriented Aranzadi's anthropological work away from defining the

Spanish race and focusing on the more nettlesome issue of Basque identity. Aranzadi wanted to provide a portrait of the Spanish nation first sketched out in his 1899 *Etnología*, where he stressed not only physical identification of the Spanish, but also comparative analysis of cultural output. Through an understanding of both processes, Aranzadi argued, the true history of contact and fusion could be told. For Aranzadi, ethnology, the comparative study of all races, and ethnography, the particular study of individual cultures, became the primary focus of his anthropological study. When physical anthropology failed to define fully the distinctions between races, cultural forms had to be inserted into the analysis in order to understand the roots of both cultural and physical mixture: "We could say that the part of a museum in which the objects are arranged by countries, or better by *pueblos*, is ethnographic. The part in which the objects of all countries, or at least those in which objects of countries are arranged by continent, are organized by their significance in the life of a *pueblo*, is ethnological, keeping in mind, of course, there are ethnological comparisons between the objects within a people."[13] This more wide-ranging analysis would complete the portrait of Basque differences and similarities amid the entire Spanish race.[14]

Aranzadi's increasing interest in cultural forms as a way to distinguish the Basque and thus more accurately define this relationship to the Spanish led him back to the German influences on his anthropology that had distinguished him among Spain's usually French-oriented anthropologists. Aranzadi needed to discover the mechanism that would explain why the Basque race, a composite of so many different groups, both remained different from the Spanish populations but also had become part of the overall Spanish racial mix. He returned to the German anthropologists who had influenced him when he wrote his doctoral thesis. Aranzadi was particularly drawn to German anthropology because of a debate raging at the time over the question of how cultural forms moved between peoples and were adapted to new contexts. Aranzadi saw this question of cultural movement as a way to define the uniqueness and the shared identity of the Basque people and the Spanish.

The debate that occupied some German anthropologists was rooted in a lingering question about physical anthropology. Physical attributes—part of their own wide discussion in anthropology, especially after 1900 and the rediscovery of Mendelian genetics—were generally accepted as passed from generation to generation. The actual mechanism of this passage of traits remained a source of frenzied debate.[15] Aranzadi had been a student primarily of Friedrich Ratzel, the German ethnographer who founded the diffusionist school of ethnology. Ratzel argued that all contemporary cultural attributes and ideas were rooted in an original and specific group of fundamental ideas that spread throughout the world and were altered through constant migrations of people. Ethnography for Ratzel was designed to trace how these original ideas expressed themselves within material cultures, the constructed objects, of these diverse populations of the world. This approach left Ratzel at odds with other German anthropologists, especially those in the German Anthropological Society who remained devoted to an idealist view of human development that saw a clearer and more permanent unity among all cultural elements—"a universal human nature"—that ran through all of the human past. Aranzadi saw within Ratzel's more historicist approach a potentially more open view of how distinct groups came into existence.[16]

At the same time, he placed more emphasis on the cultural habits that were unique to their context and developed in response to local conditions, in particular to the physical environment.[17] In other words, Aranzadi was more interested than other anthropologists in the actual mechanisms that brought about cultural identities in their particular contexts. For Aranzadi, the definitions of culture and racial identity were dependent on a variety of factors such as historical circumstance and social, political, and geographical context. These elements were dynamic and unstable. In addition, culture was so pervasive and distinctive in each society that it lay embedded not merely in the production of visual arts or literature, but also in its *Volkskunde*, or the material culture of a people. Thus, he argued that anthropologists needed to study not merely the most definitive or "aristocratic characters" of language or art, as some of his German colleagues had done, but also other forms of cultural output like pottery, the styles of yoke used to tether work animals to carts, or the designs of wheels used on wagons, each as evidence of cultural contact and sharing.

Such thinking, he wrote, elevated anthropology above the assertions of nationalists and writers uninterested in the scientific verity of their assertions.[18] Racial capabilities and the particular aptitude of races were only to be ascertained using numerous anthropological tools. Thus, he was suspicious of assertions of supremacy based on national categories, arguing that only anthropology was capable of defining racial stocks and racial aptitude: "The racial problem in Europe occupies the greatest number of people who write and talk about the international and national politics, who are both knowledgeable and ignorant. . . . Only anthropological methods, applied independently and with true sincerity, can shed any light on the problem with all disclaimers that others refuse to offer when they discuss this problem."[19]

Aranzadi viewed nations as compendia of racial groups. He began to present Spanish regions as essential elements of the anthropological study of national identity. Aranzadi argued that Basques were a people with some unique attributes that were mostly cultural, and that they also shared with the rest of the Spanish population other elements that were mostly physical.

This approach responded to both anthropological perspectives on the Basques that Aranzadi had encountered up to that point. On the one hand, Aranzadi was working against the European anthropological assumption that the Basques were an autochthonous race, almost entirely pure in its racial lineage, based on what Aranzadi thought were specious or, at least incomplete, racial measurements.[20] On the other hand, Aranzadi opposed Spanish anthropologists, including Manuel Antón, who argued for the inherent mixture that underlay the Basque race even though its racial origins were distinct from other Iberian groups. The Basques did display unique ethnological characteristics, according to Aranzadi, that spoke to greater differences from the rest of the Spanish population than other anthropologists were willing to allow.[21] For Aranzadi, the issue of the Basques represented in microcosm the general purpose of studying anthropology: to understand physical anthropology as the basis for identifying races, and ethnology and ethnography as the bases for determining how racial mixture was capable of manifesting itself in cultural, sociological, and national realms. Aranzadi still assumed a fundamental link between the two approaches, for cultural or ethnic qualities would always mirror the physical, or racial, formation. As he wrote in 1899, "culture is the spirit of race."[22] Racial ideology for Aranzadi was complex; rather than claiming race as a purely spiritual quality, he thought culture was a mere manifestation of a biological reality.

Again, though, Aranzadi's liberal allegiance to a modern Spanish state made him cautious about carrying arguments about the historical uniqueness of regional groups too far. The point of his work was to demonstrate how minority populations survived and thrived amid larger national entities. While he might not have been happy with the contemporary Spanish state, he was not opposed to the idea of a Spanish state that exercised control over the Basques, or any other regional group. He did not want this anthropological focus on unique characteristics to strengthen regionalist or separatist political programs. In fact, he had already written that anthropology and politics should not be linked. The anthropological idea of mixture was important in this context for it provided Aranzadi a framework with which to present Basques as partially unique and partially similar to the rest of the Spanish population in its racial lineage, but not necessarily as rebellious or naturally anti-Spanish, as his mentor Manuel Antón had done. Racial and cultural fusion countered the argument that any kind of difference would necessarily beget separatist, antinational feeling. Antistatist separatism was the product of central state policies, not of inherent regional dispositions. For Aranzadi, how a nation dealt with its internal racial and cultural differences was the key for understanding the development of nationalist and centralizing sensibilities or regionalist, separatist ardor.

One problem with states that attempted to destroy internal distinctions was that they alienated these regions and thus fostered separatist movements. This process was both predictable and inevitable. Nations, as he had written in his 1899 *Etnología*, were not natural entities. National feeling was not an inherited characteristic. Regions, on the other hand, with their much more ancient racial and cultural heritage, were. Thus, Aranzadi warned, when states imposed national programs to limit manifestations of regional cultures, as Spain had done in 1897 with the outlawing of the use of the Basque language, such efforts would lead ineluctably to national division. Cultural differences, of which language was an important part, could easily be minimized via the forging of common interests. Whether these common interests were political, economic, or cultural he never fully specified. Yet, given their historical and anthropological roots, cultural differences could not be suppressed without an obvious cost to national unity: "An unhelpful distinction is made in Castile when people say that someone 'doesn't speak Christian' when they mean to say someone who does not speak Spanish. Even worse is that these people do not understand that non-Spanish speakers can actually understand each other. But solidarity of interests can always triumph over these problems. Only the hypocrisy of states that say they support linguistic expansion, when they actually work to suppress them, awakens separatist movements."[23]

Lastly, Aranzadi wanted to sound the alarm against any association of his ideas with a more socialist reading of racial fusion. He conceded, for example, that class distinctions were also important culprits in producing regionalist ideas that led people away from their natural, ethnic feeling and toward potentially revolutionary and antistatist feeling. But Aranzadi argued that a people (*pueblo*) was a historically linked, physically and culturally organized entity that transcended social divisions. This entity could become a national body when the various regional groups fused through common interests to become nations. Thus, class distinctions that were too strongly wrought were yet one more hurdle for the proper formation of ethnic feeling and nationhood. Because the process of mixture was ongoing, national bonds were not immutable. These common interests were no less permanent and capable of change. In other words, antiregionalist acts were dangerous to national unity. If certain social conditions existed, especially in cities where people mixed with a variety of other cultural groups and racial groups, then certain ethnic differences and cultural proclivities could be overcome. Citing a craniological study of inhabitants of Madrid prepared by two military doctors working from the collection of Olóriz at the Medical Faculty at Madrid's Central University, Aranzadi noted that racial distinctions disappeared more rapidly in urban contexts and especially among laboring classes.[24] If such seemingly immutable characteristics could change, so too could cultural ones. Thus, Aranzadi argued that the development of modern work forces, which had been the cause of migration to cities, would lead to the development of a social system that provided a class identity that would supersede the ethnic one. With regional racial qualities disappearing in cities, uneven social distinctions could overcome ethnic alliances. This disappearance could foster divisions among people who were otherwise united by cultural and racial attributes: "The 'ethnos' is not the 'demos.' The 'ethnos' includes all classes of society if they are congenital. It is true that the character of the historical 'ethnos' is most concentrated in the educated classes, but it does not disappear from everyone. In the most extreme cases, the disinherited classes of the great cities create conflicts, indeed antagonisms, between the 'ethnos' and a certain image of a 'demos,' between the faithful, or 'pure-blooded' (castizo) and the revolutionary, so much so that they can lead to national suicide."[25] The muting of regional differences in the city had allowed a class system that was just as divisive and inheritable as national, pure-blooded bonds. Even worse, this rigid class system managed to overwhelm older racial characteristics and threaten the racial strength of the "faithful." Aranzadi's language here, of course, is interesting for its running together of faith and pure-bloodedness. But more important is the clear threat that cities posed to the nation. Cities could apparently crush the important differences that gave life to a nation. For Aranzadi, the "loss of arcadia" in the city was the loss of regional sensibilities that helped create the conditions for national disintegration.

The disappearance of this regional feeling at the hands of a class-based system posed a particularly serious threat to Spain as a fused nation. Urban homogenization weakened states whose strength derived from the interaction of different physical and cultural entities. Aranzadi thought that nations functioned well when they became the expressions of their distinct ethnic components. This fusion and proper understanding did not guarantee the permanent success of a nation. Instead of fostering racial strength with the proper culling of physical characteristics from the Spanish populace, Aranzadi argued that racial strength was determined by a nation cognizant of its racial makeup. A successful nation allowed these diverse cultural and racial groups to remain vibrant within the city and the nation.

But Aranzadi also found that fusion was a multiform process capable of producing good results without following any one particular line of development. He did not deplore the reality of cities, but the fact that so few cities existed in Spain. Fewer urban contexts forced Spain's many diverse elements to only a few places, thus heightening the strains of homogenization. The solutions rested in better appreciation of the anthropological understanding and delineation of the Spanish people. Ethnography would diagnose the source of social and regional unrest. Linguistic differences, manifold varieties of cultural practice, and differences in the forms of social organization all fell under the purview of anthropology, and only anthropology could sort out the methods that could unify the nation. As Aranzadi wrote in 1917: "unity is only produced organically when each part understands itself in relation to other parts and when all of these parts are conjoined into a larger singular entity."[26]

Hoyos and Antón: Finding the Unitary Spirit or Ethnic Factor in the Spanish Race

While Aranzadi's colleagues, especially Hoyos and Manuel Antón, did not disagree with their colleague's sentiment, their own approach to the study of Spain's ethnography minimized the important role that Aranzadi gave to regional identities in forging the nation. For Aranzadi, ethnology and ethnography would help solve the seemingly intractable social problems facing Spain by understanding the mechanisms of fusion rather than by focusing solely on muting regional identities. For Antón and Hoyos, the particular mission of studying the ethnology and ethnography of different regional identities was not to better understand the regions but rather to trace how the "personality of a nation" came into being.[27] The difference between these anthropologists was one of emphasis. Aranzadi argued for mutual understanding; Hoyos and Antón argued for group identity. They all emphasized the importance of national unity, yet one side did so by arguing that unity came from the suppression of regional groups while the other argued that it arrived through the enhancement and proper nurture of them.

This difference was especially evident in the course of study that Aranzadi's former teacher Manuel Antón and colleague Luís Hoyos y Sáinz pursued in the first decades of the twentieth century. Rather than following the inductive process preferred by Aranzadi—which focused on the region as the building block of the nation—Hoyos preferred to view the anthropology and ethnography of Spain deductively, taking already accepted national characteristics and tracing their incursion and dominance in Spain's regions. Interestingly, this emphasis did not lead to vastly different conclusions about the nature or reality of Spanish racial mixture. Instead, it led to a vastly different attitude and approach toward dealing with regionalist movements and sentiment. Aranzadi's folklorist, for example, would become Hoyos's violent separatist. Citing the work of the nationalists like the philologist Marcelino Menéndez y Pelayo and the sociologist Joaquín Costa, Hoyos argued that national histories were most illuminating when they allowed one to gaze on the "unified vision of the Iberian Olympus" in any region in the country.[28] For Hoyos, the goal of anthropology was to provide a glimpse of the cultural heredity of any nation. This language of inheritance was intentional for Hoyos considered the transfer of cultural traits as fundamental and as clearly observable as physical attributes: "Regional spirits, the products of a homeland and cultural inheritance, that go along with other traits are the sources of countless monographic investigations even though scientific severity obliges us to separate the wheat from the chaff, but not from the great harvest of ethnography. . . . [T]he progress [of ethnographic studies] consists in the domination of nature, not in the submission to it, recognizing the primary unities from a nation's past, and aspiring to form a superior complex of knowledge about a nation, rooted in a wide and expansive notion of what this national integrity is."[29] These "primary unities" were identified by Hoyos as ancient manifestations of culture—the texts, music, artifacts left behind in various regions—clearly linked together in form or content. Whereas Aranzadi's diffusionist perspective allowed him to view such manifestations as the product of a slow accretion, via contact and mixture, Hoyos emphasized the direct and inexorable path these cultural forms took after contact to form the contemporary Spanish nation.

Both Hoyos and Aranzadi agreed that cultural forms developed as the result of migration, with the give-and-take of human contact forming the basis of cultural evolution. In this way, both were diffusionists, like Adolph Bastian and Ratzel in Germany. Yet, like Bastian and Ratzel, who disagreed about the mechanisms of cultural appropriation but agreed about the basic historical, national, and cultural purposes of it, Hoyos and Aranzadi appropriated diffusionism for the social meanings it gave to nationalism.[30] Hoyos agreed with Bastian's belief that despite unitary human culture, some elements of cultural differentiation were the products of a unique force that produced independent inventions. This approach asserted that some, if not all, cultural forms developed independently, in response to the needs of that particular group based on an environmental imperative or on random or spontaneous generation. While Aranzadi was interested in describing local cultures, specifically the Basque, in depth, Hoyos worked in the opposite direction, preferring to research how the characteristics that made contemporary nations unique were rooted in their racial past. What made nations and cultures different was reducible, Hoyos argued, to an "ethnic factor" (el factor étnico) of a nation, the unifying characteristic traceable throughout history that ultimately gave nations their unique character. The ethnic factor was the independent invention that defined a region and, later, a nation.

This idea linked Hoyos to the more nationalist and supremacist line of anthropological thought. The term "ethnic factor," used to signify national spirit, appeared throughout Hoyos's writing. Aryan supremacist anthropologists like Otto Ammon or Vacher de Lapouge also wrote of ethnic factors that helped Aryan races spread and dominate northern Europe. While Hoyos sought to distance himself from the original use of the concept by Gobineau, who argued that the mixture of national spirits was inherently weakening, Hoyos did not deny their supposed importance in forging nations. His problem with Gobineau was that the French pseudo-aristocrat was "not a true anthropologist." He "exaggerated" the basic value of ethnic factors by focusing only on the Aryan identity. One could not assess the true components of the ethnic factor with such a small set of national spirits.[31] Hoyos did not believe this ethnic factor came from only one dominant group. Fusion and difference underscored his definition of the unifying ethnic factor. He believed that a variety of characteristics could shape any one area's ethnic factor. For some regions, the ethnic factor was most clearly physical; in other areas, it was moral. The components of ethnic factors were local phenomena. But, for Hoyos, the ethnic factor of a nation could make regional ethnies into nations. Regional groups had to unify around a national set of ideas, a national purpose—not necessarily a random course of events and fusions—which honed each region into the larger national group. This process was top-down from the state to the region. It was also a historical inevitability as long as the national unifying characteristics were strong enough to hold regions together.

For Hoyos, fusion was an inevitable process, but not all fusion produced successful results. Failed states were the product of a failed cultural transmission of the ethnic factor from the top down to the disparate peoples. Hoyos was applying Bastian's idea of natural peoples (Naturvölker) to the Spanish context. Bastian had argued that any group whose members looked and acted human but did not seem to possess the unitary cultural elements was not fully human. Bastian called these people Naturvölker, arguing that they represented a kind of living snapshot of the earliest and most primitive humans. Hoyos extended the idea of Naturvölker to those groups in a nation who seemed most resistant to the unifying spirit of ethnic factors. There was a primitive recalcitrance in defying the historical and racial process of fusion. Hoyos transposed the racial hierarchy implicit in Bastian's ideas to the Spanish context of racial fusion. Groups who did not fuse properly were racial threats who weakened the entire process of national formation. Unifying factors, both cultural and physical, had to coincide with the larger process of fusion to create nations or civilizations. Hoyos lamented that, as of the early twentieth century in Spain, the Spanish state had failed in this imposition of the ethnic factor: "this organized system of creations and forms is what Ethnography considers a civilization. It is clear that all civilizations tend to become nations; that is, they make themselves concrete in time and space. At times, however, these nations do not squeeze into a four-sided territory or a chronological timeline. . . . To some degree, a civilization is also spiritual entity in which various national groups and pueblos each give over elements of themselves to the larger nation."[32]

Much of Hoyos's work, like that of Aranzadi, was a reinterpretation of the ideas of his mentor, Manuel Antón. In his 1909 analysis of Morocco, Antón had argued that Catholicism had caused the disparate elements in Spain's racial past to fuse into the present Spanish nation.[33] Hoyos offered a similar but more secular vision of Antón's thesis. The ethnic factor was a concept not easily boiled down to a spiritual component of faith. Determining the nature and effects of these ethnic factors remained the focus of Hoyos's anthropology throughout the remainder of his career. Ethnic factors were clearly the element of a national identity honed over generations by both physical and cultural development. Environmental and biological factors, representing two distinct poles of anthropological study, were both essential in the development of such ethnic components of nations.[34]

Still, Hoyos struggled to locate and define the actual content of a nation's ethic factors. He continued to express his belief in the reality of ethnic factors, but he was tentative about defining their actual content. Hoyos did caution against fixating on any one approach as the sole method of identifying such ethnic factors and racial characteristics. Such a reductive focus lent itself to relying on national stereotypes and claims of national supremacy. Science had to lead the way in defining ethnic factors:

> In response to the negative assertions of sociologists from pure, historicist perspectives, like Finot or Fouillée, whom I cite not because of their great authority, but because they seem so well known in Spain, it is very clear that the ethnic factor intervenes intimately in the evolution of *pueblos*, so much so that one cannot discount the work of true anthropologists like Ammon, Reese, Lapouge, or Thompson among others. One must simply ignore the predictably misguided ideas they base on Gobineau's exaggerations. If one acknowledges that even in scientific construction total prudence is not possible, one has to exercise even more caution in relation to Anthroposociology, because even purely objective anthropological data can occasionally unite with political passions, not only in international and inter-regional politics, but also in terms of social classes.[35]

Certainly anthropologists could work to falsify specious nationalist or supremacist claims of scientists and nonscientists. Yet, Hoyos suggested it would be more beneficial to deny no scientific approach and to accept as a basic assumption that ethnic factors existed and would, through unbounded scientific analysis, eventually be described by anthropology. To fail would lead to national decline: "in spite of these inductive generalizations, processes of stagnation can overtake nations, peoples, races, and even the progress and conquest of modern life . . . leading to the stagnation of human development, which then depends on the superiority or inferiority of ethnic factors to overcome."[36]

Hoyos did not discount the possibility that there were elements involved in the formation of ethnic factors or national personalities that scientists had yet to uncover through experimentation or observation. His approach was still materialist and determinist. Even a solitary element of identity could corrupt the nation and would require some kind of treatment. Science, he felt, could uncover these negative qualities. This kind of determinism left the door open for any number of views of what components were dangerous interpretations of this ethnic factor and its means of control. For example, because Hoyos removed the fundamental role of Catholicism, he expanded the range of influence of his ideas, especially among critics of the Restoration government. In a letter from the Spanish philosopher José Ortega y Gasset to Hoyos, Ortega explained that his reading of Hoyos's work had convinced him that Spain's perpetual experience of poor government was a product of "our ethnic substance."[37] When Ortega later wrote of Spain's national woes as a product of it being invertebrate, or without a solid government or leadership class, the biological language and the idea of Spain missing its historical glue remained quite close to Hoyos's idea.[38] In fact, Hoyos himself offered a hint of the pessimism that later defined Ortega's 1922 work. Hoyos agreed with Ortega's notion that ethnic factors could contain negative elements and corrode the nation. In 1917, Hoyos argued that the world war "demonstrates the power of these ethnic unities to make *pueblos* overcome *entente* and create friction between races and nations."[39]

Such an assertion was perhaps not surprising given the state of contemporary Spanish anthropology. Though popular as a theme in contemporary debates, anthropology as a discipline remained relatively underrepresented in the country.[40] The few people in Spain devoted to the actual study of anthropology were left to rely either on their own productivity or the work of Europeans to test the theoretical bases of their work. Thus, Hoyos's recommendations for an ecumenical approach to anthropological research was a response to the sense that, for work to advance, anthropologists could not specialize in a particular sphere of anthropological study, whether physical, ethnological, folkloric, etc. Rather, anthropologists would have to be expert in, and publish in, all fields. But the clear tone of eugenic concern for ethnic factors and their diagnosis and treatment hinted at the possibility of a wide array of social programs that could use science as the justification to intervene in the reproduction of the Spanish population.

The Legacy of Hoyos and Aranzadi: Racist Francoism, or the Republican Melting Pot

Despite their differences, Hoyos and Aranzadi both worked to expand the field of anthropology and its public role in the years following World War I. From his position as professor of physiology and school hygiene in the College of Teachers (Escuela Superior de Magisterio), a position he obtained in 1909, and as director of the Science Section in the Madrid Athenaeum, which he held from 1914 to 1919, Hoyos reentered the practice of anthropology, producing more than one hundred works almost exclusively on physical anthropology. After 1920, Hoyos maintained his preference for physical rather than cultural analysis, turning toward biometric study after establishing contact with Karl Pearson and his journal *Biometrika* in London. He served as the main contact between this group and a growing number of Spanish anthropologists interested in eugenics.[41] This eugenic approach was an outgrowth of his deterministic approach and served as the basis for later thinking about race and national enemies, which will be discussed in the next chapter. Hoyos devoted the remainder of his career to a kind of biological determinism that most clearly distinguished between groups: the various blood groups of Spain. Though he remained personally disappointed at the lack of support for and research on the subject in Spain, his approach remains influential even today, with some still relying on blood types as a physical means of differentiating between regional groups in Spain.[42] Physical anthropology dominated Hoyos's work through the 1930s and 1940s until his death in 1951.

Aranzadi also devoted the remainder of his career to anthropology, though his focus resettled on the work with which he began his career, sketching an overview of the original races that composed the Basque population.[43] From his position as a botany professor at the University of Barcelona and then, after 1920, as chair of anthropology, Aranzadi became a dominant voice in the establishment of anthropological approaches to Spanish identity. His work for the Espasa-Calpe Enciclopedia universal ilustrada was particularly important for establishing links between scientific approaches to Spanish identity, and popular notions of Spanish national and regional identities.[44] In the 1939 supplementary edition, written in the midst of the Civil War, Aranzadi reiterated the Spanish view that race could not be understood solely in biological terms, as Nazi racial scientists were doing: "In reality, the search for purely hereditary racial qualities serves only a quantitative purpose, not a functional one. This search also relies on a kind of Romanticism, studying only ideal 'Natural People,' since it does not present them in relation to their social reality or to their own history or the history of their race."[45] Still, as testimony to Spanish anthropologists' eclectic approach, Aranzadi continued to use German racial theorists including Eugen Fischer—the then head of the Kaiser Wilhelm Institute of Anthropology, Human Heredity, and Eugenics— to explain the genetic bases of race. Aranzadi implied that his Nazi colleagues were wrong in the application and conclusions of their race science, but not in the methods that underscored it.[46]

Despite their concentration in a variety of anthropological fields, the theme of mixture remained constant in the work of Antón, Hoyos, and Aranzadi. How they differed lay in identifying the galvanizing agent that brought these groups together and allowed them to form cohesive bonds. For Aranzadi, this cohesion was unsteady; efforts at cultural suppression could undo or weaken the centuries of physical fusion that had taken place. Because cultural and physical cohesion were both natural processes, tampering with them via artificial means of state policy meant undoing the larger political unity of Spain. Aranzadi's frustrations lay with nationalist attitudes that sought to mute regional differences rather than view them as essential parts of nations. These ideas made Aranzadi's work popular among regionalist organizations. His volume on ethnology, where he first made these arguments, became a famous and widely reviewed book in Catalonia.[47] He also attended the much-discussed Orthographic Conference of Hendaye in the Basque country in 1901, the purpose of which was to provide the first orthography of the Basque language. This conference served as an ideological battleground for an increasing but disparate number of Basque nationalists then appearing in the Basque country, including the most famous proponent of Basque racial purity, Sabino de Arana Goiri. Sabino de Arana had already argued against miscegenation between Spaniards and Basques and counseled separation of Basques and Spaniards.[48] While Aranzadi argued against the hazardous effects of suppressing regional identities, he also was careful not to assert the supremacy of regional identities. The formation of a nation could be a natural process of absorption, allowing differences to remain within the nation while fostering the political formation of a central state and guaranteeing its unity through acknowledgment of ethnic factors or the development of shared interests.

Hoyos spent the remainder of his career charting the physical and cultural formation of Spaniards. Yet, the purpose of charting this fusion was to understand the uniqueness of the Spanish race. Despite his concerns with the Aryanism of his German colleagues, Hoyos maintained a steady faith in the existence of determinative racial characteristics and ethnic factors. In his work for nonspecialized audiences, Hoyos stressed the need for anthropology to be empirical. Yet, at the same time, by defining anthropology as the science that coordinated all of the knowledge gathered by history, sociology, medicine, anatomy, and, later, biology and genetics, Hoyos often used as his sources thinkers whose view of Spain's history of racial fusion had far more ideological connotations than Hoyos readily admitted.

Anthropology in Wartime: Luís de Hoyos Sáinz

Luís de Hoyos Sáinz provided the clearest example of the wide political range that racial mixture allowed Spanish racial thinkers to traverse in the first half of the twentieth century. In 1943, during his acceptance speech to the Academy of Sciences in Spain, Hoyos argued that regionalism posed the greatest threat to national unity and that Spain's ethnic spirit could only be guaranteed by the new regime of General Franco. For proof of this ethnic spirit and the national unity that guaranteed it, he suggested that people study his own anthropological work, the histories of Spain provided by the Catholic traditionalist thinker Marcelino Menéndez y Pelayo, the Catholic unionist historian Ramón Menéndez Pidal, and the Spanish neurologist and Nobel laureate Santiago Ramón y Cajal. This odd union of figures featured individuals who had argued for Spain's unity based on the supposed timeless Spanish Catholic tradition and also those who represented Spain's scientific prowess in the modern world. Spain's history, in Hoyos's rendering, was the story of a constant mingling of distinct features, all studied and understood contemporaneously using the tools of science. Nations were a natural end point of ethnological and cultural evolution. Regionalism was an atavistic reminder of earlier forms of human development:

> Looking at this century, one can see two great epochs having formed that are completely contradictory: one was that of the Great War, dissociating great States and creators of Nations, and was motivated by an idea that was parasitic to humanity. This epoch caused in Spain the creation of intense regionalist movements that reduced the country to the pursuit of the primitive vice of localism and cantonalism. But in the less than a quarter of a century that has since passed, the corrective forces of history have integrated peoples and nations again into great states, one of which, with its double base of common race and universal language, is, should be, and will always remain Spain.[49]

It is important to acknowledge the pressures Hoyos might have faced speaking on such topics in the early years of the Franco regime. As a result, one might conclude that Hoyos was merely aligning his science to fit the new political context. Yet, despite his true motives, Hoyos continued well into the 1950s to present an anthropological image of Spain that conformed to Francoist ideology.[50] He still worked to define the Spanish regional map in terms of biological makeup.[51] He continued his analysis of skulls, especially recently unearthed prehistoric skulls, to identify later regional types reflected in them. He was particularly excited about studying the "proto-madrileño," who as a true cosmopolitan reflected the array of "Spanish racial mixture: African, Neanderthal, Mediterranean."[52] He concluded his professional career with a long article proving the anthropological roots of the important Francoist theme of Hispanidad, i.e., Spain's supposed historical affinity and, in some sense, parentage of Latin American culture and history. Hoyos argued at length that two races came together in the Western Hemisphere, the Spanish and the Indian. Again echoing the older ideas of Menéndez y Pelayo, Hoyos provided a history of racial fusion that improved rather than destroyed the world's racial heritage. The contemporary world was now made up of the various castes that were formed after Spaniards had brought a fusionary spirit of "fraternity, universal and catholic equality to all people."[53] Hoyos only lamented that Spanish anthropologists were never able to establish a firm enough discipline to re-create the former glories of Pedro González de Velasco's museum and Anthropology Society. Sadly, he wrote, the physical evidence of this fusion remained scattered in too many anthropology museums throughout the world instead of resting in a Spanish site for all to see and study.

Conclusion

Spanish racial thinkers almost universally accepted the idea of fusion, that Spain represented the coming together of a variety of traits. Yet, how they deployed this idea of fusion to discuss larger issues of political or social importance revealed wide differences in the political implications they saw in racial mixture. Trained under the tutelage of French anthropology with its positivism and empiricism, both Hoyos and Antón maintained the argument throughout their careers that only verifiable facts were reliable enough to support anthropological assertions about racial makeup or racial hierarchies. Linguistic analysis, for example, was too easily adulterated by nationalist sensibilities. Yet, this reliance on verification did deter Antón and Hoyos from attributing meaning and significance to the history of racial mixture that celebrated a centralized Spanish nationalism. As a result, they searched for elements like "ethnic factors" that were demonstrated with difficulty and ultimately, according to Hoyos, perhaps only with the hope of "future analysis."

Antón asserted much more boldly the uniqueness of the Spanish race, attempting to rewrite the European racialist assertions that rooted Western civilization in Aryan ancestors in northern India. Not only was Spain the product of racial mixture from the south, from Africa as much as from Europe, he wrote, but it took the cultural, or religious, phenomenon of Catholicism to work as the binding agent for this racial fusion. For both Antón and Hoyos, the reliance on verifiable proof led them to a scientific method that was dependent only on what they considered objective criteria, observable fact. Interestingly, despite the two anthropologists' slightly divergent approaches, they had similar political resonance. Anton's belief in the importance of

Catholicism and Hoyos's call for top-down fusionary process provided an anthropological proof of the absolute necessity of Spanish national unity.

Aranzadi's version of the anthropologically defined Spanish nation departed from his Spanish colleagues' ideas. Influenced by his position as a Basque within the Spanish state, and during a period of intense nationalist fervor, Aranzadi saw Spanish regional groups as similar physically and, more importantly for the purposes of national health, as distinct culturally. His allegiance to German ethnology allowed him to focus on these supposedly distinct cultural attributes as important elements in the formation of nations. As with many of the German anthropologists of this period, especially Adolph Bastian's student Franz Boas, Aranzadi saw difference rooted in both space and time, in geographical location and cultural practices of different groups that came into contact with each other. As a result, he confronted the eternal verities implicit in Hoyos's search for an ethnic factor in national formations and argued instead that the secret of national development was incidental only to how these national groups treated regional groups within a nation. While Hoyos was describing national unity as a racial imperative verified by Spanish history, Aranzadi was writing that national unity was an entirely artificial product created by a government that understood the racial differences in its diverse population.[54] Aranzadi wanted the state to be the crucible—indeed, the melting pot—of regional differences, forging a stronger nation that acknowledged regional differences. These differences were not threatening to national unity; they were, in fact, its superstructure.

Racial mixture was the undercurrent that ran through all of these analyses of Spain's racial history. Yet, the various meanings and uses ascribed to the idea of racial amalgamation demonstrated its political and ideological malleability. Anthropological interpretation and examination of the concept was just one example. The idea of fusion was a compelling metaphor for both liberal and conservative thinkers during the Restoration. For conservatives, fusion harkened back to a tradition of Catholic conversion and subsequent cultural unity. For others, the idea of fusion was perhaps better understood as hybridity: the valorization of the racial mix of the contemporary Spanish nation would lead to the formation of a Spanish state devoid of separatist sentiments.

Lastly, despite this reliance on the concept of racial fusion, Spanish anthropology and its external applications demonstrated an increasing interest in applying these ideas to Spain's own internal context. Race was not being defined in terms of an "other" that was identifiable by clear differences in appearance. Rather, Spanish racial thought was increasingly defined in regional terms. Race was deployed in Spain in an effort to define a national entity composed of the fused elements of Spain's mixed racial past. Others described Spain's racial mixture as a permanent condition, one that provided the source of its national strength because the state was capable of organizing, not subjugating, these various racial groups with diverse abilities, cultural habits, and behaviors under its own aegis. The concept of racial mixture, verified by physical anthropology in the late nineteenth century and adapted to the changing approaches of cultural anthropology at the turn of the twentieth century, served to link together a wide range of political and social thought in Spain. The primary engines of development of Spanish anthropology, Manuel Antón, Luís de Hoyos Sáinz, and Telésforo de Aranzadi, represented in microcosm the larger range of possible applications of this idea in the Spanish context. The next chapter explores how the malleability of the idea of racial mixture in Spain played a role in the establishment of actual social policy, as Spain's anthropologists of the generation following the formulators of the discipline moved into bureaucratic positions in the state.

2 | Applying Race

6. Recruiting the Race
Military Applications of the Racial Mix

At the end of the nineteenth century, the Spanish military appeared to be the reverse image of many other European fighting forces. Spain's once vast overseas empire was consigned to history as Spain lost its colonies in Cuba, the Philippines, and Puerto Rico in 1898 in a devastating rout by the United States. This loss—still known succinctly today as the "Disaster"—provided the capstone to an already energetic national soul-searching among Spain's intellectual, political, and cultural elite. This wide-ranging and quite energetic search to find the "problem of Spain" or to "regenerate" Spain contained many of the dominant European intellectual strains of turn-of-the-twentieth-century Europe—conservative traditionalism, scientific positivism, Romantic nationalism, regional development, and economic and political modernization. Nevertheless, many military leaders responded in a tradition formed over the previous hundred years, with a scorching indictment of the Madrid politicians who mishandled the war and maligned the ancient martial values that had made the Spanish empire. This response had defined much of the nineteenth-century military when it developed a liberal, praetorian tradition that saw its primary role as guardian of a true Spain that needed occasional pronouncements or *coups d'état* when governments seemed to lose their way.[1] But as some historians have recently begun to point out, the military, with its once liberal tradition, had developed some modern, reformist sections that sought to frame the Disaster as an opportunity to modernize the military and, in turn, to regenerate the Spanish nation.[2] In fact, the military modernizing effort relied upon the new racial sciences that were developing in Spanish anthropology.

Race helped account for the nettlesome issue that emerged from the Disaster: why, despite overwhelming numerical supremacy, did the Spanish fighting force in Cuba fare so poorly in the war? One clear problem was the health of the Spanish soldier in Cuba. Disease accounted for over 20 percent of the Spanish fatalities. At any moment during the three-year conflict, about 20 percent of the active fighting force was lying in a hospital bed attempting to overcome diseases contracted in Cuba. Even worse from the Spanish perspective was the fact that disease accounted for only 3 percent of the U.S. fatalities in the conflict.[3] The effort to deal with the apparently poor health of the Spanish soldier fell to the small but important Military Sanitary Corps (Sanidad Militar), the group of medical doctors who had experienced and treated the soldiers most directly in the field.[4] Some military doctors, increasingly aware of racial ideas from Spanish physical anthropology, saw the high mortality from disease as a sign of racial, or physical, weakness, in the Spanish soldier. Instead of having kept up-to-date on available medical knowledge of the insect vectors of the most virulent diseases, Spain's military doctors saw as far more modern and advanced the consideration of Spain's problem as a product of the racial stock from which these soldiers emanated.[5]

Racial arguments proved appealing because they also pointed to a new direction for reform. Rather than blaming the poor decision making of military leaders or the apparent ineffectiveness and obsolescence of Spanish warships vis-à-vis the American ironclad, anthropological explanations provided an optimistic hope that what had disappeared from the Spanish fighting force could be resurrected. Military officials could begin to argue that racial fusion had been derailed at some point in the Spanish past, a historicist explanation that really served to provide military men a road forward by suggesting that problems in Spain were endemic but not insurmountable. Also for these empirical doctors, the causes of this racial derailment remained quite evident in the broader social and political turmoil that befell Spain in the aftermath of the colonial defeat. As in anthropology, the military investigation of race pinpointed regionalism and working-class organization as corrosive to the nation. As a result, military doctors offered a means of rehabilitating the image of the military from failed overseas colonizer to internal colonizer, seeing its own population as the seedbed both of traditional martial values of strength, valor, and honor, along with weakness, decline, and separatism.[6]

The racial explanation for the Disaster also afforded the usually sedate and small medical corps an opportunity to expand its role in military decision making. In this sense, military doctors were hoping to join a trend toward modernization of military technique and technology taking place in other European countries. Certainly, the Spanish military was not alone in its growing reliance on anthropology to modernize its administration and policy. Here again, however, the historical context is important. The lessons of such anthropological awareness would seem most applicable where the needs of "racial management" were greatest. In France, England, and Germany, racial management unfolded in colonial contexts. Historians of French colonization have demonstrated that, especially in North Africa, military leaders were quite reliant upon racial theories to administer their colonies in a supposedly more modern and efficient manner. The military was usually the leading edge of contact with other peoples, as invasions unfolded and colonial armies began to set up camp. Military figures had to address the most nettlesome, fast-changing, and difficult administrative concerns as armed forces marched into unknown territories.[7] The military responses to these new contexts were usually not elegant or well-thought-out models of efficiency. In fact, it is the assumption of the conservatism of military responses, and the usual reliance on force, that generally prevents the historian from probing military thought in these colonial moments.[8]

In Spain, racial sciences would be implemented in the opposite direction, in the context of military retrenchment and the return of Spanish soldiers to the peninsula. As a result, the medical expertise directed to the management of racial problems focused on the Spanish population, not on the colonized other but on the deficient Spaniard who did not measure up to other European or U.S. forces. Here awareness of the new racial studies examining the Spanish past and the paradigm of proper and improper fusion would help refashion the Spanish soldier and hopefully the Spanish nation. The typologies that Spanish anthropologists like Federico Olóriz and Manuel Anton had offered were now reconfigured to define "the useful Spaniard" and thus to help cull a far stronger, fitter, and more racially representative Spanish fighting force. The shock of defeat overseas and the conquest of lands in North Africa meant that military figures responded quickly to address the supposed racial weaknesses demonstrated in Cuba so they could be corrected in Morocco.[9] Not surprisingly, therefore, race's role in the military, especially in the Sanitary Corps, produced an active and energetic area of application of racial thought in Spain.

To plumb the racial past that was producing such poor soldiers, military doctors mimicked the eclectic approach that came to define Spanish social sciences and medicine more broadly.[10] Foreign sources provided important templates. Did the French, to whom military doctors had traditionally turned for medical and surgical expertise, provide an equally compelling belief in

racial typology and environmental conditions? Or were biological determinist models more appealing, gleaned from England, the United States,
or Germany? Or were the problems really more psychological and spiritual?
In studying the Spanish scientific context, in which Spanish scientists were
aware of their nation's delayed scientific development, one sees that these
dichotomies between European scientific approaches to race really did not
exist as cleanly as historians have generally asserted. No racial thinker firmly
rejected the role of environment while making biological determinist models,
nor did neo-Lamarckians discount all biological bases for racial formation.
The actual mechanisms of transfer (otherwise thought of as inheritance) of
racial identity—including thought, memory, culture, and appearances—represented a complicated world of ideas that some thinkers attempted to align,
others only crudely confronted, and some just ignored entirely.[11] Throughout
the nineteenth century, whether the basis for racial identity was cultural or
physical was constantly debated, but rarely were such discussions the site of
sharp confrontation. Racial thinkers of this period, as enlightened men of science, considered their ideas to be as universal as those of any other scientists.
Thus, debates were energetic but neither rancorous nor sharply partisan.

Spanish racial ideas in the military demonstrated this open and wide definition of race. In the years immediately following the Disaster, military leaders dispatched doctors to address what one military doctor called both "spiritual and material" ailments in the military that festered after the defeat in the
Spanish-American War.[12] In the years after the war, the military engaged in a
series of efforts to reform its institutions, training, and equipment, often with
uneven success. This process has been recently studied in much the same way
as other areas of Spanish reform. The influences on military figures were not
only conservative or liberal but drew from a multifaceted array of political
and social ideologies. Not surprisingly, military thought was a steeped in the
kind of modernist pull to combine rational and scientific solutions with more
Romantic, spiritual, and mystical realignments that typified fin de siècle Europe.[13] As a result, this chapter concludes with an analysis of how this racial
thinking at the turn of the twentieth century fit with the kind of broad intellectual formation open to both scientific modernism and the traditionalist
conservatism that fueled later Francoism. Like many of the technological and
political modernizing impulses of this era, the Spanish military's modernism
relied on a number of contradictory impulses to resuscitate ancient traditions
by using modern technique and universal science to reinvigorate the nation.[14]

Anthropology fit well into this dualistic paradigm for it provided a portrait of the ancient Spaniard, the cultural practices, and the customs—all the components that had driven the conquering Spaniard around the world—that conformed with the historicist teaching about the nation that officers were experiencing in military academies.[15] Anthropological inquiry would also provide a scientific portrait of the physical makeup of the Spaniard that would serve the more utilitarian purpose of defining and fostering "useful Spanish soldiers."[16] In the military examination of race, all the themes of racial mixture from Spanish anthropology reappeared: Spain's particularly long experience of Spaniards occupying foreign lands; Spain's ability to intermix with occupied peoples; and Spain's success in convincing others of the value of Spanish colonization and civilization. And also like the larger anthropological project, military racial studies sought to identify the home population's racial diversity and diagnose areas of improper fusion.[17] The military's Sanitary Corps, entrusted with the mission to identify the "useful Spanish soldier," took as its mission the improvement not of colonized peoples, but of soldiers who seemed unable to control or conquer them.

Making the "Useful Soldier" a Racial Program: Doctors' New Place in the Military

Interest in improving the Spanish soldier began to be expressed immediately after the end of the war in 1898. This interest coincided with a concerted effort to expand the role of the military doctors in making military decisions. In 1900, one doctor wrote that that medical care had to make up at least one-half of the "fundamental plan" of all future military engagements; tactics would be the other half.[18] Some well-placed anthropologists moving into the government bureaucracy also helped expand the voice of science and medicine in military reforms. In 1909, the anthropologist and then senator Ángel Pulido made calls on the Senate floor to increase the military's budget for research into the Spanish soldier's high morbidity from disease. The Sanitary Corps in particular was pleased with Pulido's appeals for he described their role as central in modernizing the military. Pulido had argued on the Senate floor that without "maintaining the health and vigor of soldier . . . the machine gun, cannons and rifles, horses, tactics and all of the abundant munitions will not be worth anything." Taking care of soldiers, he continued, "is and will forever be the *leitmotiv* of war."[19]

The defeat also inspired an effort to expand the range of European science available to Spanish doctors in their main professional journals. After 1899, an obvious increase took place in the number of new translated and excerpted European medical texts. In addition, current anthropological views of race had already made their way into intellectual circles within the military and civilian life through the military journals and speeches in the Madrid Athenaeum and the Military Athenaeum.[20] Physical anthropology proved particularly interesting to members of the Sanitary Corps. Most military doctors were trained to treat individuals. Military doctors thus were more interested in diagnosing why the individual soldier seemed so uniformly susceptible to these diseases. Increasingly, the attention paid to the Spanish soldier as somehow weaker and more susceptible to disease shifted attention away from the now well-understood role that bacilli—typhus, yellow fever, and cholera—played in Cuba and the Philippines in the deaths of so many soldiers.[21] The Spanish soldier was now the problem. Medical doctors could treat the soldier's body, and anthropology would provide what they thought were insights into why the Spanish soldier, as representative of his *patria*, seemed so much more susceptible to enervating disease. As a result, the effort to define and locate the source of Spain's military decline took on a decidedly racial cast. The definition of this race modeled on Spanish anthropology's definition was a wide-ranging one.

Felipe Ovilo y Canales and the Biological and Spiritual Race

The most influential arguments for racial investigation came from doctors who had served in the field in Spain's colonies. One doctor, in particular, laid out the clearest explanation of racial decay as a cause of military failure in Cuba. Felipe Ovilo y Canales, who had served in Cuba both before and during the war, Ovilo y Canales emerged as the first voice after 1898 to argue that the failings of the military emanated from its inability to apply modern science and medicine to military practice. As a member of the Royal Academy of History, which he had joined after he left the army in 1897, he wrote two important reports on the "hygienic state" of the Spanish military and the effects on its soldiers.[22] For Ovilo, the clearly depleted physical condition of the Spanish soldier bespoke a deeper physical and spiritual breakdown. Rather than as a result of mistaken tactics or strategy, the Spanish military had failed in Cuba because of an entrenched racial decline. For Ovilo, this decay was a reflection of internal Spanish weaknesses, not the product of diseases whose vectors were mosquitoes, fleas, and poor sanitation: "Without hygienic individuals, there are no sane and healthy *pueblos*. The history of racial decay affirms this because the ties between the physical and the psychological are so intimate and influence each other so reciprocally that it would be difficult to define the boundaries that separate them. Hygiene unites all the medical and natural sciences with those of political and social economy. . . . In turn, military hygiene not only affects armies, but also the country as a whole."[23]

Most racial theories have proven to be a complicated mixture of mystical belief in an imagined past and a sense that this past, with its values and attitudes, were somehow stitched together and reflected in a more temporal and material appearance of the body or its health and welfare. Clearly, these two stances ran together for Ovilo. Race represented a biological fact and a spiritual problem. Race connected Spain's soldiers to their ancient forebears and reflected not just the *esprit de corps* but also the quality and strength of the fighting force of the contemporary military. In turn, the overall strength of the nation was reflected in the quality of fight the Spanish soldier offered in combat. Thus, race had to be an essential element of the biological and medical effort to elicit the true causes of Spain's military failures. Rather than a more routine focus on the failure of tactics and strategy, Spanish military doctors thought the appropriate subject of study would be the individual soldier, who represented both a microcosm of the nation and the determining factor in the success of the nation in war. Because the Spaniard had proven to be such an effective soldier in the past, Ovilo assumed that a glitch had appeared in Spanish history that weakened the soldier. This mis-intervention into Spanish racial fusion was perpetrated at the level of recruitment. Perhaps, then, it is not surprising that Ovilo saw the crux of the racial problem both resting in and later to be cured at the moment of recruitment. Examining new recruits had been one of the first and most important functions of the Sanitary Corps since its official inception in the late eighteenth century.[24] Recruiters were taking soldiers too young to fight not because of their inexperience but because their bodies had not yet fully formed. This one mistake had lasting repercussions that culminated in the "decay of the race." Worse, this decay was two-sided and required specialized knowledge to reverse. "The psychological and the biological are so intimately related," Ovilo wrote, that even doctors struggle to "to know where the boundary between them exists."[25] The result was that soldiers too young to fight in the first place were then physical and morally depleted in combat, returning to Spain not energized and patriotic, which in Ovilo's liberal reading meant ready "to build a modern nation," but as "weakened and miserable beings who are only capable of producing further puny, ruined, and sickly generations of people."[26]

If the state and the nation were to improve, Ovilo argued, a radical reform of recruitment policies had to be undertaken with the use of modern anthropology. Of gravest concern was the fact that Spanish military recruiters failed to consider the ethnic makeup of the recruit as an essential factor in culling a healthy and strong fighting force. It was a mistake, Ovilo noted, to assume that all Spanish soldiers emerged from a "common mold." Borrowing from Pulido and Olóriz, Ovilo wrote that "diverse ethnographic elements" composed the Spanish military, and, as a result, such elements would need to be factored into the new recruitment procedures of a reformed Spanish military.[27] Like many of his colleagues, Ovilo used racial language in an ambiguous and inconsistent manner, and he did not clearly cite any of the anthropological works of his era to which he had access. Yet, this article had been vetted by Ángel Pulido, the former secretary of the Spanish Anthropology Society and disciple of Pedro González Velasco. More importantly, Pulido, serving then as Spain's director of public health, offered the customary follow-up comment to Ovilo's lecture at the Military Athenaeum in 1899.[28] Certainly, the speech appeared to have a scientific imprimatur if not a rigorous framework. In fact, demonstrating his own awareness of Spanish anthropology, Ovilo's speech even echoed the split that was beginning to divide Spanish anthropology into ethnography and physical measurement in the years surrounding the Spanish-American War. Ovilo maintained the historicist argument that a unique and virile fighting spirit united Spanish soldiers to their ancient forebears. Yet, the physical makeup of the soldier and the degeneration of his body clearly disconnected the present from the past and rendered the Spanish soldier into the sickly, yellow, and weakened conscript who was lucky enough to return from Cuba at all.

Ovilo stated clearly that his speculative piece needed to be seconded by rigorous scientific research. Not surprisingly, the Sanitary Corps, which had experienced firsthand the ravages of yellow fever, typhus, and cholera, had little difficulty accepting physical decay as a symptom of historical deficiencies afflicting the Spanish soldier. Even though the Sanitary Corps never existed at the forefront military decision making, the infamous mortality rates from the Spanish-American War proved that military sanitation and the conditions of the Spanish soldier could not easily be ignored.[29] The military press was quite clear that the Sanitary Corp's former function of staffing field hospitals, tending to battlefield injuries, and assessing recruits was now inadequate. Even

clearer were the complaints about the iniquities of military funding that kept
the Sanitary Corps behind its European counterparts in research, especially
in epidemiology. Yet, as in other areas of Spanish science, there were a few
well-trained figures who had kept well abreast of wider debates in and out of
Spain about health of soldiers in the field and in peacetime.

After the Disaster, these doctors saw their roles as much more than
providing mere prophylaxis. They called for greater funding of the Sanitary
Corps and succeeded in having financial resources expand in the first decades of the twentieth century. While much of this funding went to improving medical facilities and equipment, some was directed to improving the
Spanish soldier. The emphasis on anthropological expertise at the important
moment of recruitment became increasingly evident after Ovilo's speech. A
royal decree issued in August 1899 demanded that military recruiters send
any soldier potentially made "useless" as a result of dementia or mental infirmity to a "medical-military" tribunal for further assessment.[30] Given the
anthropological interests of many of these military doctors, and the apparent
disparity of Spain's vulnerability to disease as compared to other militaries,
the focus on the soldier's bodies gave this study a racial edge in the effort to
explain Spain's unique condition among its European counterparts. Part of
this process was movement of the Sanitary Corps to a site more appropriate
for the kind of anthropological and racial study they were to perform. The
military requested that the building that had housed Pedro González de Velasco's Anthropology Society become the headquarters of the Sanitary Corps.
The Sanitary Corps even requested that Velasco's anthropological collections
be included so that they could use "his historical evidence" to begin the process of identifying the medical provenance of the Spanish recruit. The request
was denied, but not for lack of fundamental support for such medical and
anthropological study. The state granted the building to the Central University medical faculty, who had long complained of their inability to teach their
full curriculum for lack of adequate facilities in the university's buildings.[31]
But the military received funds for its own museum and collections in 1900,
with a royal decree noting that such a museum and study was important not
just for scientific progress but for "the exact understanding of the principal
examples of our nation and any foreign materials that affect them."[32]

Yet, this association of goals to improve the health of the individual with
the anthropological concern for defining and understanding the condition of
the whole population was clearly present within the medical corps. In the few
months after Ovilo's talk, a royal decree demanded an expansion of the "ser-

vices and responsibilities of the military health corps."[33] Three years after Ovilo's talk, the military responded more specifically to his suggestions. In 1902, General Valeriano Weyler, the minister of war in the liberal government of Práxedes Sagasta, approved a four-year anthropological study to devise a prototype of the "useful Spanish man" to serve in the military.[34] Weyler himself was notorious for his efforts to modernize military practice. He earned the nickname the "Butcher of Cuba" partly because of his order to create the world's first concentration camps in Cuba to more effectively and efficiently separate the insurgent soldiers from Cuban populations not yet radicalized by the independence movement.[35] Indeed, the attraction of racial explanations for figures like Weyler was their appeal to a supposed ancient martial prowess in the Spaniard and their apparent scientific modernity. Racial problems also assuredly distracted reformers from more structural problems like a bloated officer staff, shoddy strategy, and the poor training exemplifed by figures like Weyler.

Interestingly, though, the power of military prejudice affected how doctors defined the problems afflicting the Spanish population. Despite being filled with perhaps the most politically liberal and progressive members of the military, the Sanitary Corps saw these physical maladies through the lens of the social prejudices felt among military leaders and taught in military academies.[36] Their studies demonstrated that the causes behind so many "useless men" were rooted in the weakness of Spanish nationalism and the ineffectiveness of state policies to protect and nurture its citizenry. Not surprisingly, the notion of racial decay these figures used to explain the failures of military performance in Cuba really reflected the general military preoccupations of the postwar period: the rise of regional separatism—the bane of traditional integrist nationalism in the military—and working-class violence.

Defining the "Useful" Spaniard

A military doctor, Luis Sánchez Fernández, performed the study to define the "useful Spanish man." In many ways, Sánchez Fernández was an obvious candidate to conduct the research. He had practiced combat medicine in the Philippines in 1887 and in Cuba from 1895 to 1898. He had also been stationed in Spain's African colony in Melilla in 1893. Perhaps more importantly, he had trained outside Spain and was familiar with European military and civilian medical training. Six months after the war's end in Cuba, the Sanitary Corps sent Sánchez to Germany and Italy to acquire "modern" military surgical technique that was thought to be lacking in the Spanish medical corps.[37]

In terms of scientific training, the decision to send Sánchez to Germany signaled a broader intellectual shift within the Spanish military officer corps. Throughout the eighteenth and nineteenth centuries, the Sanitary Corps generally relied on French medical traditions to train its personnel.[38] By the last few decades of the nineteenth century, especially after the Franco-Prussian War, Spanish military personnel increasingly turned to Prussian models, especially in terms of training. For Spaniards, recent Prussian success undeniably demonstrated the value in having blended modern military technique and traditional martial values.[39] The attraction did not reside solely in the technological advancement or surgical technique. Especially after the Franco-Prussian War, Spanish military officials saw Germany as having tethered the ancient fighting spirit of the Teuton with positivist science and technique. The "historicist" Spanish nationalism that dominated in military circles at the turn of the twentieth century sought ancient signs of foreboding and glory in the Spanish past. The military historian Geoff Jensen has recently pointed out that it was an easy intellectual shift for liberal military leaders to also support illiberal imaginings about reviving ancient military prowess in the present.[40]

Hence, in the military Sanitary Corps, doctors like Sánchez Fernández were drawn to their German colleagues not just for the content of their science but also because the Germans were able to reconcile their medical expertise and modernity with their national psychology—their ancient traditions and psyche. Modern medicine helped resurrect the past rather than destroy it. According to the journal of the Sanitary Corps, the German medical corps had perfected the use of its medical expertise to complement the fighting spirit of German soldiers.[41] This Germanophilia among the Sanitary Corps lasted well into the twentieth century. For example, despite Spain's neutrality in World War I, Spain's military doctors went exclusively to Germany to serve as military attachés and neutral observers precisely so that they could train with German doctors.[42] Certainly, some of this interest was the product of Spanish military figures who had just suffered defeat gravitating to the supposed winning military practices of Germany. But this interpretation rested on the belief that success emanated from the alignment of transcendent national values amid materialist perfection of technological and scientific expertise.[43] Germans succeeded because of their ethnic capacity to conquer. Spanish saw many similarities between the warrior spirit of the Teutonic hordes and the ancient Iberian tercio. Further, this warrior spirit did not ignore the needs of the soldier's body. Thus, for Sánchez and other military doctors, the goal to align the warrior spirit with modern scientific practice was an exercise in racial improvement of the Spaniards. The martial values were the same; Spain's defense of them needed perfecting.

Here again, the Spanish historical context was important. Unlike the German, French, or British militaries, whose territorial expansion focused their military concerns toward understanding "foreign" subjects, the Spanish military directed their anthropological attention to the Spanish recruit. This focus on the home population followed Spanish anthropology's widespread concentration on regionalism. The concern with separatism in a sense overwhelmed the larger, seemingly more intractable and less easily solved, "problem of Spain" and instead offered a far more fixed object of concern, the Spanish soldier and, in particular, his body.[44] Military doctors borrowed a normative view of Spanish body types from Spanish anthropology and used them as templates to assess and diagnose the poor condition of the Spanish soldier. While the entire Sanitary Corps saw its budget increase throughout the first decade of the twentieth century, again the historical experience of assessing recruits drew the attention of military doctors to the deficient quality of the raw fighting force arriving in recruitment stations. Luís Sánchez Fernández's study of the "useful Spanish soldier" reflected this new medical concern for the health of the individual soldier and also the anthropological concern for historical or inheritable forces that were producing these individuals.

Between 1903 and 1904, Sánchez culminated his European training with nine months studying in the Military Medical Academy in Berlin. He then returned to Spain by way of Italy, where he spent a few weeks observing work in military hospitals. Setting about the study of the "useful man" in Spain, Sánchez first decided that the recruitment problem with was rooted in the anthropological origins of the Spanish soldier. For example, Sánchez was one of many doctors to complain about the frailty and small size of recruits being sent off to war. These soldiers, he noted, were not even strong enough to endure training.[45] As a result, he agreed with Ovilo that the problems had to do with recruitment procedures that had not been updated for decades with new scientific knowledge. Unlike Ovilo, however, Sánchez laid out a specific plan to reverse the racial decay brought on by nonanthropological recruitment practices. To devise the prototypical Spanish soldier, Sánchez first wanted to perform an anthropological analysis of all recruits between 1903 and 1906. The goal of the study was to provide the military a framework for culling only useful, healthy, and vigorous soldiers from the Spanish population, something that it had seemed incapable of doing. Sánchez finished with measurements of more than 119,000 soldiers, a sample that dwarfed those in most other European studies of conscripts.[46]

Sánchez's study analyzed the ethnic components of the recruit and their effect on that person's usefulness as a soldier. Sánchez published two versions of the study, the first in 1908, and the other in 1913.[47] In the first version, he ventured very few conclusions about the raw data he had gathered. He only argued that recruitment policy needed to be informed by the recent work of anthropology and the array of racial mixtures then present on the Iberian Peninsula. He said that, first and foremost, the size of the human body had to be calculated using an index of many measurements, as Olóriz, Hoyos, and Aranzadi had done for the civilian population. He quoted Olóriz's inaugural lecture to the Royal Academy of Medicine, in 1896, in which he argued that human size did betray racial lineage and that measurements of the Spaniard indicated enough mixing to produce a standard measurement, a mean with which to define the Spaniard.[48] He also wrote that nations themselves could be made up of a variety of racial groups that were in turn affected by both endemic and acquired characteristics. These variations ultimately led to the disappearance of most original racial or physical attributes and made for a certain uniformity among recruits that was otherwise lacking in Spain.[49]

Sánchez also relied on Antón's 1895 lecture on the races and nations of Europe to argue that all Spaniards ultimately emerged from a single racial conglomeration of Celtic, North African, and indigenous Iberian races, to form the uniquely Spanish Libyan-Iberian race. Using the measurements he had culled over the four years of the study, Sánchez argued that the lack of ethnic considerations in the recruitment process had led to the gradual weakening of Spain's military fighting force. The effects of such ignorance were detrimental not only for the military but also for national stability. Echoing Federico Olóriz, Sánchez argued that racial fusion produced a variety of racial types, the mean average of which would represent a final stage, an end point, in racial development. This end point, according to Sánchez, usually conformed to that society's cultural conception of beauty: those who measured closest to the mean were seen as the most beautiful members of society. The most average in their measurements were the most beautiful in appearance. "In science," Sánchez wrote, "the medians express the intimate fusion of all of the evidence that is studied, and represent the 'true type,' but not necessarily the most beautiful."[50] Sánchez argued that those who represent the median rather than the most beautiful are the best representatives of the race, for they were produced as a result of natural selection that led invariably to the melding of different racial types through evolution. The attempt to produce artificially these more mixed, and thus more perfect, types based on an "artist's sense of beauty," rather than on scientific measurement, usually resulted in the isolation of some positive qualities, but not always in a complete racial mixture that contained all of the desired elements of the country's racial components.[51] Thus, careful grooming of racial characteristics was successful when it was informed by specific anthropological knowledge and carried out with massive enough alterations to affect the overall average measurements of a country. He cited, for example, the right-minded but ultimately failed attempts of Fredrick I, in early-eighteenth-century Prussia, to glean only tall, and thus strong, soldiers for his army. The Prussians did not succeed because they attempted the change with too small a sample.

> That fact that today one simultaneously encounters all over the globe races of dwarves and giants, the sickly and the vigorous, the ugly and the beautiful, makes us assume that the most perfect races are the product of natural selection and the multiple and fortuitous influences of nature. Improvements are possible through artificial selection, as in the breeds of pigeons, dogs and horses. . . . [T]he attempts of Catherine of Medici or Frederick William I of Prussia to produce races of dwarves and giants did not provide any great lessons because of the small number of samples. Yet, these efforts did produce some improvement. . . . [I]t is therefore possible to say that active artificial selection with proper knowledge of the anthropological facts, can improve races.[52]

Yet, the problem for Sánchez was not that Spain was removing the best elements of the Spanish race, but rather that they were removing a component of the racial mix. Military recruitment practices disconnected from these obvious anthropological lessons had affected the proper fusion of racial characteristics in Spain. Recruitment officials tended to accept the most robust, physically attractive people who appeared before them. As a result, they were unwittingly removing from the population an important segment of Spain's racial composition. They were inadvertently performing a type of artificial selection that weeded out a racially positive element. If mixture had produced a median as the most perfect specimen of a race, then the selection of only the most robust, the tallest, and the widest actually was causing a general decay in the process of fusion that had produced the Spanish race. The natural process of Spanish racial fusion was lost to inadvertent racial tampering that removed an important segment of the racial mix.

To counteract these unintentional manipulations of the racial stock, Sánchez suggested that Spanish anthropologists determine the ethnic median for each region of Spain. Once these measurements were revealed, recruitment officials could then begin to draft soldiers whose absence from their home regions would not enfeeble its racial makeup or that of the nation. A proper racial array from each region needed to be recruited, not just one section of the racial mix, in order to perpetuate the continued fusion of racial characteristics in that region. Because a perfect example of a Spaniard was an average and not an extreme, the removal of extremes during the recruitment process was selecting out important elements of the racial fusion. Recruiters inadvertently left behind only the smallest, shortest elements, producing over time a general decrease in the physical size and prowess of the Spanish population and presumably of the army as well. Proper recruitment required taking a cross-section of physical attributes, tall, short, fat, thin, ugly, beautiful, so as not to leave only enervating groups behind.

Here, Sánchez Fernández was working with an idiosyncratic view of the racial thought of the period that accepted a wide range of distinct views and positions. As others have pointed out, however, this grazing across scientific approaches was not so uncommon among European anthropologists.[53] Sánchez Fernández followed Quartrefages' belief that racial types were fixed into certain set of specific groups but from there had transmogrified over time. He added a neo-Lamarckian sense that climate and geography also affected distinct groups, so much so, in fact, that, over time, races were the product both of a timeless biological link to a primordial past and of a more recent adscription to their climate. Thus, the Spanish race was both the agglomeration of attributes unique to Spain but also variable throughout the peninsula. Sánchez's views were a compendium of diverse influences. The acknowledgments in his work testified to his intellectual breadth. He listed well over 100 names and works, ranging from Baxter's 1864 study of U.S. Civil War soldiers, to Rudolf Virchow's 1884 study of German schoolchildren, and Rodolfo Livi's 1895 study of Italian recruits. His list of Spanish influences included more than 180 names.[54]

His approach firmly expressed the eugenic belief that despite a race's unalterable core, states had to manage and administer their racial stock to keep it supple and healthy. First, he needed to present a method to identify proper racial array for each region. He attempted via his measurements of Spanish recruits to devise charts for proper anthropological recruitment. He calculated general body sizes, which included the measurement of head shapes, height, girth, and thoracic measurements. Physical size was a racial characteristic, he argued, that could be determined in the same manner as other racial characteristics, by studying the average type from that region:

> When one arrives in a country, one contemplates the multitudes and notices first off the great differences in individual stature. It seems then that height is not a racial characteristic that is relatively permanent or immutable and is suitable for racial classification. But when one looks more closely, one sees a country where tall people predominate and another where short people do. It is even clearer during the more exacting operations of recruitment, when one measures thousands of men down to the millimeter, obtains averages that can be compared with measurements from other countries, that size is an important factor in the characterization of races.[55]

According to Sánchez, Spain itself was divided into three main racial groups. One racial group in the north was defined by its "small stature, wide midriff, and high weight," and its "round heads" (brachycephalic), characteristics that were attributed to Celtic invasions in the northeast of Spain two thousand years earlier. The second racial group predominated along the eastern shores of the peninsula. It was characterized by its height, "regular weight and size," and longheadedness (dolichocephaly). This group represented the best example on the peninsula of what Antón had called the Libyan-Iberian race, from which, Sánchez wrote, all contemporary Spaniards had taken the greatest portion of their racial makeup. The third racial group that composed the Spanish race lived in the center of the peninsula, on the vast plains of Castile and Extremadura. They tended to be the smallest and thinnest Spaniards.[56]

Once these racial types were identified in each region, the military could forever ensure that it was taking a properly diverse array of recruits from each regional racial group, and not necessarily seeking recruits who fit an ideal image used for the entire peninsula. Basing recruitment throughout Spain on conformity to an ideal image, he argued, was inappropriate for different regions, weakening the racial stock of the nation as a whole and the army in particular, which relied on the fortitude of this racial stock. Previous recruitment practice had applied an ideal image to the entire Spanish nation and had consequently depleted Spain's racial stock. Anthropological understanding dictated that if medians were the inevitable and desirable end point of racial mixture and fusion, then the average obtained via the measurement of all recruited soldiers should be the same as the racial average of the entire

Spanish population. Soldiers were to be recruited from various regions, taking the definitive elements of those areas, those closest to the mean of that region, not necessarily the largest or most developed. By recruiting under these guidelines, the Spanish army would develop a racially representative sample of the Spanish population and would thus be stronger, taking presumably much healthier and more durable people to compose its fighting force.

More importantly, Sánchez hoped this modern technique would resuscitate the ancient Spanish warrior that seemingly was lost in the contemporary Spaniard. In Sánchez's view, the results of this physically and racially informed recruitment policy would also lead to a more stable Spanish nation, one where the internal threats of regionalism and working-class violence would disappear as proper recruitment would manufacture only resolute and engaged Spaniards. As had already been demonstrated by earlier anthropologists, Sánchez argued, regional separatist movements had their roots in the anthropological makeup of Spain's diverse regions. Recruitment had inadvertently fostered the regional separatist movements that the state usually called on the military to suppress. Previously, when the military recruited only the tallest from the nation, rather than selecting based on the ethnic mean of that region, they invariably left behind the racial characteristics of the smallest inhabitants.[57] Sánchez argued that never allowing those left unrecruited to experience the world from any perspective other than that of the region in which they lived led them to overvalue the importance and uniqueness of their home regions. As a result, they developed a social view that only included their own region and did not expose them to the nationalizing effects of military service: "In the nations where diverse races with different sizes live together, military selection ends up leaving intact the shortest races. Some sociologists argue that this particularity can contribute to the fomenting of regionalist ideas among those in the races that remain, because of their stunted experiences, not enlivened by travel to different social and cultural environments, or by the possibility of marriage with previously unknown people."[58] Like Aranzadi in his Etnología (1899), Sánchez was offering a possible anthropological solution to the regional nationalist movements that were increasingly becoming the main focus of the Spanish military. In turn, he was suggesting anthropological roots for the weakness of the Spanish state. Without an army developed with an anthropological understanding of the nation's racial makeup, the nation itself would be beset with regionalist factionalism.

Sánchez's study was but one of many attempts to apply anthropological ideas to military practice. Before the minister of war sponsored Sánchez's study, other doctors had already begun to publish calls for the necessity of using anthropological models in recruitment practices.[59] In some recruitment centers, doctors had begun their own studies of anthropological elements of their recruits for the purpose of applying them in the future to larger national studies.[60] Despite the support Sánchez received, funding remained incomplete for these kinds of studies, with one group of doctors noting that they had had to borrow anthropometric tools and instruments from Olóriz. Professional concerns also would impede their efforts. They noted that Olóriz's help was not easily obtained nor voluntarily offered. Instead, they noted mysteriously, Olóriz helped only when it was "spontaneously and delicately" negotiated.[61] It was clear that these anthropological efforts in the military drew from the work of the first institutionalizers of anthropology in Spain. In addition to Sánchez's use of the studies of Olóriz, Antón, Aranzadi, and Hoyos, other military doctors acknowledged their debt to these anthropologists in their own work.[62] One in particular noted that his 1909 nosology of Spanish diseases was based on the idea that variations in the occurrence of disease in Spain were the product of distinct regional or ethnic proclivities. His demarcation of regional, ethnic identities was based on the lines already advanced by Olóriz, Antón, and Sánchez Fernández.[63]

Once again, racial thought proved quite malleable as it served a wide range of political and social opinions among military decision makers. Much as race provided a flexible template for other conceptions of the nation and Spain's social problems among regenerationists outside the military, the rational and mystical facets of a good or useful Spanish soldier could easily be cobbled in any number of combinations to provide particular prescriptions for improving the Spanish fighting force. Sánchez diagnosed regionalism as the unfortunate by-product of nonanthropological recruitment afflicting Spanish soldiers. The assumption that the military needed to reflect a national psychology that was reflected in the Spanish body or its health remained a recurrent theme in military and civilian medical circles that also attempted to explain the political instabilities and regime shifts of the next four decades in Spain. Villamartín's own study of the Spanish history had already demonstrated that the Spanish past was a mixed one, and that the soldier was in the avant-garde of a fusionary process. Later military intellectuals, some quite influential in providing the later ideological framework for Francoism, flirted with and refined racial thinking adapted from other Europeans and from Spanish sources themselves.

The Legacy of Military Thinking about Race in the Twentieth Century

The praetorian tradition in nineteenth-century Spain—the belief that the military was the sole protector of the Spanish nation especially against the politicians who ran its government—began as a decidedly liberal endeavor in the 1820s and lasted well into the Spanish Civil War era, motivating Franco and the military rebels.[64] Recent work has suggested that the Spanish military did not just magically transform into a bastion of Catholic traditionalism and integrist Spanish nationalism that the Francoist forces represented as a result of the failures of the 1898. Instead, military politics and intellectual culture was bound up in the larger divide between liberal, modernist traditions and Nietzschean irrationalism and violence that dominated the fin de siècle. For example, Francoist authoritarian notions of the state relied on important elements of European modernism—the celebration of technology and industrialism, for example—to build their ideological apparatus, much as what Jeffrey Herf called "reactionary modernism" or the "accommodation of opposites" supported the intellectual framework of Nazism or French fascism.[65] The use of modern scientific methods to improve the military was an important case in point. Valuing the Romantic qualities of character and national spirits implicit in the historicist nationalism of the military did not necessarily mean that more material factors, like physical condition, diet, and—in the lexicon of the time—race, were fundamentally excluded. Thus, the eugenic approach of Sánchez Fernández symbolized a turn-of-the-century modernist faith in the ability of science, medicine, and rationality to improve the Spanish soldier and in turn improve the Spanish nation.

Yet, Sánchez Fernández and his colleagues were not merely a few interested figures engaging in isolated scientific efforts. Their work was state-funded and also ideologically linked to later decidedly more illiberal efforts. The anthropological and racial thought of military doctors had a national purpose of regeneration that relied on both historicist notions of national identity and a modernist faith that technology and science could help reinvigorate it. Recent revelations about psychiatric experiments in Francoist prisoner-of-war camps and other atrocities during the Spanish Civil War have focused on the aberrant behavior of a few seemingly depraved men, especially the main psychiatrist responsible for these experiments, Antonio Vallejo-Nájera. Perhaps this explanation is not surprising given the oft-voiced Francoist mantra that Spanish fascism was fundamentally different from its European counterparts because of the absence of intense racial rhetoric or Nazi racist excess. Even Vallejo-Nájera liked to distance his own racial thinking from that of his Nazi colleagues (whom he otherwise adulated) by calling for a supposedly unique form of Spanish eugenics that was "racial but not racist."[66]

Yet, part of the inconvenient truth of the discoveries is that Vallejo had much contact with the German scientific community throughout and after the Spanish Civil War. He presented his work in Germany to audiences composed of scientists, and he was also a great admirer of the Nazi willingness to allow science to directly guide social policy. There is no doubt that Vallejo differed from the Nazis in the methods of treatment he pursued—an essential difference. Yet, understanding Vallejo as one depraved individual rather than as part of a group psychosis or as the result of ideological training ignores the fact that, like his Nazi colleagues, he viewed his experiments on human beings as logical and rational. He and many of his colleagues also shared with the Nazis a fanatical hatred of the wartime enemies.[67] Indeed, the focus on individual behavior, especially among Nazi doctors, has long since given way to a broader view of the corruption of science with political values, social pressures, and propaganda well before the start of the Nazi regime.[68]

A better way to understand Vallejo's behavior is to view him as part of the continuum of thought about Spanish racial fusion that preceded the Spanish Civil War and even the political fractionalization of the Second Republic. Vallejo's politics were quite clearly informed by the conservative political values on which Francoism was based. Vallejo believed that anti-Spanish behaviors, read as Marxism and regionalism, could be treated through changes in the environment (medio ambiente) of those suffering from these supposed maladies. The eugenic measures he promoted focused on behavioral and environmental manipulation that included the forced adoption or removal of infants and young children from birth parents deemed politically unacceptable. The Francoist rendering of the Spanish nation—with its fanatical anticommunism and integrist nationalism—still did not place Vallejo very far away from a more progressive and liberal figure like Sánchez Fernández, who shared the goal of a positive manipulation of the Spanish populace through such small measures as recruitment practices. Liberal and progressive forces, too, relied on eugenic means to sponsor social reforms that focused on ameliorating social conditions and fostering greater equality of opportunity for citizens not afflicted with racial deficiencies.[69]

The differences rested in the political values that informed the policies and science, not in the acceptance of modern science as a useful tool for social manipulation. One colleague of Vallejo's in the psychiatric division of the Sanitary Corps, César Juarros, saw Spanish workers' uprisings as a reflection of the sexual deficiencies from which all the Spanish suffered. Indolent, lazy Spaniards longed for government aid (the support of a father) because of a lack of sexual drive that Spanish religious education inculcated.[70] Oddly, his response was not further repression of workers' uprisings but rather the rooting out of the problem through the imposition of more secular education that would alleviate the sexual guilt and other tensions created by too much Catholic moralism. Juarros, who trained under Sánchez Fernández and Ovilo, promoted a kind of behavior modification similar to that proposed by Vallejo; only the political values that informed his work were different. Like his scientific forebears, Juarros argued for further research. At the start of the Spanish Second Republic, he argued that Spaniards required strong collectivist political ideologies to overcome their ingrained culture of individualism. He remained unsure, he wrote, after a visit to Mussolini's Italy whether any of the dominant collectivist ideologies—Italian fascism, German Nazism, or Soviet communism—were appropriate in the Spanish context. What would decide the issue, he concluded, were good scientists who would define, "in good clinical spirit, the Spanish racial characteristics (*características raciales*)" that would fashion the appropriate the government.[71]

Clearly, medical professionals saw protection of the race at least in the same instrumental sense as their counterparts elsewhere. Vallejo's eugenic policies were not mere products of the social and political upheavals of the Spanish Civil War.[72] They were part of an early-twentieth-century view in the military that Spain's problems were internal and the product of a historical formation rather than the incursion of a foreign enemy. But with race defined in these terms, the racial enemy became the supposed process of racial formation rather than a specific group of people. Some Spaniards were rendered racially dangerous but not irredeemable. Certainly this heightened concern for the process of racial formation—and the subsequent focus on populations who were otherwise potentially Spanish—meant that less barbarous forms of social engineering would take place. The worry over who should be stitched into the social fabric or who had unbound themselves from it gave Spanish racial thought a more hopeful tone, implying that racial inclusion was a possibility through statewide policies.[73] Yet, as some recent theorists have suggested, even racisms of inclusion—intended to bring a diverse population together— are not necessarily free of exclusive forms of thought.[74] Defined by behaviors or fusion, race still serves to leave certain people out of the community.

The impulse to compare historical contexts has generally been used to exculpate the Spanish flirtation with Nazism and eugenics during the Franco era. As one historian of Spain's experimentation has written, Francoist studies somehow stopped short of the Rubicon that the Nazis passed because they took "the logic of positivist medical research [only] so far."[75] Other historians of the Spanish Civil War also are beginning to see the shades of gray that existed among the actual views and attitudes of Spanish military and civilian figures who felt a "near racist contempt" for their opponents and held a "more or less racist vision" of the nature of the conflict.[76] This general historical assessment that Spanish programs approached other countries' evils but in the end were not as barbaric as others, while true, misses the point. The era of George Mosse's assumption that all racial thought must necessarily lead to the gas chamber if it is to be categorized as racial is well passed. While it is true that Spanish thinkers were not direct imitators of their Nazi colleagues, despite the actual ideological affinities of the doctors engaging in these programs, it is not necessary to deny that these efforts exist on a continuum of eugenic and racial thought that only the contingencies of historical context alter.[77] These Spanish ruminations on and experimentations with race serve to complicate the expectation of historians that their subjects neatly fit into such categories as "fascist racial theory" or "neo-Lamarckian freedom from racial thought."

Throughout the first two decades of the twentieth century, the idea of mixture at the heart of racial formations was still the dominant theme in Spanish anthropology. Spain's regions continued as the bases upon which anthropologists charted the development of Spain's racial mixture. Yet, after 1900, as attention increasingly focused on the populations of the peninsula, the meaning ascribed to mixture became a contested topic.

7. Race Explains Crime
The Emergence of Criminal Anthropology, 1870–1914

The scientific study of race in late-nineteenth-century Spain found its most active application in the fields of criminology and penal law.[1] This was, in part, the result of the impact that anthropology and, to a larger degree, science were beginning to have on Spanish social and political discourse. In Spain, as in other European countries, politicians, intellectuals, and scientists presented their images of a proper, healthy, and successful society by identifying those who most threatened it.[2] Science, and specifically anthropology, became the primary tools in the late nineteenth century to identify criminal behavior and diagnose methods to eradicate it. In Spain, however, criminal anthropology differed from its European counterparts. How Spanish criminal anthropology was distinctive both in terms of the scientific ideas that constituted it and the political purposes to which it was put are the subjects of this chapter.

Devised along anthropological lines that promoted rather than rejected the idea of racial mixture, Spanish criminal anthropology did not view the criminal as the product of decayed, retrogressive, or atavistic racial components.[3] Instead, Spanish criminal anthropologists came to see criminal behavior as the product of missteps, breaks, or derailments in the process of the proper racial fusion that characterized the noncriminal Spanish population. Thus, criminals were missing an element or had a corrosive ingredient in their particular racial composition that led them to commit criminal acts. Like their colleagues in the larger field of anthropology, however, Spanish criminal anthropologists saw the process of racial fusion not solely as the product of immutable, inexorable biological identity, but also as a process affected by environmental conditions. Thus, when Spanish criminologists spoke of racial roots they were not necessarily limiting themselves to physical lineage. Borrowing from their anthropological colleagues outside criminology, Spanish criminal anthropologists saw race and indeed racial fusion as promoted or inhibited by the social or cultural makeup of the groups that composed them. They saw the physical environment in which both individuals and large groups of people developed also as playing formative roles in their racial makeup. This multisided view within Spanish anthropology of how races developed was part of the more general tendency in the Spanish sciences of the late nineteenth century to borrow and adapt various European approaches from much better-defined and institutionalized scientific disciplines. One effect of this open appropriation of different European approaches to criminal anthropology was that it allowed Spanish criminologists to mix a variety of explanatory models, often considered contradictory outside Spain, to be used to explain criminal behavior. As such, crime came to be viewed as the product of a breakdown of one or more of the physical, social, or environmental elements involved in racial fusion. Race still was the underlying cause of crime, the totalizing explanation for criminal behavior. It was incumbent on Spanish criminal anthropologists to diagnose what corrupted aspect of the various elements of Spain's racial fusion was causing criminality.

The large number of available explanations for crime allowed for an equally large number of political and social ideas to seep into the scientific analysis of criminal behavior. In fact, criminality became, like race, a flexible, prismatic category reflecting a wide array of the social and political views, interests, and prejudices of those who studied it as a discrete field of scientific inquiry.[4] This study closely examines the diverse visions and ideologies that underlay, and indeed constructed, the criminological ideas of late-nineteenth- and early-twentieth-century Spain. The criminal anthropologists presented a liberal and nationalist view of Spain that they saw as congenitally in need of national unity and requiring scientific means of controlling crime and suppressing working-class political agitation. At the same time, these scientists, all trained as anthropologists, attempted to combine a biological model of European criminology, most famously asserted by the Italian criminologist Cesare Lombroso, with French models favoring environmental determinism, using methods they thought unique and therefore appropriate for the Spanish context. In the end, they claimed space in the public debate about crime, both for science and for the idea of racial fusion. The larger goal was to promote an organic, evolutionary image of a unified Spanish populace devoid of regional separatist inclinations and revolutionary working-class politics.

Criminology on the Threshold of Science: Before 1880

Spanish criminology as a specialized sphere of scientific knowledge had roots in the early nineteenth century. A Spanish school of phrenology appeared in the 1840s led by a Madrid-based doctor, Mariano Cubí.[5] Cubí followed quite faithfully the phrenology of the Viennese doctor Franz Joseph Gall. Lecturing throughout the country, especially in Barcelona and Madrid, Cubí attracted a small but active group of Spaniards to study the links between criminal behaviors and observable physical structures of the head.[6] Rather than being charged with the task of forming from scratch new scientific disciplines, Spanish scientists enjoyed the benefits of building upon or adapting foreign ideas in the development of their sciences. Especially important for these scientists was the idea of developing disciplines attuned to the needs and requirements of their particular national context. Cubí, for example, was always interested in forming not only a Spanish group that followed the ideas of Gall, but also a uniquely Spanish version of phrenology rooted in and suited for the Spanish context. It was in this endeavor that Cubí had his greatest success attracting followers.[7] Nevertheless, critics remained, both of phrenology and of the adaptation in Spain of any aspect of European sciences. Among these critics was perhaps the most famous and influential doctor in nineteenth-century Spain, Pedro Mata Fontanet (1811–1877), president of the College of Medicine and also Spain's first professor of forensic medicine (1843). Mata succeeded in keeping phrenology from developing into a larger scientific subfield. His attitude toward the study grew out of his fundamental skepticism toward foreign scientific ideas and his caution about translating them to the Spanish context. Mata's most famous admonishment to Spanish scientists was to ensure that all scientific explanations were rooted in reason and empirical science, and not based on "metaphysical" underpinnings like those he associated with phrenology.[8]

The 1868 Revolution changed the fortunes of criminal scientists. They had been active in the formation of the First Republic and suffered professionally after its failure. Those who had lost positions in the universities during the university crisis of the 1860s saw their positions re-created in the 1870s, only to lose them again after the Restoration of the monarchy in 1874.[9] Newly formed intellectual circles and societies and an increasingly powerful body of scientific experts exerted significant influence, if not on the setting of public policy, then on the establishment of a public discourse on criminality, insanity, and the nature of individual and social behavior rooted in scientific terms.[10] The people most active in this effort were doctors linked to Pedro González de Velasco's Anthropology Society of Spain.[11] For these figures, the roots of criminological behavior were overwhelmingly physical. They wanted to identify the physical features they believed were most closely association with criminal behavior. Like their counterparts in the wider field of anthropology, scientific and political proclivities drew Spanish criminologists in the 1870s and 1880s to France.[12] There they were exposed to the psychiatric tradition that had driven French penal reform throughout the nineteenth century. The debate about crime's roots had actually begun earlier in the century with the development of psychological discussions of crime and the efforts, predominantly of French psychologists, to identify the etiology of criminal pathologies via the development of case studies of individual criminals.[13] The work of the French doctors Phillipe Pinel and his student Etienne Esquirol and later Jean-Martin Charcot to categorize criminal behaviors and thus devise systematic treatment for them was adopted in Spain by a small group of doctors who had returned to Spain during the revolutionary period after 1868.

In the new open university atmosphere after the revolution, doctors increasingly attempted to insert the new science of psychiatry and medicine into the legal system. They succeeded in the passage of the new penal code of 1870, which stipulated in Article 8 that insanity and "uncontrollable urges" were possible grounds upon which to sentence criminals to asylums for treatment rather than to prisons or execution (in capital cases).[14] This change in the penal code signaled the beginning of the permanent inclusion of psychiatric and medical knowledge into the judicial process in Spain. However, the significance of this incorporation was ambiguous. For the next two decades, doctors complained ceaselessly about the failure of their expert testimony to sway judges or juries to acquit on the grounds of mental illness and sentence prisoners to asylums for treatment.[15]

The failure of psychiatric ideas in the courtroom did not necessarily mean these ideas were not widely discussed. In fact, legal journals and also the popular press turned their attention to arguments of Spanish criminologists who suggested that criminals were ill rather than merely morally corrupt. Causes célèbres like that of the curate Cayetano Galeote, who had murdered the head of the Madrid Archdiocese, or that of the serial rapist and murderer El Sacamantecas (Juan Díaz de Garayo), who was Spain's first nationally feared mass murderer, along with the medical testimony offered in these cases, were widely covered. Even though Garayo and Galeote were both executed for their crimes despite the efforts of doctors and psychiatrists who testified at the trials to their mental incompetence and need for treatment, the cases led to fervent discussions about the issue of criminal responsibility and the predictability of criminality within individuals.[16] One other effect of this debate was the difficulty lawyers and judges had incorporating this new medical information into the binary requirements of guilt or innocence in the Spanish legal system. Doctors argued that figures like Garayo and Galeote killed indiscriminately as a result of an affective disorder that could be treated, rather than as a result of a moral, religious, or individual failing that rendered them at least permanently suspect and at worst permanently lethal. Lawyers experienced problems assimilating this idea into their juridical arguments, which depended on, as one historian has noted, clear definitions of transgressions and clear requirements for their punishment.[17] This conflict took place along nascent disciplinary boundaries and signaled the growing rift between doctor and lawyers—or, in a larger sense, natural science versus legal philosophy—in the setting of Spanish social policy.[18]

Doctors, of course, were aware of the difficulties their ideas were posing for the judicial system. The effort to make medicine more applicable in legal matters defined the 1870s and 1880s. In 1880, the most famous of Spain's specialists in legal medicine, José María Esquerdo Zaragoza (1842–1912), delivered a lecture on the new science of criminal psychiatry. A student of Pedro Mata, Esquerdo had opened his own private asylum in Carabanchel, on the outskirts of Madrid. Here, Esquerdo became the Spanish champion of Pinel's and Charcot's psychiatric approach, which he had learned from Mata.[19] Most importantly, Esquerdo believed that the insane were curable only after long and individually focused psychiatric treatment. Yet, given the complexity and number of forms of insanity, Esquerdo argued that the courts had to allow doctors first to diagnose the type of insanity that the patient displayed. Too often lawyers and judges assumed that insanity existed only in quite visible forms, especially in outrageous behaviors in the courtroom, or when the convicted clearly posed an uncontrollable danger to fellow prisoners.[20] This approach, Esquerdo noted, had encouraged outbreaks in the courtroom often more theatrical than real to win the sympathies of the judge or just to intimidate him.

After having testified in numerous trials, Esquerdo was invited in 1880 to defend the psychological roots of criminal behavior in the Madrid Athenaeum. In his paper "The Insane Who Do Not Appear to Be" ("Locos que no lo parecen"), Esquerdo argued that insanity could only be a medical diagnosis, recognizable to those trained as doctors. Esquerdo's lecture was important for it signaled a shift in the approach of Spanish doctors to crime. Esquerdo's definition of criminal behavior began to show hints of the mixture between French psychiatric ideas and the burgeoning Italian positivist school of criminology associated with Cesare Lombroso.[21] Esquerdo argued that the insane were not only recognizable through physical traits like wide-set eyes or low-slung ears, notions borrowed from Lombroso's L'huomo delincuente, which he had read in French translation. Instead, he wrote that there were insane people who did not betray telltale physical markers of their mental condition. Esquerdo transplanted to psychiatry the commonly accepted idea from anthropology that extremes indicated a departure from the average, and averages always represented the norm. Esquerdo added mental acumen and tendencies toward illegal behaviors to this equation. Thus, great size and weight were always associated with unrepresentative elements of a race; in the same way, incalculable stupidity betrayed a mental "disorder, irregularity, or departure from type."[22]

Yet, while many forms of mental disorder were expressed in physical anomalies, as Charcot had argued, Esquerdo was more perplexed by those with unstable minds who were not necessarily recognizable, displaying no clear deformation or obvious physical anomaly.[23] These figures, he wrote, could only be recognized by a doctor trained to spot a person's "mental capacity hidden away in the depths of our cerebral formations."[24] By 1880, when Esquerdo was presenting his paper to the Madrid Athenaeum, mental illness, delirium, and monomania were all conditions already accepted by most members of the Spanish judicial system as disorders that affected or caused an individual to commit crime. Despite the 1870 changes in the penal code, Esquerdo lamented that such acceptance had been inconsequential. He faulted the legal community for not allowing psychiatric treatment of criminals in asylums. The preference, it seemed, was imprisonment.[25] Still, Esquerdo's lecture symbolized an important moment in the reform of legal treatment of criminals in Spain and the attack on lawyers' dominance in the formation of political and social policy in Spain. Esquerdo was complicating the usual debate between doctors and lawyers. By raising the question of motivation as a potential factor in determining guilt, he also was complicating the standard legal issue of individual responsibility versus "uncontrollable urges" that governed one's actions.[26] This issue came to underline the major elements of the debate on the nature of crime and treatment of criminals in Spain in the late nineteenth and early twentieth centuries. Not only were doctors and the natural scientists associated with Spanish anthropology interested in studying the natural or medical bases of criminal behavior, they were also devoted on a more philosophical and political level to removing the force of legal and church influence over the penal system. These latter groups had long argued for personal responsibility in punishing criminals rather than admitting the possibility of uncontrollable urges caused by mental disease as the cause of criminal acts.

Throughout the late 1870s and 1880s, the issue of insanity came to dominate the debates in criminal anthropology. Despite the occasional reference to Cesare Lombroso or the Italian positivist school, the focus of debates on criminality remained fixated on the issue of whether individuals could on occasion be free of responsibility for their acts. As other historians have noted, this focus represented a victory for doctors and natural sciences in at least incorporating into the legal system and in penology new ideas about the scientific, rather than immoral or irreligious, basis for criminal acts.[27] In addition, it represented the victory of reformist ideas rooted in liberal political discussions of the immediate post–First Republic period. Most of these figures remained radicals only in spirit, shifting their political allegiances to factions of the Liberal Party that shared power with the Conservative Party in the brokered *turno* system of the Restoration.

This focus on insanity in the 1880s, rather than on the more general definition of criminal identity that dominated Italian positivist discussions, was partly attributable to the medical and psychiatric makeup of Spain's first scientific criminologists. In addition, the focus on insanity—and, in turn, sanity, consciousness, and free will—was part of a wider philosophical reorientation of figures associated with the Revolution of 1868, republican politics, and their dénouement in 1874. Historians of Spain have long asserted that the peculiar development of positivism in the last quarter of the nineteenth century was part of a general accommodation of various ideological and political positions during the Restoration of former republican or radical figures. Chastened by the failures of the First Republic and in search of political and social visions more usable within a particular Spanish context, Spanish positivists sought out politics and social ideas substantiated by scientific study but rooted in theocratic or moral terms.[28] Thus, Spanish positivism was remarkable because it was less radical or revolutionary than its French forebears. Spanish positivism allowed for a much wider range of political, theological, and moral viewpoints to be verified under its scientific auspices. For example, Spanish positivists did not argue against the legitimacy of the monarchy or its support from theocratic groups.[29] One historian concluded that in Spain positivism was both progressive and conservative, assuming, on the one hand, an antirevolutionary posture opposing both anarchism and socialism, which were seen as rooted in materialist first principles rather than more moral or spiritual ones, and, on the other hand, a liberal individualism that promoted free thought and mass participation in politics.[30]

As a result of this particular intellectual milieu, Spanish criminologists of the 1870s and 1880s were generally focused on resolving a contradiction between free will, individualism, and the scientific basis for criminal behavior. This scientific view saw crime as the product of disease that stunted or destroyed a person's capacity for free agency. The lessons of European criminology that presented criminals as potentially unfree agents, unable to control their own impulses, were forced to work in tandem with political programs that favored the protection of individual rights and the treatment of citizens as autonomous individuals. In part, the history of Spanish criminal anthropology was the failure to work out the tensions that grew out of their scientific agenda and their political ideology.

This tension was particularly acute in the Free Institute of Education (ILE; Institución Libre de Enseñanza), founded in 1876. Criminal anthropology was one of the formative courses of study in the ILE beginning as early as 1878.[31] The ILE trained many of Spain's second generation of criminologists, who were active during the 1890s and the first decade of the twentieth century, and determined the unique approach that was later to define Spanish ideas about criminal identity and treatment. The ILE's peculiar version of liberal politics and scientific practice grew out of its intellectual grounding in the work of an obscure German idealist, Karl Christian Friedrich Krause (1781–1839), whom some Spaniards elevated as the torchlight of Spanish thought. Krausists in Spain strongly argued for the removal of church authority from education, stressing the need for secular scientific education as the one path to invigorating and modernizing Spanish society. Yet, this secularism was rooted in a German idealist notion promoted by Krause that science and the secular knowledge of the world served a divine purpose. According to Krause, humans needed to understand the human condition in order to create a moral, or what they called harmonic, world where rational debate would ultimately uncover a divine plan.[32] This goal served an ultimately religious purpose, promoting a universal harmony that bound the body and spirit of the individual to the social organism and a divine plan. Religion, which represented the prescientific elements of humanity, could work in conjunction with the scientific understanding of human relations and physical composition and thus composed the unity of spirit and body.[33] As a result, Krausists pursued anthropology and sociology as methods of uncovering the laws that demonstrated physical health to be a precursor of social health and healthy living conditions of individuals as prerequisites for moral societies.[34] As one historian has noted, anthropology within the ILE was designed as a distinct scientific discipline to promote a moral society. From its inception, anthropology in the ILE was focused more on social organization of human groups than on the purely physical comparisons of different human groups common in the anthropology taught in Spanish universities.[35] Professors encouraged their students to perform ethnographic analyses of different peoples. When they traveled inside or outside Spain, they were admonished to note the social roles that people played and the effects on the health, or stability, of the individuals and on the group as a whole. Although some lessons were offered in physical anthropology, it was clear this knowledge was borrowed from the anthropologists working outside the ILE in the Anthropology Society.[36]

Given the social purpose of Krausist anthropology in the ILE, interest in criminal anthropology increased throughout the first decade of the ILE's existence. Most Krausists, trained as lawyers rather than as doctors or psychiatrists, were initially resistant to the idea of disease separating people from their rational desires and thus absolving them of responsibility. Morality and criminal responsibility could not be separated, as Giner de los Ríos had written in 1878, indicating that insane people were always immoral. Their punishment required they recover both their sanity and morality to atone for their criminal acts.[37] Yet, by the early 1880s, even Giner began to question this distinction between moral reform of criminals and the position of Spanish positivists, who were pointing to the organic, physical roots of criminal activity. In 1886, he sent one student, Pedro Dorado Montero, a lawyer having just completed his studies at the ILE and at the University of Salamanca, to Bologna to study with Lombroso's most famous disciple, Enrico Ferri. Dorado sent monthly letters to Giner promoting the validity of the Italian positivist school of criminology and suggesting possible methods of incorporating these ideas into Krausist thought. He described to Giner the ideas of various Italian criminologists and at the same time was updated by Giner on publications of recent Spanish criminologists.[38] It was clear from the letters that Dorado functioned as Giner's tutor in what was becoming known as criminal anthropology in Italy, or the study of the racial or physical roots of crime. Criminal anthropology, unlike its medical and psychiatric predecessors, saw the criminal as the product of a flawed evolution.

Thus, this science would use then contemporary analyses of race and ethnic makeup of nations to represent criminals as anomalies in a particular nation's evolution.

As in the larger discipline of anthropology, criminal anthropologists saw the signs of this evolutionary decay in physical characteristics. Cesare Lombroso and the Italian positivist school of criminology were the first practitioners of this science, providing now infamous charts that categorized the various head shapes and physical markers emblematic of the criminal. For most of the criminal anthropologists writing in the 1870s, criminals were lost within evolutionary development, permanently removed from the progressive flow of racial development.[39] Giner and the ILE were increasingly forced to confront this new science of penology and the lessons that anthropology posed to more morally rooted approaches to criminal treatment. Dorado's mission in Italy was to study with Enrico Ferri and the second generation of Italian positivists. In addition to Ferri, Dorado studied with Giusseppe Sergi, a physical anthropologist in Rome who became famous for his study of what he called the "Mediterranean race."[40] Dorado also came to be the main translator for Giner of criminological ideas developed within Spain. Félix de Aramburu, a professor of medicine at the University of Oviedo, in northwestern Spain, sent Giner a copy of his book, *La nueva ciencia penal* (1886), which was the first comprehensive presentation of Italian criminal anthropology in Spanish. Giner forwarded the book to Dorado in 1887.[41] Thus, by the middle of the 1880s, criminal anthropology was emerging as a sphere of knowledge essential to Spanish intellectuals and reformers interested in dealing with crime. In addition, it was clear that the reformers themselves would need to analyze in greater detail their own assumptions about personal responsibility and free will in order to absorb foreign notions of criminality into their own calls for reform.

While historians have considered how criminological ideas came into Spain from Italy and from France, most have assumed that these ideas were translated mutatis mutandis into the Spanish context. These historians also assume that the translated ideas themselves were somehow coherent and comprehensive.[42] Most analysts of Italian positivist criminology have long agreed that the use of racial language in this work was rather slipshod and often inconsistent.[43] A closer look at how these ideas were absorbed into the particular Spanish criminological milieu, either in the ILE, among Spanish positivists, or among those figures like Dorado who were trained more in one school but increasingly attracted to another, indicated a far more complicated appropriation of these ideas, which were sometimes interpreted in terms of what Spanish thinkers wanted them to say rather than as their authors intended.

Crime and the Obsession to Explain It: Spanish Criminal Anthropology in the 1880s

The great revelation that Italian criminologists offered was that not all criminals were deranged or morally bankrupt. Rather, some were the organic product of their racial lineage, a class of people who through evolution had inherited characteristics of criminality. Spanish recipients of these ideas rarely accepted the argument that these characteristics were permanent elements of a person's makeup. While historians usually suggest that Lombroso maintained a strong hold on Spanish criminology, the work of his student Enrico Ferri proved to be the most influential. Ferri had forced Lombroso to incorporate more thought on the role of social environment and background in the etiology of crime. These influences were most apparent in the subsequent editions of L'huomo delinquente (1st ed. 1876), especially the 1887 French translation, the edition most commonly read in Spain.[44]

One important explanation for Ferri's alterations of Lombrosian biological determinism was that Ferri was originally trained as a lawyer and not as a doctor. As a result, he did not necessarily believe that the inheritance of physical traits was the sole basis of criminal behavior. He did, however, find physical characteristics to be reliable markers for identifying criminals. Ferri used a wider net in his analysis than did Lombroso, considering social and cultural inheritance, what he called "racial energies and attitudes," as plausible factors in the creation of criminal behaviors.[45] Interestingly, doctors were not the first to assimilate Ferri's ideas or the Italian school in general in Spain. Lawyers initially seized upon Italian criminology and especially Lombroso's own writings as a model for Spanish reform. Lawyers tended to find solace in the less fungible strictures that physiological determinism offered in defining guilt and responsibility.[46] If the accused looked like criminals, they were criminals. Doctors had only clouded the issue of criminal responsibility to a judicial system that relied upon certainties to determine guilt or innocence.

As early as 1880, however, physicians were trying to incorporate systematically the more nuanced approach of Ferri in Spanish medical conceptions of crime. One of Esquerdo's students, José María Escuder, was the first to engage seriously with Ferri's criminological ideas, attempting to fuse them with those of his own mentor. Escuder portrayed criminals as diseased mentally and also as products of the environment from which they emerged. While at first echoing his teacher's calls for more asylums and better treatment of the insane, Escuder argued that lunacy, if left untreated by society, would become a national pathology, a disease affecting the entire race. Spain's lack of asylums and the doctors to staff them were signs of the weak defenses against these potential pathogens. He wrote with concern: "The level of civilization of a nation is in direct proportion to the number of asylums in it. . . . [In Spain] our lack of reason is agitating."[47] Borrowing from Ferri, Escuder wrote that the problem with insanity left untreated was its inheritability. Leaving insanity untreated would lead to an ever more insane nation: "At least one-quarter of all neuroses are transmitted from parents to children, always reappearing in each one of these descendants with the same or different signs of mental perturbation. More than 75 percent of the insane are made that way because of inherited characteristics."[48] Escuder concluded that only mixture between the sane and insane could disrupt this potentially retrogressive lineage. A motley crew of supposedly pure lineages proved to Escuder that seclusion of biological characteristics in unmixed lines was destructive: "Such is the end of the aristocrats who only mix among themselves, as is true with royal lines. In the same way, have bandits, gypsies, Jews, the insane, and thieves all met their end; because of their resistance to cross, they degenerate."[49]

Escuder was indicating new stakes in the discussion of criminal behaviors. He emphasized the potential national effects of insanity on the Spanish race. He also suggested that racial mixture served as a bulwark against the effects of insanity on a society. The novelty of Escuder's argument was based on his particular reading of Italian criminology. For Lombroso, criminals represented evolutionary atavisms in human development, dangerous to society by their mere presence and requiring isolation from society in order to allow the line to die out. Escuder built on this argument, adding the possibility of reform, arguing that if the insane were treated, their threat to society would disappear. If left unreformed, however, the insane would spread the disease of insanity throughout the population. A colleague of Escuder's and also a student of Esquerdo's, Ángel Pulido y Fernández, who was also Pedro González de Velasco's secretary in the Anthropology Society, wrote a book to buttress these claims in 1882. Pulido described his visits to Esquerdo and Escuder's asylum, describing in great detail the successfully reformed patients who were given positions of authority in the asylum. Esquerdo's assistant, who once suffered from extreme melancholia, now exercised an "ingenuous goodness in all of his actions," ever since he had been "bathed by science."[50]

The context in which Escuder was writing seemed to explain this esca-
lating rhetoric surrounding penal reform in Spain. Escuder was writing in
defense of reforms of the penal code under debate in the Spanish Congress in
late 1882 and eventually passed in 1883. These reforms to the code increased
the role of doctors in Spanish jurisprudence. They required the testimony
of at least three doctors in any murder trial relating to the sanity of the de-
fendant and to any forensic evidence.[51] The actual impact of these reforms
was again ambiguous. On the one hand, the Royal Academy of Medicine
was increasingly enlisted to prepare dossiers on criminals, testifying to their
mental state and possible exposure to inherited mental illness. At the same
time, while doctors were testifying in a variety of important trials, including the sensationalized trial of the aforementioned Galeote, their testimony
failed to convince the judges to sentence the defendants to asylums for treatment rather than execution.[52] But Spanish criminologists had succeeded in
changing the terms of the penal code if not its actual legal application. One
barrier remained. Throughout the 1880s, no clear consensus had emerged
among the relatively small number of criminologists about the purpose of
criminological reform. By the next decade, an increasingly large group was
beginning to ask anthropological questions in an attempt to solve Spain's
criminal problem: Were criminals the products of an inexorable lineage of
deviance? Were they created in conjunction with a social and environmental
background that lent itself to the appearance of those without social feeling
or respect for the person or the property of others? How could people who
were congenitally criminal be reformed? Was the criminal a person devoid of
free will? If so, how could they be reformed? Krausists wondered how a moral
society based on the idea of redemption could be created from irreversible
physical conditions that created criminal behavior. Positivists pondered how
certain criminals behaved so detestably even though they were aristocrats
or did not have the physical hallmarks of criminality.[53] Escuder's work had
clearly opened the door for other writers to explore criminal anthropology
and apply its lessons to what they considered to be Spain's unique context.[54]

Spanish anthropology's focus on the effects of racial admixture helped
frame the expansion of this interest in criminal anthropology. With criminals
most commonly defined as aberrant elements of racial development, criminal
anthropologists set about explaining the nature of Spanish crime in terms
of the fusion of distinct racial types.[55] If fusion was the hallmark of Spain's
racial strength, criminal behaviors reflected certain negative elements in this
racial mix. Since only a small percentage of Spaniards were criminals, the

idea that some moral or physical quirk had been infused into the Spanish racial mix sometime in the past seemed the obvious solution to criminologists. Armed with the new anthropological analysis, criminologists began to explore the different elements of Spain's racial past to identify those corrosive ingredients in the Spanish racial mix that were contributing to the appearance of crime in the nation. By the 1890s, the identification of this racial anomaly began to occupy much of the scientific inquiry into crime.

The reform of the penal code in 1883 might not have brought many changes in the actual application of criminal law in Spain.[56] But changes in the code reflected a sea change in the willingness of the Spanish legislature to allow scientific or medical ideas to play decisive roles in the function of the legal process in Spain. Coupled with increasingly intense press coverage of criminal acts that transformed them into public spectacles, a much more energetic debate about the nature and makeup of criminals began to spread out from medical and psychiatric settings into public discourse. Thus, the early 1880s represented the moment when the effort to designate criminal acts became methods of defining pathological behavior, and in turn, following one of Foucault's most lasting insights, of prescribing codes of normal or proper social behaviors for society in general.[57]

By defining aberrant Spaniards and detailing the origins of their difference, Spanish criminologists worked to define, at least indirectly, a supposedly normal Spanish type.[58] As a result, the appeal to anthropology was part of an effort to substantiate scientifically the idea of a typical and deviant Spaniard. How then did the concepts of mixture and fusion come to define normal and deviant behaviors? How did the idea of races intermixed in the Spanish past come to support criminological ideas of the mixed roots of Spanish criminals and the possibility of bad mixes and good ones? And, finally, how did the emergence of regionalist ideas, working-class political groups, and trade unions that confronted head-on the "naturalness" of a unified state and of the social order come to inform the anthropological notions of proper, law-abiding behaviors, and of criminal ones?

Crime as a Product of National Evolution: Criminal Anthropology between 1885 and 1895

A supporter of criminal anthropology entered the Spanish government in 1885 with the appointment of Manuel Alonso Martínez, a lawyer, to be minister of grace and justice. As a minister, Alonso Martínez worked to modernize the Spanish penal code by expanding the uses of science in the jurisprudence and penology of Spain. In 1886, he introduced to the Cortes a series of amendments to the penal code that allowed for greater discretion for magistrates and judges in sentencing criminals. The reforms called for expanding the list of extenuating circumstances to be taken into account for sentencing. Judges, for example, needed to accept that the causes of crime were natural and to allow for treatment of criminals in hospitals or asylums rather than placing them into prisons.[59] Interestingly, the debates in the Cortes focused more on the implicit reduction of the power of lawyers in these reforms by allowing for greater sway of medical testimony and doctors over the court system. Opponents tended not to concern themselves with the scientific ideas that underlay the reforms.[60]

Although the amendments failed to pass, the effort of the minister emboldened Spanish criminologists to argue more publicly for the penal reform. In the same issue of the newspaper that announced these reforms, an official in the Ministry of Grace and Justice working specifically in the Section on Prisons and Asylums (Dirección General de Establecimientos Penales) decried the piecemeal nature of the 1883 penal reforms and the present efforts of the minister.[61] The official, Rafael Salillas y Panzano, argued that debates about the power of lawyers over doctors were more political bluster than conscientious efforts at actual reform. Such debate denied the public a more complete hearing of the recent developments in criminal anthropology and legal medicine. Instead, the public was fed generous portions of confusing, fear-inducing scientific discussion of the incorrigibility of born criminals and the "insane who did not appear to be."[62]

Attention should be paid instead, Salillas argued, to "recent scientific discoveries" that pointed to differences between the "insane" who represent the "degenerative path" of evolution, symbolized by Lombroso's born criminal, and those who were curable.[63] Salillas wrote that too many scientists were misreading foreign ideas, leaving the impression that criminals were not treatable, and that the threats they posed to society were endemic. He suggested instead that "mental medicine and criminal anthropology were doing quite the opposite, . . . reducing considerably the limits of our definition of evil, metaphysically speaking.[64] Salillas's article had greater salience because, unlike his predecessors, Salillas had trained both as a lawyer and as a doctor. As a result, he came to be an important voice in the formal development of criminal anthropology in Spain. His interest in criminal anthropology began precisely during the 1886 penal code reform debates.[65] Though he has remained associated with the introduction of Lombrosian ideas in Spain, Salillas himself, as he expressed in this article, attempted to bridge a variety of approaches in the application of criminal anthropology in Spanish society.[66] In fact, historians have accused Salillas of being a champion of almost every criminological position that existed in Europe between 1890 and 1914.[67] The one constant in Salillas's approach was the desire to adapt any foreign criminological idea into what he considered a uniquely Spanish setting.

After beginning work in the government ministry, Salillas was increasingly interested in criminal anthropology as a means not only to reform the treatment of prisoners, but also to understand their makeup. He was originally attracted to the ideas associated with Lombroso. Yet, his reactions were not those of an avowed Lombrosian. Instead, he found that the overall rejection of what he called materialism in Spanish jurisprudence had been based on a misreading of both Spanish and classical history. The most blatant example of this misreading occurred in 1887, when, during the debates on Alonso Martínez's reforms, the chief of the Spanish Supreme Court commented during the September opening of the court's session that anthropology and doctors had destroyed the judicial process in Spain and were thus a threat to the social order.[68] Salillas instead suggested indigenous elements of Spanish literary and philosophical history had provided the foundation of contemporary European criminal anthropology. Criminological ideas associated with science in the late nineteenth century were first adumbrated in Spanish literature dating back hundreds of years. Quevedo and Cervantes had a seemingly intuitive sense of what drove criminals, describing both the physical features of their criminal characters and their typical psychological pathologies. Salillas also noted that the Greeks, among them Socrates, Plato, and Aristotle, were all aware of the physical manifestations of diseased minds, "the misshapen heads, the possessed expression, or the primal bodies, that is the phrenologic, physiognomic, and degenerative" elements of the criminal.[69]

One aspect of this past criminal understanding was the older Spanish openness to new ideas. Salillas was optimistic about furthering the less developed modern criminal sciences in Spain by adding new sciences to their older methods. He noted that most of the leading Spaniards preoccupied with Spanish crime had accepted certain claims of the scientists who explained crime in terms of "the natural elements of human development" without adopting a fully biological deterministic outlook: "Spanish juridical sciences have never had an intransigent temperament. . . . [T]hey appreciate the reciprocal relations between physical man and moral man."[70] Salillas

argued that this cautious open-mindedness was exemplified in Alonso Martínez's efforts to reform the penal code. No fan of determinism, Salillas wrote,
Alonso Martínez was nevertheless willing to "press into service the science . . .
that recognizes the energy of the forces that block a person's free will."[71]
Even those who confused "rights with morals, crime with sin" occasionally
broke from their metaphysical proclivities to recognize "that contradictions
still produced reality," contradictions explained by the force of scientific understanding of insanity and the effects of it on the body.[72] This cautious acceptance of determinist ideas in Spain was an attribute celebrated even by the
Italian school. Lombroso openly celebrated Spanish participation in the new
science at the first Congress of Criminal Anthropology in Rome in 1885. In
addition, Salillas argued that such a response represented a unique element
of the Spanish character, which was entranced by foreign ideas but did not
work to develop any of them in a systematic, comprehensive way. This failure
to develop a school of criminology in Spain was due to a more sharply divided
political world in which the religious convictions of some made them hesi-
tant to allow such foreign science into the realm of social policy. Perhaps it
was this hesitation that Salillas hoped to overcome by finding ancient Spanish
roots of scientific progress.[73]

Still, Salillas argued that, despite this groundwork, one could overesti-
mate the impact of these new sciences on Spanish jurisprudence. Intellectual
development was evolutionary, slow, and adaptive, conforming to social settings rather than necessarily upsetting them. Because of the late development
of the Spanish sciences, scientists were able to absorb, reject, and assess
ideas in a rational, judicious manner. Salillas described this Spanish process:
"sometimes things are organized along ordered lines, without demanding
great leaps from spiritualism to positivism, or asking them to arise spontaneous out of conjunctures. . . . [P]eople will accept doctrines in a piecemeal
fashion, others in their totality. . . . [T]his process is the success of intellectual exchange not the conquest of ideas; so that anticipating ideas and their
applications is not to actually put them in practice, nor reduce them to their
simplest forms."[74] Salillas had been promoted to head the Department of
Penal Institutions just two months prior to delivering this address.[75] After
making a historical and cultural case for Spain's slow but willing acceptance
of all new approaches to crime, Salillas suggested the need for a cautious
plan to incorporate the lessons of criminal anthropology in a manner inoffensive to Spanish political and social sensibilities. In fact, the plan would
be closer to a reincorporation of native Spanish traditions with the tools of

modern science: "Now that the various fields are defined, one can say that anthropological doctrines are not really new but quite ancient. In fact, they have their origins in genuinely Spanish philosophy and traditions. Now, instead of fearing science as the destruction of our social fabric, one can see that our own instincts for conservation have kept it alive."[76]

The problem for Salillas with the Spanish penal code was that it treated people properly but for the wrong reasons. For example, the code allowed for people younger than fifteen years old to be considered not culpable for the crimes they committed since their moral development had not been completed and, as a result, they lacked free will. Yet, the problem for Salillas was that the code was still motivated by moral values rooted in family relations and individual improvement rather than scientific deduction. The code called for their return to their family, entreating the parents to be "watchful over the child and to educate him."[77] Salillas noted that many eighteen-year-olds still lacked free will. Only anthropology offered the possibility of complicating this simple binary division of "normal" (with free will) and "abnormal" (without free will). He suggested that such binary divisions were not scientifically verifiable, but were rooted in the legal need of the jurist to distinguish between guilt and innocence. The tendency in the Italian school was to devise explanatory models that were equally reductive and simplistic. Salillas instead argued that different types of criminals required analyses based in different fields—anthropology, psychology, and medicine—many of which were still too undeveloped to devise clear and concrete reforms to penal codes in Spain. Instead, Salillas wrote, Spain needed to begin the formal study of criminal anthropology in institutional settings so that it was prepared when the science developed enough inside and outside Spain to rewrite the penal code with confidence that it would be applied effectively.[78]

Salillas's lecture spurred a wide public debate on Lombrosian criminology and its application in Spain.[79] After 1888, Lombrosian ideas, as in the rest of Europe, began to appear not only in the popular press, but also in literature and in fictionalized accounts of criminal activity.[80] By 1891, books and journals devoted to the "new juridical sciences" began to emerge in Spain as forums to discuss Lombrosian ideas. Some worked to adapt Lombroso's work on the born criminal, devoid of any choice over his own fate or actions, to Catholic notions of free will. Others attempted more secular readings to clean up discrepancies between Lombroso's assertion of certain fixed physical signs of inescapable criminality with discussions of physiological and behavioral variance among those committing crimes.[81] In 1894, a spirited exchange took place between the anarchist Ricardo Mella and Lombroso, with Mella criticizing Lombroso for arguing that anarchists were figures lost in evolutionary development, evolved just enough to express their primitive and barbaric instincts in political terms and in political acts.[82]

This public debate also seemed to foster a desire to formalize the new science in institutional settings. Salillas began discussions with the director of the ILE, Francisco Giner de los Ríos, to open a school devoted solely to the "science" of penal law. Salillas had reported to Giner that the Ministry of Grace and Justice had been receptive to the idea of a normal school for penitentiary workers that would serve two purposes: to "educate students of penal science in theoretical and practical matters" and in turn to create the need for a new discipline for a university chair.[83] Giner had demonstrated interest in this discipline, having already interviewed the Austrian criminologist Moritz Benedikt a few months earlier in Madrid. His notes indicated that Giner succeeded in soliciting a comprehensive view of the various European schools of criminology from Benedikt, replete with a national breakdown of the interests and approaches that predominated in each country. This interview helped Giner to complete new lectures on criminal anthropology to replace those he had already prepared that he felt presented only a small selection of the criminological ideas available in Spain.[84]

Between 1891 and 1900, Salillas and groups emerging from the ILE advanced criminal anthropology in legal journals and in other popular intellectual and cultural periodicals. Salillas formed the *Nueva Ciencia Jurídica*, a journal that advanced Lombrosian ideas, including an anthropometric analysis of a murderer deemed by Salillas to be "a born Spanish criminal."[85] Despite the failure of this journal, Salillas joined the anthropologist Luís de Hoyos Sáinz at José Lázaro Galdiano's *España Moderna* as both a scientific editor and as the criminal anthropological consultant. It was through his connection with Hoyos Sáinz that Salillas began to explore the specific anthropological—or physical and evolutionary—roots of the Spaniard and the Spanish criminal. Salillas's first introduction to specifically Spanish anthropology came from the work of Federico Olóriz y Aguilera. Olóriz's first lectures at the Athenaeum on his research into the cephalic indices of Spain had concluded that extremes of measurement did not exist in Spain as they had elsewhere, as a result of Spain's history of racial mixture. As a result, Lombroso's idea that in the extremes of physical measurement lay the criminal type did not seem to fit in the Spanish context. The lack of clear-cut extremes would make distinguishing the criminal difficult, but not, as it turned out, impossible.[86]

Attempts were made to ferret out from the anthropological statistics a portrait of the Spanish criminal type. In 1892, a royal decree was issued calling
for each prison to take anthropometric measurements of prisoners' heads
and bodies to define their personality types upon their admission to the
prison.[87] By 1895, the measurements had begun for all prisoners entering
Spanish prisons.[88] Another royal decree of 1897 required all prisons to perform statistical analyses of this information, and thus to provide the government with anthropological data about criminal makeup. Despite complaints
from many of the directors of Spain's largest prisons, the anthropometric
measuring and statistical analysis of prisoners continued throughout the
1890s and expanded in 1901, when Olóriz himself was named inspector general of identification in prisons.[89]

By the 1890s, however, criminal types, like racial types, were neither
seen solely as the product of a physical evolution nor as physical types visible through anthropological measurement. The first volume of the Spanish *Lecciones de antropología* written by Hoyos and Telésforo de Aranzadi was
published in early 1891. In these volumes, the anthropologists first argued
that local environments, social settings, and cultural makeup also were determinants of the success of a racial group. The effects of racial fusion might
have been written in physical markings and characteristics, but the success of
the fusion was dependent upon its relationship to the environmental conditions in which it took place.[90] Salillas publicly advanced these ideas between
1888 and 1898, publishing only in popular journals like *España Moderna* and
in legal journals. It was clear that Salillas had a two-part mission in this journalistic work. The first was to expand public awareness of the potential uses
of anthropology in the adjudication of crime in Spain. Public awareness was
needed because the introduction of medical testimony had failed to alter sig-
nificantly the outcome of any trial. The solution lay in the empanelling of juries composed only of people trained in medicine for, as he wrote, it was clear
that judges and lawyers who gathered testimony and the juries that heard it
did not know how to ask the proper questions or understand the answers
medical experts provided.[91]

Salillas also began to establish criteria for discerning national differences
in criminal behavior. Reporting on the conviction of a well-publicized British
murderer in 1894, Salillas used the trial to explore the differences between
Spanish and British criminals. For example, he voiced an old trope of phrenology that crimes against property characterized more advanced nations.
Where this type of crime predominated, a more advanced racial development

had taken place and a more developed civilization existed. Crimes against people—violent crimes and murder—were thought to be the hallmarks of less advanced civilizations.[92] These differences were rooted in the "natural, biological development of a nation."[93] Salillas's ideas remained inflected with Lombrosianism, yet it was clear that, by 1894, his notions about the roots of criminal behavior had become infused with other environmentally based ideas emanating from France. Still, criminals represented an atavism, or a backwards or incomplete step in the evolution of a particular population of a nation, an idea borrowed from Lombroso. Such atavisms were not necessarily passed down through biological inheritance; they also developed. How then did criminals develop differently in different national contexts?

Salillas enlisted the monist evolutionary thought of Ernst Haeckel, arguing that in every organism individual physical development passed through the various stages of the evolutionary development of that species. Thus, to be born human meant that a person had passed through each stage of humanity's evolution, transforming from one-celled organism through reptile, primate, and finally homo sapiens. Degeneration took place when an event interrupted this evolutionary development: "A break in development has to be seen as the cause of the stagnation of the character, explained by the idea that ontogeny (genesis of the individual) is an abbreviated phylogeny (genesis of the species)."[94] Environmental conditions, not just racial heritage, affected this evolutionary progression. The environment, the levels of nourishment and care one received at the liminal moments of development, as one passed between various stages, were the most important in ensuring proper, healthy racial formation. Deficiencies in these moments helped create human beings who were degenerate, or delayed, in their physical development. The same process defined mental or emotional development as well. Salillas extrapolated from the Haeckelian notion of ontogeny recapitulating phylogeny that the stages of social and moral development also followed a certain pattern, with breaks or deficiencies along the way causing interruptions in the makeup of not only an individual's character but also of society's.

> Humans run through a series of stages that mimics that of the species, in uterine life: cell, ovum, embryo, etc. In extrauterine life, the process is completed with people passing through the stages of primate and savage, until the process ends with the conversion into a human. To say it with more common language, upon birth, man is not born a man of his time, but of times very remote. As he develops, man passes through the centuries, slipping by distant stages in evolution, from the most primitive tribal lives, to the end point of his present race and family.

Looking at his own development, man sees himself overcome his previous infe-
rior nature.[95]

The repercussions of these breaks in evolution affected not only the individual but also the society in which these individuals lived. Here, Salillas combined the Haeckelian idea of individual development with Spencerian notions
of national evolution, arguing that certain national characteristics could cause
these breaks in individual development to occur. Individual degeneration was
then closely linked to national degeneration. One way to see how national
characteristics were affecting criminal activity was by analyzing the kinds
of crime that were committed in each national context. Degenerate nations
created an increased number of degenerate individuals committing violent
crimes. Nations with a predominance of crimes against property had at least
fostered the expression in crimes that were thought to betray the ingenuity
and civility of the person committing it: "In countries like England where
one can live by force of his own initiative or reason, this force is inherited
and guaranteed by custom or by law. Here, where one cannot even divorce legally, we respond to our needs by the force of our own southern character, the
product of our excitable nature and the historic commotions of our past."[96]

According to Salillas, the process of degeneration was self-replicating.
Criminals sowed the seeds of further degeneration of that nation by creating
an atmosphere where crime, insecurity, fear, and antisocial behaviors fostered
further criminal acts. As a result, criminal anthropologists needed both to diagnose the sources of the specific environmental factors that elicited degenerate individuals and also to determine the elements of the nation that fostered
these environmental conditions. It was important to see criminals rooted in
the society that produced them but also as distinct elements to be removed
from society: "[W]hat matters for our social interests is not to avenge ourselves on them, but to defend ourselves from them and, more importantly, to
defend ourselves without a sense of superiority. It would be a shame that in response to the degeneration of those who commit crime, we allowed ourselves
to be dragged down the same path by virtue of our methods of punishment."[97]

In a subsequent article, Salillas lamented the lost opportunity to explore
the particular interaction between environment and physical decay in an infamous murder that had just taken place in the Spanish military. A captain in
the Spanish army had murdered his commanding officer, a general, in what
investigators said was an unpremeditated moment of insanity. Salillas argued

that the captain's temporary murderous lunacy had been created over a vast period of time, the result of an acute mental decay and also the constant environmental stimuli that the military had failed to recognize. The environmental factors had caused an actual physical change in the captain's brain. The problem for Salillas was that in the army's zeal to execute their criminal they did not leave adequate time for criminal anthropologists to examine the patient or establish a case history in order to diagnose the environmental factors leading to his insanity.[98]

Race as the Root of Crime: Salillas after 1898

While Salillas's journalistic endeavors attempted to explain the mechanisms of criminal development, they did little to elaborate how Spanish criminals were created. To construct this specific view, Salillas turned to the anthropological work of Telésforo de Aranzadi and Luis de Hoyos Sáinz. Salillas's physical and social analysis of criminal development was similar to the approach that Aranzadi and Hoyos had brought to the study of the Spanish race. Context, history, and environment all functioned as the driving forces in the creation of Spanish criminals. In 1898, Salillas published the first book-length study of the unique national characteristics of the Spanish criminal, El delincuente español. For Salillas, race mixture proved to be the mechanism that brought about the creation of the Spanish criminal. Salillas began the study by noting that the kinds of crime prevalent in Spain showed that criminal populations were among the most retrograde in development among Europeans. The prevalence of murder and political violence indicated that, at least among criminals, some racial element was creating a lag in the development of Spanish civilization. In El delincuente español, Rafael Salillas argued that this racial element was the direct result of a historic infusion of gypsy populations into the Spanish race.[99]

This racial component combined with the inhospitable environment of southern Spain to create what Salillas called nomadic instincts within Spanish criminals. These nomadic instincts led Spaniards to feel, despite the realities of their surroundings, a certain desperation about finding sustenance and shelter. Criminal behaviors, both violent and nonviolent, emerged out of this desperation. Thus, the mixture of nomadic populations into the Spanish racial stock had left a unique mark on Spaniards, a mark observable in "sociological, psychological and even anatomic characteristics."[100]

In order to make precise the affinities between our people and theirs, we must recognize that these affinities have come to be constituted by virtue of certain national habits and types, a fused personality. This fusion has resulted in the coupling of picaresque and gypsy, that is, of the blood relations of gypsy and criminal. This affinity can only be explained through the intermingling of characteristics between one people and another. Such a strong intermingling, of course, would indicate a similar nature in the constitutive groups, a similarity rooted in one clearly shared trait, nomadism.[101]

If the criminal underworld in Spain emerged from gypsy populations and as a result of the effects of the rugged environment in the South, Spain's law-abiding population was the product of continued fusion with other more advanced populations and the dispersion of these populations to other more hospitable areas of Spain. Like his anthropological colleagues, Salillas suggested that the advanced fusion of the law-abiding citizens emerged not only in physical makeup but also in cultural and political behaviors. Unlike the work of Olóriz, Salillas argued that this fusionary process was not a mere evolutionary inevitability, free from the influence of human action. Rather, Salillas argued that evolution was mutable. In fact, the racial fusion could be artificially skewed to rework the combination of ingredients and the environments in which they mixed to create a more desirable human product. In this sense, Salillas was closer to adopting the ideas of anthropological development that Telésforo de Aranzadi had advanced: tracing racial fusion not only through physical measurements but also through alterations in cultural practice, social organization, language, etc. Salillas, who had read Aranzadi's work, argued that in terms of reducing the criminal population, one could not directly weed out the racial mixture of the past in a physical sense.[102] What humans could alter were the environmental conditions that fostered and reinforced the psychological traits associated with nomadism.[103]

If nomadic instincts and the desperate sense of survival they engendered were the product of fusion with nomadic populations and interactions with an inhospitable environment, Salillas argued, political and social reforms, the will of the state, had to be enlisted to overcome some of the most lasting and corrosive effects. Securing more access to property ownership and providing sustenance via education in cultivating the land, for example, would all be effective measures to weed out the lasting negative effects of mixture with nomadic populations. Gypsies were unredeemable by state intervention because they preferred separation from larger populations, resisting the beneficial aspects of racial mixing. Yet their effects on the Spanish racial mix, though physically indelible, could be altered socially and culturally. Gypsies were a block in an otherwise successful racial fusion. Gypsies, in fact, suffered too from their own, albeit self-imposed, lack of intermixture:

> the present population of Spain does not have a complete homogeneity, and in fact, offers quite a diversity of types, costumes, customs, of related peoples and origins. The work of national unity centered on fusing all of these diverse elements into a politico-religious configuration to which even many Jews and Moors, who were not expelled, submitted. But the gypsy, who does not have a political personality . . . who loves nothings else but his independence and wandering life, does not fuse, but rather holds on his customs and way of life. . . . [T]he representatives of that people who remain in Spain do not constitute a true community, a nation, but rather an aggregate of all the influences acting on it, the product, it must be said, of some of the vicious indifference of Spanish society.[104]

The number and variety of reactions to Salillas's book demonstrated that a burgeoning school of criminology had formed in Spain. Reviewed in the popular, political, and legal press, Salillas's study was hailed as the catalyst of a distinctly Spanish brand of criminological study, one that examined the individual not solely as a product of his environment and racial past, but in relation to it, as potentially reacting to it.[105] One reviewer attempted to define this work as emblematic of the Spanish method of treating the "physiological, cultural, sociological and psychological" roots of crime all with equal weight.[106] Another suggested that criticisms of Salillas as a "little Lombroso" were unfounded; El delincuente español was not "a mere translation of Lombroso with a smattering of other Italians, like Ferri, Garofalo, and others thrown in," but rather a work "with its own personality well defined and well developed. . . . Lombroso need not have been born for this work to have been written."[107] The most consistent critique, however, focused on the fact that, despite its five hundred pages, the study failed to perform formal "scientific anthropological analysis," detailing only through secondary works the psychological and "anatomo-physiologic" bases of criminal behavior.[108] Salillas had hoped to forestall such criticism, referring to his five-hundred-page book as a "pamphlet," suggesting that it was a call to arms rather than a formal plan. Some reviewers agreed, noting that Salillas spent too much time on the theoretical basis of the causes of crime, and not enough on the actual methods of treating prisoners, the role he was supposed to fill in his ministry position.[109] This lacuna in Salillas's anthropological analysis apparently provided the impetus for Spanish criminologists to research anew the postulates of El delincuente español. Over the course of the next seven years, Spaniards published more than twenty studies of criminal anthropology, specifically the physical, psychological, and environmental analysis of criminals and their backgrounds.[110] These studies were translated and published outside of Spain as representatives of a growing body of Spanish literature on the subject of criminal anthropology.[111] Reviews also were generated of Spanish works, with Salillas's El delincuente español receiving favorable attention from Max Nordau and from Johannes Näcke in France and Germany respectively, and with Näcke arguing that Salillas's book was the first to provide a comprehensive scientific rendering of "the roots of the psychology of a people."[112]

Students of Salillas and his colleague Pedro Dorado Montero were the first to launch formal plans for the application of their teachers' ideas. In many ways, these approaches differed very little from those of their mentors, conflicting only in relation to specific calls for reform of the penal code or prison management. Dorado, who as an early anarchist was politically more radical than Salillas, had already sparred with Salillas over the issue of how to apply the criminal anthropology upon which they otherwise agreed. Dorado argued that knowledge of the roots of crime meant nothing if the criminal could not be treated.[113] Dorado especially attacked Salillas's desire for special juries trained in medicine or the natural sciences to hear cases involving medical testimony.[114] His reasons, however, for disagreeing with Salillas did not focus on the content or validity of the ideas as much as they did on the scope and potential use of the criminology Salillas presented. Dorado maintained the Krausist belief that whatever the particular roots of crime were, the potential existed for the treatment and moral reform of the individual. The racial and psychological roots that Salillas pointed to, even if accurate, could not be so deterministic that one sacrificed the hope of treating the individual because of their history and environment. In his criticism of El delincuente español, Dorado argued against the deterministic criminology of the Italian school of Lombroso or Ferri. The value he saw in Salillas's book was that the author never firmly averred a pure Lombrosian biological determinism. Rather, he had accepted elements of Lombrosianism but had infused them with more subtle and nuanced ideas. The book was comprehensive but still incomplete: "I consider this the most profound of all books like it for the following reasons: crime, it says, is the product of atavisms, an effect of degeneration, neurasthenia, of deficient nutrition of the central nervous system, of epilepsy, in sum, of an organic and psychic inferiority of the criminal in relation to other citizens, due to the effects of economic misery, lacking or bad education, etc. etc. To all of this I say: 'good, right, and what is there to do about it?'"[115]

Dorado's criticisms, of course, represented differences much closer to shades of gray than to vastly divergent theoretical positions. Ultimately, Dorado concluded that Salillas's view of the role of racial mixture and its function in the division of the Spanish population into parasitic nomads and productive, sedentary people who stabilized the nation was probably accurate. Still, more research was needed that focused on the psychological, cultural, and physical—that is, anthropological—roots of crime.[116] Only after this research was finished could criminologists turn to the social application of these ideas to control crime by reforming the elements of Spanish society that produced crime, and by identifying the potentially irremediable elements of Spanish society. Scientists needed to foster a "living sense of obligation to employ all of our forces to make hygienic and safe a society that continues and stop the production of nomads, or individuals whose attacks on civilized sedentary society lead to persecution rather than care."[117] He concluded with a rousing: "To work, gentlemen!"[118] An explosion of both nationwide and site-specific studies of crime and criminals throughout Spain followed Dorado's comments. These studies all revealed the continuing mixture in the appropriation of European ideas in Spanish criminology. Following Salillas's approach, most criminologists in Spain performed anthropological studies that focused on both the physical identifiers of criminal identity, and also on environmental factors that were thought to determine criminal behaviors. Yet this dual approach worked to complicate the application of these ideas, offering little specific or concrete information for policymakers, government officials, jurists, and the police to apply them.

Crime and Race Defined: The Search for Applications, 1895–1907

Those who followed Salillas, Dorado, and the first practitioners of Spanish criminology tended to align themselves with the political approach of Salillas. They sought methods to identify the criminal that looked at physical hallmarks of criminal identity, and also offered possible paths and treatments for their reform. Unlike the Italian positivists, many of whom were socialists like Lombroso, Salillas and the growing Spanish school of criminology did not assume that the removal of criminals would eliminate the disease from society and consequently produce an equal, just, democratic, socialist, or communal society of good, healthy citizens.[119] They sought scientific technique to reform and redeem criminals devoid of a religious purpose. Salillas summed up this position writing a eulogy for a Spanish Carmelite nun, Concepción Arenal, whose *Letters to Delinquents* (1865) and *Estudios penitenciarios* (1877) had helped draw attention to the deplorable conditions and inhumane treatment of criminals in Spanish prisons that had activated the first efforts in prison reform in the 1870s. Arenal did not favor new medical treatment of prisoners; their criminality was the result of moral degeneration due to poor living conditions or improper religious training. As a result, she long supported religious education in the prisons rather than medical or psychiatric treatment. Salillas considered her the founder of modern criminology because her writing was marked by the same kind of two-sided approach that later came to dominate Spanish criminology. She focused on the need to save the soul by improving the conditions in which the body lived. Criminal anthropologists replaced the soul with environment and psychology and saw the body in terms of its racial history. Salillas did not quibble with calling a person's psychological and temperament their soul. In fact, he noted that this terminology might be the only workable one for Spain. The lessons of criminal anthropology in Spain, he wrote, were that in the treatment of crime, saving the soul included understanding the body of the criminal.[120] After an early flirtation with anarchism, Pedro Dorado Montero remained ardently anticlerical in his rhetoric and goals for solely secular reform of the criminal. Yet, Dorado ultimately failed to attract many followers because he continued to be thought of as too radical for Spanish criminology.[121]

The success of Salillas's approach and the failure of Dorado's were evident in the ILE, which remained the key center of instruction in criminal anthropology. Students followed Salillas's approach, exploring both the physical and environmental roots of criminal behavior, only studying Dorado's more philosophical jurisprudential writings on civil and criminal law.[122] The most prolific student to emerge from the ILE who attempted to expand upon and organize Spanish criminology into its own national discipline was Constancio Bernaldo de Quirós, who worked under Salillas in the Ministry of Grace and Justice.[123] In 1898, Quirós wrote the first textbook of criminal anthropology in Spain, entitled *Modern Theories of Criminality*. The work was designed to be an introduction to the field for both the student and the general public, presenting all of the various European schools of thought on criminality. The book offered subtle support for the Italian school of Lombroso and especially his disciples. The school itself was then under attack from the followers of the French criminologists who favored purely behavioral and environmental explanations for criminal behavior. The attacks particularly aggrieved Spaniards like Salillas because of their assumption that Lombroso could only be read one way.[124]

Quirós's book represented the typical appropriation of an international scientific discipline by Spanish scientists. Despite the focus on particular Spanish ideas, the work functioned much better as a compendium of European ideas selected to provide a view of criminology that was both comprehensive in its presentation of the various schools, but also idiosyncratic in its application in the Spanish context. The work was translated into English by the American Institute of Criminal Law and Criminology in 1912. The committee, composed primarily of the representatives of legal sociology like Roscoe Pound and Ernst Freund at the University of Chicago, chose Quirós's work precisely because of its synthetic quality: "The great work of Señor de Quirós . . . reveals all the shades of thought which have marked the development of the science and constitutes a compendium that no student of the subject can ignore without disadvantage."[125]

Quirós had already established this international reputation with a study published in 1901 entitled *The Low Life in Madrid*.[126] Later translated into German and Italian, with an introduction by Lombroso, Quirós's book presented a view of the criminal in Madrid as the mixed product of the various racial influences on the Spanish population. The urban context of Madrid fostered the creation of criminals. The city's unhygienic living conditions for the poor and the ingathering of criminal elements from all of Spain, who were able to avoid the scrutiny of the police within the city's large population, exacerbated the nomadic, parasitic tendencies of those few who already had the "protoplasm of criminal life" in their racial mix.[127] The argument had already been introduced in the craniological studies of a Dr. Porpeta and a military doctor, Carlos Slocker, among them the most famous *Capacidad craneana en Madrid*. After measuring the crania of both living and dead Madrileños, these doctors concluded that the process of racial fusion took place in cities at a much faster rate. They added, however, that certain racial elements were more robust than others and better resisted this fusion.[128] Criminality was one of these elements. Despite this evolutionary view of criminality in Madrid, Quirós's idea also relied on the Haeckelian approach of Salillas, suggesting that even during the life of a criminal, certain stages of development were linchpins in the creation of different criminal behaviors: "Thus it happens that, adopting as a definite occupation one of the said modes of life and practicing it habitually, [criminals] become identified with delinquency, prostitution, or criminality, producing the delinquents, the prostitutes, or the beggars."[129] Quirós's theory relied on a hodgepodge of scientific views of evolutionary development. He adopted Haeckel's stage theory of development, yet added the neo-Lamarckian perspective that criminals acquired characteristics over the course of their lives that were then passed on to successive generations of criminals.

Quirós was presenting the argument that criminal development could potentially be curtailed with treatment, or some form of medical, psychological, or social intervention. For if certain aspects of criminality were acquired, then perhaps intervention in peoples' lives prior to their acquisition would thwart criminal development. What differentiated Quirós's view from other environmental arguments was his belief that people who exhibited criminal traits, either behavioral or physical, had indeed followed not only a different social path, but had entered that path already predisposed to criminality because of their racial lineage. Criminals were, in fact, either a distinct species born to criminal life or a people once altered by circumstances. The criminal was a "product of vagabond temperament, of early neglect and social decadence, the outlaw lives as a parasite of the social organism, devoting himself to theft, prostitution and beggary. We find in him the aptitude and, at times, even the practice of these three phases of life. . . . [W]hen [criminals] become settled in any of these differentiated states, they experience also a series of changes and transformations related to the adaptation to the new mode of life. . . . [T]he differentiation [between criminals] is never so complete as to atrophy altogether the primary aptitudes for every kind of parasitism. . . . [B]iological species abandon or hide the characteristics for which they are persecuted and imitate others in order to mask themselves."[130]

In his textbook, Quirós discussed over a dozen books and articles on Spanish criminals published after Salillas's El delincuente español. The portrait that emerged from these studies, he wrote, was of a Spain still dominated by violent, or "blood," crimes and "assaults and insults against authority and public functionaries."[131] Spanish criminals, given their retrogressive fusion with gypsy populations and the inhospitability of the environment that nurtured them, were lower down in this evolutionary scale. Yet, using a statistical analysis of Spanish crime, Quirós noted that the intensity of violent crime varied throughout the nation. He concluded that this variation provided further evidence of incomplete racial fusion and the possibility of localizing and thus isolating the particular corrosive influences within Spain's regions. The variation of intensity within the peninsula indicated that racial fusion was not uniform throughout Spain. Even more, these variations were brought about by the peninsula's distinct environments. He wrote, for example, that the uneven intensity of violence in Spain was "generally due to racial distribution. In the Northwestern provinces of Lugo and Oviedo, where the brachycephalic (eurasian) type prevails, there is a minimum intensity of crimes of blood; while in the regions mainly inhabited by dolichocephalics (eurafricans), including the upper plateau of Castile, the lower Ebro, the eastern slope and the elevation of Andalucia, there is a maximum intensity, especially in the second and last places."[132]

This mapping of the racial distributions in Spain duplicated the ethnological studies of Federico Olóriz, Hoyos, and Aranzadi. Yet Quirós came to slightly different conclusions about the effects of racial mixture than did his anthropological colleagues. In fact, it is interesting to note that Quirós evaluated the effects of the infusion of African peoples in the peninsula quite differently than did his colleague Manuel Antón y Ferrandiz, the holder of the chair of anthropology at the Central University in Madrid. Antón had argued that the influence of African races brought a fiery sense of independence, a character that served Spain well in foreign wars and in the conquest of the Americas, but had aroused regional aspirations within the country.[133] Quirós placed more emphasis on the negative effects of this mixture, connecting the infusion of African races with an increase in violent crime and the proliferation of retrograde behaviors.[134] Yet, the method for dealing with the effects of this mixture was not simply extracting this fused element from the Spanish race. Such an unbinding of the racial mix could also be detrimental to Spanish racial health. Quirós, like Antón, found certain qualities inherent in the African race. Since crime could be understood as rooted in physical differences, Quirós argued that other influences, more controllable and mutable elements of crime, would be the criminologists' focus. Following Salillas's argument, Quirós wrote that these other factors also helped fashion Spain's criminal element: "the influence of culture and of the density of population is sufficiently noticeable in the distribution of criminality; but what determines it better are the natural forces, like temperature and humidity."[135]

Quirós displayed a distinct resistance to following any one particular school of thought, preferring instead to blend different approaches. For example, when data appeared to contradict his arguments about environment's role in creating crime, he used race, now defined in terms of permanent biological inheritance, to explain such contradictions. He observed, for example, that the province of Logroño, which had normal humidity, a climate usually associated with less criminal activity, also had a very high level of violent crime. The explanation for this apparent anomaly lay in the fact that Logroño existed in a "zone . . . which preserves in sufficient purity the ancient, impulsive and violent Iberian race."[136] The Basque race that lived in proximity to the region surrounding Logroño was the ostensible culprit in this improper racial fusion.

Almost all Spanish criminologists agreed that Spain's criminals were the product of Spain's unique racial past. Yet, other European criminologists and anthropologists offered plans for removing criminal elements from society (and curtailing their ability to propagate) that Spaniards found useless given its complicated history of racial mixture. Ambivalence defined the interactions between Spanish and other European racial scientists. Spaniards were drawn to the sociological approaches of some German anthropologists, for example, valuing their connection of racial history with social strength. Yet, the concomitant German arguments about Aryan supremacy were difficult for Spanish scientists to accept given their own promotion of racial mixing. One interaction stood out. The German racist and antisemitic anthroposociologist Otto Ammon, whose correspondence with Federico Olóriz had demonstrated the support of the German for Spanish anthropology, attracted Spanish criminologists to his theories about the relationship between racial provenance and superiority.[137] Quirós, for example, argued that Ammon was correct to study social factors as signs of the superiority of race.[138] In fact, Quirós wrote, the German and French school of Aryan supremacists, like Gobineau and Vacher de Lapouge, were not wrong to assume that racial superiority did exist and could be observed in social structures. Their error lay in the assumption that access to Aryan blood was the only basis of superiority and, in turn, that inferiority, as exemplified in criminals, was a clear indication only of non-Aryan lineage. Ammon's mistake resided in his consideration only of the content of the racial stock and not social factors in the generation of crime: "We believe the most complete and accurate truth on the genesis of criminal phenomena (and that of all social phenomena) resides in the approach of the positivist school of criminology and its exploration of the causative role of anthropological factors (both organic and psychic) and of the environmental factors (both physical and social)."[139] Still, despite the "Aryan fantasies and exaggerations" of Ammon and Vacher de Lapouge, Quirós seemed to support the eugenic logic gleaned from anthropology. One needed to devise laws steeped in this anthropological knowledge to better the Spanish race and improve Spanish society: "one certainty is that this great torrent of ideas invading all scientific fields does not seem to be affecting official orthodoxies; the laws of any country cannot crystallize in past molds but have to adapt themselves to the evolution of scientific thought."[140] He favored, for example, new laws in the United States against marriage of the insane, "imbeciles, and weak of spirit." He also celebrated other European nations' new associations that devised laws of proper selection for each country, noting with a tone of optimism that, in Spain, "some time will have to pass in order for us to be able to pass legislation based on these new ideas. But, the process has started and now it is impossible for us to evade the 'invasion' of these ideas."[141] Despite Quirós's faith in the inevitability that criminal sciences would take hold in Spain, Spain's criminologists never offered clear, comprehensive plans for their implementation as government policy. This last passage shows that Quirós was not averse to making a case for the logic of eugenic measures in society, even while arguing that social factors, nutrition, and class status all played formative roles in the creation of crime. This failure to offer consistent and coherent programs for criminology was partially due to the complicated, multileveled view of criminal causation they presented. Were criminals congenitally programmed to commit crime? Or were criminals the products of a particular social milieu that often served as the catalyst for a criminal who might have developed with a degenerate lineage?

The requirements of the Restoration system also denied criminologists the political space to argue for any more than the mildest of reforms, especially the more fundamental changes they thought would diminish criminality in Spain. For most criminologists, a program of social reform, land redistribution to increase wealth in rural areas, and various calls for urban reforms to make the city more hygienic were potential methods to confront the psychological elements of criminal behavior, to ameliorate the desperate conditions in which people lived. Yet, these kinds of reforms were considered far too radical for the brokered and fundamentally conservative Restoration system to consider, much less to promote. These reforms also focused too much on criminals and their cure, and not on the damage they inflicted on society. Certainly, Dorado's example was illustrative; Dorado was often labeled a revolutionary (even by fellow criminologists) for arguing that only through an analysis of a criminal's intent, with its implication that crime was sometimes the rational response to desperate circumstances, could the state accurately impose punishment. Such a reaction certainly did not represent a hopeful sign for the large-scale application of the criminal sciences that was promoted by Spanish criminologists in turn-of-the-century Spain.[142]

During the first decade of the twentieth century, clear signs of political and scientific will emerged among scientists to expand upon the criminal sciences already being developed in Spain. In response to the recent assassinations of Conservative Party head Cánovas del Castillo (1897) and an attempt on the lives of the Spanish monarchs (1906), government officials suspended ideological resistance to aggressive scientific endeavor and pushed for the creation of centers to educate police and prison officials to understand the roots and causes and ultimately the methods of prevention of criminal behavior. These calls for the expansion of the anthropological study of crime were joined between 1900 and 1905 by most Spanish criminologists, who had long demanded the creation of schools in which to train a future corps of experts and practitioners in the criminal sciences. Salillas and Quirós both made efforts to create schools through private initiative, with Salillas hoping his could be an adjunct of the ILE. Salillas had also negotiated from his position within the Ministry of Grace and Justice for the creation of a school.[143] Demonstrating again that science alone was not anathema to conservative thinkers, Salillas had the most success negotiating with a conservative government, obtaining in 1903 a royal decree under the Minister of Grace and Justice Eduardo Dato that created the School of Criminology (Escuela de Criminología). The government, however, wanted some control over the school. Salillas noted in a letter to Giner de los Ríos that the government had been far more interested in the people who were going to teach in the school than in the curriculum. Concessions had to be made only in terms of participants.[144]

The most important compromise apparently was not having Salillas's friend Dorado participate in the school. It remains unclear how strenuously Salillas fought to have Dorado included, though in his letters he seemed to express more anger and shock to Dorado than to Giner about the exclusion of Dorado from the faculty.[145] Dorado did leave an impact on the curriculum of the school, which focused as much attention on the individual study of criminals and their motives as on the physical and environmental characteristics that functioned as predictors of criminal behavior.[146] The faculty of the school, which was given space in Spain's first penitentiary, Madrid's Model Prison, was comprised of the country's leading psychologists, anthropologists, and criminologists. Federico Olóriz, with whom Salillas had petitioned for the school, was charged with teaching anthropometry. Manuel Antón, who held the chair of anthropology at the Central University of Madrid, taught ethnology and anthropology. The Spanish psychiatrist Luís Simarro, who at the same time became an active member of the European Free Thinkers League, taught experimental psychiatry, stressing the role of brain lesions in the creation of criminal insanity. Salillas and Manuel Cossío, both instructors in the ILE, taught criminology and legal philosophy. The curriculum was thus designed to provide a wide-ranging view of criminal anthropology, focusing not only on the causes and nature of crime and criminals but also on their identification and treatment once in custody.[147]

The reason most often cited for why the school was needed was to train a corps of prison and police personnel. Much to the continued frustration of the school's founders, however, the school's curriculum, approved by the conservative government's Ministry of Grace and Justice, concentrated only on the methods of identifying prisoners and criminals.[148] The school might have had a wide-ranging curriculum in the new criminal sciences, but the jobs that awaited the graduates were mostly in the anthropometric offices of Spain's prisons. While the anthropological and scientific press, for example, bemoaned this small step in the expansion of the criminal sciences, the specialized prison and police journals, most of which maintained a critical stance toward criminal anthropology, celebrated each instance when anthropological measurements were used to identify repeat offenders who might otherwise have escaped notice with more traditional police identification procedure.[149] Despite the misgivings of its professors, the school enjoyed a substantial and long-lasting supply of students throughout the first two decades of the twentieth century. In a speech to the Royal Academy of Medicine in 1911, Olóriz discussed how the school had succeeded in making knowledge of the criminal sciences as common among Spain's educated elite as knowledge of medicine and psychiatry. Even more, the school and the anthropologists working in it had helped disperse to a wider public the general awareness of the role of race in the ranking of European nations and the knowledge therefore of Spain's racial position in relation to the rest of Europe.[150]

Yet what racial ideas about Spain did the school present? One can assume that, with the control over anthropology courses exercised by Olóriz, Antón, and Salillas, the anthropological perspective offered to students focused both on Spain's mixture of races and the role this mixture had on Spanish culture. Olóriz, who had been the first to define physically the contours and nature of Spain's racial mixture, wrote that the ideas presented in the school in part had allowed him to understand that racial difference formed in the same way as differences between criminals. Thus, criminals were not solely the products of physical lineage, an idea that Olóriz had long debated with Lombroso.[151] Rather, criminals emerged out of the confluence of different causes, with environment often the catalyst that triggered the beginnings of criminal behavior: "I believe that criminality is something so complicated and varied that the process of understanding it cannot be reduced to simplistic schemes, or absolute formulas. In fact, even when it becomes possible to accept as certain universally applicable criminological ideas, they will still have to have the flexibility to explain each particular, individual case, without destroying aspects of the general principle. The system I would support would be the Doctrine of Opportunism, a general principle that would sustain and explain all contingencies with its ample set of explanatory tools."[152]

The school labored throughout the first two decades of the twentieth century under the threat that its funding would be cut off if the political mission of the teachers began to conflict with state policy. Attention was to be focused primarily on understanding the appearance of anarchists and terrorists within the Spanish population.[153] Yet, the faculty of the school did not seem to adhere too closely to this admonition. In one letter to the director of the school, Manuel Cossío, the anarchist writer Joan Montseny asked Cossío if he could spare a teacher to instruct students at a satellite school, in Andalucía, of Francisco Ferrer's Modern School. Ferrer had made this request to Montseny from prison, where he was completing his sentence for allegedly conspiring to assassinate the king in 1906, a crime for which he was eventually executed despite the lack of evidence and a large-scale Europe-wide protest.[154]

Clearly, the goals of the government that ran the school and the political mission of the school's faculty often conflicted. In 1917, Salillas, Cossío, and Luís Simarro were all forced out of the School of Criminology for allowing "permissive ideas" and an air of radicalism, revolution, and anarchism to reign.[155] Writing four years later to the newly reformed Spanish Association of Anthropology, Ethnology and Prehistory, Salillas commented that the school troubles were not the result of its faculty's abilities or the state-imposed goal of suppressing anarchist violence. Rather, he noted the problem lay in the lack of funding and any real possibility of work outside prisons' anthropometric labs for the graduates of the school. Often the repressive forces of the police and the army destroyed evidence essential for anthropological analysis. At other times, they ignored suggestions from the prison officials about how to prevent crime using anthropological data that predicted who and where likely candidates for criminal activity came from or lived. One other complaint focused on the lack of interest in the school among the students. The director, Manuel Cossío, complained that the school had become a repository for children of Spain's elite who placed them in the school in order to guarantee a profession and status for their children. Requests to administrators from parents for the school to overlook cheating on exams or failing grades seemed to prove this point.[156] Salillas also complained that students were pulled out of the school before their education had been completed because the state wanted some procedure, most commonly the identification of criminals using anthropometric analysis, to be conducted without regard to the nonphysical causes of criminal behavior.[157]

Conclusion

Speaking to the new Spanish anthropological society more than two decades after the publication of *El delincuente español*, Salillas did not disavow any of the racial interpretations of criminal development he had offered in his earlier book. In fact, the members of the society—including Luís de Hoyos Sáinz as its secretary, Salillas as its vice president, and Ángel Pulido, the former secretary of González de Velasco's 1874 Spanish Anthropology Society—still promoted racial investigation of the Spanish population using both the physical and cultural methods they had presented twenty years earlier.[158]

At the same time, the ethnographic approaches of Telésforo de Aranzadi and Manuel Antón also seemed to have attracted the attention of some of the anthropologists in the society. Studies were commissioned to identify the various styles of cultural artifacts in Spain, to locate the essential elements in these diverse styles, and to identify the characteristics of the fused Spanish type.[159] Antón y Ferrandiz presented new measuring tools for acquiring the most accurate craniometric measurements of people.[160] He also counseled the new society to look toward North Africa for the racial roots of the Spanish population. After decades of stalemated colonial wars, Antón suggested that better anthropological understanding of the enemy could be the most effective weapon for the Spanish military. Interestingly, he argued that this understanding would not only work to devise military strategy to defeat the enemy but also to find the common links between Spanish and North African races and cultures that would be used to quiet the insurgent colonial subjects.[161]

The work of the society highlighted the trajectory that Spanish anthropology, including the criminal sciences, followed throughout the late nineteenth and early twentieth centuries. While a group of scientists worked successfully to create a discrete scientific discipline and a self-sustaining profession, their research struggled to find outlets into actual political and social policy. The discipline certainly developed and even within criminal anthropology found actual sites for its public use in prisons and police identification procedures. Among the small group of anthropologists, the exploration of racial mixture and the shifts in the more general development of anthropology throughout Europe led scientists to use a variety of approaches to analyze and ultimately to define the various components of the Spanish racial mix. In addition, these scientists attempted, like their counterparts elsewhere, to lend social and political significance to their ideas about mixture and to give them a certain social force to change the way Spaniards managed civil society.

Yet, the theme of mixture allowed different members of the scientific and then the larger intellectual community to point to distinct behaviors as problematic while never agreeing upon an image of the national body they were attempting to define. Salillas's efforts highlighted the growing scientific consensus that mixture was the key element of Spain's racial heritage. His work, and the school of Spanish criminology that it inspired, did not, however, fashion a unified view of how this mixture created criminals or a prescription for how to treat them. For Bernaldo de Quirós, the antirevolutionary member of the Liberal Party, the cities and the working-class neighborhoods seemed to breed criminals because there, in the congested and closed urban world, racial atavisms from throughout Spain would be introduced into and dispersed among a much wider array of the population than if these racial groups remained isolated in their regions.[162] For Salillas, anarchists were the unfortunate heirs of atavisms left by intermixture with gypsy populations. Yet, he had found so many other factors that contributed to criminal behavior that Salillas himself long advocated for the humane treatment of prisoners and the amelioration of the poverty-ridden social conditions that he thought activated racial atavisms that might otherwise remain dormant.[163]

The lack of consensus as to the meanings of Spanish racial mixture continued among Salillas's and Quirós's disciples. One student—and later head of the Spanish Criminological Institute, a state-funded laboratory that performed both physical and emotional testing on criminals—wrote that criminals in fact had become a distinct race, the product of nomadic isolation and subsequent interbreeding.[164] However, a few years later, he also moved away from the conclusions made from his craniometric study, arguing that such data were not informative without the psychological study of criminals to complete them: "The physical environment and the organism itself are nothing but wrappings that cover our spirit. . . . [W]e believe over all that the environment, the cranium and the brain are not so dense and impenetrable that we cannot glimpse in all its brilliance and solemnity the human soul."[165]

The failures of Spanish criminal anthropology to persuade the Restoration governments, either liberal or conservative, which all proved interested in cultivating the science and altering actual police policy and jurisprudence, were attributable primarily to the inability of the system itself to enact what would have been wide-ranging reform. However, the large-scale development of an infrastructure for scientific study of particular social problems laid the groundwork for future thought on the Spanish racial makeup and its social meanings. Figures active in later Spanish eugenics movements began their studies in the classrooms of the School of Criminology.[166] Influential literary figures who later wrote compellingly of the power and strength of the Spanish racial mix were trained in the anthropology classes of Spain's universities.[167]

Questions then remain as to how the racial thought at the turn of the twentieth century came to form the basis of later Spanish racial ideas. The later central focus of Spanish eugenics on changing the physical environment of people needs to be examined in relation to the anthropological and criminological sciences from which later eugenicists emerged.[168] In addition, the conservative racial thought of the 1920s and 1930s that sought to divest itself from its physical basis but also relied on the idea of the Spanish racial mixture as an important and beneficial element of the Spaniard must be examined in relation to its forebears at the turn of the century.

8. Remaking a Good Fusion, Excising a Bad

The Jewish Repatriation Movement in Spain, 1890–1923

The previous chapters have demonstrated that racial identity, as defined in anthropology and criminology, was a rather flexible concept. Most often the racial characteristics that were thought to define the nation or region reflected as much the particular interests and prejudices of the racial theorist as any objective interpretation of the scientific evidence. Race sometimes referred only to the physical characteristics of individuals in a national group. At other times, race was a compendium of cultural and social attributes of the individual or a region, defined partly by a vague sense of inheritance and partly by environmental conditioning. Underlying all of these positions was the assumption that fusion best characterized Spain's racial past. Though the idea of racial fusion was widely shared, certainly what caused this fusion and what qualities were ascribed to Spaniards fluctuated depending on the racial theorist and to what political or social purpose the idea of racial fusion was put. These scientific positions did not necessarily conform to any one political ideology. In fact, liberals were drawn to racial identities conditioned by social environments because they implied that individuals could somehow alter their own destinies with a simple change of scenery or economic status. Catholic traditionalists, like Marcelino Menéndez y Pelayo, saw the anthropological view of racial fusion as verification of the value of conversion. Anarchists, like the criminologist Pedro Dorado Montero early in his career, thought racial identity proved that societies were shaped by social and economic forces.

This final chapter explores the multiplicity of meanings and historical trajectory that racial fusion had in Spain through the experiences of one figure whose conclusions about race transcended a variety of the political positions.

His ideas led him to direct a movement to restore Spain's racial health by reintroducing a racial group that had been needlessly excised from the racial mix in the fifteenth century, Sephardim, or Jews of Spanish origin. This effort merits attention for several reasons. One, it was defined as a project to regenerate the Spanish race; in other words, it was a racial project of national reformation. Two, the Jewish repatriation movement in Spain overlapped in time the development of anthropological and criminological discussions of race. Three, the movement's leader used his racial ideas to defend a variety of political projects and to serve different political agendas throughout his career. Yet his basic sense of the value of racial fusion and its effects on Spaniards remained the same. As a result, Ángel Pulido y Fernández and the Jewish repatriation movement provide an good case study of how racial fusion supported a number of different political positions—especially because the individual who consistently supported this notion of race saw his own interests and ideas change quite a bit during the turbulent decades between 1890 and 1920.

The vast changes in the professional pursuits of the movement's leader, Ángel Pulido, provided an important backdrop for the evolution of his racial ideas. Pulido began as one of Spain's first modern anthropologists. He subsequently turned to criminology and then served in a variety of administrative and bureaucratic offices within the Spanish government. Among these were his most famous roles as a senator and a director of the Spanish postal system and Department of Public Health. He was an early advocate of public immunization (in response to the flu pandemic of 1918–19), the abolition of capital punishment, and the promotion of women's health.

Political changes matched career changes. Pulido began as a republican and an initial critic of the Restoration system. He remained throughout his life a close confidant of one of the Restoration's greatest enemies, Emilio Castelar. Later, he became supportive of the Liberal Party of the Restoration, as well as a great advocate of scientific interventions in social problems, specifically the expansion of scientific education and public hygiene. He ended his career still identified with the Liberal Party, but working closely with ideas more commonly associated with the Conservative Party and Catholic traditionalism. As a result, Pulido's exploration of the racial sciences and his efforts to use race to fix social and political problems mimicked the pattern traced in the previous chapters. The scientific ideas about race that he advocated were used to support a variety of political positions. The effort to repatriate Spanish Jews, a pursuit Pulido initiated in 1880 and that ended only with his death in 1932, was one example of how racial ideas were used to justify what were fundamentally political and social goals. Thus, this chapter explores in microcosm the larger shifts discussed earlier in political and scientific meanings of race during this period.

Ángel Pulido and the Early Conception of Race

Pulido's efforts to repatriate Jews began in earnest in 1903, when his career as a doctor and anthropologist had given way to more political pursuits as a result of his election to the Spanish Senate.[1] Most scholars have focused on his leadership of Jewish repatriation as a reflection of his politics and not of the scientific training that had occupied the previous three decades of his professional life.[2] This chapter assumes, however, that his political ideas cannot be divorced from his scientific ones. Instead, the issue is approached here with a sense that the two sets of ideas were far more interdependent, informing each other throughout his career. The repatriation of Jews for Pulido was always defined as a political act: to rejuvenate Spain by reintroducing an element of the Spanish racial fusion inherent in its makeup, the removal of which, with the expulsion of Jews from Spain in 1492, had caused the decay of the Spanish nation. However, Pulido's mission to repatriate Sephardic Jews must be viewed through the lens of the racial ideas that underlay them. Encouraging fusion and counteracting racial decay were Pulido's two primary motives for repatriating Jews. For Pulido, this act would in turn foster a healthy and thus prosperous Spain. Pulido's motives, then, were no different from the other members of what José María López Piñero called the Generation of the Learned (la Generación de los Sabios), which envisioned science not only as a profession but also as a tool for political, social, and even economic progress in Spain.[3]

Like other members of this group, Pulido's professional career started in medicine and quickly led to anthropology. Trained initially as a doctor, Pulido left Madrid in 1873 upon graduation from medical school and settled in the northern town of El Ferrol to serve in the army's medical corps.[4] Exhausted from his medical studies, Pulido had entered military service hoping for a tranquil experience in this small coastal city. After only a few months, Pulido recovered from his fatigue and grew weary of the quiet life in this provincial outpost. In 1873, he began to seek work in Madrid that would allow him to use both his medical training and his artistic abilities.[5]

Pulido was put into contact with Pedro González de Velasco, the founder of the Madrid Anthropology Society, by their mutual friend Emilio Castelar, the head of a republican party. González hired Pulido to be the society's first secretary and an illustrator for the journal *Anfiteatro Anatómico Español*.[6] Pulido's interests lay, like those of the society in general, in physical anthropology and morphology, the study of the relationship between physical structures and biological function. Yet Pulido also saw early on within anthropology the potential source for understanding "the origins, viability and sociability of nations," which had long been considered the purview of historical and political study rather than anthropological measurement.[7] Pulido began to study and promote craniometry as the most effective tool in acquiring such information about nations. Emerging as the most vocal proponent of craniometry in the society, Pulido was drawn earlier than most to the comparisons of physical differences between the races, a study becoming known then as ethnology, and taught at the same time by Manuel Antón at the Museum of Natural History.[8] In forming such comparisons, Pulido argued that differences in religious practices and what he called "cultural attributes," like folk customs and diet, also played an as yet unknown role, either determinative or merely regulative, in shaping racial differences: "The comparative study of the various races that populate the Earth revolves around the question of similarities and differences, and the most accurate assessments of their abilities. It is important, gentleman, to identify the as yet undetermined ascendance of our human species. We must determine scientifically whether this development was of a unique lineage or had multiple influences, if different races come from common or different origins, and if the differences among them are due to nutrition, social custom, religion . . . and finally how much development can be influenced by physical and moral changes."[9]

Pulido considered Spanish anthropologists as especially qualified for this type of multidimensional analysis of the races. Because anthropological study was developing after other competing European schools had already taken shape, Spain had the benefit of combining different kinds of study. Spanish anthropologists could filter out the elements of these methodologies that he thought were tinged with national chauvinism. He thought Spanish anthropology provided a potential midpoint between the competitive and contradictory conclusions of Broca and his disciples in the French school and those of the leader of the German school, Karl Vogt.

> With respect to various theories of civilizing tendencies, it is important to determine the relative accuracy of all of the portraits provided. Does Civilization exist

only in relation to a specific atmosphere and environment, as the French would have it? Or is the truth closer to the specific physiological ideas of Vogt, who as member of the Germanic Race, with a much more pronounced and desirable dolichocephalic cranium, considers the French conclusions as examples of their vanity and confusion since they also say that this environment has produced an medium-sized mesocephalic heads, hallmark of Civilization.[10]

As his prestige grew as secretary of Velasco's Anthropology Society, Pulido began to present his developing definitions of anthropological study to a much larger audience. He became an editor of the dominant medical journal El Siglo Médico.[11] He became a member of the Royal Academy of Medicine in 1884, and he also emerged as an important voice in the debates surrounding criminology of the 1880s.[12] Yet, here, too, Pulido viewed the Spanish criminal sciences as benefiting from the perspective its later development made possible. Spaniards were able to avoid the overly technical and rational treatment of criminals whose crimes were so heinous that their scientific explanations, which, in many cases, argued for treatment rather than punishment, were easily ignored in favor of rapid execution or long prison sentences.[13] In fact, Pulido had long argued that all science must be reflective of the national context in which it developed. He faulted many of Spain's scientists for mindlessly applying European sciences in a resistant and inequivalent Spanish context. For example, Pulido directed trenchant critiques toward his mentor José María Esquerdo, with whom he had studied in medical school, for his efforts to instill biological determinist criminology in Spanish jurisprudence. Writing in 1881, Pulido criticized Esquerdo not only for testifying for the defense of José Díaz Garayo (El Sacamantecas), a serial murderer and rapist, most of whose victims were young women and girls, but also for misrepresenting the role and value of science to a Spanish populace that associated any defense of Garayo as condoning or excusing his murders.[14]

A more nuanced understanding of the Spanish populace with its racial proclivities would have elicited a more effective strategy. Spaniards, he wrote, were by nature democratic and open to free exchange of ideas. Thus, a more discreet airing of Esquerdo's arguments, situated in a discourse accessible to Spanish viewers, who were resistant to positivist ideas, would probably have convinced the nation to treat Garayo as a sick person in need of humane and scientific treatment. It was not the value of the science but its misapplication in the Spanish context that drove Pulido's criticism. Pulido suggested that a scientific discussion cloaked in religious terms would probably have helped achieve Esquerdo's goals: "Success belongs not to the passionate ones who confuse and silence opponents but to the believer who explains and persuades . . . not to the atheistic rationalist who wants to impose his ideas for what are truly heretical goals, but to those with the serious spirit of that most sanctified Father, who wants to cure with love an insane person and liberate the insane with the tool of human justice."[15] Pulido was not merely recommending strategies to Esquerdo for accommodating rational criminal sciences to a fundamentally irrational religious Spain. Rather, Pulido was presenting the historical context of Spain, the formation of its cultural attitudes and religious moral viewpoint, as important, scientifically verified aspects of Spanish social thought. Spaniards were not congenitally resistant to science; they only fought its antireligious, anti–free will implications. For Pulido, cultural and religious attributes of a nation were as systemic as their physical features. As a result, Pulido assumed that the democratic spirit of the Spanish produced a nation ever open to new ideas and willing to debate them in this "new era of free public debate."[16] Scientists could only aid in the acceptance of science if they couched its application in religious imagery. Pulido's view of the essence of Spain did not just emerge from his anthropological analysis. It was also shaped by his political ideas. The next section explores Pulido's political formation and how it dovetailed with his scientific conception of Spain's racial composition and temperament.

Pulido, Politics, and the Jews

Pulido's political views were formed between 1868 and 1876, a time span that included Spain's Revolution of 1868, the year he entered medical school; the declaration of the First Republic in 1873; its end in 1874 with the Restoration of the Bourbon monarchy; and the signing of the constitution of 1876. He graduated from medical school in 1878 having been taught by some of the most famous scientists associated with republican politics in the period, Pedro Mata, Pedro González de Velasco, Francisco María Tubino, and José María Esquerdo. In addition, Pulido had formed a close friendship with and served as the personal doctor for the leader of one faction of republicanism in Spain, Emilio Castelar.

Among the various parties that made up Spanish republicanism, Pulido aligned himself with one of its most conservative wings throughout the Restoration.[17] Castelar's possibilist republicans gathered around the themes of democracy, individual rights, and free markets, departing from the more radical republican groups that argued for decentralizing the Spanish state, creating public and secular education, and even instituting a federated division of political power in Spain.[18] Castelar's faction supported a pragmatic promotion of reforms that members thought had a chance of being implemented, considering the size and strength of the opposition and the lack of commitment from a quiescent populace. Pulido was attracted to Castelar's argument, viewing it as a natural approach more attuned to the slower, evolutionary pace of national development. As societies evolved, their politics became freer and more democratic, according to Pulido. Borrowing from the catastrophists of evolutionary biology and geology, Pulido argued that civilization was not created in rapid, massive leaps.[19] Revolutions did not remake societies; they merely initiated shifts in the long evolutionary development of nations. Yet, Pulido did not think that all nations shared the same evolutionary future or end point.

Perhaps reflecting his recent reading of the French philosopher Hippolyte Taine, who was already wildly popular in Spain, Pulido saw each society as endowed with certain local or indigenous characteristics that governed the pace and type of political and social transformation that could take place. For Pulido, these characteristics were scientifically verifiable facts, not, as Taine asserted, the esoteric idea of nation characterized in its artistic production: "The life of a people is dependent on a number of local circumstances. It happens so frequently that upon examining aspects of the native land, one sees the psychological disposition of a particular civilization emerging from its locale. . . . [B]iology, anthropology and natural history have all demonstrated this as a scientific fact; history and sociology have amplified the importance of these scientific lessons."[20]

Influenced by discussions of degeneration, especially those of the Italian criminological school, Pulido did not consider positive evolution a scientific certainty. Rather, he thought rapid political changes could potentially derail a nation's evolutionary progress. In fact, over the course of the Restoration, Pulido lost the vestiges of the revolutionary ardor he had developed in the university and medical school in the late 1860s and 1870s. By the 1880s and 1890s, he had become an advocate of slower change, arguing that Spain's particular history, its past glory, and its present decay in the late nineteenth century were the products of predictable, diagnosable problems in its evolution. This view of Spanish history did not grow solely out of Pulido's idiosyncratic scientific imagination. Pulido adapted ideas first presented by republicans during Spain's liberal *sexenio* (1868–1874) to justify in part his effort to repatriate these Spanish Jews.

Castelar, Pulido, and the History of Spain

In 1870, Emilio Castelar wrote that democracy and liberty were the two most enduring products of Spanish history. Castelar presented Spain as a fusion of Celto-Roman influences with Visigothic blood. This combination, in his view, forged a people fundamentally democratic, egalitarian, and Catholic, an aggregation of their Roman descent. Spain began its national history as a democracy, conquering the aristocratic and hierarchy-loving Visigothic strains among Spaniards: "Liberty began to form the soul of our people. Popular rights, the seed of democracy, the fecund seed that saturated the blood of our parents, and enveloped itself in their viscera. An athletic race, valorous, resistant to any foreign yoke, disposed toward liberty, incompatible with foreign control, without social distinctions, with religious or political privilege."[21] Yet, Visigoths and later Arab incursions had left behind stains of aristocratic feeling, love for hierarchy, and social domination in the Spanish racial mix. As a result, the reign of Charles V—grandson of Spain's Catholic Monarchs, yet raised in Flanders and of "Visigothic descent"—had destroyed the very democratic institutions that had become tangible expressions of Spain's racial spirit. Charles V introduced absolutism, a monarchical framework that "weakened our blood . . . and sold us vilely to a foreign influence."[22] Writing immediately after the Revolution of 1868, Castelar declared that the recent abdication of Isabel II and the debates about forming a republic in Spain reflected the reconquest of Spain's racial spirit.[23]

Castelar's presentation of Spanish ancient and early modern history as a struggle between Celto-Roman blood and Visigothic blood was not novel. In fact, his version was one of many alternatives that presented Spain's political makeup emanating from its racial heterogeneity. However, the defining role that democracy played in Castelar's history and the racialism of his discourse were clear markers of the republican politics he was advocating. Its historic and racial links to Rome left indelible impressions on the Spanish makeup, influences strong enough that, after lying dormant for centuries, were rekindled when political circumstances changed. Spain was programmed for democratic institutions.[24] Within a year of writing his racial history of Spanish democracy, Castelar gave his first speech on the floor of the Cortes, arguing for the revocation of the Edict of Expulsion and the inclusion of a provision in the constitution to assure religious tolerance in Spain. This 1869 speech presented a view of Sephardic Jews as intrinsically linked to Spain's era of world supremacy. Castelar thought democracy and heterogeneity were synonymous concepts. Thus, the desire for religious purity that drove the expulsion order offered the first intimation that Spanish leaders were working against the racial spirit of the nation: "[Ideas that] had as yet not succeeded in the world—one religion for all and one nation for all . . . Alexander, Caesar, Charlemagne, Charles V and Napoleon tried to accomplish the second and failed. The idea of variety conquered the conquerors. The variety of consciences conquered the Pontiffs and the variety of people conquered the warriors."[25]

Part of Castelar's support for heterogeneity and variety as hallmarks of Spanish greatness were conditioned by experiences ten years earlier during Spain's first colonial wars in Morocco in 1859–60. During this conflict, Sephardic Jews living in Morocco had famously come to the aid of Spanish soldiers. Some requested the opportunity to convert to Catholicism so they could legally enter Spain as Spanish citizens.[26] Others, citing their ancient ties to Spain, requested permission to reenter Spain and establish trading and financial centers. In addition, the Spanish press on the peninsula, relying on scattered eyewitness accounts, provided constant reports of Sephardic Jews greeting Spanish soldiers with cries of support in Spanish.[27]

The effect of this contact, whether real or imagined, among Spanish liberals was an increased interest in exploring the potentials of a population that seemed to have preserved the Spanish language and Spanish culture over such a long period. In addition, some Spanish liberals saw these Jews, whom they associated with finance and capital, as potential sources of international commerce for Spain. Turning the usual antisemitic trope on its head, Spanish liberals hoped that because Jews were good with money and finance, and Sephardic Jews were no exception, their associations and clear identification with Spain could be used to jump-start Spain's moribund international trade relations with Europe and the East.[28] A newfound interest in Spanish Jewry began to proliferate within literary and intellectual circles. The first critical histories of Spain and Sephardic Jews were written in which Jews were presented not solely as deicides but also as contributing elements of Spanish civilization in the Middle Ages.[29] In addition, writers like Benito Pérez Galdós, Emilia Pardo Bazán, and Leopoldo Alas (Clarín), began to incorporate Sephardic Jewish characters into their works, presenting them as instructive, rational counterpoints to fanatic, misguided Catholic characters.[30]

In fact, as one historian has noted, this interest in Sephardim was not just a reflection of an actual interest in Jews themselves and their contributions to Spanish society. Rather, Sephardic Jews became in the nineteenth century a marker that delineated the larger political divide in Spain between liberal and conservative, Left and Right. The role Jews had played and, for some, could still play in Spanish society became a vehicle for discussions of what was wrong with Spanish society. Spanish liberals saw Jews as potential modernizers replete with a cultural attachment to Spain. Conservatives still saw Jews as deicides and potential threats to Spain's Catholic unity.[31] While Castelar's historical vision was steeped in racial rhetoric, his ideas lacked scientific support. For him, race was a cultural concept that implied inheritance, relying on the idea that temperaments and political sensibilities were somehow transmitted over the generations. Yet, even without scientific substantiation, Castelar's racial view did not contravene the racial ideas being fostered by republican colleagues in the nascent fields of anthropology, among them his disciple, Ángel Pulido. Pulido tested his mentor's ideas in the scientific realm. For Pulido, Jews had a greater role to play in Spain than to be used in diagnosing the nation's larger problems. Rather, Pulido was the first to argue that the return of the Jews to Spain represented an important and scientifically justifiable project that could lead to the recovery of Spain's racial health. If Jews had been an important element of the Spanish racial mix when they were removed four hundred years earlier, Pulido argued, their return would make whole the fractured and moribund Spanish race.

Pulido's Crusade to Repatriate Sephardic Jews

In the period following the Restoration in 1874, Pulido heeded Castelar's advice to break with the republican party and join forces with Práxedes Mateo Sagasta's Liberal Party. By so doing, Pulido argued, he was in a position to work within the Restoration system to begin the scientific improvement of Spain.[32] This break was important for it led to Pulido's election to the Cortes and then the Senate, in 1893 and 1903, respectively.[33] As a result, Pulido acquired a political pulpit from which to advance his efforts to repatriate Spanish Jews.

His first contact with Sephardim came during a cruise along the Danube between Budapest and Vienna in 1883. Three Sephardic businessmen approached Pulido upon hearing him speak Spanish. Their conversation with Pulido was the first he had ever had with Jews. They informed him of the large Sephardic community in the Balkans and in Asia Minor that still spoke what Pulido thought was an ancient or broken form of Spanish rather than the Sephardic dialect, Ladino.[34] Recounting the event two decades later, Pulido noted that the first confusion he had upon meeting these men was whether they were in fact Spaniards since they appeared to be. They first approached Pulido, asking if he was a Spaniard:

> "Yes sir, I am. And by the looks of you, I assume you are too."
>
> The other responded: "Yes, I am but not from Spain. I am a Spaniard from the East . . . a Jewish-Spaniard."
>
> "Ah, I see . . . ," I exclaimed, trying to figure out at the same time what kind of Spaniard that is.[35]

This contact took place early in Pulido's own career, and, despite an occasional mention of issues relating to Spanish Jewry in El Siglo Médico or El Liberal, it did not seem to have much impact on Pulido's active political interests or his medical activities. He did advocate, however, for the licensing of a kosher butcher shop for the roughly three hundred Jewish families living in Madrid whose requests had been ignored.[36]

Of greater significance for Pulido was a longer conversation he had more than two decades later, again while cruising the Danube between Budapest and Belgrade. In August 1903, while visiting his son, who was attending medical school in Vienna, Pulido met Enrique Bejarano (Heinrich Bejarano), who was traveling with his wife, also a Sephardic Jew. Bejarano was the Romanian director of a Sephardic school in Bucharest that he had modeled on the Alliance Israélite Universelle in Turkey and Eastern Europe.[37] Bejarano informed Pulido about the more than 2 million Sephardic Jews spread throughout Asia Minor, the Middle East, the Americas, and the entire Mediterranean littoral. Their maintenance of the Spanish language, according to Bejarano, was the product of their underlying cultural allegiance to Spain.[38]

Pulido returned to Spain in 1903 and began a campaign to inform his countrymen of this substantial population of what he thought were hitherto unknown fellow Spanish speakers and former compatriots. He wrote a succession of newspaper articles for both the Spanish and Latin American press, all of which he collected in his first book on the subject, Los Israelitas españoles y el idioma castellano (Spanish Israelites and the Castillian Language, 1904). Dedicated not only to the minister of state, but also to the Academy of the Language, business associations, and groups of writers and artists, the book represented Pulido's first efforts to defend a plan of repatriating Spanish Jews to improve Spain's racial stock. Pulido also made famous speeches in the Senate in defense of Sephardic repatriation and began a movement that would have repercussions throughout the remainder of the twentieth century.[39] What most struck Pulido about Sephardic Jews was that they had maintained the Spanish language throughout their four-hundred-year exile from Spanish-speaking lands. For him, their persistent use of the language bespoke a deeper connection with Spain and specifically the Spanish peninsula of the fifteenth century. Like discovering a long-lost tribe fully isolated from the world, Pulido considered Jews of Spanish origin to be a repository of Spanish attributes from the period of its greatest national success, of the democratic tolerance that dominated the period beginning with the formation of its empire and the unity of the separate kingdoms prior to 1492. Unlike Castelar, Pulido approached the expulsion of the Spanish Jews in scientific terms, as an excision from the national body. As a result, Pulido wanted to reintroduce Jews to the Spanish mix. This effort would help reconstitute the Spanish race with the same ingredients and in the same proportion it had during its greatest historical moment.[40]

His method was first to perform ethnographic studies of Spanish-speaking Jews throughout the Mediterranean basin, the Balkans, the Middle East, and the Americas. In 1904, he prepared a questionnaire modeled on the 1902 ethnographic study of Spain published by the Madrid Athenaeum. The questions focused on the levels and quality of Spanish spoken in Sephardic communities, the numbers of Sephardic Jews living in the area, their folk customs (dances, songs), the level of instruction offered in "Jewish Spanish," and their knowledge of the Spanish homeland, or "patria."[41] Bejarano aided in the creation of these questionnaires and provided addresses for Sephardic cultural centers throughout Europe and among Turkish Sephardic communities.[42] Pulido hoped the questionnaires would elicit a portrait of the Jewish community of Spanish origin with a special focus on the "Spanish content of their identities."[43] Pulido also pointed out that the purpose of the study was to reacquaint Spaniards with a part of their racial past that clearly had not benefited Spain since its excision: "When we were children, we also believed that Jews were an abominable race, filled with all species of intellectual, moral, and even organic horrors, including even having a tail, things that ignorant and simple people could not countenance. To reacquire a sense of the exact nature and usefulness of Israel, many distant travels, constant study of *pueblos*, our own national disasters, and finally a burning desire to serve our Patria, Progress, and Humanity was required to overcome our previous ridiculous prejudices."[44] The effort to reintegrate Jews into Spain was thus a dialectical process: learning about Spanish Jews also provided knowledge about Spain and remediation for the national disasters that afflicted it. The repatriation of Jews would lead to the "reconstitution of the Spanish race and improvement of the patria."[45]

In fact, throughout Pulido's career, he expended as much energy tracing the effects of the expulsion on the Spanish populations left behind as on the Sephardic Jews who actually left. Of especial importance was the effect of this removal on the Spanish racial mix. Excising Spanish Jews had left Spain bereft of a key component of its racial mix, with the resulting homogeneity producing disastrous effects: "The resulting frightful and miserable homogeneity of Spanish cities, as closed off to cosmopolitan life as they are to the pacifying and edifying effects of having people in all of their infinite racial derivations and beliefs; one other odious result has been the belief in our ignorance and fanaticism with which advanced nations have judged and condemned us."[46] Mixture was a delicate process, according to Pulido. Spanish Jews and Spaniards had clearly intermixed and improved each other; however, not all mixtures were productive and healthy. In fact, Jews and Spaniards shared a kind of robustness engendered by racial mixing that had led other nations to decay.[47] Pulido went further, suggesting that a hierarchy existed among races when mixture predominated. Among all of the nations where Jews mixed with the home population, the Sephardic groups added the best qualities to the admixture of Jewish and non-Jewish blood. Other European nations experienced racial degeneration as a result of racial mixture. In Spain, Sephardic Jews clearly had prospered as a result of blending with the Spanish populations. Jews of German and northern European descent were "degenerate because of their mixtures." Spanish Jews had emerged as the most beautiful of all Jewish peoples as a result of their mixture with Spaniards.[48]

Physical characteristics were not the sole indication of racial affinities between Spaniards and Spanish Jews. Following Telésforo de Aranzadi's and Luís de Hoyos Sáinz's additions to Olóriz's cephalic index studies of Spaniards, Pulido considered physical markers to be mere signs of a shared racial past.[49] Other characteristics, especially cultural and environmental ones, determined the success and value of racial mixture. Sephardic Jews clearly shared physical characteristics with their Spanish brethren. Yet, more important for Pulido's calls for repatriation was that Jews and Spaniards shared similar forms of comportment, dress, and behaviors that demonstrated the value of their former intermixing: "Even personal impression shows the exact physical similarities between Sephardim and the Spanish type. They are tall and short, blond-haired and brunette, wide-nosed and flat-nosed, hairy and bald, outgoing and dry, lively and calm. Even looking at their expressions, dress, and personal aspect, nothing indicates that they are from a race different from the Spanish."[50]

For Pulido, these racial similarities provided the basis for his calls to bring the two groups back together. If racial affinity was proven in the past, the separation of the races had to have had negative consequences for one or both races. Mixture had led to a sharing of the positive qualities of both races and to a form of racial fusion that had allowed both groups to prosper together. The expulsion disrupted this racial fusion and had led to decay:

> Israelite surnames and first names shine throughout our genealogical tree. One can still see in our cities the distinct signs of their old neighborhoods. In their synagogues, they still pray with the same honest devotion as we do. Their words pepper our speech. Their philosophical, medical and literary works have been sprinkled all across our intellectual fields. At the height of our Reconquest, their blood and heroism also shined. In our public and financial life, we were privileged to learn from their expertise. In the continuous and powerful nutritive sharing that underpins universal existence, such mixtures always make superior, even if sometimes strange, some from the more unfortunate, isolated few. Only God knows how and how much mixture has defined life; or, how much two peoples linked to the same land for centuries have struggled together to make successful coexistence against the pain and misery that torments so many other people.[51]

He also noted that Spaniards and Jews had become so racially linked that once separated, they underwent similar transformations.[52] Following Aranzadi's claims about the effects of social environment on racial development, Pulido noted that Spaniards languished with the expulsion of Jewish learning and financial acumen, while Spanish Jews suffered isolation living in an alien environment far from Spain. This inability to adapt to a new environment led them to retain their Spanish as a defense against new cultures or racial influences.

> It is always our adversaries and never us who best define. It is not our desire or will that forms us but rather our environment, telling us what we are going to be and why. Thus, this conservation of Castilian and our ancient customs says more about Spanish Jews and their links to us than any spirit of retention, or instinctive resistance, or elements of their race, or religious traditions. . . . [O]ne should attribute it to the fact that any place Spanish Jews found themselves after they left was unbearable for them spiritually. It was like mixing two unblendable or repellant liquids. Thus, they maintained what was instinctively good for them, knowing they could not establish the same roots in the places they found themselves.[53]

Thus, Pulido was launching a defense of Jewish repatriation along the grounds that it would mutually aid both Sephardic Jews and Spaniards. Jews had been members of Spain's elite. Losing this aristocracy, Spain experienced a concomitant loss of its medical, scientific, agronomic, financial, and industrial expertise. These elements that, he noted, no society could live without needed to be reincorporated into a moribund Spain. The country had, in fact, lost the war precisely because of the lack of scientific acumen that had afflicted the nation. Thus, returning Jews to Spain would reintroduce the catalyst—the racial energy and creativity—needed for Spanish modernization.[54]

Pulido was certain to cast this racial argument in what he called nonracist terms. He, like his anthropological colleagues in Spain, attacked the racist writings of other European anthropologists on the grounds that they misguidedly sought to define racial strength in terms of pure lineages and racial hierarchies. Pulido argued that such a racial history was impossible, that all races were conglomerations. What distinguished them was the nature of the mixture and the particular relations between racial background and social and geological environment, an argument advanced by Hoyos and Aranzadi two years earlier in a study partially funded by Pulido.[55]

> We have always believed that circumstance and education are the factors that most distinguish one people from another. The ability to be educated is not an aptitude reserved for any one group or peculiar to any particular race. When one looks at the history of nations, especially when it was long, one can appreciate through the ups and downs of their power or through the ebbs and flows of their culture, that the success is defined by the morality of the governing bodies, by the levels of civilization a nation's neighbors have achieved, and by the genius of its public figures.[56]

Pulido followed this diagnosis of Spain's racial problems as being based in the loss of its aristocratic elite during the expulsion with some official efforts to reclaim Jews of Spanish origin. In 1904, he initiated debates in Congress calling for the expansion of Spain's naturalization laws to facilitate Spanish Jews becoming Spanish citizens. However, since Spain had lost its economically proficient aristocracy, he argued, it needed an infusion only of elite Jews. Especially in speeches to foreign audiences, Pulido emphasized the fact that Spain could not afford the influx of impoverished Jews.[57]

Pulido did have some success in these efforts. Changes to Spain's naturalization laws did begin the process of allowing some Sephardic Jews to request and in some cases receive Spanish citizenship.[58] The requests arrived mostly from Morocco from Sephardic Jews living in the Spanish colonies in Ceuta and Melilla. Pulido had noted that Moroccan Jews especially deserved citizenship because, with already established commercial ties, they would act as a vanguard for Spanish commerce into Europe and Latin America.[59] Pulido had greater success attracting intellectuals and writers to the cause of Sephardic repatriation. Max Nordau, who had befriended Pulido in 1904, and who would stay with Pulido during his exile from France during World War I, argued that Pulido's efforts would fail more from a lack of funding from Spanish authorities than a lack of will.[60] The liberal press in Spain, especially the newspaper Pulido helped direct, El Liberal, focused increasing attention on the plight of Sephardic Jews. These groups were especially drawn to Pulido's idea that the reinsertion of Jews would lead to a revivification of Spanish business and international commerce. As one historian noted, Pulido's efforts had "acclimatized" liberal Spain to the idea of Jewish repatriation as the key to Spanish modernization.[61] The results of these efforts were widespread. By 1915, the Central University of Madrid endowed a chair of Hebraic language and literature, appointing the German Sephardic Jew Abraham Shalom Yahuda. Both the king and Fidel Fita, a Jesuit priest and the director of the Real Academia de Historia, sponsored Yahuda's appointment. Nordau called the event the "Spanish surprise."[62]

Other intellectuals organized groups to help Sephardic Jews outside Spain, with the most famous incident taking place in 1913, after the Greek seizure of Salonica. The Sephardic population of about eighty thousand, which had always allied with Turkey in the region, began to suffer reprisals from Greek troops. Spanish intellectuals petitioned the king to grant these Sephardim Spanish passports. The outbreak of World War I forced many of these Turkish Jews to flee to France and Italy. Many Sephardic Jews begged Spanish consulates to intervene on their behalf, knowing that foreigners with ties to a neutral country would receive better treatment than those from enemy countries. A group of Spanish intellectuals and politicians, among them the scientists Santiago Ramón y Cajal, Luís Simarro, the Radical Party leader Alejando Lerroux, Rafael de Labra, Manuel Azaña, and Benito Pérez Galdós, wrote to the French and Italian prime ministers citing the Turkish Jews' unique links to Spain. The safe treatment of Turkish Jews, especially in comparison to other enemy aliens in France and Turkey, has long been credited to these efforts.[63]

Pulido's efforts also had an impact on the particular nonscientific discussion of race prevalent in Spain at the turn of the twentieth century.[64] Pulido's

reliance on the Sephardic maintenance of the Spanish language as evidence
of their conservation of Spanish cultural identity did attract other Spanish
intellectuals to the cause. Indeed, Miguel de Unamuno, who had read the anthropological work of his cousin Telésforo de Aranzadi, supported Pulido's
efforts but not quite in the scientific racial terms in which Pulido had placed
them.[65] Unamuno, who by the early 1900s had begun to reject scientific positivism as an "un-Spanish" form of thought, wrote to Pulido in 1904 agreeing that Sephardic Jews were repositories of the essence of Spanish culture
from the period of its imperial greatness.[66] He saw, for example, the repatriation in terms of a reinstallation of "pure, uncontaminated" Spanish values,
ideas, and energy lost after the 1492 expulsion. He wrote that Jews possessed
the language of a "youthful Spain" in the period of its greatest vitality and
strength before its decline in the fifteenth and sixteenth centuries. His efforts
to reinvigorate the Spanish race by reincorporating Spanish Jews were, he
wrote, a worthy goal.[67] Unamuno, however, having trained as a philologist,
saw the evidence of the Jewish maintenance of Spanish culture only in the
preservation of spoken Spanish and not in the physical attributes to which
Pulido also pointed. Language, he wrote, was a truer marker of racial identity
than any other characteristic: "You know the great value I confer on language;
much more than that of race. Scientifically, we still know so little about races.
. . . [E]ven though an anthropologist might discuss consanguinity, we know
that language is really the blood of the spirit."[68] Yet, Unamuno did not seem
to differ with Pulido on the nature or the explicit purposes of Jewish repatriation. It is important to note that, in 1904, Unamuno still had not rejected entirely the possibility that these anthropological bases existed. He wrote only
that they were as yet impossible to uncover.

In subsequent years, however, Unamuno provided fuller meaning to the
idea of racial identity being bound up in the health and dispersion of the
Spanish language. By 1920, he argued that the Spanish language was the sole
measure of the diffusion of the Spanish race. He disavowed more actively an
anthropological definition of race. At the same time, he seemed to accept the
position of scientists who had proven, he wrote, that racial history was the
story of fusion. Language was the key in racial concepts of Spaniards because
their physical legacy had disappeared via various fusions in Spain and in Latin
America. The only racial differences that were discernible were linguistic and
therefore cultural: "It would be best to stop using this error-prone term race,
or just give it a historical and human meaning rather than a naturalistic or
animal-based idea. . . . [W]here these animals races have persisted one has

seen them fuse into a human race, developing then a history, a civilization, rooted in language and its progeny, culture.[69]

Between 1910 and 1929, the movement itself focused more on the economic benefits of Jewish repatriation than on the explicit racial purposes outlined earlier by Pulido. Other intellectuals joined Pulido's efforts to repatriate Jews, yet their arguments were more attuned to Unamuno's linguistic racial arguments. Most followers also were more pointed in their arguments in favor of Jewish repatriation. Some, for example, wanted only to mimic the efforts of the Alliance Israélite Universelle in Spanish Morocco. Spaniards needed to acculturate the Sephardic Jews living nearby to solidify an economic vanguard for Spain into international commerce.[70] Between 1910 and 1923, a number of groups formed to guarantee that in the race to acculturate Sephardic Jews, Spaniards would quickly begin to set up cultural centers and Spanish language institutes to rival the Alliance system that was attracting Sephardic Jews to the French language and culture. In 1908, during the inaugural events for the Jewish-Hispanic Alliance (Alianza Hispanohebrea), the writer Carmen de Burgos (Colombine), a friend of Pulido's, expressed this mission in terms of national competition. Spain's success in spreading Spanish around the world would have no lasting benefit for Spain unless speakers remained bound culturally and economically to Spain: "Unfortunately, the truth remains that israelites who in spite of maintaining Spanish, actually use French, English, Italian, and German more correctly and with more proficiency. We have to engage in an effort of pure patriotism, concord, and fraternity to make Sephardic Jews love Spain by teaching them Spanish, filled with faith in the beneficial future effects of this effort."[71]

There were clear political purposes for the various arguments that justified the Jewish repatriation movement. For Pulido, the return of Jews was an avowed effort to enact the vision of his political mentor, Emilio Castelar. The expulsion of Jews caused an unhealthy excision of an otherwise healthful element of the Spanish racial mix. Spain degenerated without them. To regenerate, especially via colonial projects, Spain needed to retie "bonds between the two races."[72] Pulido, unlike Castelar, cast this process of degeneration in scientific and racial terms. The 1492 edict represented the triumph of religious intolerance and exclusion in a race that had actually formed as a result of opposing sensibilities: religious tolerance, democratic ideals, and a Spanish awareness of the need for economic acumen that Jews possessed and used to foster Spanish development. In a fitting allegory borrowed from histories of Spain written by Antonio Llorente and the American historian

William Prescott, Pulido illustrated how Spanish values were torn in different directions and eventually conquered by the religious fanaticism of the
Inquisition. Immediately after the expulsion decree, a group of Spanish Jews
approached King Fernando and Queen Isabella asking to buy back the right
of Jews to live in Spain. The king and queen, clearly convinced by the force of
the argument and compassion, began to sign papers to nullify the decree. At
that moment, the Grand Inquisitor Torquemada rushed into the room filled
with "religious fury," saying Jews sold Jesus to Pilate for money and now the
Catholic Kings were again falling prey to these malefactors: "And, uniting
action with word, he threw a crucifix on the table and rushed out. Frightened
and made uncertain by this audacious act, and also by the fact that the fre-
netic Torquemada was Doña Isabella's confessor, they decided not to fight
this religious fanaticism, and pursued the proscription of the Jewish people
from Spain."[73] The moral of this story was clear. The king and queen, guided
by reason to see the error of Jewish expulsion, were once again convinced by
a fanatic religious figure disdainful of the financial benefits of keeping Jews
in Spain, to split asunder the components of the Spanish race.

Race Becomes Class: Pulido, Politics, and a New Prescription to Combat Spain's Degeneration

Despite Pulido's successes in developing support for Jewish repatriation,
the movement did not catapult Pulido to positions of governmental power
where he could enact legislation to guarantee their return.[74] There were still
people unconvinced by Pulido's efforts. During the moments of his widest
acclaim, Pulido was appointed a senator for life, an appointment that gave
him a pulpit from which to defend the interests of Jewish repatriation. In a
more general sense, Pulido also used his position to expand scientific education so that more could be trained to understand the movement's purpose.[75]
Private practice and senatorial service dominated Pulido's life between 1905
and 1916. During World War I, Pulido suffered what he called a "nervous sickness" that led to his remaining in his apartment in the Royal Academy of
Medicine in Madrid for three years.[76]

This period of illness ended with the publication of new books on the
links between Jews and Spaniards. Pulido maintained the arguments he first
outlined in 1905, only focusing greater attention on the similarities in cultural
practices of Spaniards and Sephardim. Among them he noted correspondence in the two groups' reverence for motherhood, dance styles, and dress.[77]

Pulido also enjoyed the benefits of the maturing Sephardic associations that he helped found from 1910 to 1919.[78] He published increasingly with the *Editorial Ibero-Americana*, which had been founded by the scion of one of the few prominent Jewish families in Spain, the anthropologist Ignacio Bauer. Pulido helped direct Bauer's Universal Home of Sephardim (Casa Universal de los Sefardíes), an organization founded in 1920 and designed to compete with the Alliance Israélite Universelle by establishing a network of schools in the Spanish protectorate of Morocco.[79]

With the Jewish repatriation movement thus on firm institutional ground, Pulido turned his attention to social problems within Spain that he also thought were the product of Spain's racial development. Pulido's study *El cáncer comunista o la degeneración del socio-sindicalismo: Necesidad de su regeneración higiénica y moral* (The Communist Cancer; or Degeneration Caused by Social-Syndicalism and the Necessity of Moral and Hygienic Regeneration) tied together a series of newspaper articles he had written over the previous decade, published in the form of a doctor's case file for a sick patient. He dedicated the book to the then head of the Conservative Party, Camilo Calleja y García, hoping to elevate the book's analysis to the level of public policy recommendations. Two years earlier, Pulido had written that doctors needed to combine social analysis with medical and scientific knowledge in the aid of quelling the political violence and evolutionary disruptions of working-class organizations.[80] This study, Pulido's last major published work, detailed the process of Spanish degeneration based on the uncoupling of Spain's racial fusion. Yet, while his arguments mimicked in structure those used to defend Jewish repatriation, he deployed them in a contrary sense. Instead of remaking Spain's racial fusion by reincorporating a lost component, Pulido argued in 1921 that Spain's racial health could only be promoted by excluding elements that had found their way into Spain's racial makeup.

The period between 1917 and 1921 was particularly unsettled in Spain. Protests over military action in the colonies, general strikes, political assassinations, including that of the conservative prime minister Eduardo Dato, a friend of Pulido's, all culminated in the devastating military defeat in 1921 in Morocco. These developments brought Pulido to a conclusion about contemporary Spanish problems similar to one Castelar had reached in 1868. Pulido considered the root of the problem to be a foreign invasion of ideas, this time not from the Austrian Habsburg monarchy, but from syndicalist and communist ideas entering through Spanish ports, especially the capital of Catalunya, Barcelona. Unlike Castelar, however, Pulido suggested that these

foreign elements upset the racial fusionary balance within Spain. This disruption caused the peaceful social conditions that had been the hallmarks of
the healthy Spanish race to degenerate. The increasing allegiance to regional
nationalist movements and the ever more virulent working-class trade union
movement, the socio-syndicalists, as he called them, provided the clearest
evidence of this degeneration. According to Pulido, Barcelona had once been
the most idyllic representative of the positive qualities of the Spanish race:
vigor, intelligence, industry, and kindness. Barcelona was the "prototype of
the fusion of all of our excellent organic roots." Yet, the Catalan bourgeois
elite, seduced by its own success, began to argue that its prosperity was the
product of "autocthonous" and not Spanish qualities.[81] This elite had created a city with themselves as leaders, making reference to the victory of the
Lliga Regionalista, the conservative Catalan nationalist group that won parliamentary elections in the Generalitat in 1920. Pulido wrote that Catalonia
was turning into an "animal with the body of a lion and the head of a rat."[82]
They falsely considered their leadership qualities as the product of their separate lineage, when, according to Pulido, their successes were rooted in the
more general racial fusion beginning with the mixtures of Hellenic people
and indigenous populations.[83]

Even more corrosive to the Spanish racial blend was the increasing impact of foreign ideas on the working classes. For Pulido, it was not surprising
that "foreign pathogens" had taken root in industrial Barcelona, a port city.
Lying at the contact point with Europe, Africa, and Latin America, Barcelona
had absorbed a variety of invading forces, like communism, anarchism, and
socialism, that were ideological but also had biologically degenerative effects.
That ideas were degenerative in a physical sense was proven, according to Pulido, by the fact that clear violations of ethics and morality, like violations of
national unity and social order, had grave repercussions on the nation: "a vio-
lation of these essential ethics and organic functions, which characterize the
principal biological essence of life, leads to degeneration that is obvious in
the patient we are examining. These attacks have led to the fatal decay, a state
of degeneration, atavism and sterility, so serious that death of the patient,
without treatment, is assured."[84] Worse for Pulido were the signs that the
infection was spreading and beginning to threaten the entire nation. Pulido
focused on cities where recent general strikes and pitched battles between
trade unions and the military had taken place: "It was the worst possible case
that having been incubated and cultivated, a pathogen, a germ has infected

social life in so virulent, contagious a way that one can see it spreading to other cities, like Zaragoza, Seville, Valencia. They have destroyed the essential personality of these cities. Even more, they have begun to send Spain itself into the abyss of inferiority, delay, and barbarity that will determine the final insult and ruin of our Patria."[85] More than mere metaphor, Pulido saw this problem as a disruption of the positive process of racial fusion that had characterized the Spanish past. He viewed the nation as an organism capable of fighting off pathogens based on the strength of its racial stock. Yet, the world of 1921 provided far more threats to the Spanish national immune system than it had ever before experienced:

This type of morbidity is the result of infections and exotic diseases. Never before has Iberia or have the ethnic elements that constitute the Spanish Race—nor for that matter have the immigrant groups that have invaded and dominated here—carried the blood-borne symptoms of such a malignant condition as now dominates in our country. In contradistinction to the usual effects of mixture of the germs from the distinct races that have come here, now pathogenic germs require us to search in bacteriology for a polymorphous vaccine to prevent, alleviate, cure the grave sickness with which this same mixture of germs is now afflicting us. From Italy, France, Russia, Germany, and the Devil knows where else! have come numerous miscreants, fanatics, and lunatics who, resembling all terrorists, have developed and spread anarchistic, criminal doctrines that have infected the working class and created a vanguard bent on social destruction, committing hundreds of crimes, deteriorations, and incalculable ruin that has made Barcelona, for example, suffer for years.[86]

Regional nationalisms and the workers' organizations represented for Pulido the most malevolent potentials of a national disposition for racial fusions. These disruptions affected not only the social order but, more importantly, the sense of nation, national pride, and common purpose that normally was the product of a successful nation's racial history. The problem was that these pathogens directly attacked the exact qualities that the Spanish racial fusion had produced.

Patriotic feeling . . . is nothing more than a rigorous biological expression of the survival instinct that exists in the spirit as well as in the organism. Physically we are composed of that which our ancestors have passed in their carnal legacy, and also of that which nourishes us in each of our particular regions. In the same way, our soul is the inheritance of other elements that have been modified over the years by psychological nutritive elements that mold it, condition it, and imprint upon it a determined character made up of certain modalities, tones, vibrations, feeling, and impulses. . . . Our soul is a synthetic accretion of the secular soul of the nation, as our body is the synthetic, carnal accretion of material and ethnic factors that nourish it.[87]

The cure for these pathogens lay in fortifying the aspects of the Spanish character that other anthropologists had already outlined as beneficial for positive fusion. Of these aspects, religion was the most important. Pulido, who long described himself as a "practicing Catholic," presented Catholicism as a balm for revolutionary politics because it seemed to promote a love for democracy and national unity: "Religions tend to promote a certain social placidity. This is because the spirit of religion compels a certain healthful and beneficial democratic sense, in which the proletarian classes are indeed favored and protected."[88] It is important to notice how similiar this idea was to Manuel Antón's argument that Catholicism had helped soothe the more warlike characteristics of the important African races absorbed into the Spanish mix.

Pulido's ideas relied on the assumption that outward behaviors, political ideologies, and actions were the expressions of inherent biological characteristics conditioned both by the nation's racial past and its contemporary environmental conditions. As a result, Pulido could envision, like Castelar, enduring characteristics of the Spaniard that transcended centuries of Spanish history. Such characteristics, like the inherently democratic predisposition of the Spanish populace that had grown out of the indigenous and Greco-Roman admixtures of the previous millennium, and the basic attitude of tolerance, all lay buried within the Spanish race. Occasionally these characteristics were muted by foreign, environmental stimuli, as in the Austrian Habsburgs for Castelar, or in anarchism and communism for Pulido.

However, Pulido maintained the idea that changes in contemporary conditions, like the excision of these foreign pathogens, could help effect changes in Spain's current political and economic state. These changes, in fact, would help return the nation to racial status quo ante, when its positive racial spirit would flourish. As an anthropologist, Pulido had worked to define this inherent racial temperament of the Spaniard. He, like his other anthropological colleagues, saw this racial temperament as the product of a fusion of many different groups, in combination with geological, environmental, and social conditions. Reared at first in a revolutionary republican context and then in more a moderate liberal setting, Pulido assumed this racial fusion had produced a race of people predisposed toward democracy and tolerance of difference. He also saw the Spaniard as desirous of national unity and as a part of a social system governed by a scientifically derived natural order.

Trained as a doctor, Pulido associated any change to this image of Spain as an indication of an infection caused by a foreign-born pathogen. At the midpoint in his career, as he engaged with the issue of Jewish repatriation, Pulido counseled treatment that required reinserting Sephardic Jews back into the racial mix. The equilibrium of Spain's racial fusion had been disrupted by the expulsion of Jews. As a result, their qualities and their maintenance of spoken Spanish led Pulido to conclude that Sephardic Jews were the repository of Spanish cultural attributes of the fifteenth century, at the moment of Spain's worldwide ascendance. Thus, their return to Spain would signal the return of much-needed attributes that had long been lost. By the end of his career, Pulido began making this same argument in the obverse. If the return of Sephardic Jews was salutary, the removal of foreign ideas that threatened or weakened the healthful Spanish temperament needed to be excised. The two arguments were not contradictory. Rather, they relied on the same premise: Spain's temperament produced through racial mixture and environmental context required national unity, Catholicism, and a respect of the social order that was rooted in nature. Any threat was therefore the product of a biological menace that required medical treatment.

Pulido's ideas did seem to reflect the historical context in which he was writing. During the relative stability of the Restoration, Pulido responded to the losses of the Spanish colonies and its perceived economic backwardness with the hope of recapturing aspects of Spain's liberal, economically advanced, and powerful past. During the 1920s, in response to further military defeat, but more importantly to class unrest in the form of larger working-class movements and political violence, Pulido emerged as equally concerned with tackling these threats to social order with biological weapons. It is important to note that the structure of his racial ideas remained the same. What changed was the perceived threat to the Spanish nation that these racial ideas were enlisted to combat.

The epilogue considers the legacy of this racial premise, especially in terms of the political viewpoints that it came to serve, demonstrating the malleability of the concept of race in late-nineteenth- and early-twentieth-century Spain. Rooted in the revolutionary moments of the Glorious Revolution of 1868, in the First Republic, and in the Restoration, the scientific development of racial theories in Spain was still capable of serving a rather conservative agenda. The epilogue also examines how the legacy of the racial ideas discussed in the previous chapters came to be expressed in the 1920s and 1930s, during the particularly fractured period of the Second Republic and the Civil War. Eugenics movements and the desire to cure society via scientific means were the offspring of these efforts to define the Spanish race between 1880 and 1930.

Epilogue

The Concept of Race Lingers

This book has presented race in late-nineteenth- and early-twentieth-century Spain as a "mode" of viewing human differences that clearly did not rely on ideas of purity or obvious physical differences in appearance. Racial thought is contextual and dynamic, reflecting both the era in which it is expressed as well as an ever-shifting evaluation of the importance of human differences. Yet, in contemporary Spain, there still continues a strong effort, the legacy of Franco-era efforts to distance Spain from its wartime alliances, to shelter Spanish society from charges of racial thinking or its social practice, racism. As a result, an important impediment to confronting the existence of racial thought remains. A controversy over some photos appearing in a Spanish newspaper in 2008 serves as an important reminder of the complex ways in which the dominant view of Spanish history as magically free of racism collides with events that offer seemingly uncomfortable counterexamples.

During the 2008 Summer Olympic Games held in Beijing, an advertisement appeared in a Spanish sports newspaper in which the Spanish Olympic men's and women's basketball teams were posed with their hands pulling their eyelids to the side in an apparent attempt to resemble Asian facial features. The international reaction to this advertisement concentrated on whether the act reflected inadvert or intentional racial insensitivity. Rather than decry the gesture and the advertisement, many Spanish newspapers of different political positions condemned the reaction in the "Anglo-Saxon" press for criticizing a clearly "humorous" but certainly not "malicious" act.[1] One player noted that many of his good friends in the Canadian city in which he plays in the NBA are Chinese.[2] Another journal defended the act as inoffensive because a Chinese representative of the company for which the advertising photo was taken was not offended. The head of Spanish basketball noted that there could be no racist intent in the Spanish team's acts because, among other reasons, "the mixture of races in the world of basketball is total."[3]

The defenders of the image seemingly ignored any connection between the obvious stereotyping of Asian facial features and the idea of representing human differences in potentially demeaning, grotesque ways. Instead, they defended the image with an assumption garnered from Spanish history: that Spain could not harbor the same racist malice that countries with more racial historical baggage did. According to some Spanish commentators, other nations, the "Anglo-Saxon ones," with prolonged histories of racism like the United States and the United Kingdom, should not judge another nation's racial sensitivities. This subtle contrast assumed other nations' histories of racism left little room for them to condemn a country like Spain with a history relatively free of racial thought and racism. Again, the reaction reflected more the historical sense of Spanish freedom from racism than a more judicious and complex understanding of racial thought and racist stereotyping.

One goal of this work is to complicate this notion that Spain is historically free from racial thought. Rather than arguing that racism existed in Spain, this work has suggested that histories of nineteenth- and twentieth-century Spain need to take into account a far more complex relationship between racial thought and historical memory. In fact, some of the most important historical debates in Spain over the last half century have evolved over the issues of race, assimilation, and tolerance even if the participants themselves were unaware of it. These relatively recent debates about Spanish identity have generally focused on far more remote times, especially over the formation of Spanish identity in the ancient or medieval world. For example, Spain's position as the crossroads of Europe and Africa and its multiethnic society elicited one of the most strenuous debates about Spanish history and nationalism in the 1950s and 1960s. Américo Castro started the historiographical battle in 1948, arguing that different groups, specifically Jewish, Arab, and Christian populations in medieval Spain, all helped forge the components of Spanish national identity.[4] Others, even earlier, like Marcelino Menéndez y Pelayo and, in this century, Nicolás Sánchez Albornoz, had made nationalist claims that obliterated the role of different population groups in Spanish history, arguing that the expulsion of these groups in the fifteenth and sixteenth centuries allowed the true and original genius of Spain to burst forth from its mixed past. In the end, the debate has been about the meaning of difference and its larger implications for constructing pluralist societies and/or rigid racial classifications—even if Américo Castro and Sánchez Albornoz did not see this discussion in such terms. Not surprisingly, perhaps, U.S. scholars beginning in the late 1950s were quick to evaluate this conflict in Spanish historiography as a debate over the role of different ethnicities in shaping the nation.[5] Nevertheless, those who study this period usually end their discussion with the seventeenth century, the point at which they say Spain declined into an imperial, silver-addled decadence.

Equally interesting is the question of how the memory of this past historical mixture continued to play out in the formation of Spain's mass political system and the modern state in the late nineteenth and early twentieth centuries. With the loss of the last remnants of Spain's overseas empire and the rise of nationalist liberal and conservative parties, antistatist anarchist parties, and hypernationalist fascist parties, the past treatment of difference provided a fertile ground for debating the present state of Spanish internal affairs. This work attempts to lay the foundation for understanding not only the role of racial ideas in Spanish society but also the shared political pool from which these ideas originated in the late nineteenth century.

As discussed at the end of chapter 6, a spate of works have appeared quite recently that detail how Spanish scientists working within the nascent Franco regime expressed a strange and unique racial thought, notably different from racial ideas developed elsewhere. The recent publication of such works has proven inordinately shocking to Spain's present-day population, especially as the revelations have played out sensationally in the modern media, particularly television.[6] The immediate formation of research centers to study these wartime activities testifies to this interest. Certainly, this reaction is partially the product of a long-delayed confrontation with many of the crimes of the Franco regime.[7] But there is a stronger tendency underlying this bewildered and horrified reaction. The shock is abetted by the discovery that some Spaniards seem to have behaved much like other Europeans in that era, committing crimes against populations, experimenting on human subjects, and creating eugenics programs. These endeavors have astonished a Spanish population conditioned to believe that "*no somos racistas*," and that Spain is different.[8] As a result, even the historians who attempt to recover and document experiments designed to manipulate and reconstruct the Spanish population have engaged with the racial thought of these figures as if it were sui generis a bizarre manifestation of some individual's particular psychopathology or intellectual formation.[9]

This book reorients this approach, demonstrating that the roots of racial thought emerged from earlier Spanish sciences. Franco's scientists did not invent the world they inhabited. Indeed, many of these eugenic programs were rooted in Spanish thought from an earlier period. The infamous search for the red gene as performed in Francoist concentration camps was not the product of the strange racial view of one man, an argument both facile and ultimately exculpatory for the intellectual traditions from which it sprang. Rather, this racial thought was the product of a developing discourse of race that was forged throughout the late nineteenth and early twentieth centuries in the various cross-sections of Spanish political and social debate. The discovery of this wartime behavior, and the particularly pernicious and violent forms of wartime and postwar repression that relied on collective punishment and rhetorical excess that dehumanized the enemy, have reanimated some discussion of the place of Francoism amid the pantheon of pernicious European regimes of the 1930s and 1940s. For the same reasons that Soviet historians continuously explore the "vexed issue of comparison" of Stalin's Soviet Union and Nazi Germany, historians of Spain quite rightly want to consider now the "social utopia" that the Franco regime wanted to manufacture.[10] Franco and his regime had, at least, the pretension of totalitarian control over Spain's population. Spain was not unique in that its dictator saw as essential to the installation of his Movement the manipulation of the composition of the nation's population.

The question that has engaged historians of Spain is whether this manipulation makes Francoists like Nazis. As mentioned in chapter 1, an important component of Spanish historiography of the early Franco regime is the basic assumption that Francoism differed from Nazism in the key area of racism. Stanley Payne, for example, defined the deciding factor separating German fascism from the practice of fascism in other nations as the "basis in biological determinism."[11] Even the most recent contemplation of the treatment of prisoners and manipulation of the Spanish population during the Franco regime continues to be mired in the "vexed historical comparison" with the Nazi government. Most recent work concludes that Spanish scientists and the programs they directed did not exhibit the characteristics that would identify them as racist. Yet, this argument fails to recognize that racial thought, as presented here, existed along a spectrum of different kinds of racial policy and thought in the early twentieth century. Thus, these Spanish scientists and their programs are better explored as products of similar racial thought that existed elsewhere but followed different trajectories, with different outcomes and consequences.

The effort to place Spanish racial thought on a separate and sui generis trajectory rather than on a broader continuum of racial thought remains common among historians. For example, the eminent historian of Spanish eugenics, Raquel Álvarez Peláez, has shown increasing interest in Spanish conservative eugenics and Francoist wartime policies. Recently, she used Antonio Vallejo-Nájera's notion of racial hygiene as proof that subtle but fundamental differences exist between the fascism of the Nazis and the "conservative authoritarianism" of the Francoists. Any real similarities existed for superficial propagandistic purposes only, to maintain the appearance of ideological similarity despite philosophical differences. The actual policies Francoists produced reflected the Catholic, spiritualist strictures placed on true biological determinism. "Vallejo wanted to analyze the situation with the new knowledge [of the relation between science, biology, and the decay of the race]."[12] According to Peláez, Vallejo, attempting to align this new science with the Catholicism of the new regime, abhorred the potential of eugenics to upset familial structures and to impose divorce laws and controls on birth, the supposedly "left-wing," or modern, aspects of eugenics. In the end, Vallejo's policies were not fascist for his ideas of race were too "philosophical and spiritual."[13]

To dismiss Vallejo and others in this fashion is to assume that ideology alone shapes policy rather than to acknowledge that contingent political circumstances help shape policies as much as ideology does. In other words, to dismiss Vallejo and others for being only superficially modern and biological assumes that all the policies they supported were intentional, the logical product of a coherent ideology. How Vallejo and others defined race determined which policies they advocated and which they abjured. Michael Richards, again studying the historical formation of Vallejo's scientific and political views, argues that the actual content of the ideas with which Spaniards worked controlled the ultimate expression of them in political and social policy.[14] Richards often notes in his excellent work on psychiatry that Vallejo was fundamentally ambivalent about pursuing more "negative eugenics," caught as he was between pursuing what he believed to be scientifically derived "racial hygiene" and avoiding the liberal, positivist pursuits of eugenicists of the Left.[15] In other words, despite the actual creation of programs to manipulate the Spanish population, the content of the basic ideas led to a differing logic of Spanish eugenics. The ideology of the regime ultimately halted the more pernicious and negative policies that might have emerged from Francoist eugenics. Again, ideas prefigured policies.

With a more dynamic and contextualized definition of race that considers not just the content of the racial idea but also how it shifted in time and was configured to fit historical circumstances, one sees that the behavior of Francoist military figures was far less ambivalent toward, and more of a piece with, policies enacted elsewhere. The motivation and drive to implement policies to manipulate populations were the same. The assumption that this manipulation must be done—or at least aided through and proven by scientific means—was also similar. As examined in chapter 1, racism can exist without a clearly formulated concept of race. The question historians should ask is, how did events and ideas come together to produce this kind of behavior? The forced adoption of children away from republican mothers or the testing of political prisoners to find out if they harbored a "Marxist gene" are shocking and interesting practices both because they existed and because of the rationale for them. They exist along a spectrum of policies of the era, not as counterexamples, the motives for which have to be explained away.

Clearly, ambivalence toward racial science born of Catholic antipathy for the supposedly scientific basis of identity was quite easily overcome by historical circumstance. The era of the Second Republic and the Spanish Civil War sharpened the belief in fundamental differences between opposite political groups, and as a result, policies and notions of treatment coarsened in the context of the actual Civil War. Even Raquel Álvarez Peláez concedes clear "contradictions" between the ambivalence of Vallejo toward fascist policies in Nazi Germany before the Spanish Civil War and his more full-throated celebration of Nazi eugenics during the actual conflict between 1936 and 1939.[16] It is hard to argue against the attempt among Spanish fascist intellectuals and doctors to align Francoist thought and policy with that of their Nazi compatriots. Vallejo lectured in Germany in 1938 about eugenic policies.[17] The Spanish fascist writer Ernesto Giménez Caballero, speaking in Berlin in 1941, referred fondly to the mutually reinforcing "marriage" of Nazism and Francoism, with the racial and historical missions of the two countries driving both forward. Germany offered the world the "racial impetus" for understanding race as the basis of national strength, and Spain provided its age-old "racialist virtue" of spreading this idea to the world.[18] Clearly, the historical moment of the early 1940s allowed for a greater sense of shared ideas, shared mission, and shared purpose than we might in retrospect assume existed between Spanish and German fascists. From this perspective, one can then argue that the Civil War helped transform and radicalize the otherwise more passive racial and scientific thought of Francoist doctors.

In the recent effort to understand the particularly vicious and sanguinary treatment of the enemy during the Spanish Civil War and the postwar repressions, answers to how these ideas were transformed in a new context have begun to emerge. Certainly, it will always be difficult to know what truly inspired the torture and slaughter of prisoners, or the reprisals that ballooned out from attacks on individuals to collective punishments against families, villages, and cities during the Spanish Civil War.[19] But Paul Preston and, more recently, Michael Richards, have targeted the military figures that murdered their wartime opponents and then justified and explained their behavior along medical and scientific grounds. Here a promising new line of thought is showing the potential lineage of racial thought from the period discussed in this book to later manifestations in the 1930s and 1940s. The promising conclusion of these works is that historical context in a sense plays a definitive role in determining how ideas ultimately manifest themselves in behaviors. Paul Preston recently has suggested that through a more diachronic analysis of the ideas that existed among the Spanish military officers corps, these leaders were rendered more radical and vicious in the context of the Civil War. Ideas bent to the whims and needs of people in their historical context.

Richards and Preston have both shown how the historical moment of the Spanish Civil War helped radicalize the Francoist forces' own definitions of the enemy. As demonstrated in chapter 6, Spanish military figures had applied a neocolonialist view of the enemy to the peninsular Spanish population. By the start of the Spanish Civil War, this internal population now harbored an internal enemy that needed to be rooted out. Spanish military figures, some in medical fields, others not, radicalized this hatred by adding biological explanations of their enemies' unredeemability. Political views transformed into pathological conditions that rendered the enemy into an immutable foe. As a result, the kinds of collective punishments common during the Spanish Civil War and the postwar repression, including mass rapes and mass murder and retaliatory violence, became exercises in social, political, and even ethnic cleansing. The justification was usually presented in racialist terms: "liberalism was a poison acting like a German virus . . . incurable and infectious," or working-class dissent was the product of "slave stock" being given access to sewers, which saved them from diseases and thus saved "Red leaders [who] would have died in infancy instead of exciting the rabble and causing good Spanish blood to flow."[20]

Ironically, despite being one of the few historians to place this kind of biological language in the proper context of what historians of race call racialist discourse, Preston continues to apply this racial language to a zero-sum rigid contrast with Nazi-like language. In the end, Preston qualifies this biological language as "near-racist" rather than racist.[21] If the language assumes transmissible, immutable differences and makes decisions about life or death based on them, then why do historians of Spain still qualify the racial qualities of this kind of thought? There still exists the "vexed" tendency to assume a basic definition of racism that is defined solely by Nazism and to excuse other manifestations. The resulting barbarity in Spain obviously did not mimic the scale, organization, or even legal apparatus that defined Nazi crimes, but, as in the debates about the Holocaust, functionality, the context of the ideas, matters in making ideas lethal. The needs of the moment often determine the manner in which political figures—or, in this case, medical personnel responding to political figures—interpret ideas. Perhaps it is not surprising that two recent books have approached the efforts to recover the memory of the crimes of the Civil War by discussing the repressions during and after the war as "Spanish Holocausts."[22] The Civil War proved that defining difference in biological and behavioral terms helped brutalize the treatment of the enemy.

As interesting as the wartime behavior itself is the fact that this radicalization of racial thought did not simply die off when the war and repressions ended. The desire to make comprehensive and verifiable the association of political behavior and biology continued long after the end of the Civil War. This task was the domain of anthropologists and doctors, figures who had been trained by the anthropologists discussed in earlier chapters. In 1942, the Spanish Society of Anthropology, Ethnography and Prehistory, still linked historically to and housed in Pedro González de Velasco's museum, folded as a discrete institution. During the Civil War, however, its focus of study had clearly drifted from the liberal designs of its original members and focused particularly on "the memory of the empire and the study of race."[23] Yet, this mission, linked as it was to the Francoist political imagination, troubled some members of the society, and the failure to continue as a society seemed to reflect the confused and difficult political position of the members in the midst of the coalescing Franco regime.

Even though the society folded, its journal, *Actas y Memorias de la Sociedad de Antropología, Etnografía y Prehistoria*, continued to be published well into the 1950s with a clearly schizophrenic attitude toward race. While the journal continued to chart blood types as the newest mode of distinguishing different racial groups in Spain, authors also tended to attack other Spanish anthropologists more closely aligned to the regime whose racial claims seemed rooted more in political wishful thinking than in clear scientific evidence. For example, one anthropologist was critical of a Francoist doctor, the anthropologist and Nazi sympathizer Misael Bañuelos, who concluded that the great Spanish writer Miguel de Cervantes was an "almost entirely pure Nordic type." The society member's complaint had to do with Bañuelos's use of evidence—a painting of Cervantes of unknown provenance that demonstrated the writer's Nordic features—not so much with his conclusion.[24]

The regime, perhaps fearing criticism from members of this older society regarding the newer Francoist definitions of racial health, established its own anthropological institute in Madrid, with offices throughout the country, through the large state-funded research organization the Consejo Superior de Investigaciones Científicas (CSIC). The Instituto Bernardino de Sahagún de Anthropología y Etnología (IBSAE) was created in 1941 and came to use Velasco's museum as a research center. The focus of this institute clearly resonated with the kinds of political and racial politics of other regimes of the era. The IBSAE would engage in "the study of the sane and normal Spanish man, his regional variations, and his relations with neighboring countries, in order to establish the limits of the normal and the pathological and to undertake efforts of the greatest national importance like the improvement of the race (el mejoramiento de la raza)."[25] The institute would contain two sections, one devoted to the study of anthropobiology, and the other to ethnology. The former was further subdivided into sections that studied, for example, raciology, human inheritance, and hematoanthropobiology (the study of racial blood groups). There were sections of the institute interspersed throughout the country, including one in Barcelona led by Santiago Alcobé, and another in Valladolid led by Bañuelos, who had trained with Ramón y Cajal and had written a textbook on pathology and race.[26]

For a few years, the IBSAE helped fund a number of studies that clearly reflected the Francoist associations of race and political preferences. In fact, the participants in the IBSAE also tended to write for the Falangist journal of "social medicine," SER, which published extensively in the 1940s on eugenics and race. The links between these figures in the IBSAE and their anthropological forebears were never very distant. According to recent studies, these organizations clearly operated with a notion of race that is defined, as always, in contradistinction to the Nazi notion. The Spanish body was in decay, but defunct racial spirits were the culprit. Nevertheless, the evidence of decline was somatic, physical, and visible. Even if the causes were "spiritual" in the lexicon of doctors associated with the Francoist social medicine sectors, all of which were controlled by the Falangists, treatments were prescribed. Topping the list also were reeducation and ideological cleansing. According to one member of the Falange's social health division, "there is no better eugenics than the education of the people (el pueblo)."[27]

Again, context matters. Education and its forms depend largely on the perceived social needs they serve and the political climate in which they operate. The "didactismo por el terror" (education through terror) used by Francoists during the Civil War to justify murder became, after the Civil War, the desire to staunch the racial decline through reeducation that took the forms of forced adoptions, long prison sentences, starvation, torture, and "moral and ideological" retooling.[28] The broader definition of what constitutes actual racial health provided in this study makes it evident that racial thought in Spain operated much closer to the experiences of many other European countries. The professed philosophical and religious standpoints of the doctors did not obviate their desire to construct and apply racial policies. Whether Francoist doctors and institutions actually supplied the programs of national value to improve the race matters less than the fact that a group of racial thinkers did exist and work to create such programs.

The expanded definition of racial thought presented here also links the discussions of race in the 1930s and 1940s with a deeper past. Race was a mode of thought that identified perceived differences in behavior and cultural and physical characteristics that were considered transmissible and transgenerational. Spanish racial thinking fits this definitional model. Even biographical links over time are not difficult to uncover among racial thinkers. In addition to his work in Germany during World War I, Vallejo-Nájera worked as Ángel Pulido's personal physician throughout the 1930s. Misael Bañuelos studied in the Central University of Madrid while Manuel Antón and Hoyos Sáinz taught there. Jose Albiñana, a doctor and political figure of the 1930s and 1940s and clear fellow traveler of the Nazis, was trained along with Bañuelos in Madrid's Central University and was a member of the Royal Academy of Medicine. Their anthropological knowledge was derived from the work of the figures presented in this study. Further research will help explain the diachronic development of racial thought in Spain.

These chapters have grounded the study of Spanish racial thought within particular historical contexts to demonstrate that this story is as European as it is particularly Spanish. The study of race in Spain upends the usually bifurcated view of Spain as fundamentally and almost permanently divided between the forces of modernity and the forces of tradition and conservatism. Spain also experienced a crisis of liberalism, a rejection of rationalism and positivism manifested in political ideologies and a conservative revolution.[29] Race entered the scene in the late nineteenth and early twentieth centuries as a tool of liberal, modernizing, and secularizing discourse, reappearing later in far more conservative garb. This conservative view of race, suggested in the epigraph at the beginning of this work from Franco's screenplay *Raza*, comprised a broad coalition of cultural values and memories of Spain's imperial greatness, spreading not only the Spanish language and culture into the Western Hemisphere, but also transplanting Western civilization and Catholicism throughout the world.[30]

For Spanish historians only now recovering from the simplistic division of Spanish political history into that of "two Spains," race can be used to provide fruitful examples of the interplay of ideas among Spanish political traditions. As early as 1966, Raymond Carr identified a streak of "biological racialism" in Spanish conservative thought. Carr was particularly taken with Marcelino Menéndez y Pelayo, in whom he sensed a contradictory impulse to ground traditional conservative rhetoric of Spain's imperial past in quasi-biological metaphors despite the fact that Menéndez y Pelayo blamed European Enlightenment thought for much of Spain's decline. Menéndez y Pelayo's notion that Spain had been "poisoned by eighteenth-century philosophy" and needed to "find again her true, Catholic self" was appropriated later by Falangists who considered Menéndez y Pelayo an intellectual fountainhead. Carr quotes Menéndez y Pelayo's clarion call that was later reiterated by early-twentieth-century conservatism: "Spain, evangelizer of half the planet: Spain, the hammer of heretics, the light of Trent, the sword of the Pope, the cradle of St. Ignatius. This is our greatness and glory: we have no other."[31] Subsequent consideration of racial thought in Spain continues to hesitate over the issue of whether these ideas were racial. Paul Preston once qualified the nationalist propaganda effort to link the Spanish Civil War to the "crusading spirit" of the battles between Christians and Moors and the imperialist conquest of the Americas as a "more or less racist vision" of the conflicts that preceded the army insurrection against the Second Republic.[32] Certainly more research can illuminate how much of a gulf exists between the "racist vision" of Francoist forces as white European Crusaders and their opponents as dark-skinned heathens, and whether this vision translated into the wider understanding of the Spanish opponents as "racial others." As exemplified by the quotation from Franco's screenplay *Raza*, there was clearly a wide range of meaning of race operating in the Francoist imaginary. This work is an exploration of this apparent contradiction that both provides a historical explanation for it and links it to the story of racial thought everywhere.

Notes

1. THE RACIAL ALLOY

1. Ramón Gubern, *Raza: Un sueño del General Franco* (Madrid: Ediciones 99, 1977); Stanley Payne, *The Franco Regime, 1936–1975* (Madison: University of Wisconsin Press, 1987), 402–3; Paul Preston, *Franco* (New York: Basic Books, 1994), 417–18.

2. Preston, *Franco*, 418.

3. On national Catholicism, see Alfonso Botti, *Cielo y dinero: El nacionalcatolicismo en España, 1881–1975*, trans. Botti (Madrid: Alianza Editorial, 1992).

4. In every year between 1875 and 1936, for example, at least one journal with the word *Raza* in the title appeared in Spain, and during this period in Madrid alone at least ten journals were published with titles that mentioned the Spanish race.

5. The classic debate relates to the supposed model of the bourgeois revolution. The literature is quite extensive, but the most important criticism remains David Blackbourn and Geoff Eley, *The Peculiarities of the German Past* (Oxford: Oxford University Press, 1984). On Spain's place in the bourgeois revolution debate, see Isabel Burdiel, "Myths of Failure, Myths of Success: New Perspectives on Nineteenth-Century Spanish Liberalism," *Journal of Modern History* 70, no. 4 (December 1998): 892–912.

6. Neil Macmaster has written recently that the racism today in the post–World War II world has been "re-coded" away from biological to cultural forms of "new racism" that "may not be so new, but it mark[s] an important strategic shift in the way in which not only fascists and overt racists, but many other groups, from conservatives to liberals have sought to legitimate exclusionary forms of difference or identity" (Macmaster, *Racism in Europe* [London: Palgrave, 2001], 193).

7. José Antonio Primo de Rivera, *The Spanish Answer* (Madrid: Artes Gráficas Ibarra, 1964), 194–98. This assertion also has a long pedigree for histories of European fascism. Stanley Payne, one of the first historians of Spanish fascism and later typologist of European fascist movements, maintains that racism and biological determinism remain the definitive aspects of fascism, leaving Nazism as the only true representative of fascism, with Italian and Spanish variants as, at best, competing recipes lacking the fundamental ingredient (see his older *Fascism: Comparison and Definitions* [Madison: University of Wisconsin Press, 1981], 149–51). He qualifies this assertion somewhat in his more recent *History of Fascism, 1914–1945* (Madison: University of Wisconsin Press, 1995), 11, 242.

8. Ronald Fraser, *The Blood of Spain: An Oral History of the Spanish Civil War* (New York: Pantheon Books, 1986), 315.

9. Ernesto Giménez Caballero, *Genio de España* (Madrid: Ediciones de "La Gaceta Literaria," 1932), 92. Franco heeded Giménez Caballero's counsel when he formally reinstituted October 12 as El Día de la Raza, a national holiday.

10. Saul Friedländer lays out a number of instances when the exactitude of racial purity thinking led to muddled and inconsistent policies, in his *Nazi Germany and the Jews* (New York: Harper-Perennial, 1998), 1:195–96; see also Robert Proctor, *Racial Hygiene: Medicine under the Nazis* (Cambridge: Harvard University Press, 1988), fig. 20.

11. Eric D. Weitz, "Racial Politics without the Concept of Race: Reevaluating Soviet Ethnic and National Purges," *Slavic Review* 60, no. 1 (Spring 2002): 8

12. Etienne Balibar and Immanuel Wallerstein, *Race, Nation, Class: Ambiguous Identities* (London: Verso, 1991); Weitz, "Racial Politics without the Concept of Race," 7.

13. Peter Wade, *Race and Ethnicity in Latin America* (London: Pluto Press, 1997), 20.

14. See Weitz, "Racial Politics without the Concept of Race," 1–2.

15. Ibid., 6.

16. See Peggy Pascoe, "Miscegenation Law and Ideologies of 'Race' in Twentieth-Century America," *Journal of American History* (June 1996): 48.

17. Quoted in Paul C. Taylor, "Appiah's Uncomplete Argument: W.E.B. Du Bois and the Reality of Race," *Social Theory and Practice* 26, no. 1 (Spring 2000): 103.

18. Antonio Vallejo-Nájera, *La política racial del nuevo estado* (San Sebastián: Editorial Española, 1938), 15.

19. George Fredrickson's work is a recent effort to refocus the debate away from tautology (see Frederickson, *Racism: A Short History* [Princeton: Princeton University Press, 2003]).

20. Alaina Lemon, "Without a Concept? Race as Discursive Practice," *Slavic Review* 60, no. 1 (Spring 2002): 54–61.

21. Laura Otis, *Organic Memory: History and the Body in the Late Nineteenth & Early Twentieth Centuries* (Lincoln: University of Nebraska Press, 1994), 92.

22. Quoted ibid., 91–92.

23. Macmaster, *Racism in Europe*, 193.

24. See the recent work by Aaron Gillette, *Racial Theories in Fascist Italy* (London: Routledge, 2002); Roberto Maiocchi, *Scienza italiana e razzismo fascista* (Scandicci: La Nuova Italia, 1999); and Jonathan Steinberg, *All or Nothing: The Axis and the Holocaust* (London: Routledge, 1990).

25. José Álvarez Junco examines this sharing of ideas in some detail in a new work on Spanish nationalism that seeks ideological commonalities instead of the usual view of division and fracture within nineteenth-century Spanish nationalism (see Álvarez Junco, *Mater Dolorosa: La idea de España en el siglo XIX* [Madrid: Taurus, 2001], esp. chap. 5).

26. Jon Juaristi has written a number of recent histories of Basque nationalism informed by the most recent historiography of the nation in Europe (see for, example, *El linaje de aitor* [1987; Madrid: Taurus, 1998]; *El bucle melancólico: Historias de nacionalistas vascos* [Madrid: Espasa, 1997]; *Vestigios de Babel: Para una arqueología de los nacionalismos españoles* [Madrid: Siglo Veintiuno de España Editores, 1992]).

27. Payne, *The Franco Regime*, 402 n. 19; emphasis added.

28. Payne once wrote that outbursts of antisemitism in Second Republic Spain were "stupid" acts "because there were no Jews for Spain to contend with" (Payne, *Falange: A History of Spanish*

Fascism [Stanford: Stanford University Press, 1961], 126). This argument seems merely to beg the question of why such antisemitic or racial ideas appeared at all when lived experience with the objects of these hatreds, Jews, were not present in the Spanish population.

29. That race is a social construction, not a biological fact, has become such an obvious assertion in racial historiography that a long bibliography here seems unnecessary. A good argument for seeing race as a tool for social analysis remains Joan Wallach Scott, *Gender and the Politics of History* (New York: Columbia University Press, 1988), esp. 28–52. Other studies of race that portray it in terms of its social rather than its supposedly biological meanings, especially in the context of Europe, include Elazar Barkan, *Retreat of Scientific Racism* (Cambridge: Cambridge University Press, 1991); Nancy Stepan, *The Idea of Race in Science: Great Britain, 1800–1960* (Hamden, Ct.: Archon Books, 1982); Ivan Hannaford, *Race: The History of an Idea in the West* (Washington, D.C.: Woodrow Wilson Center Press, 1996); George Stocking, *Race, Culture, and Evolution* (1968; Chicago: University of Chicago Press, 1982); and the now classic George Mosse, *Toward the Final Solution* (1978; Madison: University of Wisconsin Press, 1985).

30. The term is borrowed from Zygmunt Bauman's discussion of Jews as a prismatic group through which different political and social thinkers could refract their ideas about society, nation, and politics (see Bauman, *Modernity and the Holocaust* [Ithaca: Cornell University Press, 1989], 42–45).

31. See Jorge Cañizares Esquerra, "New World, New Stars: Patriotic Astrology and the Invention of Indian and Creole Bodies in Colonial Spanish America, 1600–1650," *American Historical Review* 104, no. 1 (February 1999): 34.

32. James Sweet, "The Iberian Roots of American Racist Thought," *William and Mary Quarterly* 54, no. 1 (January 1997): 143–66.

33. Anthony Pagden described this transformation in *The Fall of Natural Man* (Cambridge: Cambridge University Press, 1982), 57–108. José Piedra looks at the language of inclusion within Spain in literary presentations of the indigenous populations of the New World (see Piedra, "Literary Whiteness and the Afro-Hispanic Difference," in *The Bounds of Race*, ed. Dominick LaCapra [Ithaca: Cornell University Press, 1991], 278–311). Cañizares discusses the polarities of Spanish discussions of indigenous groups in "New World, New Stars," 65.

34. A participant in these debates, Yosef Yerushalmi was also a good chronicler of how the debates unfolded among principals like Cecil Roth and Henry Lea (see Yerushalmi, *Assimilation and Racial Anti-Semitism: The Iberian and the German Models*, Leo Baeck Memorial Lecture no. 26 [New York: Leo Baeck Institute, 1982]). Not included in this discussion is the latest contribution by Benzion Netanyahu, *The Origins of the Inquisition in Fifteenth Century Spain* (New York: Random House, 1995). On the blood purity statutes, see Albert A. Sicroff, *Les controverses des statuts de "pureté de sang" en Espagne du XVe au XVIIe siècle* (Paris: Didier, 1960).

35. *Convivencia*, as a description of Spanish society in the medieval and early modern eras, emerged out of the famous Américo Castro–Nicolás Sánchez Albornoz debates. For Thomas F. Glick's arguments about the lack of interrelation, or sharing, of cultures in medieval, Islamic, and early modern Spain, see Glick, *Islamic and Christian Spain in the Early Middle Ages: Comparative Perspectives on Social and Cultural Formation* (Princeton: Princeton University Press, 1979), 6–13. David Nirenberg also explores the concept in *Communities of Violence: Persecution of Minorities in the Middle Ages* (Princeton: Princeton University Press, 1996), 8–9.

36. Yerushalmi concluded in his remarks that perhaps the best description of Spanish lineage laws would be "proto-racialist," in *Assimilation and Anti-Semitism*, 21; see also Jaime Contreras,

"Aldermen and Judaizers, Criptojudaism, Counter-Reformation and Local Power," in *Culture and Control in Counter-Reformation Spain*, ed. Anne J. Cruz and Mary Elizabeth Perry (Minneapolis: University of Minnesota Press, 1992).

37. See, for example, the efforts to cling to a racial difference in Pedro Gorospe, "Arzalluz subraya que la raza vasca es un hecho y que manipular eso es de cínicos," in *El País* (Madrid), 31 January 1993.

38. See William Montgomery McGovern, *From Luther to Hitler: The History of Fascist-Nazi Political Philosophy* (Boston: Houghton Mifflin, 1941).

39. Nirenberg, *Communities of Violence*, 4–6.

40. Nirenberg put it this way: "any inherited discourse about minorities acquired force only when people chose to find it meaningful and useful, and was itself reshaped by these choices" (ibid., 6).

41. On this continuum, see Wade, *Race and Ethnicity in Latin America* , 14. See also Aline Helg, "Race in Argentina and Cuba, 1880–1930: Theory, Policies and Popular Reaction," in *The Idea of Race in Latin America, 1870–1940*, ed. Richard Graham (Austin: University of Texas Press, 1990), 37–71; and Benedict Anderson's "Creole Pioneers," in *Imagined Communities* (1983; London: Verso, 1991), 47–66.

42. For recent discussions of *Hispanidad* and *Hispanismo*, see the classic work that first presented the topic as worthy of study, Frederick Pike, *Hispanismo, 1898–1936: Spanish Conservatives and Liberals and Their Relations with Spanish America* (Notre Dame: University of Notre Dame, 1971); and its recent progeny like Eduardo González Calleja and Fredes Limon Nevado, *Hispanidad como un instrumento de combate* (Madrid: CSIC, 1988).

43. Howard Winant has recently written: "the boundaries of racially defined groups are both uncertain and subject to change. Indeed whole groups can acquire or lose their racialized character as historical and social circumstances shift" (Winant, "Race and Racism: Overview," in *New Dictionary of the History of Ideas*, ed. Maryanne Horowitz, vol. 5 (1987; Detroit: Scribner's, 2005).

44. Fredrickson, *Racism*, 9.

45. Ada Ferrer shows the use of "cross-racial" alliances in Ferrer, *Insurgent Cuba: Race, Nation and Revolution, 1868–1898* (Chapel Hill: University of North Carolina Press, 1999), 15–42.

46. For a discussion of Freyre, see Magnus Mörner, *Race Mixture in the History of Latin America* (New York: Little, Brown, 1967), 13–14.

47. The classic analysis of this system itself remains Mörner, *Race Mixture in the History of Latin America*. See also Claudio Esteva Fabregat, *El mestizaje en Iberoamérica* (Madrid: Editorial Alhambra, 1988). One can also turn to the classic debates about the differences between the role of race in the slave systems of the United States and Latin America (see Carl N. Degler, *Neither Black nor White* [Madison: University of Wisconsin Press, 1971], 16–20).

48. Wade, *Race and Ethnicity in Latin America*; Alejandra Bronfman, *Measures of Equality: Social Science, Citizenship and Race in Cuba, 1902–1940* (Chapel Hill: University of North Carolina Press, 2004), chap. 1; Lilia Moritz Schwarcz, *The Spectacle of the Races: Scientists, Institutions, and the Race Question in Brazil, 1870–1930*, trans. Leland Guyer (New York: Hill and Wang, 1999). For a more positive view of the implications of *mestizaje*, see Marilyn Grace Miller, *Rise and Fall of the Cosmic Race: The Cult of Mestizaje in Latin America* (Austin: University of Texas Press, 2004).

49. Matthew Frye Jacobsen, *Whiteness of a Different Color: European Immigration and the Alchemy of Race* (Cambridge: Harvard University Press, 1998), 1–12.

50. José María López Piñero, introduction to *La ciencia en la España del siglo XIX*, ed. López Piñero (Madrid: Marcial Pons, 1992), 17. Human sciences have come to signify for historians the host of disciplines that are devoted solely to human existence: anthropology, medicine, sociology, etc. Their formation as discrete disciplines took place throughout Europe and the United States in the late nineteenth century. Though studying this phenomenon in a comparative perspective has only just recently begun, see Dorothy Ross, ed., *Modernist Impulses in the Human Sciences 1870–1930* (Baltimore: Johns Hopkins University Press, 1994). Most scholars still agree that national context gave each manifestation of these disciplines unique attributes that require specific study (see Jan Goldstein, "Foucault among the Sociologists: The 'Disciplines' and the History of the Professions," *History and Theory* 23 [June 1984]: 170–92).

51. The new system guaranteed by the constitution of 1876 was known as the *turno*, with two parties alternating in power despite the efforts to make these shifts under the guise of democratic elections (see José Varela Ortega, *Los amigos políticos: Partidos, elecciones y caciquismo en la Restauración (1875–1900)* (Madrid: Alianza, 1977).

52. A number of Spanish historians have considered the development of larger intellectual discourses in Spain. Temma Kaplan has presented this process as energetic but ultimately doomed to insignificance by a largely unsupportive political and intellectual environment (see Kaplan, "Luís Simarro and the Development of Science and Politics in Spain, 1868–1917" [Ph.D. diss., Harvard University, 1969], 5–36). For a particularly Foucaldian approach, see Fernando Álvarez-Uría, *Miserables y locos: Medicina mental y orden social en la España del siglo XIX* (Barcelona: Tuquets, 1983).

53. See Thomas F. Glick, "Spain," in *The Comparative Reception of Darwinism*, ed. Glick (Austin: University of Texas Press, 1974), 207–15.

54. Francisco Villacorta Baños, *Burguesía y cultura: Los intelectuales españoles en la sociedad liberal, 1808–1931* (Madrid: Siglo XXI, 1980), 53–89.

55. New work by Andrew Zimmermann has demonstrated that anthropology developed in Germany because of its connection to mass culture. It appealed because of its accessibility to the masses. This work does not examine such popular notions of race, but the study is needed (see Zimmermann, *Anthropology and Anti-Humanism in Imperial Germany* [Chicago: University of Chicago Press, 2001]).

2. FINDING A SCIENCE IN THE MYSTERY OF RACE IN SPAIN

1. Though there are many books on Spanish conservative ideas, Eduardo González Calleja and Fredes Limón Nevado offer a good discussion of how these ideas were used in the propaganda efforts of conservative groups to define Spain's historical, cultural, and racial identity (see González Calleja and Limón Nevado, *La hispanidad como instrumento de combate* [Madrid: CSIC, 1988]).

2. See George L. Mosse, *Toward the Final Solution: A History of European Racism* (1978; Madison: University of Wisconsin Press, 1985); and Ivan Hannaford, *Race: The History of an Idea in the West* (Washington D.C.; Woodrow Wilson Center Press, 1996), chap. 4.

3. George Stocking, "The Idea of Race in the American Social Sciences" (Ph.D. diss., University of Pennsylvania, 1960), 24–26; Joan Corominas and José A. Pascual, *Diccionario crítico etimológico castellano e hispánico* (Madrid: Editorial Gredos, 1981): 800–802.

4. See González Calleja and Limón Nevado, *La hispanidad como instrumento de combate*, 11–13.

5. On conversion as an option, see Anthony Pagden, *The Fall of Natural Man* (Cambridge: Cambridge University Press, 1982), 109–18. On linguistic appropriation, see José Piedra, "Literary Whiteness and the Afro-Hispanic Difference," in *The Bounds of Race*, ed. Dominick LaCapra (Ithaca: Cornell University Press, 1991), 279–85.

6. The comparative observation, though unexplored in the literature of either Jewish expulsion or colonial contact, is not meant to quibble with well-developed historiographies of either historical event. Nor does it attempt to argue that language alone was the ideological or practical basis of either event. Rather, the call for comparison follows the suggestion of Yosef Yerushalmi, who argued that racism was not the sole driving force of the Jewish expulsion and that assimilation pressures placed on society by entrenched and new populations also played a role (see Yerushalmi, *Assimilation and Racial Anti-Semitism: The Iberian and German Models*, Leo Baeck Memorial Lecture no. 26 [New York: Leo Baeck Institute, 1982]; and David Niremberg, *Communities of Violence: Persecution of Minorities in the Middle Ages* [Princeton: Princeton University Press, 1996]).

7. José Álvarez Junco traces the formation of the idea of "España" and the "españoles" "to antiquity and the Middle Ages" but argues that it had real political meaning after the unification of the peninsular kingdoms in 1469 (see Álvarez Junco, *Mater Dolorosa: La idea de España en el siglo XIX* [Madrid: Taurus, 2001], 45, 49). On Maimonides and the language of walls, see Hannaford, *Race*, 105–26.

8. Real Academia Española, *Diccionario de la lengua castellana*, 12th ed. (Madrid: Imprenta de los Sres. Hernando y Compania, 1884), 900.

9. See Margaret R. Greer, Walter D. Mignolo, and Maureen Quilligan, introduction to *Rereading the Black Legend: The Discourses of Religious and Racial Difference in the Renaissance Empires*, ed. Greer, Mignolo, and Quilligan (Chicago: University of Chicago Press, 2007), 13.

10. David Niremberg, "Race and the Middle Ages," in Greer, Mignolo and Quilligan, eds., *Rereading the Black Legend*, 77.

11. Ibid., 79.

12. Quoted ibid., 78.

13. Ibid.

14. Yerushalmi, *Assimilation and Racial Anti-Semitism*.

15. Christiane Stallaert, *Ni una gota de sangre impura* (Barcelona: Círculo de Lectores, 2006), 14.

16. Gonzalo Álvarez Chillida, *El antisemitismo en España: La imagen del judío (1812–2002)* (Madrid: Marcial Pons, 2002), 43–44.

17. Greer, Mignolo, and Quilligan, introduction to *Rereading the Black Legend*, 12.

18. Ibid.

19. Niremberg, "Race and the Middle Ages," 79.

20. The term "organic unity" is borrowed from Niremberg, "Race and the Middles Ages," 86.

21. Carolyn P. Boyd, *Historia Patria: Politics, History and National Identity in Spain, 1875–1975* (Princeton: Princeton University Press, 1997), chap. 1.

22. Other concepts were used as well to express this unity between Spain and Latin America. *Hispanismo, hispanoamericanismo*, among others, asserted the cultural ties extant among all Spaniards (see Pike, *Hispanismo, 1898–1936*, 1, 3–5).

23. Ibid.

24. See Hannaford, *Race*, 235–76; Mosse, *Toward the Final Solution*, 77–93; and Michael Banton, *Racial Theories* (Cambridge: Cambridge University Press, 1987), 65–92.

25. Hannaford, *Race*, 229–32.

26. Paul Preston has recently noted the colonialist language with which military officials began to describe internal Spanish populations during the Spanish civil war. This chapter suggests a longer timeline (see Preston, "The Answer Lies in the Sewers: Captain Aguilera and the Mentality of the Francoist Officer Corps," *Science and Society* 68, no. 3 [Fall 2004]: 277–312).

27. "Europeanization" (*europeanizar*) is a term taken from the language of the period, and from the regenerationist debates at the turn of the twentieth century. The term, first coined by Ángel Ganivet, was employed always in contradistinction to those who wanted to "*españolizar*" Spain via Catholic orthodoxy and antagonism to scientific endeavor and liberal parliamentary democracy. *Españolistas* were generally more conservative, traditionalist, and welcoming of church control. *Europeanistas* usually called for less church control, for strengthening more democratic, often republican, forms of government (see Rockwell Gray, *The Imperative of Modernity* [Berkeley and Los Angeles: University of California Press, 1989]; H. Ramsden, *The 1898 Movement in Spain* [Manchester: Manchester University Press, 1974], 12–15; and Sebastian Balfour, *The End of the Spanish Empire* [Oxford: Oxford University Press, 1997], 64–91).

28. See Vicente Cacho Viu, "Efervescencia intelectual bajo la paz política," in *La Institución Libre de Enseñanza* (Madrid: Ediciones Rialp, 1962), 1:3336–59; and José Luís Abellán, "Una manifestación del modernismo: La acepción española de 'raza,'" *Cuadernos Hispanoamericanos* 553–54 (July–August 1996): 203–14.

29. Santos Juliá, *Historias de las dos Españas* (Madrid: Taurus, 2004), 63–64. On this tendency to return to the *pueblo* and the central myth, as cited by Juliá, see Jon Juaristi, *El bucle melancólico* (Madrid: Espasa Calpe, 1997), 93–100, esp. 98.

30. Quoted in Boyd, *Historia Patria*, 130.

31. Laura Otis, *Organic Memory: History and the Body in the Late Nineteenth and Early Twentieth Centuries* (Lincoln: University of Nebraska Press, 1994), 130–31.

32. José Ortega y Gasset, *El tema de nuestro tiempo*, 3rd ed. (Madrid: Revista de Occidente, 1934), 68; see also Joshua Goode, "La contradicción como arma: Ortega y Gasset y el concepto español de la modernidad," *Foro Hispánico* 18, no. 18 (September 2000): 99–122.

33. Preston, "The Answer Lies in the Sewers," 288.

34. Juliá, *Historias de las dos Españas*, 84–85.

35. Carlos Serrano, "Conciencia de la crisis," in *Más se perdió en Cuba*, ed. Juan Pan-Montojo (Madrid: Alianza Editorial, 1998), 342.

36. Otis, *Organic Memory*, 89.

37. See her short story "The Blood Bond," in Emilia Pardo Bazán, *The White Horse and Other Stories* (Lewisburg: Bucknell University Press, 1993) 76–79; see also Otis, *Organic Memory*, 139–46.

38. See Juan Pan-Montojo, introduction to *Más se perdió en Cuba*, ed. Pan-Montojo, (Madrid: Alianza Editorial, 1998), 22–24 ; see also Boyd, *Historia Patria*, chap. 1; and Diego Núñez Ruiz, *La mentalidad positiva en España: Desarrollo y crisis* (Madrid: Tucar Ediciones, 1975), 23–58; and Juliá, *Historia de las dos Españas*, chap. 2.

39. Most estimates of the Jewish population in Spain in 1900 range around two thousand people. Today the number hovers around twenty thousand people, most of whom were born in Spain (see José Antonio Lisbona, *Retorno a sefarad: La política de Espana hacia sus Judíos en el siglo XX* [Barcelona: Rio Piedras, 1993], 19; and Álvarez Chillida, *El antisemitismo*, 21).

40. Álvarez Chillida, *El antisemitismo*, chap. 2.

41. See Stephen Jacobson, "A Mixture of Spaniards," in *Times Literary Supplement*, 3 October 2005, 28. On the use of such enemies in the formation of revolutionary politics on the Right, see, for example, Ze'ev Sternhell, *Neither Right nor Left* (Berkeley and Los Angeles: University of California Press, 1987).

42. Gobineau was read with a certain amount of irritation among Spaniards, though not with any great attention. The first translation of Gobineau's *Essai sur l'inegalité des races humaines* (1855) in Spanish seems not to have appeared until 1937, and by then it was seen as a work that actually demonstrated Spanish racial superiority by showing that all of the praised qualities of the Aryan were demonstrated by Spaniards long before, in the fifteenth century (see El Conde de Gobineau, *Ensayo sobre las desigualdad de las razas humanas*, trans. Francisco Susanna [Barcelona: Editorial Apolo, 1937], 1–12).

43. See Hannaford, *Race*, 292–94.

44. Lily Litvak, *Latinos y Anglosajones: Orígenes de una polémica* (Barcelona: Puvill Editor, n.d.), 15–28.

45. "A nuestros lectores," *La Raza Latina* 11, no. 21 (15 January 1875): 1. For further statements summarizing this position, see Matías Rodríguez Sobrino, "La raza latina," *La Raza Latina* 1, no. 13 (13 July 1874): 4–6.

46. Active in such publications were Anatole France, George Sand, Juan Valera, Leon Gambetta, and Cánovas del Castillo. The first attempt in anthropology to define the contours of this racial group, the Latin race, was made by Giussepe Sergi in 1896 in a book that proliferated in the debates and was once referred to by William Ripley in his "Racial Geography of Europe" as filling a great void in the knowledge of Latin races. On Sergi, see Giussepe Sergi, *Origine e diffusione della stirpe mediterranea* (Rome: Soc. Ed. Dante Alighieri, 1895). For Ripley's work, see Ripley, "The Racial Geography of Europe," *Appleton's Popular Science Monthly* (February 1897): 456–58. For a list of the most prominent journals involved in the movement, see Litvak, *Latinos y Anglosajones*, 33, 38–39.

47. Spanish historiography still lacks a wide discussion of the impact of Darwin and Spencer on social thought. Some analysis exists in Thomas F. Glick, "Spain," in *The Comparative Reception of Darwinism*, ed. Glick (Austin: University of Texas Press, 1974), 207–345 .

48. Mosse first discussed the science and mystery of race as a way of describing the philological and scientific approaches in *Toward the Final Solution*, chaps. 6–7.

49. See Miguel Ángel Puig-Samper and Andrés Galera, *La antropología Española del siglo XIX* (Madrid: "Instituto Arnau de Vilanova," CSIC, 1983), 40; Paul Weindling, *Health, Race and German Politics between National Unification and Nazism, 1870–1945* (Cambridge: Cambridge University Press, 1989), 52; and Aleš Hrdlicka, "Preface," *American Journal of Physical Anthropology* 1, no. 1 (January–March, 1918): 1.

50. Ángel Pulido y Fernández, *El Doctor Velasco* (Madrid: E. Teodoro, 1894), 80.

51. Carmelo Lisón Tolosana, *Antropología social en España* (Madrid: Siglo XXI de España, 1971), 147–48.

52. See Diego Núñez Ruíz, *La mentalidad positiva en España* (Barcelona: Tucar Ediciones, 1975), 86–87; and Puig-Samper and Galera, *La antropología*, 73.

53. Though there are many books on Spanish conservative ideas, the discussion in González Calleja and Limón Nevado, *La hispanidad como instrumento de combate*, offers a good discussion of how these ideas were used in the propoganda efforts of conservative groups to define Spain's historical, cultural, and racial identity.

3. RACE AND THE EMERGENCE OF PHYSICAL ANTHROPOLOGY

1. This distraction among anthropologists was noted in Germany in Andrew Zimmermann, *Anthropology and Antihumanism in Imperial Germany* (Chicago: University of Chicago Press, 2001), 44; and in France, in Joy Dorothy Harvey, "Races Specified: Evolution Transformed: The Social Context of Scientific Debates Originating in the Société d'Anthropologie de Paris, 1859–1902" (Ph.D. diss., Harvard University, 1983).

2. Francisco Tubino, *Revista de antropología*, as quoted in Carmelo Lisón Tolosana, *Antropología social en España* (Madrid: Siglo XXI, 1971), 108.

3. Ibid., 107.

4. See Lisón Tolosana, *Antropología social en España*, chap. 2; see also Miguel Puig-Samper, *Crónica de una expedición romántica al Nuevo Mundo* (Madrid: CSIC, 1988); Alejando R. Díez Torre et al., eds., *La ciencia española en Ultramar: Actas de las I jornadas sobre "España y las Expediciones Científicas en América y Filipinas"* (Aranjuez: Doces Calles, 1997); and *Historia de un olvido: La expedición científica del Pacífico (1862–1865): Museo de América, diciembre 2003–mayo 2004* (Madrid: Ministerio de Educación Cultura y Deporte, 2003), 15–16.

5. Photographs and material from these exhibits still exist in the archives of the National Ethnological Museum in Madrid (see Pilar Romero de Tejada, *Un templo a la ciencia* [Madrid: Ministerio de Cultura, 1992], 50–51).

6. Diego Núñez Ruíz, *La mentalidad positiva en España* (Madrid: Tucar Ediciones, 1975), 86–87; José María López Piñero et al., *Medicina y sociedad en la España del siglo XIX* (Madrid: Ediciones Rialp, 1964).

7. Vicente Cacho Viu, *La Institución Libre de Enseñanza* (Madrid: Ediciones Rialp, 1962), 1:282–318; Ángel Pulido y Fernández, *El Doctor Velasco* (Madrid: Establecimiento Tipográfico de E. Teodoro, 1894), 10–12; Temma Kaplan, "Luís Simarro and the Development of Science and Politics in Spain, 1868–1917" (Ph.D. diss., Harvard University, 1969), 23–36.

8. Quoted in Harvey, "Races Specified," 111.

9. Kaplan, "Luís Simarro and the Development of Science," 40–59.

10. Pulido, *El Doctor Velasco*, 33–37; José María López Piñero, "Pedro González de Velasco," in *Diccionario histórico de la ciencia moderna en España*, ed. López Piñero et al. (Barcelona: Ediciones Peninsula, 1983), 1:417–18.

11. George W. Stocking, *Race, Culture, and Evolution* (1968; Chicago: University of Chicago Press, 1982), 40–60.

12. López Piñero, "Pedro González de Velasco," in *Diccionario histórico de la ciencia moderna en España*, 1:418.

13. Patricia M. E. Lorcin, *Imperial Identities: Stereotyping, Prejudice and Race in Colonial Algeria* (London: I. B. Tauris, 1999), chap. 5; see also Ivan Hannaford, *Race: The History of an Idea in the West* (Washington, D.C.: Woodrow Wilson Center Press, 1996), 260–69.

14. Harvey, "Races Specified": 115–16; see also Stephen Jay Gould, *Mismeasure of Man* (New York: Norton, 1981), 66–85.

15. Lorcin, *Imperial Identities*, 153.

16. As quoted in Harvey, "Races Specified," 116, 117; see also Gould, *Mismeasure of Man*, 84.

17. Gould, *Mismeasure of Man*, 86–87.

18. Harvey, "Races Specified," 17–20.

19. Stocking, *Race, Culture, and Evolution*, 42–68; Harvey, "Races Specified," chap. 2.

20. It would be a criticism on these grounds that eventually led not so much to the decline of polygenist arguments but to the desire to perform large national studies of populations, like those undertaken by Rudolf Virchow on German schoolchildren in 1869; by Rodolfo Livi in the Italian military in 1894; and by Federico Olóriz in Spain in 1894. On Olóriz, see Elvira Arquiola, "Anatomía y antropología física en el positivismo español," *Asclepio* 33 (1981): 3–22.

21. In a sign of the rather insular Spanish scientific community, this passage appeared in a prologue that Letamendi wrote for Pulido, who was then writing about one of Spain's then most illustrious doctors (see Ángel Pulido y Fernández, *La medicina y los médicos* [*Mosáico de discursos, artículos, correspondencias, semblanzas, pensamientos . . .*], prologue by Dr. José de Letamendi [Valencia: Librería de P. Aguilar, Caballeros, 1883], xiv).

22. Harvey, "Races Specified," 135–36.

23. In contrast, Broca struggled during the empire to work without the attention of police spies, who often infiltrated the meetings of the anthropological society (see Harvey, "Races Specified," 10–15).

24. Ibid., 111.

25. See "Felicitación," *Anfiteatro Anatómico Español* (hereafter cited as AAE) 1, no. 2 (15 February 1873): 1.

26. Pulido, *El Doctor Velasco*, 57–85.

27. Lisón Tolosana, *Antropología social en España*, 104–5.

28. Like other private, or "free," institutions, the ILE had relationships with many anthropologists who shuttled between teaching positions at the ILE and their other positions (see Sandie Holguín, *Creating Spaniards* [Madison: University of Wisconsin Press, 2002], chap. 2).

29. Kaplan, "Luís Simarro and the Development of Science," 55

30. "Extracto de las actas de 14 de marzo de 1874," *Revista de Antropología* 1 (1874): 1–4.

31. Dr. Pedro González Velasco, "Adelante," AAE 1, no. 1 (15 and 30 June 1873): 2.

32. For an analysis of the comparative effects of external and internal immigration into U.S. and Spanish cities, see Acosta, "Cosmopolitismo humano," AAE 1, no. 2 (15 February 1873): 21–22. For a discussion of European public health programs and their application in Spain, see Eduardo García Perez [director gerente], "Salubridad publica," AAE 1, no. 1 (15 and 30 January 1873): 7–8

33. Unsigned editorial, *Revista de Antropología* 1 (1874): 75.

34. Thomas F. Glick, "Spain," in *The Comparative Reception of Darwinism* (Chicago: University of Chicago Press, 1988), 207–345; Ángel Pulido Martín, *El Doctor Pulido y su época* (Madrid: F. Domenech, 1945), 172–79.

35. Francisco Maria Tubino, "De la unidad nativa del género humano o del parentesco por consanguinidad universal entre todas las razas de la especie humana, diseminadas por todas las regiones de la Tierra," *Revista de Antropología* 1 (1874): 51–52. For further definitions of anthropology in this period in Spain, see Miguel Angel Puig-Samper and Andrés Galera, *La antropología española del siglo XIX* (Madrid: "Instituto Arnau de Vilanova," CSIC, 1983), 11–13; and Lisón Tolosana, *Antropología social*, 108.

36. Arquiola, "Anatomía y antropología física," 8.

37. Ángel Pulido y Fernandez and Pedro González Velasco, *Discurso leído en la apertura del Museo Antropológico y Escuela Libre del Dr. Velasco* (Madrid: Imp. Juan Aguado, 1875), 45, 64.

38. Ibid., 47.

39. For Broca's insistence on physical bases, see Gould, *Mismeasure of Man*, 85–87. For debates within French anthropology on the uses of craniological differences, see Harvey, "Races Specified," 59–69.

40. The French Société de Observateurs de l'hommes was the first to use this designation of their study. The Spanish attempted in the same spirit to continue with their long ethnological traditions of observation of the habits and customs of their colonial inhabitants. Spanish success in such ethnological expeditions ebbed in the nineteenth century, however, suffering from a lack of government funding, the dearth of worthy vessels, the failure of Spain's one main expedition to its African colonies, with the ship sinking upon launch, and also the lack of colonies to visit after the 1820s era of independence. For the French society, see George Stocking, "French Anthropology in 1800," in *Race, Culture, and Evolution*, 42–68; for Spanish expeditions, see Lisón Tolosana, *Antropología social*, 1–96.

41. Pulido was also the personal doctor of Emilio Castelar, one of Spain's leading republican politicians and the leader of the Republican Party from the First Republic.

42. Ángel Pulido, *Discurso leido en la inauguración del año académico de 1875–1876 en la Sociedad Española de Antropología* (Madrid: Imprenta de T. Fortanet, 1875), 13.

43. According to Temma Kaplan, Luís Simarro reached a similar conclusion (see Kaplan, "Luís Simarro and the Development of Science," preface).

44. Pulido, *Discurso leido en la inauguración*, 6; see Ángel Pulido y Fernández, "Orígen e importancia de la craneometría," in *De la medicina y los médicos (Mosáico de discursos, artículos, correspondencias . . . pensamientos)* (Valencia: Manuel Alufre, 1883), 39–66; and Federico Olóriz y Aguilera, "Recolección de craneos para estudios antropológicos," *El Siglo Médico* 31, no. 1594 (13 July 1884): 444–46.

45. Arthur de Gobineau, *The Inequality of Human Races* (New York: Howard Fertig, 1999, 29 (originally translated 1915).

46. Pulido, *El Doctor Velasco*, 86–87.

47. Karl Vogt, an acquaintance of Velasco's, had been read in Spain in French translation by members of the institute and was also a corresponding member (see Puig-Samper and Galera, *La antropología española del siglo XIX*, 32–35).

48. Paul Topinard, "On 'Race' in Anthropology (1892)," in *This Is Race*, ed. Earl. W. Count (New York: Henry Schuman, 1950), 176.

49. Pulido, "Origen e importancia de la craneometria," 65.

50. Ibid., 55, 66.

51. Other related institutions did not, however. The Free Society of Histology led by Aureliano Maestre de San Juan continued to function, though its success had more to do with its lack of ambition. Little experimentation occurred directly within the confines of the society, probably owing to its lack of a building. The society really existed as a discussion group albeit an important one. Santiago Ramón y Cajal, the first Spanish recipient of a Nobel Prize in the sciences, was an active member, as were Luís Simarro and Ángel Pulido (see Carlos Maria Cortezo to the Royal Academy of Medicine [Real Academia de Medicina], December 1932, Papers of Angel Pulido, Biblioteca de la Real Academia Nacional de Medicina, Madrid). Also, Rudolf Virchow's cell theory was introduced in Spain via this society (see "Sociedad Histológica Española: Boletín de las asociaciones científicas," *Revista Europea* 1 [22 March 1874]: 4).

52. E. [pseud.] "Academia de Medicina: Recepción del Sr. Pulido," *El Porvenir* (23 June 1884): n.p.

53. Kaplan, "Luís Simarro and the Development of Science," 63–66.

54. See Luís Simarro, "La enseñanza superior en París: La escuela de antropología: Curso de Mr. Matías Duval," Boletín de la Institución Libre de Enseñanza 4 (3 December 1880); and Luís Simarro, "Colegio de Francia, el curso de Anatomía general de Mr. Ranvier," Boletín de la Institución Libre de Enseñanza 5 (19 January 1881).

55. Julian Calleja was to be chair of anatomy briefly in the medical school of the Central University in Madrid.

56. See Pulido, El Dr. Velasco, 64.

57. Ramón J. Sender and Juan Antonio Cabeza both wrote fictional works as late as the 1960s featuring Dr. Velasco and his daughter. For more on this reputation, see Pilar Romero de Tejada, Un templo a la ciencia, 10.

58. Robert Proctor, "From Anthropologie to Rassenkunde in the German Anthropological Tradition," in Bones, Bodies, Behavior: Essays on Biological Anthropology, ed. George Stocking, History of Anthropology Series no. 5 (Madison: University of Wisconsin Press, 1988).

59. Elvira Arquiola, "Broca y el positivismo en la antropología francesa," Asclepio 28 (1976): 51–92.

60. Elvira Arquiola, "Paul Topinard: Médico y antropólogo físico," Asclepio 30–31 (1978–79): 41–44.

61. Suzanne Marchand, Down from Olympus: Archaeology and Philhellenism in Germany, 1750–1970 (Princeton: Princeton University Press, 1996), chap. 1.

62. Topinard once wrote that regardless of whether mixed races or pure races exist, the only way to ferret out racial differences would be through anthropometric exercises: "we cannot deny them, our intelligence comprehends them, our mind sees them, our labor separates them out; if in thought we suppress the intermixtures of peoples, their interbreeding, in a flash we see them stand forth—simple, inevitable, a necessary consequence of collective heredity" (quoted in Stocking, Race, Culture, and Evolution, 59).

63. Glick, "Spain," 315–17.

64. Class notes for Pedro González de Velasco's lectures on anatomy, dated 1872, Box 7, uncatalogued papers, Archivo Federico Olóriz (hereafter cited as AFO), University of Granada.

65. Diploma of Federico Olóriz from Medical Faculty at the University of Granada, June 1875, uncatalogued papers, AFO, University of Granada. See also Elvira Arquiola, "Anatomía y antropología en la obra de Olóriz," in Dynamis: Acta Hispánica ad Medicinae Scientiarumque Historiam Illustrandam 1 (1981): 165.

66. Loose sheets of paper entitled "Manual de técnica anatómica destinado principalmente a servir de guía a los alumnos en la cátedra de disección con notas sacadas de los trabajos inéditos del eminente anatómico, Dr. D. Rafael Martínez Molina por Federico Olóriz" (undated but prior to 1883), uncatalogued papers, AFO, University of Granada.

67. Arquiola, "Anatomía y antropología física," 12–13.

68. José Gómez Ocaña, "Elogio del Don Federico Olóriz y Aguilera," Memorias de la Real Sociedad de Historia Natural 7 (1913): 364.

69. Pulido, El Doctor Velasco, 118.

70. Romero de Tejada, Un templo a la ciencia, 15

71. For more on impact of Haeckel on European scientists, see Daniel Gasman, Haeckel's Monism and the Birth of Fascist Ideology (New York: Peter Lang, 1998).

72. Puig-Samper and Galera, *La antropología Española*, 13; Kaplan, "Luís Simarro," 62–65. The implications of Haeckelian monism would find expression in psychiatry, anthropology, physiology, and other burgeoning human sciences of the period (see Daniel Gasman, *Haeckel's Monism and the Birth of Fascist Ideology*).

73. Stocking, *Race, Culture, and Evolution*, 57.

74. Federico Olóriz y Aguilera, *Recolección de cráneos para estudios antropológicos*, Trabajo publicado en la Gaceta Médica de Granada (Granada: Librería de Paulino Ventura Sabatel, 1884), 3–4. He added to these calls in other scientific journals, providing instructions in medical journals for the preparation of skulls and cadavers for anthropological analysis (see Olóriz, "Recolección de cráneos," 444–46).

75. Olóriz, *Recolección de cráneos*, 9.

76. Olóriz, *El siglo médico*, 444.

77. Federico Olóriz y Aguilera, *Manual técnica de anatomía* (Madrid: Editorial Cosmos, 1890), 48. Olóriz originally wrote this manual in 1886 as a textbook for his anatomy classes. He published it four years later.

78. José María Jover Zamora discusses the phenomenon of social penetration of liberal ideas in Spain as one legacy of the First Republic. In this sense, public discussion of science, and expansion of the forums in which these discussions took place, was given more latitude than previously seen in Spain (see Jover Zamora, *Realidad y mito de La Primera República* [Madrid: Espasa Calpe, 1991], 65–71). For a similar, though less optimistic, presentation of this scientific penetration, see Francisco Villacorta Baños, *Burguesía y cultura: Los intelectuales españoles en la sociedad liberal, 1808–1931* (Madrid: Siglo Veintiuno de España, editores, 1980), 80–89.

79. Olóriz was allowed to enter the medical school and perform his measurements on those bodies marked for his studies according to the letter he received from the medical school dean ("Autorización para aumentar las colecciones antropológicas de la Facultad de Medicina de Madrid 1.0 de mayo 1889. Signed by the Decano, Jose de Letamendi," Box 2, uncatalogued, AFO, Universidad de Granada). For more on Letamendi, see Juan Riera, "Letamendi y Turró: Romanticismo y positivismo en la medicina catalana del siglo XIX," *Asclepio* 17 (1965): 117–53.

80. Federico Olóriz, "El laboratorio de antropología de la Facultad de Medicina," *Revista Ibero-Americana de Ciencias Médicas* 1 no. 1 (March 1899): 78.

81. Olóriz, *Recolección de cráneos*, 5.

82. Federico Olóriz to the Director General de Instruccion Publica, Madrid, 6 May 1891, Box 2, uncatalogued, AFO, Universidad de Granada.

83. Ibid.

84. "Plan de un Trabajo sobre el índice cefálico comparado en el vivo, el cadáver y el craneo fresco y seco," Box 7, uncatalogued, AFO, Universidad de Granada.

85. Research notebook, "Coloración: 1 Octubre 1891, Ideas," Box 1, uncatalogued, AFO, Universidad de Granada.

86. He wrote: "in the future one might be able to study all 100 municipal schools in Madrid and the military academies . . . to obtain the first important statistical study of pigmentation in Spain. Would that I could make my dream come true one day" (Research Notebook, "Coloración parte 2, Octubre 1 1891: Proyecto de Investigación," Box 1, AFO, Universidad de Granada). He received this permission to conduct measurements in 1899. See Junta Municipal de Primera Ensenanza de Madrid to Federico Olóriz, 25 April 1899, granting permission "to enter the afore-

mentioned schools and . . . conduct the scientific study that the doctor has requested," in Box 3, uncatalogued, AFO, Universidad de Granada.

87. Ramón y Cajal wrote to Olóriz telling him that the tasks facing descriptive anatomy—the subject of the anatomical textbook Olóriz was then writing—had already been completed. He suggested that Olóriz pursue physiognomy and morphology: "the topic is vast and open, and so little studied" (Santiago Ramón y Cajal to Federico Olóriz, 12 March 1886, in Rafael Sánchez Martín, "El epistolario [1886–1912] de Federico Olóriz [1855–1912]" [Ph.D. diss., Universidad de Granada, Spain, 1979]; available in the Archivo Federico Olóriz, AFO).

88. Federico Olóriz y Aguilera, Distribución geográfica del índice cefálico en España deducida del examen de 8.368 varones adultos: Memoria presentada al Congreso Geográfico Hispano-Portugués-Americano, en sesion de 19 de octubre de 1892 (Madrid: Imprenta del Memorial de Ingenieros, 1894), 5–6.

89. Ibid., 278.

90. Ibid., 220–21; emphasis added.

91. Ibid., 221.

92. Ibid., 218.

93. In a letter to Olóriz, the head of the Musée d'Histoire Naturelle, the Russian-born polygenist Joseph Deniker, commented how he had presented Oloriz's study to the Société d'Anthropologie, where it was published in the society's bulletin. Olóriz then sent a letter asking Leon Azoulay, a member of the society, who was also a friend of Santiago Ramón y Cajal, if he thought the work suitable for the Prix Godard. A week later, Azoulay sent Olóriz a request for his permission to submit his study for consideration for the prize. Olóriz received word of his reception of the prize in November from Azoulay (see Joseph Deniker to Federico Olóriz, 4 October 1894; Federico Olóriz to Sr. Dr. Azoulay, March 1895; Azoulay to Federico Olóriz, 3 April 1895; and Azoulay to Olóriz, 14 November 1895, in Sánchez Martín, El epistolario [1886–1912] de Federico Olóriz [1855–1912]).

94. See J. Ranke to Federico Olóriz, 6 February 1895; F. Yagor, Berlin, to Federico Olóriz, 10 October 1894; Cesare Lombroso to Federico Olóriz, 25 December 1894, in Sánchez Martín, El epistolario (1886–1912) de Federico Olóriz (1855–1912).

95. Certainly Oloriz would have raised the eyebrows of the anthroposociological school with his assertion that Spaniards as a nation represent the same racial superiority that his German aristocrats and scientists do (see Stocking, Race, Culture, and Evolution, 60, 163).

96. For more on anthroposociology, see ibid.

97. On his critiques of Olóriz's cephalic index, see Otto Ammon to Federico Olóriz, 4 July 1895; for offers and requests to Olóriz, see Otto Ammon to Federico Olóriz, 5 March 1896; and Olóriz to Ammon, 8 March 1896, in Sánchez Martín, El epistolario (1886–1912) de Federico Olóriz (1855–1912).

98. José Luís Abellán, "Una manifestación del modernismo: La acepción española de 'raza,'" Cuadernos Hispanoamericanos 553–54 (July–August 1996): 203–14.

99. See Luís de Hoyos Sáinz, "Crónica científica," La España Moderna 8, no. 65 (May 1894): 186.

100. E. Inman Fox, La invención de españa; José Álvarez Junco, Mater Dolorosa: La idea de España en el siglo XIX (Madrid: Taurus, 2001), 199–204.

101. Quoted in Cacho Viu, La Institución Libre de Enseñanza, 347.

102. Ibid., 350–51.

103. Marcelino Menéndez y Pelayo, Historia de los heterodoxos españoles, 2nd ed. (Madrid: Librería General de Victoriano Suárez, 1911), 208.

104. Marcelino Menéndez y Pelayo, *Historia de los heterodoxos españoles*, 4th ed. (1948; Madrid: Editorial Católica, 1986), 1037. The passage first appeared in the 1881 edition, Marcelino Menéndez y Pelayo, *Historia de los heterodoxos españoles* (Madrid: Librería Católica de San José, 1881), 3:833.

105. Carolyn Boyd, *Historia Patria: Politics, History and National Identity in Spain, 1875–1975* (Princeton: Princeton University Press, 1997), 104.

106. Raymond Carr, *Spain: 1808–1975*, 2nd ed. (Oxford: Clarendon Press, 1982), 355.

107. Federico Olóriz y Aguilera, "La talla humana en España," in *Discursos leídos en la Real Academia de Medicina para la recepción pública del Académico Electo Ilmo. Sr. Dr. D. Federico Olóriz y Aguilera el día 24 de mayo de 1896* (Madrid: Nicolás Moya, 1896), 9.

108. Ibid., 53, 99, 106.

109. Ibid., 8–9.

110. As he wrote in his opening speech: "Of the causes which modify growth, some are physiological and internal. Some of these are constant, like dental growth, puberty, while others are variable like the evolutionary roots of race and family, transmitted by inheritance, and those individual predispositions whose roots are unknown like dwarfism or gigantism. Others are caused by external factors outside of the organism, like the hygienic conditions in which they live, or eating habits, exercise, climate, and some of these last are pathological like fevers, infirmity and illnesses of the skeleton [sic]" (ibid., 15).

111. There are signs that Olóriz's interests in applied sciences were piqued early, including his position as an adviser to a government commission on urbanization and public works. See the letter from the minister of government (Ministro de Gobernación del Reino) to Federico Olóriz, dated 16 June 1894, appointing him Vocal de la Junta de Urbanización y Obras, Box 3, uncatalogued, AFO, Universidad de Granada.

112. Puig-Samper and Galera, *La antropología*, 71–72.

113. Manuel Antón y Ferrándiz, *Razas y tribus de Marruecos* (Madrid: Sucesores de Rivadeneyra, 1903), 5.

114. Harvey, "Races Specified," 22–23.

115. Ibid., 40–41; Stocking, *Race, Culture, and Evolution*, 59–63.

116. As quoted in Harvey, "Races Specified," 40.

117. Polygenists, of course, had to confront the fact that some populations were capable of intermixing despite the fact that they seemingly belonged to distinct species. Broca's response was to identify what he called hybrid species, those composed of different groups. Yet, he argued, as did Topinard with less vigor, that most of these hybrid species eventually failed or died off by creating weaker mixtures. Topinard's correction of this idea, via the notion of racial types, turned Broca's assertions on their head, stating that all racial groups were mixtures of ancient pure races, with contemporary races exhibiting various and differing physical and cultural signs of racial health (see Stocking, *Race, Culture, and Evolution*, 55–65; and Harvey, "Races Specified," chap. 1).

118. Manuel Antón y Ferrándiz, *Doctorado de medicina: Conferencias de antropología dadas por el Catedrático de esta asignatura y tomadas taquigráficamente por el alumno E. F.* (Madrid: Sánchez Covisa, 1892).

119. Manuel Antón y Ferrándiz, *Programa razonado de antropología* (Madrid: Imprenta de la Viuda de M. Minuesa de los Ríos, 1897).

120. These materials were not available to the author but are held in the Museo Nacional de Etnología in Madrid (see María Dolores Adellac Moreno, "La formación del Archivo Fotográfico en el Museo," in *Anales del Museo Nacional de Antropología* 3 [1996]: 246–47).

121. Antón, "Lección 6ª," in Doctorado de Medicina, 79–80.

122. Antón, Programa razonado de antropología, 7.

123. Boyd, Historia Patria, 100.

124. Antón, Doctorado de Medicina, 87–88.

125. Ibid., 10–11.

126. Antón, Programa razonado, 32.

127. Ibid., 35–55.

128. Ibid., 17.

129. Echoing Quatrefages, Antón wrote: "When one sees that in all anthropological and linguistic questions that develop within the heart of a historian, the serenity of the scientist is disturbed by patriotic feelings that infiltrate even in the most elevated of intelligences. Thus, the hopes of those who wish that education will destroy the grandest and most sublime of human feelings, like religion, are destroyed for that which differentiates us from beasts, religion and intellect, are both fundamental elements of our heritage" (Manuel Antón y Ferrándiz, Razas y naciones de Europa: Discurso leído en la Universidad Central en la solemne inauguración del curso académico de 1895–1896. Catedrático de Antropología en la Facultad de Ciencias (Madrid: Imprenta Colonial, 1895), 14.

130. Manuel Antón y Ferrándiz, "Fernando Póo y el Golfo de Guinea, por Osorio," Antropología 15 (Madrid, 1891).

131. See Francisco Villacorta Baños, El Ateneo Científico de Madrid (1885–1912) (Madrid: CSIC, 1985), 289–91; and Olóriz, La talla humana, 2–3.

132. Manuel Antón y Ferrándiz, "La raza de Cro-Magnon en España," Anales de la Sociedad Española de Historia Natural 13 (1884).

133. Antón, Razas y tríbus, 5.

134. Ibid., 6.

135. A term that recently had been coined by the Italian anthropologist Giuseppe Sergi. For Sergi, however, the Mediterranean race was composite of both European and North African and Middle Eastern racial groups, while Anton, in an attempt to isolate the Spanish racial type, had previously argued that the Spanish race had undergone little transformation as a result of the invasions of northern Europeans.

136. Antón, Razas y tribus, 6. For more on this notion of the beauty myth and the view of classical Greek statuary as the model of such myth, see George Mosse, Toward the Final Solution (1978; Madison: University of Wisconsin Press, 1985), 1–2.

137. Antón, Razas y tribus, 10.

138. Ibid., 12; emphasis added.

139. José Gómez Ocaña, Elogio de Don Federico Olóriz y Aguilera (Madrid: Fortanent, 1913), 380.

140. Manuel Antón y Ferrándiz, "España: Sección Segunda Antropología," Enciclopedia universal ilustrada: Europeo-Americana (Barcelona: Hijos de J. Espasa, 1923), 406–7.

141. Even as late as 1948, the conclusions reached by Olóriz were still cited as proof of the power of Spain's historical and cultural legacy and its race. While denying the inferiority or superiority of races based on biological categories, the anthropologist José Pérez de Barradas celebrated Olóriz's conclusions as proof of Spain's racial strength and cultural cohesion over the centuries (see Frederick B. Pike, Hispanismo, 1898–1936: Spanish Conservatives and Liberals and Their Relations with Spanish America [Notre Dame: University of Notre Dame Press, 1971], 385). One should note that not all the praise was untempered. In 1956, Julio Caro Baroja lamented that

even in Olóriz's otherwise "magisterial" study, unfortunate "nationalist intentions" leaked into some of the conclusions that he had reached (see Julio Caro Baroja, *Razas, gentes y linajes* [Madrid: Revista de Occidente, 1957], 137).

142. See Proctor, "From Anthropologie to Rassenkunde in the German Anthropological Tradition," 141–47.

4. HOW SPAIN BECAME INVERTEBRATE

1. Luís de Hoyos Sáinz, *Técnica antropológica y antropología física*, 2nd ed., prologue by Manuel Antón y Ferrándiz (1893; Madrid: Imp. del Asilo de Huérfanos del S.C. de Jesus, 1899), 13–14.

2. For more on the makeup of the Spanish educational system at the end of the nineteenth and beginning of the twentieth centuries, see Carolyn Boyd, *Historia Patria: Politics, History and National Identity in Spain, 1875–1975* (Princeton: Princeton University Press, 1998), chap. 1; see also Temma Kaplan, "Luís Simarro and the Development of Science and Politics in Spain, 1868–1917" (Ph.D. diss., Harvard University, 1969), 68.

3. Luís de Hoyos Sáinz, "La antropología: Métodos y problemas," in *Estado actual: Métodos y problemas de las ciencias*, ed. Hoyos Sáinz (Madrid: Imprenta Clásica Española, 1916), 16–18.

4. Manuel Antón y Ferrándiz, *Programa razonado de antropología* (Madrid: Imprenta de la Viuda de M. Minuesa de los Rios, 1897), 7.

5. Societies formed in many of Spain's provinces, including Asturias (1882), Galicia (1887), Extremadura (1882), Catalunya (1885), the Basque country (1879), in addition to the variety of societies that formed in Madrid and in the province of Castile (see Carmelo Lisón Tolosana, *Antropología social en España* [Madrid: Siglo XXI, 1971], 147).

6. Ángel Goicoetxea Marcaida, *Vida y obra de Telésforo de Aranzadi* (Salamanca: Ediciones de Salamanca, 1985), 17–18. On German development, see Benoit Massin, "From Virchow to Fischer: Physical Anthropology and 'Modern Race Theories' in Wilhelmine Germany," in *Volksgeist as Method and Ethic*, ed. George Stocking (Madison: University of Wisconsin Press, 1996), 84.

7. David Ringrose, *Spain, Europe and the "Spanish Miracle," 1700–1900* (Cambridge: Cambridge University Press, 1996), chap. 2.

8. A famous discussion of this literature remains Pedro Laín Entralgo, *España como problema*, 2nd ed. (Madrid: Aguilar, 1957). A more recent look at this literature is Sebastian Balfour, *The End of the Spanish Empire* (Oxford: Oxford University Press, 1997), 64–91.

9. For the sciences, Joy Dorothy Harvey shows how French anthropology weathered the changes in government in France between the Second Empire and the Third Republic (Harvey, "Races Specified; Evolution Transformed: The Social Context of Scientific Debates Originating in the Société d'Anthropologie de Paris, 1859–1902" [Ph.D. diss., Harvard University, 1983]). The effects on scholarship and science in France after the loss to Prussia in 1871 have also been analyzed in Robert Nye, *Crime, Madness and Politics in Modern France: The Medical Concept of National Decline* (Princeton: Princeton University Press, 1984).

10. A good discussion remains Robert Wohl, *The Generation of 1914* (Cambridge: Harvard University Press, 1979), 122–24.

11. Herbert Ramsden, *The 1898 Movement in Spain* (Manchester: Manchester University Press, 1974), 12–15; Wohl, *The Generation of 1914*, 122–59.

12. The classic analysis of the critique of positivism and the search for the irrational is H. Stuart Hughes, *Consciousness and Society*, rev. ed. (New York: Vintage Press, 1977). On the Spanish

version of this modernist response, see Juan Pan-Montojo, introduction to *Más se perdió en España*, ed. Pan-Montojo (Madrid: Alianza Editorial, 1998), 13; and E. Inman Fox, *Ideología y política en las letras de fin de siglo* (Madrid: Espasa Calpe, 1988). On the view of Spain as the actual avant garde of modernist critique of positivism and reason, see Rockwell Gray, *The Imperative of Modernity* (Berkeley and Los Angeles: University of California Press, 1989).

13. The historian Manuel Túñon de Lara has written of "spaces" reserved in each generation for figures from earlier generations whose interests overlapped with those associated with later generations (see Manuel Túñon de Lara, "Grandes corrientes culturales," in *Los orígenes culturales de la II República*, ed. José Luis García Delgado [Madrid: Siglo XXI de España, Editores, 1993], 9).

14. Juan López Morillas, *Hacia el '98* (Barcelona: Ediciones Ariel, 1972), 246; see also Balfour, *The End of the Spanish Empire*, 67. The late Carlos Serrano also was critical of the generational label, noting broadly that regardless of age or shared experience, "something was in the air" linking disciplines, people, and generations together in this era (Serrano, "Conciencia de la crisis," in *Más se perdió en Cuba*, ed. Juan Pan-Montojo [Madrid: Alianza Editorial, 1998], 339).

15. Balfour, *The End of the Spanish Empire*, 67; Serrano, "Conciencia de la crisis," esp. 342–48.

16. See Vicente Cacho Viu, *La Institución Libre de Enseñanza* (Madrid: Ediciones Rialp, 1962), 1:332–36. On Miguel de Unamuno, see Carlos París, "El pensamiento de Unamuno y la ciencia positiva," *Arbor* 22, no. 77(May 1952): 11–23; and Diego Núñez Ruíz, *La mentalidad positiva en España* (Barcelona: Tucar Ediciones, 1975).

17. Thomas Glick's early work on the reception of Darwin and Einstein's theory of relativity in Spain are important exceptions (see Glick, "Spain," in *The Comparative Reception of Darwinism*, ed. Glick [Austin: University of Texas Press, 1974], 207–345; and Thomas F. Glick, *Einstein in Spain: Relativity and the Recovery of Science* [Princeton: Princeton University Press, 1988]). Sebastian Balfour has also worked to correct this gap (see Balfour, *The End of the Spanish Empire* [Oxford: Clarendon Press, 1997], chap. 2); as has Carlos Serrano, with an eye only toward the expressions of positivism among Spain's leading intellectual lights, but not necessarily from where they borrowed them (see Serrano, "Conciencia de la crisis," 347–59).

18. In *Consciousness and Society*, H. Stuart Hughes traces patterns among a variety of intellectuals in this transition in several European countries. Spanish writers are rarely included in such discussions outside Spain, and the work on intellectual transitions in Spain from positivism to later epistemologies still awaits its author.

19. For a discussion of the "two Spains" thesis, see Enric Ucelay da Cal, "The Hispanic Studies Ghetto," *Bulletin of the Society for Spanish and Portuguese Historical Studies*, 19, no. 3 (Fall 1994): 11–15.

20. Lisón Tolosana, *Antropología social*, 150.

21. One might assume these societies were linked to ethnographic thinking outside of Spain primarily because foreign anthropologists would often contact local institutions prior to their arrival in Spain and then use these institutions as home bases when they visited Spain to perform research. For example, Paul Broca encamped in the society in San Sebastian during his work in the Basque country, and the German linguist Hugo Schuhardt lived in the society in Sevilla with the support of the Spanish anthropologist González de Linares (see Lisón Tolosana, *Antropología social*, 145).

22. Ibid., 132.

23. Santos Juliá discusses regionalist, especially Catalan, criticisms of the racial makeup of Castilians in Juliá, *Historias de las dos Españas* (Madrid: Taurus, 2004), 120–37.

24. Quoted in Jacques Maurice and Carlos Serrano, J. Costa: Crisis de la Restauración y populismo, 1875–1911 (Madrid: Siglo XXI Editores, 1977), 148.

25. Juan Corazon, quoted ibid., 157.

26. As quoted in Alfonso Botti, Cielo y dinero: El nacionalcatolicismo en España, 1881–1975 (Madrid: Alianza, 1992), 37.

27. Laura Otis was writing of Pío Baroja, a distant relation of Telésforo de Aranzadi and student of the criminal anthropologist Rafael Salillas y Panzano, that his work was typical of the general nineteenth-century tendency in which "thoughts of heredity invite[d] thoughts about race" (Otis, Organic Memory: History and the Body in the Late Nineteenth and Early Twentieth Centuries [Lincoln: University of Nebraska Press, 1994], 89).

28. See, for example, Joaquín Costa, Oligarquía y caciquismo (1902; Madrid: Ediciones de la Revista de Trabajo, 1975), 4; see also Maurice and Serrano, J. Costa, 157.

29. See Luís de Hoyos Sáinz, Notas para la historia de las ciencias antropológicas en España, in Congreso de Granada 1911: Asociación Española para el Progreso de las Ciencias, (Madrid: Eduardo Arias, [1912]),14; and Francisco Villacorta Baños, El Ateneo Científico, Literario y Artística de Madrid (1885–1912) (Madrid: CSIC, 1985), 122.

30. Manuel Antón y Ferrándiz, Razas y naciones de Europa discurso leído en la Universidad Central en la solemne inauguración del curso académico de 1895–1896 (Madrid: Imprenta Colonial, 1895), 8.

31. In his 1903 anthropology textbook, Antón wrote that all history was anthropology, best presented by Greek and Roman historians, and only updated and made scientific by their nineteenth-century descendants. Much of contemporary anthropology only confirmed what had been written by Roman and Greek forebears (see Manuel Antón y Ferrándiz, Antropología o historia natural del hombre, 2nd ed. [1903; Madrid: Sucesores de Rivadeneyra, 1927], 14, 24).

32. Antón, Razas y naciones, 8–15. On linguistic assertions of Aryanism, see George Mosse, Toward the Final Solution (Madison: University of Wisconsin Press, 1985), 39–40.

33. Antón, Razas y naciones, 16.

34. Ibid., 30–31.

35. Ibid., 31.

36. Ibid., 41.

37. Ibid., 42.

38. Elena Ausejo Martínez, Por la ciencia y por la patria: La institucionalización científica en España en el primer tercio del siglo XX (Madrid: Siglo XXI de España Editores, 1993), 91.

39. Manuel Antón y Ferrandiz, Razas y tribus de Marruecos (Madrid: Sucesores de Rivadeneyra, 1903), 5.

40. Botti, Cielo y dinero, 38–40.

41. Marcelino Menéndez y Pelayo, Historia de los heterodoxos españoles (Madrid: Librería Católica de San José, 1881), 3:833.

42. Telésforo de Aranzadi, Etnología: Antropología filosófica y psicología y sociología comparadas, vol 2 of Lecciones de antropologia, 2nd ed. (Madrid: Romo y Füssel, 1899), 43.

43. Ibid., 426–27.

44. Antón, Razas y tribus, 6.

45. Aranzadi, Etnología, 539.

46. He became a dean at the university in 1905, stepping down in 1907 after a mysterious dispute with botany students about his "teaching methods." He began teaching anthropology

classes at the University of Barcelona in 1917, assuming a professorship in the new discipline of anthropology three years later (see Goicoetxea, *La vida y obra de Telésforo de Aranzadi*, 17).

47. Aranzadi wrote for the *Zentralblatt für Anthropologie* and Hoyos for the *Deutsche Anthropologie Gesellschaft* (see Telésforo de Aranzadi to Luís de Hoyos Sáinz, Granada, 29 November 1896, reprinted in Carmen Órtiz García, *Luis de Hoyos Sáinz y la antropología española*, 546, 570).

48. Telésforo de Aranzadi to Miguel de Unamuno, Granada, 29 April 1899, Legajo H$_5$/3, Correspondencia, Fondo Miguel de Unamuno, Casa-Museo Unamuno, Universidad de Salamanca.

49. See James Urry, "Englishmen, Celts and Iberians: The Ethnographic Survey of the United Kingdom, 1892–1899," in *Functionalism Historicized*, ed. George Stocking (Madison: University of Wisconsin Press, 1984), 88. Spain's association seems to have been composed of the country's entire intellectual community, including scientists, writers, politicians, lawyers, and doctors (see the membership list in *Congreso de Zaragoza: Asociación Española para el Progreso de las Ciencias*, vol. 1, pt. 2 [Madrid: Enrique Arias, (1909)], frontispiece).

50. D. Ricardo Garcia Mercet, "Memoria leida por el Secretario General de la Asociacion," in *Asociación Española para el Progreso de las Ciencias*, *Primer Congreso, Congreso de Zaragoza* (Madrid: Eduardo Arias, 1908), 1:13.

51. On Spanish educational reform and its failures in the two decades following the 1898 War, see Boyd, *Historia Patria*, esp. chap. 2.

52. See Jon Juarisiti, *El bucle melancólico: Historias de nacionalistas vascos* (Madrid: Espasa, 1997), 96–98.

53. Unamuno, for example, had written to Aranzadi asking for more literature on ethnology after Aranzadi had sent him some of his work from the 1890s. Aranzadi responded that the volume on ethnology that he had written was the most complete because it focused on Spain, and was thus more comprehensive on Spain than those that had been translated into Spanish. The later volumes on descriptive ethnography were written with "less precision" because of the lack of data (see Telésforo de Aranzadi to Miguel de Unamuno, Barcelona, 23 October 1900, Legajo H$_5$/3, no. 10, Correspondence, Fondo Miguel de Unamuno, Casa-Museo Unamuno, Salamanca).

54. Hoyos Sáinz, "La antropología," 34.

55. Lisón Tolosana, *Antropología social en España*, 159; Órtiz Garcia, *Luís de Hoyos Sáinz*, 547. On Foster's comments, see George Foster, *Culture and Conquest* (Chicago: Quadrangle Books, 1960), 6.

56. This assertion is based on others' accounts of how materials are arranged in the archives of the Museo Etnológico Nacional in Madrid. These accounts were compiled by Carmelo Lisón Tolosana, *Antropología social*, 152–53. The library of the museum houses the materials today but did not allow me to consult them.

57. See "Acta de la sexta sesión," *Actas y memorias de Sociedad Española de Antropología, Etnografía y Prehistoria* 1, no. 1 (1 May 1922): 59–61; and Lisón Tolosana, *Antropología social*, 153–54.

58. Enrique de Areilza, *Epistolario* (Bilbao: Epistolario El Tilo, 1999), 179.

5. RACE, REGIONALISM, AND THE COLONIES WITHIN

1. On Hoyos's attempts to gain an instructorship at the Institución Libre de Enseñanza in Madrid, see Luís de Hoyos Sáinz to Gonzalez de Linares, 10 October 1890, Item #1, File 1825, Box 127, Fondo Augusto Gonzalez de Linares, Archive of the Institución Libre de Enseñanza (hereafter cited as AILE); and Aranzadi to Hoyos, 7 October 1902, quoted in Carmen Órtiz García, *Luís de Hoyos Sáinz y la antropología española* (Madrid: CSIC, 1987), 574–75.

2. Hoyos was the secretary of the Section of Exact, Physical and Natural Sciences at the Madrid Athenaeum's School for Advanced Study (see Luís de Hoyos Sáinz's prologue to *Estado actual: Métodos y problemas de las ciencias* [Madrid: Imprenta Clásica Española, 1916], 5–7).

3. Luís de Hoyos Sáinz and Telésforo de Aranzadi. *Unidades y constantes de la crania hispánica. Discurso leido a la Asociacion Española para el Progreso de la Ciencias, Congreso de Granada,* 1911 (Madrid: Eduardo Arias, 1913), 3. The Parisian version is in "Notes préliminaires sur les "crania hispanica," *Bulletin et Memoires de la Société d'Anthropologie* (20 February 1913): 81–94; and the version from the Geneva conference is Luís de Hoyos Sáinz, "Caractères généraux de la "crania hispanica," Geneva, 1912, in the Archivo del Ateneo de Madrid.

4. Aranzadi to Hoyos, Granada, 7 June 1896, in Órtiz Garcia, *Luís de Hoyos Sáinz,* 569–70; see also Luís de Hoyos Sáinz, "La antropología: Métodos y problemas," in *Estado actual,* 428.

5. See his discussion of Collignon and W. A. Ripley's 1899 work in Telésforo de Aranzadi, *Etnografía: Razas negras, amarillas, y blanca: Lecciones de antropología,* 2nd ed. (Madrid: Romo y Füssel, 1900), 4:319–20, 336–37.

6. He first took up this kind of argument in his 1889 doctoral dissertation, "El Pueblo Euskalduna," and continued it in many other works, including: Telésforo de Aranzadi, "El problema antropológico vasco," *España Moderna* (July 1894): 141; and "Consideraciones acerca de la raza basca," *Euskal Erria* 35 (July and August 1896): 34. On the development of Basque nationalism, see Jon Juaristi's important *El linaje de aitor* (Madrid: Taurus, 1998); Fernando Molina Aparicio, *La tierra del martirio español* (Madrid: Centro de Estudios Políticos y Constitucionales, 2005); Marianne Heiberg, *The Making of the Basque Nation* (Cambridge: Cambridge University Press, 1989), 49–57; Juan Díez Medrano, *Divided Nations: Class, Politics, and Nationalism in the Basque Country and Catalonia* (Ithaca: Cornell University Press, 1995), 69–89; and, for a brief discussion of physical anthropology, specifically that of Aranzadi, on the development of Basque nationalism, see Daniele Conversi, *The Basques, The Catalans and Spain* (Reno: University of Nevada Press, 1997), 198–99.

7. Jon Juaristi writes of the "clumsy racist arguments" among Basque nationalists of the early twentieth century based on Aranzadi's ideas (see Juaristi, *El chimbo expiatorio* [Madrid: Espasa Calpe, 1999], 222).

8. See Conversi, *The Basques, The Catalans and Spain,* 198–99. On Arana's scientific discussions of Basque purity, see Carlos Serrano, "Conciencia de la crisis," in *Más se perdió en Cuba,* ed. Juan Pan-Montojo (Madrid: Alianza Editorial, 1998), 358.

9. Fernando Molina Aparicio describes this tension as one between "separatistas o separadores" (see Molina Aparicio, *La tierra del martirio español,* chap. 5).

10. See ibid., 262–63.

11. Telésforo de Aranzadi, "De antropología de España," *Revista Estudio* 12, no. 36 (1915): 335. See also Ángel Goicoetxea Marcaida, *Vida y obra de Telésforo de Aranzadi* (Salamanca: Ediciones de Salamanca, 1985), 129.

12. Hoyos and Aranzadi, *Unidades y constantes,* 31–32.

13. Telésforo de Aranzadi and Luís de Hoyos Sáinz, *Etnografía: Sus bases, sus métodos y aplicaciones a España* (Madrid: Biblioteca Corona, 1917), 16.

14. Ibid., 9–10.

15. Lamarckian versus Darwinian evolution and finally the reincorporation of Mendelian genetic inheritance in public discussion were all sources of debate in the late nineteenth and early

twentieth centuries (see Michael Ruse, *The Darwinian Revolution: Science Red in Tooth and Claw* [Chicago: University of Chicago Press, 1979], 6–12).

16. For a discussion of German anthropological fights over diffusionism and idealism, see Andrew Zimmermann, *Anthropology and Antihumanism in Imperial Germany* (Chicago: University of Chicago Press, 2001), 205–12

17. Aranzadi and Hoyos, *Etnografía*, 8–18.

18. Telésforo de Aranzadi, *Problemas de etnografía de los vascos* (Paris: Paul Geuthner, 1907), 3–4.

19. Aranzadi, *De antropología de España*, 5–6.

20. Aranzadi, *Problemas de etnografía de los vascos*, 45–46.

21. Ibid., 46.

22. Aranzadi, *Etnología*, 528.

23. Ibid., 459.

24. Hoyos and Aranzadi, *Unidades y constantes*, 31–32. I have not been able to locate the original study by Dr. Porpeta and Carlos Slocker, *Estudio de topografía craneocerebral* or *Capacidad craneana en Madrid* (Madrid, n.d.).

25. Aranzadi and Hoyos, *Etnografía*, 9.

26. Ibid., 15.

27. Aranzadi and Hoyos, *Etnografía*, 130. In a speech in 1915 to the Madrid Athenaeum, Hoyos wrote ,"[we] reaffirm that ethnography is the search among objects and acts for the national personality" (Hoyos Sáinz, "La Antropología: Métodos y problemas, conferencia del Ateneo de Madrid, Mayo 1915," in Hoyos, *Estado actual: Métodos y problemas de las ciencias* [Madrid: Imprenta Clásica Española, 1916], 436).

28. Aranzadi and Hoyos, *Etnografía*, pt. 2, 193. Hoyos dedicated this study to the work of Joaquin Costa, whom he called "the most profound investigator of the Spanish people" (127).

29. Ibid., 194–95.

30. Andrew Zimmermann notes that even in Germany, Ratzel's criticisms were often unfair in that all anthropologists believed that geography and time shaped the appearance and flow of cultures (Zimmerman, *Anthropology and Antihumanism*, 205). George Stocking notes this tendency in the important nineteenth-century English anthropologist Edward Tylor (Stocking, *Race, Culture, and Evolution* [1968; Chicago: University of Chicago Press, 1982], 79). Others have noted this tendency in the works of Bastian and Ratzel, the respective founders of diffusionism and independent invention (Klaus-Peter Koepping, *Adolf Bastian and the Psychic Unity of Mankind* [St. Lucia: University of Queensland Press, 1983], 68).

31. Hoyos, "La antropología," 17.

32. Aranzadi and Hoyos, *Etnografía*, 162.

33. Antón, *Razas y tribus*, 13.

34. For the significance of this reliance on environment over biology as the cause of racial differentiation, see Frank Dikötter, "Race Culture: Recent Perspectives on the History of Eugenics," *American History Review* 103, no. 2 (April 1998): 467–78.

35. Hoyos, "La antropología," 17.

36. Ibid., 17–18.

37. Jose Ortega y Gasset to Hoyos, El Escorial, 1912, reprinted in Órtiz Garcia, *Luís de Hoyos Sáinz*, 588–89.

38. José Ortega y Gasset, *España invertebrada* (Madrid: Espasa Calpe, 1922).

39. Aranzadi and Hoyos, *Etnografía*, 131–32.

40. Elazar Barkan claimed that academic appointments were the bellwether of anthropology's disciplinary status throughout England during the first two decades of the twentieth century (see Elazar Barkan, *Retreat of Scientific Racism* [Cambridge: Cambridge University Press, 1991], 19).

41. Luís de Hoyos Sáinz, "Comunicación num. 21: Los datos de la antropología penitenciaria en Bélgica," *Actas y Memoria de la Sociedad Española de Antropología, Etnografía y Prehistoria* 2 (26 February 1923): 24–33.

42. Luís de Hoyos Sáinz, *Una hoja para el estudio de la herencia en el hombre: Grupos sanguíneos y carácteres antropológicos* (Madrid: Laboratorio de Antropología Fisiológica, 1929), 426. On Hoyos's focus on blood types, see Luís de Hoyos Sáinz, "Los tipos raciales regionales actuales: Las bases para el estableciemiento de las regiones españoles," *Revista de Antropologia y Etnologia* 7 (1952): 365–412. Claims of the predominance of Rh negative factors in Basque blood continue to arise today in claims for Basque biological purity and uniqueness. For a good counterbalance of responding to claims of Basque racial purity of blood with a celebration of Iberian *mestizaje*, see Santiago Belausteguigoitia, "Jon Juarisiti elogia el mestizaje en Sevilla," *El País*, November 9, 2000, www.elpais.com/articulo/andalucia/JUARISTI/_JON_/INSTITUTO_CER VANTES/Jon/Juaristi/elogia/mestizaje/Sevilla/elpepiespand/20001109elpand_25/Tes.

43. His work with the Basque archaeologist Miguel de Barandiarán still represents the fundamental work on Basque anthropology (see José María Basabe Pardo, *La población vasca en perspectiva biológica*, lecture presented in honor of retirement of the Catedrático of Anthropology (Servicio Editorial de la Universidad del País Vasco, 1984), 8.

44. Jean-Francois Botrel y Jean-Michel Desvois, "Las condiciones de la produccion Cultural," in *1900 en España*, ed. Serge Salaün and Carlos Serrano (Madrid: Espasa-Calpe, 1991), 50.

45. Telésforo de Aranzadi, "Antropología," in *Enciclopedia universal ilustrada Europeo-Americana*, Annual Supplement 1936–1939, pt. 1 (Madrid: Espasa-Calpe, 1944), 60.

46. Ibid., 68–69.

47. See Goicoetxea, *Vida y obra Telésforo de Aranzadi*, 67–68.

48. For more on this conference and Aranzadi's tensions with other attendees, see ibid., 61–62.

49. As quoted in Órtiz García, *Luís de Hoyos Sáinz*, 195.

50. On the content of "official anthropology" during the Franco regime, see Luis Ángel Sánchez Gómez, "Contextos y práctica de la antropología 'oficial' en los fascismos ibéricos," in *Ciencia y fascismo*, ed. Rafael Huertas and Carmen Ortiz (Madrid: Doce Calles, 1997), 127–46.

51. See Luís de Hoyos Sáinz, "Los tipos raciales regionales actuales: Las bases para el estableciemiento de las regiones españoles," 365–412: Luís de Hoyos Sáinz "Análisis por partidos judiciales del acrecimiento de la poblacion de España," *Revista Internacional de Sociologia* 8, no. 29 (1950?): 1–56.

52. Luís de Hoyos Sáinz, "El primer cráneo cuarternario madrileño," *Revista de la Real Academia de Ciencias de Madrid* 63, no. 4 (1952): 435.

53. Luís de Hoyos Sáinz, *Antropólogos y zoólogos españoles en América* (Madrid: C. Bermejo, 1950), 10–11.

54. Aranzadi, "Antropología" 60.

6. RECRUITING THE RACE

1. Carolyn Boyd has written the most direct history of this tradition in her *La política praetoriana en el reinado de Alfonso XIII* (Madrid: Alianza, 1990), which is an expanded version of her *Praetorian Politics in Liberal Spain* (Chapel Hill: University of North Carolina Press, 1979). Other works that

examine the military in Spanish political and social life include Manuel Ballbé, *Orden público y militarismo y la España constitucional (1812–1983)* (Madrid: Alianza, 1983); Gabriel Cardona, *El poder militar en la España en la España hasta la Guerra Civil* (Madrid: El Siglo Veintiuno, 1983); Daniel R. Headrick, *Ejército y política en España (1868–1898)* (Madrid: Editorial Tecnos, 1981); Carlos Seco Serrano, *Militarismo y civilismo en la España contemporánea* (Madrid: Instituto de Estudios Económicos, 1984); and Stanley G. Payne, *Politics and the Military in Modern Spain* (Stanford: Stanford University Press, 1967).

2. Geoffrey Jensen has recently explored the intellectual culture of the Spanish military in the period leading up to the Spanish civil war in *Irrational Triumph: Cultural Despair, Military Nationalism, and the Ideological Origins of Franco's Spain* (Reno: University of Nevada Press, 2002).

3. John Lawrence Tone, *War and Genocide in Cuba, 1895–1898* (Chapel Hill: University of North Carolina Press, 2006), 97.

4. See Vincent J. Cirillo, *Bullets and Bacilli: The Spanish American War and Military Medicine* (New Brunswick, N.J.: Rutgers University Press, 2004).

5. On the medical approaches to treating disease, see Tone, *War and Genocide in Cuba*, 98–99.

6. Some military figures even emphasized the retrenchment of bravado and military domination in the decade following the disaster (see Sebastian Balfour, "Spain and the Great Powers in the Aftermath of the Disaster of 1898," in *Spain and the Great Powers in the Twentieth Century*, ed. Balfour and Paul Preston [London: Routledge, 1999], 13–31). Paul Preston has recently written of the Spanish military increasingly viewing the Spanish proletariat as the internal enemy, the "subject colonial race" (see Preston, "The Answer Lies in the Sewers: Captain Aguilera and the Mentality of the Francoist Officer Corps," *Science in Society* 68, no. 3 [Fall 2004]: 281).

7. Patricia Lorcin has recently examined the role of military doctors in establishing French control in Algeria in the nineteenth century (see Lorcin, *Imperial Identities: Stereotyping, Prejudice and Race in Colonial Algeria* [London: I.B. Tauris, 1999], 97–145).

8. This view is certainly under revision, especially for French imperialism (see Richard Fogarty and Michaela Osborne, "Constructions and Functions of Race in French Military Medicine, 1830–1920," in *The Color of Liberty: Histories of Race in France*, ed. Sue Peabody and Tyler Stovall [Durham: Duke University Press, 2003]: 206–36). Patricia Lorcin has examined the contribution of French military doctors to racial thinking in France in "Imperialism, Colonial Identity, and Race in Algeria, 1830–1870: The Role of the French Medical Corps," *Isis* 90 (1999): 653–79. On Spanish colonial policy in Morocco, see Geoffrey Jensen, "The Peculiarities of 'Spanish Morocco': Imperial Ideology and Economic Development," *Mediterranean Historical Review* 20, no. 1 (June 2005): 81–102.

9. Sebastian Balfour and Paul Preston wrote that, after 1898, "Morocco became the means whereby Spain re-entered international relations in a dynamic period of neo-colonial expansion" ("Spain and The Great Powers in the Aftermath of the Disaster of 1898," in *Spain and the Great Powers in the Twentieth Century*, ed. Balfour and Preston [London: Routledge, 1999], 4).

10. Carolyn Boyd notes the eclecticism of historical methodology in late-nineteenth-century Spain because of a constant battle between liberal and conservative forces to present a clear image of the Spanish past (see Boyd, *Historia Patria: Politics, History and National Identity in Spain 1875–1975* [Princeton: Princeton University Press, 1997], 70). Geoffrey Jensen describes the same, if more surprising, eclectic approach within military academies in *Irrational Triumph*, 27–30.

11. Laura Otis, *Organic Memory: History and the Body in the Late Nineteenth and Early Twentieth Centuries* (Lincoln: University of Nebraska Press, 1994), 43–49.

12. For "spiritual and material decay," see Felipe Ovilo y Canales, *La decadencia del Ejército: Estudio de higiene militar* (Madrid: Imprenta del Hospicio, 1899), 4. For a general discussion on reform efforts following the war, see Seco Serrano, *Militarismo y civilismo*, 121–26; and Payne, *Politics and the Military in Modern Spain*, 83–101.

13. Geoffrey Jensen argues strenuously for an appreciation of the kind of "accommodation of opposites" within Spanish political, military, and intellectual culture that Jeffrey Herf sees in Weimar conservatism and Nazi ideology in his book. Jensen argues that reactionary modernism, the celebration of modern technology amid a broader rejection of Enlightenment reason, is a "useful term to describe a more general European intellectual trend" in *Irrational Triumph*, 4–5. On the accommodation of opposites, see Jeffrey Herf, *Reactionary Modernism: Technology, Culture and Politics in Weimar and the Third Reich* (Cambridge: Cambridge University Press, 1984), 1–17.

14. The classic work of detailing the crisis of liberalism is H. Stuart Hughes, *Consciousness and Society* rev. ed. (New York: Vintage Press, 1977) . On this modernizing impulse in the development of modern social sciences, see Dorothy Ross, ed., *Modernist Impulses in the Human Sciences, 1870–1930* (Baltimore: Johns Hopkins University Press, 1994); on Spanish critiques among regenerationists, see Sebastian Balfour, *The End of the Spanish Empire, 1898–1923* (Oxford: Clarendon Press, 1997), 64–91.

15. Jensen, *Irrational Triumph*, 23–26.

16. The term is taken from the title of an important study of Spanish recruits discussed later in this chapter. See Luís Sánchez Fernández, *El hombre español útil para el servicio de las armas y para el trabajo: Sus características antropológicas a los 20 años de edad* (Madrid: Imprenta Eduardo Arias, 1913).

17. Military historians like Francisco Villamartín wrote as early as 1862 of the need to define the "typical Spanish soldier" using the tools of historical positivism. Anthropologists were adding a supposedly more stable and structured definition of race. For more on military history writing, see Jensen, *Irrational Triumph*, 29.

18. Military doctors often reminded military tacticians that aligning new weapons and tactics with modern medical care was part of the "'harmonic alignment' for all modern militaries" with which to head into battle (see M. Slocker, "Consideraciones generales sobre alguno de los problems sanitarios en campaña," *Revista de Sanidad Militar*, 14, no. 315 [1 August 1900]: 365).

19. This speech was reprinted in the *Revista de Sanidad Militar* over the course of four issues in 1909. On the new "*leitmotiv* of war," see Ángel Pulido y Fernández, "La Sanidad Militar," *Revista de Sanidad Militar* 3, no. 1 (1 January 1909): 16.

20. In his memoirs, the military surgeon Manuel Bastos Ansart describes the medical education he experienced in the Spanish armed forces in the 1890s and the opening up of the "unknown world" of Darwinian, Lamarckian, and Haeckelian evolution in the military academy's zoology classes (see Bastos Ansart, *De las Guerras Coloniales a la Guerra Civil* [Barcelona: Ediciones Ariel, 1969], 33, 39–49).

21. The United States succeeded partially because of its early prophylactic intervention and their awareness of the antimosquito measures (see Cirillo, *Bullets and Bacilli*, esp. chap. 4; and Tone, *War and Genocide*, 98–100).

22. For biographical information on Ovilo y Canales, see Hoja de Servicios [Personal Service File], Expediente Personal #O-25, Archivo General Militar (hereafter cited as AGM), Segovia.

23. Felipe Ovilo y Canales, *Discurso leído en la Sociedad Española de Higiene en la sesión inaugural del curso académico de 1898–1899: Consideraciones acerca de la higiene militar en España* (Madrid: Imprenta del Hospicio, 1899), 40, 43.

24. José Ma. Massons, *Historia de la Sanidad Militar Española* (Barcelona: Ediciones Pomares-Corredor, 1994), 3:11.

25. Ovilo, *Discurso leído*, 40.

26. Ibid., 43.

27. Ibid., 47, 51.

28. In a lecture given to the Royal Academy of History, Ovilo borrowed the language of Aranzadi, differentiating between the racial spirit that Spain did not lack, and the racial health that it did (see Felipe Ovilo y Canales, *La decadencia del ejército: Estudio de higiene militar* [Madrid: Imprenta del Hospicio, 1899], 9, 21).

29. José María Massons has written the most comprehensive history of the Spanish military's Sanitary Corps (see Massons, *Historia de la Sanidad Militar Española*, vols. 1–4).

30. The royal order (no. 192) was issued on 30 August 1899 (see "Real orden sobre dementes," *Revista de Sanidad Militar* 17, no. 396 [15 December 1903]: 523).

31. Unsigned and undated letter in "Folleto: Gestiones sobre cesión del Museo Antropológico del Dr. Velasco al ramo de guerra s.f.," Legajo 461, Sec. 2, Div. 8, AGM.

32. Folleto Museos y Legislacion, 16 October 1900, Legajo 461, Sec. 2, Div. 8, AGM.

33. "Sección Professional," *Revista de Sanidad Militar* 13, no. 287 (1 June 1899): 306–30.

34. Ovilo had first used the term "useful man" (*el hombre útil*) in his lecture on the military decay (see Ovilo, *La decadencia*, 7). The order for the study was issued as a royal order on 17 October 1902 (see Sánchez y Fernández, *El hombre español*, 61).

35. On the concentration camp and Weyler, see Tone, *War and Genocide*, 193–224.

36. On military education, see Jensen, *Irrational Triumph*, chap. 1.

37. Hoja de Servicios [Personal Service File], Expediente Personal, Luís Sánchez Fernández: 1857–1917, Archivo General Militar, Segovia.

38. Massons, *Historia de la Sanidad Militar Española*, 3:27–33.

39. Jensen, *Irrational Triumph*, 26.

40. Ibid., 14–16.

41. Examples abound of this philo-Germanic feeling in the Sanidad Militar. On the "perfect organization of the German military health services" developed during the Crimean War and improved upon in the "War of Succession" in 1870, see C. I. Alarcón, "Organizacion del servicio de Sanidad Aleman en tiempo de guerra," *Revista de Sanidad Militar* 17, no. 384 (15 June 1903): 254.

42. One of the most infamous of these doctors, Antonio Vallejo-Nájera helped introduce a racial dynamic to Spanish psychiatry from the work of the German doctor Ernst Kretschmer, and later directed medical experiments in Francoist prisoner-of-war camps (Michael Richards, "Spanish Psychiatry c. 1900–1945: Constitutional Theory, Eugenics, and the Nation," *Bulletin of Spanish Studies*, 81, no. 6 [September 2004]: 825–27). That Vallejo-Nájera also served as Pulido's personal doctor speaks to the large areas of overlap between between military and civilian medical and anthropological circles.

43. For the role of Germany in the turn-of-the-twentieth-century Spanish military, see Jensen, *Irrational Triumph*, 25–27; and Miguel Alonso Baquer, *El ejército en la sociedad española* (Madrid: Ediciones del Movimiento, 1971), 170–204.

44. For more on the military turn to regionalism after 1898, see Seco Serrano, *Civilismo y militarismo*, 234.

45. One national study on height of the Spanish soldier was performed in 1901 (see "Folleto reclutamiento y reemplazo: Talla oficio estados," 30 December 1901, Sección 2ª, Division 11ª, Folio

51, AGM, Segovia). For complaints about the poor state of the Spanish recruits, see "Folleto de reclutamiento y reemplazo: Traslados-Tallas," 15 March 1902, Sección 2ª Division 11ª, Folio 51, AGM, Segovia.

46. The largest was performed by Rodolfo Livi of the Italian army over a seven-year period. An initial version of Livi's study won the Prix Godard from the Société d'Anthropologie de Paris in 1896, sharing the prize that year with Federico Olóriz (see Sánchez Fernández, El hombre español útil, 3).

47. The second publication was a transcription of a lecture he had given to the Spanish Association for the Progress of Science in 1911 in Granada.

48. See Federico Olóriz y Aguilera, "La talla humana en España," in Discursos leídos en la Real Academia de Medicina para la recepción pública del Académico Electo Ilmo. Sr. Dr. D. Federico Olóriz Aguilera el día 24 de mayo de 1896 (Madrid: Nicolas Moya, 1896), 106.

49. Sánchez Fernández, El hombre español útil, 7–8.

50. Ibid., 8.

51. Ibid., 7–8.

52. Ibid., 9–10.

53. Matti Bunzl, "Franz Boas and the Humboldtian Tradition: From Volksgeist and Nationalkarakter to an Anthropological Concept of Culture," in Volksgeist as Method and Ethic, ed. George Stocking (Madison: University of Wisconsin Press, 1996), 17–78.

54. Sánchez Fernández, El hombre español útil, 3.

55. Ibid., 19.

56. Ibid., 19–20.

57. Ibid., 21.

58. Ibid., 21. This view was an interesting adumbration of the argument offered by Eugen Weber on the development of national identity via nationalizing projects like army service in his Peasants into Frenchmen (Stanford: Stanford University Press, 1976).

59. "De la formación de hojas antropométricas individuales en el ejército," Revista de Sanidad Militar 14, no. 302 (15 January 1900): 31–37.

60. "Bibliografía: Apuntes antropométricos del presidio de Melilla," Revista de Sanidad Militar 20, no. 450 (15 May 1906): 155–56.

61. L. Torremocha Téllez, "Carta Abierta," Revista de Sanidad Militar 14, no. 303 (1 February 1900): 56.

62. Sánchez Fernández, El hombre útil, 4–5.

63. Ángel Calvo Flores, "Los carácteres antropológicos y las enfermedades," Revista de Sanidad Militar 3, no. 8 (15 April 1909): 255–59.

64. See Boyd, La política pretoriana; and Jensen, Irrational Triumph, 22.

65. See Herf, Reactionary Modernism. Aspects of Ze'ev Sternhell's notion that French fascism and European fascism in general did not emerge from a hermetically sealed conservative tradition but rather combined aspects of nationalism, racism, and socialism remains widely debated but is still a compelling way of understanding the forces that fueled the rise of the radical Right in Europe in the first decades of the twentieth century (see Sternhell, Neither Right nor Left, trans. David Maisel [Berkeley and Los Angeles: University of California Press, 1986]). Enric Ucelay da Cal has made a similar argument for the rise of Spanish fascist movements, in El Imperialismo Catalan (Barcelona: Edhasa, 2003); see also Jensen, Irrational Triumph, 50–51.

66. Antonio Vallejo Nágera, La política racial del nuevo estado (San Sebastián: Editorial Española, 1938), 15.

67. Paul Preston, "The Answer Lies in the Sewers: Captain Aguilera and the Mentality of the Francoist Officer Corps," *Science and Society* 68, no. 3 (Fall 2004): 271–312.

68. This topic already has an extensive bibliography; see, among others, Mario Biagioli, "Science, Modernity and the 'Final Solution,'" in *Probing the Limits of Representation*, ed. Saul Friedländer (Cambridge: Harvard University Press, 1992), 185–205. Robert Proctor considers the relationship between Nazi political culture and medicine in *Racial Hygiene: Medicine under the Nazis* (Cambridge: Harvard University Press, 1988).

69. Michael Richards, "Spanish Psychiatry," 840.

70. César Juarros, "La emoción nomada: El pueblo neurósico," *La Raza: Revista Hispánica* 17, no. 203 (27 November 1930).

71. César Juarros, *Atalaya sobre el fascismo* (Madrid: M.a. Yagüe, 1934), 201.

72. Despite the important effort to uncover documents, recent work has tended to portray those involved in wartime atrocities as products of their moment (see, in particular, Ricard Vinyes, Montse Amengou, and Ricard Belis, *Los niños perdidos del franquismo* [Barcelona: Plaza y Janés, 2002], 31–54). Michael Richards has recently worked to show a longer historical lineage for some aspects of Francoist scientific thought and social policy (see Michael Richards, *A Time of Silence: Civil War and the Culture of Repression in Franco's Spain, 1936–1945* [Cambridge: Cambridge University Press, 1998], 57–62; and, more recently, Richards, "Spanish Psychiatry," 823–48).

73. See Mary Nash, "Social Eugenics and Nationalist Race Hygiene in Early 20th Century Spain," *Journal of the History of European Ideas* 15, nos. 4–5 (August 1992): 741–48. On eugenics within Spanish anarchism, see Richard Cleminson, *Anarchism, Science and Sex: Eugenics in Eastern Spain, 1900–1937* (Bern: Peter Lang, 2000), esp. 227–54.

74. George M. Fredrickson reframes the French sociologist Pierre-André Taguieff's distinction between the logics of racism of exploitation and extermination as racisms of exclusion and inclusion in *Racism: A Short History* (Princeton: Princeton University Press, 2002), 9.

75. Richards, "Spanish Psychiatry," 840.

76. On the "near-racist contempt," see Preston, "The Answer Lies in the Sewers," 281. On the "more or less racist vision," see Paul Preston, *The Politics of Revenge* (London: Unwin Hyman, 1990), 32. Preston's upcoming history of the repressions during the civil war—entitled, as it is, *The Spanish Holocaust*—carries this theme further (London: HarperCollins, forthcoming).

77. In addition to Vallejo-Nájera, the roster of philo-German doctors working in the Spanish military includes important figures like Misael Bañuelos, who wrote important medical textbooks on race and pathology during the early years of the Franco regime, and the doctor turned party leader of the Partido Nacionalista Español, Jose María Albiñana, who also belonged to the Royal Academy of Medicine throughout the 1930s. The role of doctors and scientists in Spanish political life still needs to be studied in more detail. Some initial work is appearing, especially Isabel Jiménez Lucena, "Medicina social, racismo y discurso de la desigualdad en el primer franquismo," in *Ciencia y Fascismo*, ed. Rafael Huerta and Carmen Ortiz (Madrid: Doce Calles, 1998), 111–26.

7. RACE EXPLAINS CRIME

1. An earlier version of this chapter has been published in the *European History Quarterly* 35, no. 2 (April 2005): 241–65, by Sage Publications Ltd. All rights reserved. An online version is available: http://ehq.sagepub.com/cgi/reprint/35/2/241.

2. Michel Foucault is probably the best known theorist to identify the process of defining the normal by defining the pathological in his studies of the development of mental health professions and of the diagnosis of madness (see Foucault, *The Birth of the Clinic* [New York: Vintage, 1994], 35–36).

3. The following represent recent work on the role these ideas played in other European criminological scientific circles. Mary Gibson explores Cesare Lombroso's particular insistence on atavism as the cause of criminal behavior in "Biology or Environment? Race and Southern "Deviancy" in the Writings of Italian Criminologists," in *Italy's "Southern" Question: Orientalism in One Country*, ed. Jane Schneider (Oxford and New York: Berg, 1998), 99–116. On degeneration as a sociobiological concept, see Daniel Pick, *Faces of Degeneration: A European Disorder* (Cambridge: Cambridge University Press, 1989); see also Robert Nye, *Crime Madness, and Politics in Modern France: The Medical Concept of National Decline* (Princeton: Princeton University Press, 1984).

4. Zygmunt Bauman, *Modernity and the Holocaust* (Ithaca: Cornell University Press, 1989), 42–46.

5. Fernando Álvarez-Uría, *Miserables y locos* (Barcelona: Tusquets Editores, 1983), 144–50; Luís S. Granjel, *La frenología en España* (Salamanca: Instituto de Historia de la Medicina, 1973); José María López Piñero et al, *Diccionario histórico de la ciencia moderna en España*, (Barcelona: Ediciones Peninsula, 1983), 1:268–69.

6. Dr. López de la Vega, 'La frenología," *AAE* 1, no. 6 (15 April 1873): 71–72.

7. Francesc Bujosa Homar, "Mariano Cubí y Soler," in López Piñero et al., *Diccionario histórico de la ciencia moderna en España*, 1:268.

8. In one article, he argued against an idea then in vogue in forensic medicine that the image of murderers became frozen on the retina of their victim at the moment of death. Mata's response reflected both his disappointment with scientists who entertained these ideas despite the structural impossibility on which they relied and with the popular press, which caused this idea to proliferate in the public mind (see Mata, "Cuestión médico-forense," *Revista General de Legislación y Jurisprudencia* 28 [1866]: 335).

9. On the university crisis and its aftermath, see Vicente Cacho Viu, *La Institucion Libre de Enseñanza* (Madrid: Ediciones Rialp, 1962), 1:134–80.

10. Substantive penal reforms were slower to develop, but the actual discussion of criminality, its causes and effects, and the general view that social and political behaviors determined the progressive and degenerate direction of a society had its first roots in this period. For example, the first articles in medicine and the law began to appear in Spanish legal journals in the 1870s, and chairs in legal medicine were created at a number of Spanish universities in Madrid in 1841 and in Oviedo in 1883.

11. Temma Kaplan, "Luís Simarro and the Development of Science and Politics in Spain, 1868–1817" (Ph.D. diss., Harvard University, 1969), 162–97.

12. Pedro Mata worked with Jean-Marie Charcot at the Salpetrière Asylum (see López Piñero et al., *Diccionario histórico de la ciencia moderna en España*, 2:42–43).

13. Jan Goldstein, *Console and Classify: The French Psychiatric Profession in the Nineteenth Century* (Cambridge: Cambridge University Press, 1987).

14. See Luís Silvela, "Sección Legislativa," *Revista General de Legislación y Jurisprudencia* (hereafter cited as *RGLJ*) 70 (1870): 339–72.

15. For examples of these complaints, see Luís de Hoyos Sáinz, "La medicina en el derecho," *España Moderna* 64 (April 1894): 178–81; [José María] Esquerdo, *Locos que no lo parecen* (Madrid: Ateneo de Internos, 1880), 4.

16. For discussions of these crimes and the popular responses, see Constancio Bernaldo de Quirós, *Figuras delincuentes* (Madrid, 1907); and Fernando Álvarez-Uría and Julia Varela, *El Cura Galeote, Asesino del Obispo de Madrid-Alcalá* (Madrid: Ediciones La Piqueta, 1979).

17. Kaplan, "Luís Simarro and the Development of Science," 162–63.

18. Temma Kaplan began the discussion of this fight in 1969, but it has not been picked up by subsequent historians (see Kaplan, "Luís Simarro and the Development of Science," 165–72). The exception to this is the recent dissertation of Stephen Jacobson, "Professionalism, Corporatism, and Catalanism: The Legal Profession in Nineteenth-Century Barcelona" (Ph.D. diss., Tufts University, 1998), 410–14. For discussions of these divisions elsewhere, see Goldstein, *Console or Classify*.

19. Esquerdo, *Locos que no lo parecen*, 14–15.

20. According to newspaper accounts, Galeote's insanity defense emerged only after his lawyer first began to notice during his pretrial conferences the curate's bizarre behavior. In court, however, his behavior did not seem to draw undue attention. See articles taken from the medical journal *El Siglo Médico* from 1887 and the reports from the Royal Academy of Medicine, in Álvarez-Uría and Varela, *El Cura Galeote*, 125–29.

21. Esquerdo had established contact with Charcot via Pedro Mata, who had studied with the French scientist in Salpetriêre Asylum in France, during his exile prior to the 1868 revolution (Kaplan, "Luís Simarro and the Development of Science, 162–97).

22. Esquerdo, *Locos que no lo parecen*, 10.

23. On Charcot's interest in physical traits, see Deborah Silverman, *Art Nouveau in Fin de Siècle France* (Berkeley and Los Angeles: University of California Press, 1989), 79–83.

24. Esquerdo, *Locos que no lo parecen*, 14.

25. Ibid., 13.

26. See Kaplan, "Luís Simarro and the Development of Science," 102.

27. Ibid., 178–85.

28. Leon Gambetta's oft-cited comment that positivism was the ideological torchlight of the Third Republic bespoke the differences with Spain. Spanish positivists, though active in the government, never succeeded in fostering an atmosphere in which a prime minister during the Restoration could make such a comment (see Diego Núñez Ruíz, *La mentalidad positiva en España: Desarrollo y crisis* [Barcelona: Tucar Ediciones, 1975], 17–18).

29. For a discussion of Spanish positivism, see ibid., esp. chap. 1.

30. Kaplan, "Luís Simarro and the Development of Science," 103.

31. See the article by the ILE's founder Francisco Giner de los Ríos, "Sobre lo moral y lo jurídico," *Boletín de la Institución Libre de Enseñanza* (hereafter cited as BILE) 2, no. 44 (16 December 1878): 175.

32. Juan López-Morillas, *The Krausist Movement in Spain* (Cambridge: Cambridge University Press, 1981), 11–22.

33. Ibid., 20; Carmelo Lisón Tolosana, *Antropología social en España* (Madrid: Siglo XXI de España Editores, 1971), 131.

34. Temma Kaplan, "Spanish Positivism," *Cuadernos Hispánicos de la Medicina y de la Ciencia*, no. 12 (1974).

35. Lisón Tolosana notes that in this way, social anthropology in Spain antedated its European cousins by almost twenty-five years. The program for social anthropology in the ILE was formed

in 1877, while in England, for example, chairs in social anthropology did not appear until the first decade of the twentieth century (see Lison Tolosana, *Antropología social*, 127). A distinction must be made, of course, between the recognition of a university discipline and the laying out of a course in a private institute, with the former indicating the institutional or official recognition of a body of literature and thought and the latter a recommendation for the particular study of such a specialized knowledge.

36. In 1881, students in the ILE were encouraged to study the "inhabitants" of Madrid, using the recently created Anthropological Museum at the Academy of Natural Sciences, which Manuel Antón y Ferrandiz directed (see Lisón Tolosana, *Antropología social*, 132). For evidence of guest lectures and the participation of non-ILE physical anthropologists in the establishment of curricula in the ILE, see, for example, the letter from Federico Olóriz to Franciso Giner de los Ríos, apologizing for not being able to attend doctoral exams for ILE students in physical anthropology that year (25 April 1887, Folder 63, Box 4, Fondo Giner de Los Ríos, AILE, Madrid). See lectures notes prepared by the anthropologist Augusto González de Linares for class on morphology and Darwinian versus Haeckelian evolution, Item 2, 4 May 1877, Folio 1873, Box 131, Fondo Augusto González de Linares, AILE, Madrid. For a view of how anthropology classes were taught, see notes taken by Manuel Cossío in Giner's 1882 anthropology classes, Folio 1421, Box 76, and Folio 1441, Box 77, Fondo Manuel Cossío, AILE, Madrid.

37. Giner de los Ríos, "Sobre lo moral y lo jurídico," *BILE* 2, no. 44 (16 Dcember 1878): 175.

38. P. Dorado Montero to Giner de los Ríos, Bologna, Italy, 15 May 1887, Folder 63, Box 4, Fondo Giner de Los Ríos, AILE, Madrid.

39. Between 1882 and 1884, more than a dozen articles appeared in the *Revista General de Legislación y Jurisprudencia* on the new Italian positivist school of criminology. This journal was the main publication of Spanish lawyers and was published by the College of Lawyers in Madrid. See, among them, E. Brusa, "Los carácteres de la Escuela Criminalista Italiana y especialmente respecto a algunas modernas cuestiones técnicas y prácticas sobre la pena." *RGLJ* 60 (1882): 210–30; Dr. Escuder, "Locos lúcidos" *RGLJ* 63 (1883): 5–40.

40. See Dorado to Giner de los Ríos, 10 May 1887, Folio 60, Box 4, Fondo Giner de los Ríos, AILE, Madrid. See also G. Sergi, *Origine e diffusione della stirpe mediterranea* (Rome: Soc. Ed. Dante Alighieri, 1895).

41. P. Dorado Montero to Giner de los Ríos, 15 May 1887, Folio 60, Box 4, Fondo Giner de los Ríos, AILE, Madrid.

42. One Spaniard complained about "these unclear Italian thinkers" despite calling for the implementation of their ideas in Spain (see E.G.A. [Enrique Garcia Alonso], "La nueva ciencia penal" *RGLJ* 70 [1886]: 656).

43. Mary Gibson, "Biology or Environment? Race and Southern 'Deviancy' in the Writings of Italian Criminologists," 102–3. In *Faces of Degeneration*, Daniel Pick interprets Lombroso's inconsistencies somewhat more positively, claiming that they indicated the openness of his approach attempting to assimilate different ideas from other countries (121).

44. Gibson, "Biology or Environment?" 105.

45. Ibid., 106.

46. Kaplan, "Luís Simarro and the Development of Science," 169.

47. Escuder, "Locos lúcidos," 10–11.

48. Ibid., 23.

49. Ibid., 24.

50. Ángel Pulido y Fernández and Manuel Tolosa, *De carabanchel al paraíso: Recuerdos de un manicomio* (Madrid: Imprenta de Enrique Teodoro, 1882), 14, 35–36.

51. See debates relating to this change in the code, in which Esquerdo was an active participant in the Cortes, in José María Escuder, "Un loco y un imbécil," *RGLJ* 61 (1882): 75–102.

52. The trial of the Cura Galeote was perhaps the most sensational and well-publicized trial in Spain during the 1880s. Little remains of the testimony other than what has been gleaned from press reports. A re-creation of the trial has been assembled by Fernando Álvarez-Uría and Julia Varela (*El Cura Galeote Asesino del Obispo de Madrid-Alcalá*).

53. One article testified to the bewilderment of criminologists who had to explain why an aristocratic woman had killed her servant and family (see Escuder, "Locos lúcidos," 6–10). For a more in-depth analysis of women criminals in particular, see Mary S. Gibson, "The 'Female Offender' and the Italian School of Criminal Anthropology," *Journal of European Studies* 12 (1982): 155–65.

54. See, for example, the Madrid lawyer Luís Morote's long disquisition on the various new methods of dealing with criminals to be applied in Spain (Morote, "El derecho penal: Capítulo de las ciencas naturales," *RGLJ* 65 [1884]: 451). See also Kaplan's discussion of the attempts of Luís Simarro to account for inoperable brain lesions while still arguing for the rehabilitation of criminals (Kaplan, "Luís Simarro and the Development of Science," 164–65).

55. This analysis of national contexts represents one method of moving away from the generalized, non–place specific Foucaldian analysis of crime. Presently, historians are accepting the idea that it is through this more comparative, site-specific approach that they can point to larger, supranational similarities in the formation criminal and in turn "normal" behaviors at different periods in the nineteenth and twentieth centuries. See, for example, the formative work in this approach, Nye, *Crime, Madness and Politics in Modern France*, esp. 26, 48; and Ted Robert Gurr, Peter N. Grabosky, and Richard C. Hula, *The Politics of Crime and Conflict: A Comparative History of Four Cities* (London: Sage, 1977).

56. Complaints about how doctors' testimony was ignored in judicial decisions abounded in the medical press (see, for example, Eulogio Ruíz Casaviella, "Martirologio Médico" in *El Siglo Médico* 31, no. 1590 [15 June 1884]: 382). Others offered advice on providing convincing testimony in a legal setting (see Ángel Pulido y Fernández, "Los informes periciales medicos en el juicio oral," *El Siglo Medico* 31, no. 1586 [18 May 1884]: 305–7).

57. As cited in Nye, *Crime, Madness and Politics*, 47–48.

58. Álvarez-Uría, *Miserables y locos*, esp. chap. 5; Julia Varela, "Técnicas de control social en 'La Restauración,'" in Álvarez-Uría and Varela, *El Cura Galeote*, 210–36.

59. "Reforma del código penal" *El Liberal*, 20 November 1886, 2.

60. Transcipts of the debates were reprinted in the *Revista General de Legislación y Jurisprudencia* over the course of six months. For the particular critiques of Alonso Martínez and his chief rival, Luís Silvela, see "Sección Legislativa," *RGLJ* 70 (1870): 339–72.

61. Rafael Salillas y Panzano, "Entre paréntesis: Los locos criminales," *El Liberal*, 20 November 1886, 2–3.

62. Ibid., 2.

63. Ibid., 3.

64. Ibid., 2.

65. María Dolores Fernandez Rodríguez, *El pensamiento penitenciario y criminológico de Rafael Salillas* (Santiago de Compostela: Universidad de Compostela, 1976), 113.

66. Salillas was a well-known figure in the Spain of 1890 to 1909, usually presented in public discourse as a fanatic champion of Lombroso. One oft-cited comment betrays the point: the Spanish writer Pío Baroja, writing in 1947, described Spain in the 1890s as "everywhere having its version of Lombroso. In Madrid, it was Doctor Salillas" (quoted in Luís Maristany, *El gabinete del Dr. Lombroso: Delincuencia y fin de siglo España* [Barcelona: Editoriales Anagrama, 1973], 40).

67. Ibid., 36–43; Fernández Rodríguez, *El pensamiento penitenciario y criminológico de Rafael Salillas*, 114.

68. Fernández Rodríguez, *El pensamiento penitenciario y criminológico de Rafael Salillas*, 114.

69. Rafael Salillas y Panzano, *La antropología en el derecho penal: Tema de discusion en la Sección de Ciencias Exactas, Físicas y Naturales del Ateneo de Madrid* (Madrid: Imprenta de la Revista de Legislación y Jurisprudencia, 1888), 9–10.

70. Ibid., 11.

71. Rafael Salillas y Panzano, "La antropología en el derecho penal," *RGLJ* 36, no. 73 (1888): 611.

72. Salillas, *La antropología en el derecho penal*, 14.

73. Ibid., 17.

74. Ibid.

75. The promotion occurred on 1 October 1888 (see Legajo 601–2, Hoja de Servicios, Expediente Personal de Rafael Salillas y Panzano, Archivo Central del Ministerio de Justicia [hereafter cited as ACMJ], Madrid).

76. Salillas, *La antropología en el derecho penal*, 18–19.

77. Ibid., 25.

78. Ibid., 29–30.

79. In addition to the published version here cited, transcripts of the lecture appeared in the newspaper *El Liberal* and in the *Revista General de Legislación y Jurisprudencia*.

80. Writers like Emilia Pardo Bazán and Benito Pérez Galdós in addition to a younger generation of writers in the 1890s like Ramiro de Maéztu, Azorín, and Pío Baroja all used characters either symbolizing or using interpretations of Lombrosian ideas. Pardo Bazán wrote in 1894, "one sees Lombroso's name everywhere, he is read sometimes, cited much more often and even translated " (quoted in Maristany, *El gabinete del Doctor Lombroso*, 30).

81. On the adaptation of Lombroso to Catholic free will, see Caesar Silió Cortes, *La crisis del derecho penal* (1891); Dorado's aforementioned *La antropología criminal en Italia* (1889); and Salillas's journal, *La nueva ciencia jurídica* (1891–92). This journal lasted two years, with Salillas becoming the criminal anthropology consultant for the publisher José Lázaro Galdiano's important journal *España Moderna* (1891–1914). See also J. Maluquer y Salvador, "Escuela positivista penal," *RGLJ* 36, no. 72 (1888): 265–66; and P. Dorado Montero "La ciencia penal en la Italia contemporánea," *RGLJ* 37, no. 74 (1889): 713–33; no. 75 (1889): 132–59, 337–60, 650–674. For more on the impact of Lombroso in Spain, see Maristany, *El gabinete del doctor Lombroso*, 31–35. On *España Moderna*, see Rhian Davies, *La España moderna and Regeneración: A Cultural Review in Restoration Spain, 1889–1914*, Cañada Blanch Monographs, 5 (Manchester: Manchester Spanish and Portuguese Studies, 2000), 87–125.

82. See Lombroso and Mella, *Los anarquistas*, 1894. In one humorous account, another Spanish anarchist wrote about the troubling existence of "born police" who patrolled Spanish society compelled by nature to leave workers subjugated and beholden to the interests of aristocracy and industrial elite (see Joaquín Romero Maura, *La rosa del fuego* [Madrid: Alianza Universidad, 1989], 194).

83. Salillas to Giner, 29 October 1889, Item 4, Folio 87, Box 5, Fondo Giner de los Ríos, AILE, Madrid.

84. Handwritten notes listing countries of origin and important ideas of European criminologists dated 1887, along with notes entitled, "Interview Notes with Benedikt, 27 April 1889," Box 29, "Notas Manuscritas Sobre Derecho Penal," Folder 615, Fondo Giner de Los Ríos, AILE, Madrid.

85. Maristany, El gabinete del Dr. Lombroso, 36.

86. Federico Olóriz y Aguilera, Distribución geográfica del índice cefálico en España deducida del examen de 8.368 varones adultos: Memoria presentada al Congreso Geográfico Hispano-Portugues-Americano, en sesión de 19 de octubre de 1892 (Madrid: Imprenta del "Memorial de Ingenieros," 1894), 114; Maristany, El gabinete del Dr. Lombroso, 38.

87. "Servicio antropométrico," Revista de las Prisiones 3, no. 19 (15 May 1895): 301.

88. After a year's worth of reporting on the building of measuring equipment and training of staff, the main journal of the Spanish prisons reported that the first anthropometric examination center opened in Madrid's Model Prison (Carcel Modelo) (see "Sueltos y Noticias," Revista de las Prisiones 3, no. 35 [15 September 1895]: 522). The first report on its construction explaining the need for it is in "Noticias" Revista de las Prisiones 3, no. 2 (9 January 1895): 30.

89. See a copy of the decree in Box 6, uncatalogued, Archivo del Dr. Federico Olóriz y Aguilera (hereafter cited as AFO), Facultad de Medicina, Universidad de Granada; see also "La Antropometría," Revista de Prisiones 9, no.4 (1 May 1901): 34–35. For complaints about anthropometry, see, for example, those from the director of the Model Prison in Madrid, who argued against anthropometric studies not because of their potential value, but because working under tight budget constraints, it was more important to feed prisoners than to measure their heads (see Fernando Cadalso, "La antropometría en España," Revista de las Prisiones 5, no. 28 [1 October 1897]: 250).

90. See Telésforo de Aranzadi, Etnología: Antropología filosófica y psicología y sociología comparadas, vol 2 of Lecciones de Antropología, 2nd ed. (Madrid: Romo y Füssel, 1899), 455–60.

91. For specific calls, see Rafael Salillas y Panzano, "El jurado médico y la causa Varela," España Moderna 62 (February 1894): 95. Interestingly, his call was seconded by Hoyos Sáinz when the guilty verdict was rendered against the person for whom Salillas testified in defense and Hoyos had also supported (see Luís de Hoyos Sáinz, "La medicina en el derecho," España Moderna 64 [April 1894]: 178–81).

92. See Rafael Salillas y Panzano, "La degeneración o el proceso Willie," España Moderna 66 (June 1894): 72. On regional differences affecting the types of crime and levels of civilization, see Gibson, "Biology or Environment?" 100–101.

93. Salillas, "La degeneración y el proceso Willie," 72.

94. Ibid., 82.

95. Ibid., 82.

96. Ibid., 95.

97. Ibid.

98. Clavijo was executed the day after his capture (Rafael Salillas y Panzano, "El Capitan Clavijo" España Moderna 7, no. 79 [July 1895]: 25–41).

99. Rafael Salillas y Panzano, Hampa: El delincuente español o la antropología picaresca (Madrid: Librería de Victoriano Suarez, 1898), 14.

100. Ibid., xii.

101. Ibid., xiii.

102. Quoted in Maristany, *El gabinete del Dr. Lombroso*, 38.

103. Salillas, *Hampa*, 517–18.

104. Ibid., 10–11.

105. See "Bibliografía," *Revista de las Prisiones* 4, no. 10 (15 May 1896): 157–59.

106. Pedro Dorado, "Sobre el último libro de Salillas," *RGLJ*, 94 (1899): 47.

107. "Bibliografia," *Revista de las Prisiones*, 4, no. 10 (15 May 1896): 157–59. This article was in part a republication of the review by Luís Morote of Salillas's book in the newspaper *El Liberal*.

108. Dorado, "Sobre el último libro de Salillas," 49–50.

109. Manuel de Cossío and G. Acebo, "El sistema penitenciario español," *Revista de las Prisiones* 3, no. 25 (1 July 1895): 391. On Salillas's comments, see *Hampa*, 518.

110. Constancio Bernaldo de Quirós, *Modern Theories of Criminality*, trans. Alfonso de Salvio (Boston: Little, Brown, 1912), 100–119.

111. Ibid., xix.

112. As quoted in Salillas to Giner, 6 May 1899, Item 2, Folder 259, Box 11, Fondo Giner de los Ríos, AILE, Madrid.

113. Dorado had been an early member of a small anarchist cell in the early 1870s, an affiliation that led to constant suspicion and harassment long after his departure from the group. For a short description of Dorado's early political life, see Fernández Rodríguez, *El pensamiento penitenciario y criminológico*, 58–59.

114. Pedro Dorado Montero, "A propósito de la causa Varela," *España Moderna* 6, no. 65 (May 1894): 92–94.

115. Dorado, "Sobre el último libro de Salillas," 68

116. Dorado's position in relation to Salillas pointed to the two-front war that Spanish scientists were fighting. On the hand, there were disagreements about scientific approaches among Spaniards, and there were also the attacks on Spanish science in general as a method for curing the ills of turn-of-the-century Spain. As he wrote in an attack on one of the most well-known books of regenerationist literature, *El problema de España* by Macías Picavea (1898), which had argued that too much European science in defiance of truly Spanish values had brought about Spain's demise: "Scientists are the ones doing the greatest number of good deeds to fix society, working in favor of abandoned children, in support of the sick, the delinquent, and workers.... [W]e are ones most capable of extending a hand to prostrate Spain, pulling us out of our tomb, and saying, like Jesus to Lazarus: Surge et ambula" (see Pedro Dorado Montero, "Noticias bibliográficas, el problema nacional de macías picavea," *RGLJ* 94 [1899]: 402–3).

117. Ibid., 78.

118. Ibid.

119. For this discourse, especially in relation to the Italian school, see Pick, *Faces of Degeneration*, 132–35.

120. Rafael Salillas y Panzano, "El alma y la cabeza del cuerpo," *Revista de Prisiones y de Policia* 6, no. 11(16 March 1898): 98–101.

121. Maristany, *El gabinete del Dr. Lombroso*, 45.

122. See Rafael Salillas to Giner de los Ríos, 19 September 1900, Item 5, Folder 282, Box 12, Fondo Giner de los Ríos, AILE, Madrid.

123. See ACMJ, Legajo 571–72, Expedientes Personales, Constancio Bernaldo de Quirós.

124. Salillas, who attended these congresses, reported back to his Spanish colleagues that the Italians remained woefully misunderstood, and the French, given their usual "snobbery," just

did not understand the Italians: "a *malentendu scientifique* reigned at the Congresses of Paris and Brussels. And worse, they kept on using this *malentendu* like a mantra. But they were wrong. The Italian school has never presented the born criminal as an anthropological type characterized only by anatomical stigmata and driven inexorably to crime, no matter what conditions they lived in or grew up within. They were just wrong. The determinants of crime *for the most part* are pathological conditions, atavisms, a physio-psychic characteristic of delinquents combined to form distinct anthropological varieties. Criminality is the result of psychic, social, and physical conditions" (see Salillas to Giner, [1903?], Folder 615, Box 29, Fondo Giner de los Ríos, AILE, Madrid). Daniel Pick discusses the debates at these congresses in greater detail in *Faces of Degeneration*, 138–43.

125. Bernaldo de Quirós, *Modern Theories of Criminality*, xv–xvi.

126. The editors of the English version of Quirós's work wrote that it was the *Mala vida en Madrid* (The Low Life in Madrid) and its international reception that had made them aware of the Spaniard and drawn them to him for their compendium (see Quirós, *Modern Theories of Criminality*, xvi).

127. As quoted in Quirós, *Modern Theories of Criminality*, 108.

128. I have not been able to locate the original studies by Dr. Porpeta and Carlos Slocker, *Estudio de topografía craneocerebral* or *Capacidad cráneana en Madrid* (Madrid: n.p., n.d.), but they were discussed widely in the anthropological and military press in the period (see, for example, Luís de Hoyos Sáinz and Telésforo de Aranzadi, *Unidades y constantes en la crania hispanica*, Presentado a la Asociación Española para el Progreso de la Ciencias, Congreso de Granada, 1911 (Madrid: Eduardo Arias, 1913), 31–32.

129. Bernaldo de Quirós, *Modern Theories of Criminality*, 108.

130. Ibid., 108–9.

131. Ibid., 104.

132. Ibid., 105–6.

133. Manuel Antón y Ferrándiz, *Razas y tribus de Marruecos* (Madrid: Sucesores de Rivadeneyra, 1903), 5.

134. Quirós was well acquainted with the anthropological works of these authors, having reviewed them for the Spanish legal press (see Constancio Bernaldo de Quirós, "Noticias bibiliográficas: Lecciones de antropología," *RGLJ* 97 [1900]: 159).

135. Bernaldo de Quirós, *Modern Theories of Criminality*, 106.

136. Ibid., 106.

137. See correspondence between Otto Ammon and Federico Olóriz, 5 March 1896, and 8 March 1896, in Rafael Sánchez Martín, "El epistolario (1886–1912) de Federico Olóriz (1855–1912)" (Ph.D. diss., Universidad de Granada, 1979).

138. Ammon had presented a field of anthropology he called "anthroposociology," arguing that societies were the reflection of their racial lineage. He devised laws that associated social makeup, the distribution of wealth, the makeup and stability of urban populations with head shapes, via cephalic indices. Dolichocephaly, considered a key characteristic of Aryan racial lineage, was associated with stable societies, intelligent leaders, and quiescent workers. Mixture with Jews, of brachycephalic head shape, was a key characteristic of areas in Germany where instability reigned (see Constancio Bernaldo de Quirós, "La antroposociología," *RGLJ* 96 [1900]: 631–32; and George W. Stocking Jr., *Race, Culture, and Evolution* [Chicago: University of Chicago Press, 1985], 60, 163).

139. Bernaldo de Quirós, "La antroposociología," 637.

140. Ibid.

141. Ibid., 638.

142. Dorado once wrote, "it is the condition of the soul that matters, because it is from the soul that all bad and all good behavior is given to us" (Dorado, "Un derecho penal sin delito y sin pena," *España Moderna* 22, no. 264 [December 1910]: 36).

143. Salillas to Giner, 12 March 1903 Item 1, Folder 336, Box 14, Fondo Giner de los Ríos, AILE, Madrid.

144. Salillas to Giner, 21 March 1903, Folder 336, Box 14, Fondo Giner de los Ríos, AILE, Madrid.

145. See letters to Dorado from Salillas in Luís S. Granjel and Gerardo Sánchez-Granjel Santander, *Cartas a Dorado Montero* (Salamanca: Europa, 1985), 17–19; and Sallilas to Giner, 21 March 1903, Folder 336, Box 14, Fondo Giner de los Ríos, AILE, Madrid.

146. Granjel and Sánchez Granjel, *Cartas a Dorado*, 17.

147. On the faculty at the School of Criminology, see Rafael Salillas y Panzano, "Comunicación número 1: La reforma científica de la criminología," *Actas y Memorias de Sociedad Española de Antropología, Etnografía y Prehistoria* (hereafter cited as AMSEAEP) (2 January 1922): 33–35; see also Kaplan, "Luís Simarro and the Development of Science," 160–65.

148. In a letter from his assistant, José Otermín, at the Model Prison, Olóriz learned that despite the constant influx of anthropometric measurements from each of Spain's provincial jails, "no judge had as yet asked for anthropological data on prisoners" (see José Otermín to Federico Olóriz, 19 September 1904, in Sánchez Martín, "El epistolario [1886–1912] de Federico Olóriz [1855–1912]," available in the Archivo Federico Olóriz, Facultad de Medicina, Universidad de Granada).

149. See, for example, "El Servicio antropométrico—Descubrimiento de un asesino," *Revista de Prisiones* 10, no. 3 (16 January 1902): 38; and "Desarrollo y difusión de los Gabinetes antropométricas," *Revista de Prisiones* 11, no. 13 (8 July 1901): 171.

150. Federico Olóriz y Aguilera, *Morfología socialística: Morfología exterior del hombre aplicado a ciencias sociales* (Madrid: Enrique Teodoro, 1911), 5, 13.

151. Olóriz did not seem to have direct contact with Lombroso, but in letters to another Italian anthropologist and disciple of Lombroso's, Enrico Ferri, Olóriz complained of unfounded generalizations to which Lombroso applied his scientific data. Craniological studies of anarchists in Spain, for example, did not yield gigantic measurements, as they did in Italy, according to Lombroso, but rather smaller ones than the Spanish norm. Thus, one could not conclude that racial heritage of anarchists included alone a propensity for large features (see notes on Lombroso's book on delinquent man, which Olóriz read in its 1887 French translation, Box 7, uncatalogued, AFO, Universidad de Granada; see also Olóriz, *Morfología socialística*, 13).

152. Olóriz, *Morfología socialística*, 23.

153. Martín Turrado Vidal, *Estudios sobre historia de la policía* (Madrid: Ministerio del Interior, 1991), 1:241–66.

154. F. Urales to Cossío, 11 March 1907 Item 4, Folder 983, Box 48, Fondo Manuel Cossío, AILE, Madrid. On the Ferrer case, see Romero Maura, *La Rosa del Fuego*, 250–58. On the European response, see Joan Ullman, *The Tragic Week: A Study of Anti-Clericalism in Spain* (Cambridge: Harvard University Press, 1968).

155. See Kaplan, "Luís Simarro and the Development of Science," 193–94.

156. Exam administrator to Manuel Cossío, Item 1, Folder 1129, Box 57, Fondo Manuel Cossío, AILE, Madrid; see also letters to Olóriz asking for his recommendation for the School of

Criminology, 16 May 1908, 16 October 1909 (Tomás Maestre to Olóriz, [1912?], in Sánchez Martín, *El epistolario (1886–1912) de Federico Olóriz (1855–1912)*.

157. Salillas, "Comunicación número," 33–35.

158. The makeup of the executive committee of the society in its first years can be found in Joaquín Sánchez de Toca, "Introducción," AMSEAEP 1, no. 1 (18 May 1921): 5–6.

159. One famous study was of houses in Spain. Salillas had argued that the home represented the fundamental cellular unit of society, thus the starting point of a particular area's evolutionary development must begin at the home (Rafael Salillas y Panzano, "La casa como celula social," in *Congreso de Zaragoza de la Asociacion para el Progreso de la Ciencias*, vol. 5, Sección 4: Ciencias Sociales [Madrid: Eduardo Arias, 1909]: 53–95). The study in the Spanish Anthropology Society was presented later by Hoyos Sáinz, who argued that in housing styles lay the "personality of races" ([Secretario Hoyos Sáinz] "Acta de la Sexta Sesión," AMSEAEP [1 May 1922]: 59–61). This look at Spanish home styles was repeated later by another group of amateur Spanish anthropologists later affiliated with the Society of Anthropology, Ethnography and Prehistory (Sociedad de Antropología, Etnografía e Prehistoria), in "La panorama humana," *La Raza: Revista Hispánica* (1930).

160. "Acta de la segunda sesion," AMSEAEP 1, no. 1(2 January 1922): 30–31.

161. "Actas de la primera sesion," AMSEAEP 1, no. 1 (21 November 1921): 28.

162. Bernaldo de Quirós, *Modern Theories of Criminality*, 106–9.

163. Salillas made this argument most forcefully in his work on the Ferrer case written five years after trial and execution of Morral, the assassin, and Ferrer, the alleged conspirator, for his supposed fomenting of the Tragic Week (*Semana Trágica*) in Barcelona (see Rafael Salillas y Panzano, *Orígenes de una tragedia: Morral el anarquista* [Madrid: Librería de los Sucesores de Hernando, 1914]).

164. See Fructuosa Carpena, *El hombre criminal: Asociación Española para el Progreso de las Ciencias, Congreso de Zaragoza* (Madrid: Imprenta Enrique Arias, 1909), 100.

165. Fructuosa Carpena, *Archivos criminológicos* (Madrid: Impr. de V. Rico, [1914?]), 10.

166. One was the later founder of the prefascist Partido Nacionalista Español, José María Albiñana, who joined the Society of Anthropology, Ethnology and Prehistory in 1923 (see "Sociedad Española de Antropología Etnografía y Prehistoria: Altas de Socios en 1922–23," AMSEAEP 2 [January 1923]: 5). For Gregorio Marañón, the later republican politician and doctor, see Gregorio Marañón to Ángel Pulido, n.d., in *Biblioteca de la Real Academia de Medicina*, Expediente Personal del Ángel Pulido y Fernández [uncatalogued].

167. In addition to earlier cited comments about Salillas, Pío Baroja discussed the influences of the courses he took in anthropology while he was a medical student. His discussion of his experiences in the courses of Olóriz and Aranzadi are in Pío Baroja, *Obras completas* (Biblioteca Nueva: Madrid, 1949), 7:932–35. The writer Azorín's (Martínez Ruíz) first book in 1887 was a discussion of the criminal anthropology and specifically the ideas of Pedro Dorado Montero and the Italian school.

168. Mary Nash, "Social Eugenics and Nationalist Race Hygiene in Early 20th Century Spain," *Journal of the History of European Ideas* 15, nos. 4–5 (August 1992): 741–48.

8. REMAKING A GOOD FUSION, EXCISING A BAD

1. The Senate was at the time the upper house of the Cortes, with representatives voted in as representatives of corporate bodies. Pulido was the representative of the University of Salamanca, for example. A small collection of Pulido's papers are at the Royal Academy of Medicine,

where he lived for the last fifteen years of his life. For the official documents relating to Pulido's election to the Senate, see uncatalogued papers of Ángel Pulido y Fernández in folder marked "Documentos Laudatorio de Angel Pulido Fernandez," in Real Academia Nacional de Medicina (hereafter cited as RANM), Madrid.

2. This interpretation has been most commonly expressed first by Julio Caro Baroja, *Los Judíos en la España moderna y contemporánea*, vol. 3, pt. 5 (Madrid: Ediciones Arion, 1961), 201; José Antonio Lisbona, *El retorno a Sefarad* (Barcelona: Riopiedras Ediciones, 1993), 23; and Isidro González, *El retorno de los Judíos* (Madrid: Nerea, 1991), 175.

3. On the generation of the learned, see José María López Piñero, "Las ciencias médicas en la España del siglo XIX," in *La ciencia en la España del siglo XIX*, ed. López Piñero (Madrid: Marcial Pons, 1992), 227–40. Dorothy Ross has argued that these processes are dependent not only national context but especially on the levels of modernization and the general intellectual disposition toward modernity and the valoration of the human sciences. This idea underscores arguments made throughout the present work (see Dorothy Ross, "Modernism Reconsidered," in *Modernist Impulses in the Human Sciences, 1870–1930*, ed. Ross [Baltimore: Johns Hopkins University Press, 1994], 23).

4. See his medical school diploma from the prestigious Real Colegio de San Carlos, in letter dated 3 October 1873, uncatalogued papers in the "Laudatorio of Ángel Pulido," RANM, Madrid.

5. His talents in art had earlier earned him scholarships to art school, a direction his father had discouraged because of its uncertain career opportunities (see the biography of Pulido by his son, Ángel Pulido Martin, *El Doctor Pulido y su época* [Madrid: F. Domenech, 1945], 46). On his military discharge, see Hoja de Servicios, File# P-3063: Expedientes Personales, Archivo General Militar (hereafter cited as AGM), Segovia.

6. Pulido once noted that his artistic ability appealed to Velasco, who wanted good anatomical drawings. Pulido, however, wanted to express other ideas via his art, and produced the impressive masthead of the journal along with those of a number of other journals (see *Anfiteatro Anatómico Español* 1, no. 1[15–30 June 1873]: 1). On his hiring at the Anthropology Society, see letter from F.M. Tubino, 25 October 1875, in separate folder of uncatalogued papers of Ángel Pulido, RANM, Madrid.

7. Ángel Pulido y Fernández, *Discurso leido en la inauguración del año académico de 1875–1876 en la Sociedad Española de Antropología* (Madrid: Imprenta de T. Fortanet, 1875), 8.

8. Manuel Antón y Ferrandiz, *Programa razonado de antropología* (Madrid: Imprenta de la Viuda de M.Minuesa de los Ríos, 1897), 5.

9. Pulido, *Discurso leido en la inauguración del año Académico de 1875–1876 en la Sociedad Española de Antropología*, 9.

10. Ibid., 28. It is interesting to note that these preliminary anthropological conclusions made by Pulido and other members of the Anthropology Society were made on the basis of the twenty skulls in the society's collection, all the property of Velasco. During the first three years of the society, Velasco succeeded in collecting an additional two hundred skulls, but the conclusions about the Spanish race and its relations to other nations were based on a small sample. This lack of research material did not seem to hinder the members of the society from making bold assertions about the nation's racial makeup. Pulido later wrote that it was fortunate that the collection fell into the hands of Olóriz who was capable of "enriching it" (see Ángel Pulido Fernández, *El Doctor Velasco* [Madrid: E. Teodoro], 94).

11. Valentín Matilla, "Cuatro secretarios perpetuos ejemplares de la Real Academia Academia Nacional de Medicina," *Anales de la Real Academia Nacional de Medicina* 98 (1981): 58.

12. This followed three years of his attending the Royal Academy of Medicine as a "corresponding member," one step below formal membership (see uncatalogued papers, Matías Nieto Serrano, Secretary of the RANM, to Pulido, 19 June 1881, RANM, Madrid). Descriptions of Pulido's entry into the staid Royal Academy suggested that his admission represented a new shift toward democratic politics and positivism in the academy (see E., "Academia de Medicina: Recepción del Sr. Pulido," *El Porvenir* [23 June 1884]: 1). For Pulido as a "revolutionary," see Miguel Moya, "Angel Pulido," *El Liberal*, 23 June 1884, 2; as an expert in racial studies, see Jose Fernández Bremon, "Pulido," *La Ilustración Española y Americana* (30 June 1884): 394; and "Notas Madrileñas," *El Adalid* (June 1884): n.p.

13. Ángel Pulido y Fernández, "Los informes períciales médicos en el juicio oral," *El Siglo Médico* 31, no. 1586 (18 May 1884): 305–7.

14. Ángel Pulido y Fernández, "Conflictos entre la frenopatía y el código penal," in *La medicina y los médicos (Mosáico de discursos, artículos, correspondencias, semblanzas, pensamientos)* (Valencia: Libreria de P. Aguilar, Caballeros, 1883), 91.

15. Ibid., 94–95.

16. Ibid., 91.

17. Carlos Dardé, "La larga noche de la Restauración," in *El republicanismo en España, 1830–1975*, ed. Nigel Townsend (Madrid: Alianza Universidad, 1994), 115.

18. The divisions that formed among the republican faction during the period of the *sexenio*, or the six-year period of non-Bourbonic rule in Spain starting in 1868 and the regency of Amadeo de Savoy and ending with the First Republic of 1873–74 are delineated in Miguel Ángel Ésteban Navarro, "De la esperanza a la frustracion, 1868–1873," in *El republicanismo en España, 1830–1977*, ed. Nigel Townsend (Madrid: Alianza Universidad, 1994), esp. 101–12.

19. See the debates between catastrophists and uniformitarians within evolutionary geology in Michael Ruse, *The Darwinian Revolution: Science Red in Tooth and Claw* (Chicago: University of Chicago Press, 1979), 37–44.

20. Pulido, *El Doctor Velasco*, 30.

21. Emilio Castelar, "Breve historia de la democracia española," in *Cuestiones políticas y sociales* (Madrid: A. De San Martín y Agustín Jubera, 1870), 3:145.

22. Ibid., 153.

23. Ibid., 167–68.

24. Spanish philologists and historians of the nineteenth century like Marcelino Menénedez y Pelayo who later supported the racial histories presented by anthropologists like Federico Olóriz, focused far more on the role that Catholicism played in the formation of contemporary Spain. Indeed, the racial histories later championed by Spanish anthropologists each followed in rough outline events and interpretations offered in these histories. But the works of Pi y Margall and Menéndez Pelayo, written at the same time as that of Castelar, also presented Spain as a fusion of different racial spirits, facilitated by the ecumenical spirit of Catholicism and Spain's democratic spirit.

25. As quoted in Caesar C. Aronsfeld, *The Ghosts of 1492*, Jewish Social Studies Series (New York: Columbia University Press, 1979), 12.

26. Caro Baroja, *Los Judíos en la España moderna y contemporánea*, 3:186–87. Caro Baroja unwittingly harkens back to Spanish fears of the "wandering Jew," arguing that most of these Jewish converts falsely represented their intentions. He wrote that they convinced "incautious" liberal

generals that they wanted to be Spanish when they really wanted leave to enter Spain and become travelling salesmen and storytellers.

27. More recent historiography has begun to explain this show of support for the Spaniards as more of a response of the Jews to their increasingly harsh treatment under Moroccan tribal leaders. In addition, the liberal Spanish generals whom Caro Baroja mentioned (among them the commander of the campaign, General O'Donnell) were also positively disposed to the potential benefits of contact with "international commerce" that Sephardic Jews in Tangier, Tetuan and Ceuta represented. On press reports, see González, El retorno de los Judíos, 68–69.

28. See María Antonia Bel Bravo, "Estudio premilinar," in Ángel Pulido y Fernández, Españoles sin patria y la raza Sefardí, facsimile ed. (1905; Granada: Universidad de Granada, 1993), xviii.

29. The most famous of these were first Adolfo de Castro's The History of the Jews in Spain (1847), first translated and released in England in 1851. Perhaps the most famous and influential was José Amador de los Ríos's 3-volume Historia social, política, y religiosa de los judíos en España y Portugal, 1875–1876. Caro Baroja wrote that Amador's sympathy for the plight of Spanish Jews rubbed off on his students, among them Menéndez y Pelayo, in their historical studies (see Caro Baroja, Los Judíos en la España moderna y contemporánea, 3:185).

30. González, El retorno de los Judíos, 69.

31. Caro Baroja, Los Judíos en la España moderna, 3:187, 193–94.

32. There is contradictory evidence about the nature of this break and whose idea it was. Pulido's son, Ángel Pulido Martin, writing in 1945 and perhaps fearing an association between his father and republicanism, never mentioned his father's politics. He argued instead that his father's political life began in association with Sagasta and the head of the Liberal Party, Álvaro de Figueroa, the Conde de Romanones. Haim Avni asserts probably more accurately that Castelar provided this advice. Pulido himself declared his allegiances to Castelar throughout his career. On Pulido's various declarations, see, for example, Ángel Pulido Fernández, "Una carta del Dr. Pulido," El Liberal, 19 December 1919, 4; for his son's comments, see Pulido Martín, El Doctor Pulido y su época, 76–77, 120–27; and Haim Avni, Spain, the Jews and Franco, trans. Emanuel Shimoni (Philadelphia: Jewish Publication Society of America, 1982), 22, 225–26.

33. One can see the official documents acknowledging Pulido's electoral success in uncatalogued papers of Ángel Pulido, RANM, Madrid.

34. As reported by his son, Ángel Pulido Martín, El Doctor Pulido y su época, 209; see also Avni, Spain, the Jews and Franco, 21.

35. Ángel Pulido Fernández, Intereses nacionales: Los Israelitas españoles y el idioma Castellano (Madrid: Imp. Sucesores de Rivadeneyra, 1904), 10–11.

36. See, for example, articles on the three hundred Spanish Jewish families living in Madrid requests for opening a kosher butcher shop, especially "Cronica: Solicitud hecha por los hebreos" El Siglo Medico 31, no. 1568 (13 January 1884): 32.

37. For more on the alliance, see Aron Rodrigue, French Jews, Turkish Jews: The Alliance Israélite Universelle and the Politics of Jewish Schooling in Turkey, 1860–1925 (Bloomington: University of Indiana Press, 1990), xi–xiii.

38. Pulido Martín, El Doctor Pulido y su época, 210.

39. A few recent histories, written as part of official efforts to celebrate of Columbus's arrival in the West Indies while acknowledging the fateful expulsion of Spanish Jews in the same year, deal with Spanish Jewish relations over the last century. One was funded by the governmental agency that coordinated the celebrations of the five hundredth anniversary of Columbus's voyage (see

Lisbona, *Retorno a Sefarad*). A more recent study focuses specifically on Spanish-Israeli relations (Raanan Rein, *In the Shadow of the Holocaust and the Inquisition* [Portland, Ore.: Frank Cass, 1997]).

40. Pulido, *Españoles sin patria y la raza Sefardí*, 11.

41. Ibid., xxix, 11.

42. Pulido, *Intereses nacionales*, 30–32.

43. Pulido, *Españoles sin patria y la raza Sefardí*, 6–7.

44. Ibid., 14.

45. Ibid., 18.

46. Ibid., 5.

47. Ibid., 30, 225.

48. Ibid., 26. This argument is repeated almost two decades later and expanded to conform to the new ideology of *Hispanidad*, the idea that Spain's legacy was a cultural diffusion throughout the world, improved as a result of Jewish intermixture: "the Israelites, upon leaving Spain, did not scrape off the dust of Spain when they left. No, they carried it in their hearts . . . constituting one of the most international of Spain's offspring" (see "En el Ateneo," El *Fígaro*, 24 February 1920).

49. Pulido had served on the provincial committee that awarded a scholarship to Hoyos to study in France and Germany. Hoyos then thanked Pulido for his "leadership in anthropological studies" in Spain (see Luís de Hoyos Sáinz, *Técnica antropológica y antropología física*, 2nd ed. [1893; Madrid: Imp. del Asilo de Huérfanos del S.C. de Jesus, 1899], 14–15).

50. Ángel Pulido, *Españoles sin patria y la raza sefardí*, 30.

51. Ibid., 32.

52. He also made this argument in the reverse, noting that Spanish Jews outside of Spain underwent similar transformations that Spaniards did during the same sweep of time. He noted, apparently with little evidence, that Spanish Jews shared the same number of dialects of Ladino, the Spanish Jewish language, as Spaniards had of regional dialects on the peninsula. There was unity among expelled Spanish Jews as well, Pulido wrote. Thus, he concluded that since all Sephardim spoke virtually the same language connected to Spanish, they all shared the same "historical connection with Spain" (see Pulido, *Españoles sin patria y la raza Sefardí*, 86, 171).

53. Ibid., 60.

54. "[T]he Hebrew race has what we might call a energetic substance, a medical condition caused strong action, the maintenance of which they are well known for and have directed in practical ways" (Pulido, *Españoles sin patria y la raza Sefardí*, 538).

55. Telésforo de Aranzadi and Luís de Hoyos Sáinz, *Lecciones de antropología: Ajustada al programa del Catedrático Don Manuel Antón por los doctores Ara. y Hoyos: Antropologia General* (Madrid: Imprenta y litografia de Los Huérfanos, 1894), 10.

56. Pulido, *Españoles sin patria y la raza Sefardí*, 568.

57. See ibid., 635–40. Twelve years later Pulido was still calling on the world Jewish community to avoid sending poor Jews: "it must not be forgotten that Spain is not yet in a material and economic position to receive great numbers of Jewish immigrants who are in need of aid, and who would require to be provided with a means of living. . . . As I believe that my country is seriously involved in this world, I intensely desire that it may have the capacity and perseverance to carry it to a happy end. The day this is realised, it will be much easier for Spain to effect the spiritual and economic reintegration of all the descendants of those who were exiled in 1492"

(Dr. Ángel Pulido, "The Sephardim in Spain," *Jewish Chronicle* [April 28, 1916]: n.p., in a scrapbook prepared by Pulido's wife contained in his uncatalogued papers, RANM, Madrid).

58. See, for example, the files from petitioners, Legajo 3987, Section: Gobernación, Archivo General de la Administración, Alcalá de Henares, Spain.

59. González, *El retorno de los Judíos*, 177.

60. Nordau, a Hungarian citizen, was forced to flee the allied country for neutral Spain. Pulido, who remained in a close friendship with Nordau, clashed with his colleague over the issue of Zionism. Pulido fought with Nordau over the issue of the eventual ingathering of Jews in one land. Perhaps they conflicted because this idea clashed with Pulido's goals of advancing Spain by reinserting its Jewish relatives, and more generally, because it ran against his biological model of the need to mix peoples rather than isolate them. For more on his relationship with Nordau, see Pulido's obituary of Nordau in Angel Pulido, "El Dr. Max Nordau, ha fallecido," *Revista de la Raza* 9, no. 95 (January–February 1923): 19–21; see also Anna and Maxa Nordau, *Max Nordau: A Biography* (New York: Nordau Committee, 1943), 223–24.

61. González, *El retorno de los Judíos*, 186.

62. The surprise, he wrote, was because the project to return Jews represented proof that Spain, "the country of the Inquisition, the expulsion of Jew and Moor, and the destruction of liberty in the Low Countries," was now emerging as a modern nation respectful of human rights (Max Nordau, "Una sorpresa española," *La Nacion*, 11 June 1916; article also noted in González, *El retorno de los Judíos*, 195; and Avni, *Spain, the Jews and Franco*, 24).

63. Haim Avni, *Spain, the Jews and Franco*, 24; González, *El retorno de los Judíos*, 197.

64. For these ideas, see Lily Litvak, *Latinos y Anglosajones: Orígenes de una polémica* (Barcelona: Puvill Editor, n.d.), 15–28.

65. Aranzadi had written to Unamuno a long letter going over the recent developments in the Spanish sciences, apparently at the request of Unamuno. Included among these is a discussion of the newest trends in anthropology, along with a promise to send Unamuno a copy of Aranzadi's book on ethnology. The card catalogue of Unamuno's personal library left to his museum and archive does contain this volume (see Aranzadi to Unamuno, Granada, 29 April 1899, Correspondencia, Fondo Miguel Unamuno, Casa-Museo Unamuno, Universidad de Salamanca).

66. Carlos París, "El pensamiento de Unamuno y la ciencia positiva," *Arbor* 22, no. 77 (May 1952): 14.

67. Letter reprinted in Pulido, *Españoles sin patria y la raza Sefardí*, 105.

68. Ibid., 104.

69. From the newspaper El *Liberal*, 15 July 1920, as reprinted in Miguel de Unamuno, *Obras completas* (Madrid: Escelicer, 1968), 4:642–43.

70. Pulido wrote in 1920 that despite the economic benefits, the key to Spanish colonial success in Morocco would be the racial affinities between Spaniard and Moroccan Jew, "because the work of colonization in Morocco, as has been said many times before, is not just a matter for governments, but a question of ethnic compatibility, that must be harmonic between public powers and the people and ultimately within the entire nation" ("Los Sefarditas y nuestra accion en Marruecos," El *Imparcial*, 9 March 1920).

71. As quoted in González, *El retorno de los Judíos*, 194.

72. "I think the object of these associations, composed of Spaniards and Jews, and united by a common ideal, is to aspire always for the tightening of the bonds between the two national races

that populate the Magreb" (quoted in "Conferencia del Doctor Pulido," *El Liberal*, 9 March 1920, from a scrapbook in Pulido's uncatalogued papers in RANM, Madrid).

73. Quoted in an obituary of Pulido, in Nicasio Mariscal y García and Joaquín Decref y Ruíz, *Discursos leidos en la Solemne Sesión Inaugural Celebrada el día 22 de enero de 1933 en la Academia Nacional de Medicina* (Madrid: Julio Cosano, 1933), 9–11.

74. His son commented that his father's dreams were to receive an appointment to head a Spanish ministry. His highest position within a ministry was the director of public health within the Interior Ministry, which he held for two years (see Pulido Martín, *El Doctor Pulido y su época*, 191–99).

75. In terms of scientific education, his efforts to increase the budgets for medical education especially within the military earned him the Gran Cruz del Mérito Militar, conferred by Alfonso XIII in 1909 (Legajo: P-3063, Item 1, Expediente Personal: Ángel Pulido y Fernández, AGM, Segovia).

76. Pulido wrote to Unamuno that "this terrible nervous sickness made me feel lost and suffering from a sense of tragic desperation." His son referred to it as a "nervous breakdown brought on by stress and the damage that the Jewish movement caused to his reputation among Catholic friends" (see Pulido to Unamuno, Madrid, 27 November 1919, Correspondencia, Fondo Miguel Unamuno, Casa-Museo Unamuno, Salamanca; and Pulido Martín, *El Doctor Pulido y su época*, 147). Interestingly, the doctor who treated Pulido, Antonio Vallejo Nájera, directed the eugenic programs under the Franco regime.

77. Ángel Pulido y Fernández, *Mica: Homenaje a la mujer hebrea* (Madrid: Ibero-Africano-Americana, 1923).

78. One aspect of these benefits was the increasing role Pulido played outside Spain as spokesman for the Sephardic repatriation. He was honored in 1920 by the Association Culturelle Orientale Israélite de Paris for his efforts to repatriate Sephardic Jews and raise awareness of their lives in Eastern Europe and Northern Africa (see Association Culturelle Orientale Israélite de Paris, *Compte rendu de la fête en l'honneur de M. le Dr. Angel Pulido* [Paris: Imprimiere H. Elias, 1920]). Pulido's disciple Ignacio Bauer also was sent to the International Federation of League of Nations' Societies, which met in Brussels in 1920. Spain was commended at this conference for its "willingness to support the struggle for Jewish rights everywhere" (quoted in Avni, *Spain, the Jews and Franco*, 27).

79. He also published in a magazine Bauer coedited with the Spanish writer Manuel Ortega, *Revista de la Raza*, published by the Casa de los Sefardíes in Madrid (see *Revista de la Raza* 8, no. 89 [July 1922]: 1).

80. Ángel Pulido y Fernández, *Relación de las cases médicas con las asociaciones cooperativas e industriales benéfico-sanitarias* (Madrid: Imprenta y Librería de Nicolás Moya, 1903), 1–4; see also Ángel Pulido y Fernández, *El cáncer comunista o la degeneración del socio-sindicalismo: Necesidad de su regeneración higiénica y moral* (Madrid: Casa Editorial de M. Núñez Samper, [1921]), frontispiece.

81. Pulido, *El cáncer comunista*, 184–85.

82. Ibid., 186.

83. He wrote of the "Helleno-Latin period of Spanish history" (ibid., 184).

84. Ibid., 345–46.

85. Ibid., 186–87.

86. Ibid., 187.

87. Ibid., 353–54.

88. Ibid., 392, 400. On his descriptions of himself as a Catholic, Pulido wrote that such affirmations were important because many doubted his Catholicism as a result of his efforts for the Jews. He wrote in 1905, "we Pulidos have descended from Old Christians." It is interesting to note that this language is taken directly from the era of the blood purity laws promulgated in the fifteenth century. Old Christians were without the taint of Jewish blood, while new Christians were descendants of Jews (see his comments in *Españoles sin patria y la raza Sefardí*, 17). Julio Caro Baroja noted in 1961 that almost all Spaniards writing histories of Spanish Jews or in the defense of their repatriation were quick to point out their non-Jewish descent (Caro Baroja, *Los Judíos en la España moderna y contemporánea*, 3:185).

EPILOGUE

1. See comments, including, Sid Lowe, "Spain's Olympic Race Row: Don't Shoot the Messenger," *Guardian* 15 August 2008: on the "Anglo-Saxon Press," see Robert Álvarez, "'No es un gesto de racismo,'" *El País*, 14 August 2008, www.elpais.com/articulo/deportes/gesto/racismo/elpepidep/20080814elpepidep_19/Tes; see also www.guardian.co.uk/media/2008/aug/15/olympicsandthemedia.pressandpublishing. For the act as a "playful gesture," in the words of one Spanish player who added that he has many Chinese friends in Toronto where he played in the NBA, see "¿Racismo or Guiño Cariñoso?" *El Mundo*, www.elmundo.es/jjoo/2008/2008/08/12/baloncesto/1218564829.html.

2. As quoted in "¿Racismo or Guiño Cariñoso?"

3. As quoted in the Spanish sports newspaper AS, Tomás Guasch, "'The Guardian' nos llama racistas y La China se ríe," AS 14 August 2008, www.as.com/baloncesto/articulo/juegos-olimpicos-verano-competiciones-deportivas/dasbal/20080814dasdaibal_1/Tes. The article defends the Spanish team's acts and argues that the players and Spaniards in general harbor no racism against "the yellow race."

4. See Américo Castro, *España en su historia: Cristianos, moros y judíos* (Buenos Aires: Editorial Losada, 1948).

5. See P. E. Russell, "The Nessus-Shirt of Spanish History," *Bulletin of Spanish Studies* 36 (1959): 219–25; and Thomas F. Glick and Oriol Pi-Sunyer, "Acculturation as an Explanatory Concept in Spanish History," *Comparative Studies in Society and History* 11, no. 2 (April 1969): 136–54. This debate has abated somewhat, but new studies, including this present one, are beginning to suggest an ethnic component implicit in Spanish nationalism that was rooted in *casticismo* (see Gonzalo Álvarez Chillida, *El antisemitismo en España: La imagen del Judío (1812–2002)* [Madrid: Marcial Pons, 2002], 43).

6. See Rodolfo Serrano, "En Busca del Gen Rojo," *El País*, 7 January 1996, www.elpais.com/articulo/espana/ESPANA/SOCIALISMO/GUERRA_CIVIL_ESPANOLA/COMUNISMO/FRANQUISMO/busca/gen/rojo/elpepiesp/19960107elpepinac_22/Tes; and Vicenç Navarro, "La Gestapo en España," *El País*, 26 February 2003, www.elpais.com/articulo/cataluna/Gestapo/Espana/elpepiespcat/20030226elpcat_8/Tes. Television shows and theatrical works have appeared dealing with these programs.

7. A recent edition of history and memory was devoted to Spain's confrontation with its own past, and, clearly, the historical consensus has emerged that forgetting long remained the strategy for dealing with Spain's recent past (see Paloma Aguilar Fernández, *Memory and Amnesia: The Role of the Spanish Civil War in the Transition to Democracy*, trans. Mark Oakley [New York: Berghahn

Books, 2002]). With King Juan Carlos proclaiming 2006 the "Year of Historical Memory" and approving a series of state laws to recover the memory of civil war and postwar crimes, the complexity of memory, historical awareness of past crimes, and the uncovering of actual buried bodies will begin to alter the pact of forgetting that dominated the post-Franco transition. The contest of memories, as elsewhere, is only just beginning. For an excellent distillation of the main themes of memory studies in Spain linked to contemporary political and historical debates, see Judith Keene, "Review Article: Turning Memories into History in the Spanish Year of Historical Memory," *Journal of Contemporary History* 42, no. 4 (2007): 661–73.

8. A common refrain, especially in reaction to racial attacks on immigrants (see, for example, "Trouble: Spain and Race," *Economist*, 24 July 1999, 27).

9. This is particularly true of those who worked diligently to uncover this material and find the archival materials. See, in particular, Ricard Vinyes, Montse Armengou, and Ricard Belis, *Los Niños Perdidos del franquismo* (Plaza y Janés/Televisó de Catalunya, 2002), 23–77. There has recently been effort to overcome this approach, including the excellent essays in Rafael Huertas and Carmen Ortiz, eds., *Ciencia y fascismo* (Madrid: Doce Calles, 1998); and Michael Richards, "Spanish Psychiatry c. 1900–1945: Constitutional Theory, Eugenics, and the Nation," *Bulletin of Spanish Studies* 81, no. 6 (September 2004): 823–48.

10. The language here is borrowed from Eric Weitz, "Racial Politics without the Concept of Race: Reevaluating Soviet Ethnic and National Purges," *Slavic Review* 60, no. 1 (Spring 2002): 24.

11. Stanley Payne, *Fascism: Comparison and Definitions* (Madison: University of Wisconsin Press, 1981), 149–51; Stanley Payne, *History of Fascism, 1914–1945* (Madison: University of Wisconsin Press, 1995), 11, 242.

12. Raquel Álvarez Peláez, "Eugenesia y fascismo en la España de los años treinta," in *Ciencia y fascismo*, ed. Rafael Huertas and Carmen Ortiz (Madrid: Doce Calles, 1998), 88–89.

13. Ibid, 88.

14. Richards, "Spanish Psychiatry," 823–48.

15. Ibid., 839–42.

16. Alvarez Peláez, "Eugenesia y fascismo," 89.

17. Hoja de Servicios [Personal Service File], 7.ª Subdivisión, Expediente Personal, Antonio Vallejo Nájera, Archivo General Militar, Segovia.

18. Giménez Caballero wrote of the "impetú racista" of Germany and of the "virtud raceadora" of the Spaniards in a speech given at the Ibero-Amerikansiches Institut in Berlin in October 1941 and printed in Ernesto Giménez Caballero, "La Espiritualidad Española y Alemania," *Ensayos y Estudios* 3, no. 5/6 (September–December 1941): 290.

19. See, for example, Santos Juliá, ed., *Victimas de la Guerra Civil* (Madrid: Temas de Hoy, 1999); and Julián Casanova, ed., *Morir, matar, sobrevivir: La violencia en la dictadura de Franco* (Barcelona: Critica, 2002).

20. Paul Preston, "The Answer Lies in the Sewers: Captain Aguilera and the Mentality of the Francoist Office Corps," *Science and Society* 68, no. 3 (Fall 2004): 286. This is also discussed in Paul Preston, *The Spanish Civil War* (London: Grove Press, 1986), 104–5.

21. Preston, "The Answer Lies in the Sewers," 281.

22. See Monste Armegou and Ricard Belis, *Las fosas del silencio: ¿Hay un Holocausto español?* (Barcelona: Plaza y Janés/Televisó de Catalunya, 2004); and Paul Preston's forthcoming, *The Spanish Holocaust*.

23. Pilar Romero de Tejada, *Un templo a la ciencia: Historia del Museo Nacional de Etnología* (Madrid: Ministerio de Cultura, 1992), 38.

24. Victoriano Juaristi, "Patología y tipo racial," *Actas y Memorias de la Sociedad de Antropología, Etnología y Prehistoria* 27 (1947): 96–102.

25. Romero de Tejada, *Un templo de la ciencia*, 40.

26. On Misael Bañuelos, see Juan Manuel Granda Juesas, *Don Misael Bañuelos, medicina, antropología y sociedad* (Valladolid: Universidad de Valladolid, 1987), 14.

27. As quoted in Isabel Jiménez Lucena, "Medicina social, racismo y discurso de la desigualdad en el primer franquismo," in *Ciencia y fascismo*, ed. Rafael Huertas y Carmen Ortiz (Madrid: Doce Calles, 1998), 122.

28. The didacticism references come from Preston, "The Answer Lies in the Sewers," 280. The discussion of "moral and ideological" education is from Lucena, "Medicina social, racismo y discurso de la desigualdad en el primer franquismo," 122.

29. On the German appearance of conservative revolutionaries, see Jeffrey Herf, *Reactionary Modernism: Technology, Culture, and Politics in Weimar and the Third Reich* (Cambridge: Cambridge University Press, 1986). Some Spanish historians have examined this process in Spain, some arguing that the Iberian Peninsula was the cradle of this reactionary modernism (see, for example, Rockwell Gray, *The Imperative of Modernity* [Berkeley and Los Angeles: University of California Press, 1989]; and Joshua Goode, "La contradicción como arma: Ortega y Gasset y el concepto español de la modernidad," *Foro Hispánico* 18, no. 18 [September 2000]: 99–122).

30. The use of memory here is not meant to suggest that depictions of the Spanish imperial past were in any way accurate. Some recent scholarship has begun to explore the "invention" of these memories, exploring the appropriation of images and measuring their political purposes as expressed in the later concepts of *la raza* or *Hispanidad* (see Maria A. Escudero, "The Image of Latin America Disseminated in Spain by the Franco Regime" [Ph.D. diss., University of California, San Diego, 1994]; and Eduardo González Calleja and Fredes Limon Nevado, *La hispanidad como instrumento de combate* [Madrid: CSIC, 1988]).

31. Raymond Carr, *Spain: 1808–1975*, 2nd ed. (Oxford: Clarendon Press, 1982), 355. For a discussion of the "two Spains" thesis, see Enric Ucelay da Cal, "The Hispanic Studies Ghetto," *Bulletin of the Society for Spanish and Portuguese Historical Studies*, 19, no. 3 (Fall 1994): 11–15; and Pamela Radcliff, *From Mobilization to Civil War* (Cambridge: Cambridge University Press, 1996), 1 n. 1.

32. Paul Preston, *The Politics of Revenge* (London: Unwin Hyman, 1990), 32.

Bibliography

ARCHIVAL COLLECTIONS IN SPAIN

Archivo Central del Ministerio de Justicia, Madrid.
Archivo General de la Administración, Alcalá de Henares.
Archivo General Militar, Segovia.
Archivo de la Institución Libre de Enseñanza, Real Academia de Historia, Madrid.
  Fondo Manuel Cossío.
  Fondo Francisco Giner de los Ríos.
  Fondo Augusto González de Linares.
Archivo de la Junta para la Ampliacion de Estudios, Residencia de Estudiantes, Madrid.
Archivo Personal del Federico Olóriz y Fernández, Facultad de Medicina, Universidad de Granada.
Biblioteca de la Real Academia Nacional de Medicina, Madrid.
  Uncatalogued Papers of Ángel Pulido y Fernández.
Biblioteca del Ateneo de Madrid.
Biblioteca Nacional, Madrid.
  Colección García-Figueras.
Casa-Museo Unamuno, Universidad de Salamanca.
  Correspondencia.
  Biblioteca de Miguel de Unamuno.
  Fondo Miguel de Unamuno.
Colegio de Abogados, Madrid.
Colegio de Médicos, Madrid.

CONTEMPORARY ARTICLES AND MONOGRAPHS
Periodical Articles

Acosta, [?]. "Cosmopolitismo humano." *Anfiteatro Anatómico Español* 1, no. 2 (15 February 1873): 21–22.
"Actas de la primera sesión." *Actas y Memorias de Sociedad Española de Antropología, Etnografía y Prehistoria* 1, no. 1 (21 November 1921): 28.

"Acta de la segunda sesión." *Actas y Memorias de Sociedad Española de Antropología, Etnografía y Prehistoria* 1, no. 1 (2 January 1922): 30–31.

"Acta de la sexta sesión." *Actas y Memorias de Sociedad Española de Antropología, Etnografía y Prehistoria* 1, no. 1 (1 May 1922): 59–61.

"Acta de la tercera sesion." *Actas y Memorias de Sociedad Española de Antropología, Etnografía y Prehistoria* 1, no. 1 (6 February 1922): 36.

Alarcón, C. I. "Organizacion del servicio de Sanidad Aleman en tiempo de guerra." *Revista de Sanidad Militar* 17, no. 384 (15 June 1903): 254.

Antón y Ferrándiz, Manuel. "La raza de Cro-Magnon en España." *Anales de la Sociedad Española de Historia Natural* 13 (1884).

"La antropometría." *Revista de Prisiones* 9, no. 4 (1 May 1901): 34–35.

Aranzadi, Telésforo de. "Antropología." In *Enciclopedia universal ilustrada Europeo-Americana.* Annual Supplement 1936–1939, pt. 1. Madrid: Espasa-Calpe, 1944.

———. "Consideraciones acerca de la raza basca." *Euskal Erria* 35 (July and August 1896): 34.

———. "De antropología de España." *Revista Estudio* 12, no. 36 (1915): 335.Bernaldo de Quirós, Constancio. "La antroposociología." *Revista General de Legislación y Jurisprudencia* 96 (1900): 631–37.

———. "Noticias bibiliográficas: Lecciones de antropología." *Revista General de Legislación y Jurisprudencia* 97 (1900): 159.

———. "El problema antropológico vasco." *España Moderna*, July 1894, 141.

———, and Luís de Hoyos Sáinz. "Notes Préliminaires sur les 'Crania Hispanica.'" *Bulletin et Memoires de la Société d'Anthropologie* (20 February 1913): 81–94.

"Bibliografía." *Revista de las Prisiones* 4, no. 10 (15 May 1896): 157–59.

"Bibliografía: Apuntes antropométricos del presidio de Melilla." *Revista de Sanidad Militar* 20, no. 450 (15 May 1906): 155–56.

Brusa, E. "Los carácteres de la escuela criminalista italiana y especialmente respecto a algunas modernas cuestiones técnicas y prácticas Sobre la pena." *Revista General de Legislación y Jurisprudencia* 60 (1882): 210–30.

Cadalso, Fernando. "La antropometría en España." *Revista de las Prisiones* 5, no. 28 (1 October 1897): 250.

Calvo Flores, Ángel. "Los carácteres antropológicos y las enfermedades." *Revista de Sanidad Militar*, 3, no. 8 (15 April 1909): 255–59.

Cossío, Manuel de, and G. Acebo. "El sistema penitenciario español." *Revista de las Prisiones* 3, no. 25 (1 July 1895): 391.

"Crónica: Solícitud hecha por los hebreos." *El Siglo Médico* 31, no. 1568 (13 January 1884): 32.

"De la formación de hojas antropométricas individuales en el ejército." *Revista de Sanidad Militar* 14, no. 302 (15 January 1900): 31–37.

"Desarrollo y difusión de los gabinetes antropométricas." *Revista de Prisiones* 9, no. 13 (8 July 1901): 171.

Dorado Montero, Pedro. "La ciencia penal en la Italia contemporánea." *Revista General de Legislación y Jurisprudencia* 37, no. 74 (1889): 713–33; no. 75 (1889): 132–59, 337–60, 650–74.

———. "Un derecho penal sin delito y sin pena." *España Moderna* 22, no. 264 (December 1910): 18–37.

———. "Noticias bibliográficas, El problema nacional de macías picavea." *Revista General de Legislación y Jurisprudencia* 94 (1899): 402–3.

———. "A propósito de la causa Varela." *España Moderna* 6, no. 65 (May 1894): 68–95.

———. "Sobre el último libro de Salillas." *Revista General de Legislación y Jurisprudencia* 94 (1899): 46–78.

E. [pseud.]. "Academia de medicina: Recepción del Sr. Pulido." *El Porvenir*, 23 June 1884.

"En el Ateneo." *El Fígaro*, 24 February 1920.

Escuder, J[osé María]. "Locos lúcidos." *Revista General de Legislación y Jurisprudencia* 63 (1883): 5–40.

———. "Un loco y un imbécil." *Revista General de Legislación y Jurisprudencia* 61(1882): 75–102.

"España: Sección Segunda Antropología." *Enciclopedia universal ilustrada: Europeo-Americana*. Barcelona: Hijos de J. Espasa, 1923.

"Extracto de las actas de 14 de marzo de 1874." *Revista de Antropología* 1 (1874): 1–4.

"Felicitación." *Anfiteatro Anatómico Español* 1, no. 2 (15 February 1873): 1.

Fernández Bremon, José. "Pulido." *La ilustración Española y Americana*, 30 June 1884.

[Garcia Alonso, Enrique]. "La nueva ciencia penal." *Revista General de Legislación y Jurisprudencia* 70 (1886): 656.

Garcia Mercet, Ricardo. "Memoria leida por el Secretario General de la Asociacion." In *Asociación Española para el Progreso de las Ciencias, Primer Congreso, Congreso de Zaragoza*. Vol. 1. Madrid: Eduardo Arias, 1908.

García Perez, Eduardo. "Salubridad Pública." *Anfiteatro Anatómico Español* 1, no. 1 (15 and 30 January 1873): 7–8.

Giménez Caballero, Ernesto. "La espiritualidad Española y Alemania." *Ensayos y Estudios* 3, no. 5/6 (September–December 1941): 290.

Giner de los Ríos, Francisco. "Sobre lo moral y lo jurídico." *Boletín de la Institución Libre de Enseñanza* 2, no. 44 (16 December 1878): 175.

Gómez Ocaña, José. *Elogio de Don Federico Olóriz y Aguilera*. Madrid: Fortanet, 1913.

———. "Elogio del Don Federico Olóriz y Aguilera." *Memorias de la Real Sociedad de Historia Natural* 7 (1913): 364.

González Velasco, Pedro. "Adelante." *Anfiteatro Anatómico Español* 1, no. 1(15 and 30 June 1873): 2.

Hoyos Sáinz, Luís de. "Acta de la sexta sesión." *Actas y Memoria de la Sociedad Española de Antropología, Etnografía y Prehistoria* 2 (1 May 1922): 59–61.

———. "La antropología: Métodos y problemas." In *Estado actual: Métodos y problemas de las ciencias*, edited by Luís de Hoyos Sáinz. Madrid: Imprenta Clásica Española, 1916.

———. "Comunicación num. 21: Los datos de la antropología penitenciaria en Bélgica." *Actas y Memoria de la Sociedad Española de Antropología, Etnografía y Prehistoria* 2 (26 February 1923): 24–33.

———. "Crónica científica." *España Moderna* 8, no. 65 (May 1894).

———. "La medicina en el derecho." *España Moderna* 64 (April 1894): 178–81.

————. "Notas para la historia de las ciencias antropológicas en España." In *Congreso de Granada, 1911: Asociación Española para el Progreso de las Ciencias*. Madrid: Eduardo Arias, [1912].Hrdlicka, Aleš. "Preface." *American Journal of Physical Anthropology* 1, no. 1 (January–March, 1918): 1.

Juaristi, Victoriano. "Patología y tipo racial." *Actas y Memorias de la Sociedad de Antropología, Etnología y Prehistoria* 27 (1947): 96–102.

Juarros, César. "La emoción nomada: El pueblo neurósico." *La Raza: Revista Hispánica* 17, no. 203 (27 November 1930): n.p.

López de la Vega. "'La frenología." *Anfiteatro Anatómico Español* 1, no. 6 (15 April 1873): 71–72.

Maluquer y Salvador, J. "Escuela positivista penal." *Revista General de Legislación y Jurisprudencia* 36, no. 72 (1888): 265–66.

Mata, Pedro. "Cuestión médico-forense." *Revista General de Legislación y Jurisprudencia* 28 (1866): 335.

Morote, Luís. "El derecho penal: Capítulo de las ciencas naturales." *Revista General de Legislación y Jurisprudencia* 65 (1884): 451.

Moya, Miguel. "Angel Pulido." *El Liberal*, 23 June 1884, 2.

Nordau, Max. "Una sorpresa española." *La Nacion*, 11 June 1916.

"Notas Madrileñas." *El Adalid*, June 1884.

"Noticias." *Revista de las Prisiones* 3, no. 2 (9 January 1895): 30.

"A nuestros lectores." *La Raza Latina* 11, no. 21(15 January 1875): 1.

Olóriz y Aguilera, Federico. "El laboratorio de antropología de la Facultad de Medicina." *Revista Ibero-Americana de Ciencias Médicas* 1, no. 1 (March 1899) .

"La panorama humana." *La Raza: Revista Hispánica* (1930).

Pulido y Fernández, Ángel. "Una carta del Dr. Pulido." *El Liberal*, 19 December 1919, 4.

————. "El Dr. Max Nordau, ha fallecido." *Revista de la Raza* 9, no. 95 (January–February 1923): 19–21.

————. "Los informes períciales médicos en el juicio oral." *El Siglo Medico* 31, no. 1586 (18 May 1884): 305–7.

————. "La Sanidad Militar: Su importancia en la salud del Ejército y en la salud pública." *Revista de Sanidad Militar* 3, no. 2 (15 January 1909): 39.

————. "Los Sefarditas y nuestra acción en Marruecos." *El Imparcial*, 9 March 1920.

"Reforma del código penal." *El Liberal*, 8, November 1886, 2.

Ripley, William Z. "The Racial Geography of Europe." *Appleton's Popular Science Monthly*, February 1897, 456–58.

Rodríguez Sobrino, Matías. "La raza latina." *La Raza Latina* 1, no. 13 (13 July 1874): 4–6.

Ruíz Casaviella, Eulogio. "Martirologio Médico." *El Siglo Médico* 31, no. 1590 (15 June 1884): 382.

Salillas y Panzano, Rafael. "El alma y la cabeza del cuerpo." *Revista de Prisiones y de Policia* 6, no. 11(16 March 1898): 98–101.

————. "La antropología en el derecho penal." *Revista General de Legislación y Jurisprudencia* 36, no. 73 (1888): 603–29.

————. "El Capitan Clavijo." *España Moderna* 7, no. 79 (July 1895): 25–41.

————. "La casa como célula social." In *Congreso de Zaragoza de la Asociación para el Progreso de la Ciencias*, vol. 5. Section 4: Ciencias Sociales. Madrid: Eduardo Arias, 1909.

————. "Comunicación número 1: La reforma científica de la criminología." *Actas y Memorias de Sociedad Española de Antropología, Etnografía y Prehistoria* 1, no. 1 (2 January 1922): 33–35.

————. "La degeneración o el proceso willie." *España Moderna* 66 (June 1894): 70–96.

————. "Entre paréntesis: Los locos criminales." *El Liberal*, 20 November 1886, 2–3.

————. "El jurado médico y la causa Varela." *España Moderna* 62 (February 1894): 95.

"Servicio antropométrico." *Revista de las Prisiones* 3, no. 19 (15 May 1895): 301.

"El servicio antropométrico—Descubrimiento de un asesino." *Revista de Prisiones* 10, no. 3 (16 January 1902): 38.

Silvela, Luís. "Sección Legislativa." *Revista General de Legislación y Jurisprudencia* 70 (1870): 339–72.

Simarro, Luís. "Colegio de Francia, el curso de anatomía general de Mr. Ranvier." *Boletín de la Institución Libre de Enseñanza* 5 (19 January 1881).

————. "La Enseñanza superior en París: La Escuela de Antropología: Curso de Mr. Matías Duval." *Boletín de la Institución Libre de Enseñanza* 4 (3 December 1880).

"Sociedad Española de Antropología Etnografía y Prehistoria: Altas de socios en 1922–23." *Actas y Memorias de Sociedad Española de Antropología, Etnografía y Prehistoria* 2 (January 1923): 5.

"Sociedad Histológica Española: Boletín de las asociaciones científicas." *Revista Europea* 1 (22 March 1874): 4.

"Sueltos y Noticias." *Revista de las Prisiones* 3, no. 35 (15 September 1895): 522.

Torremocha Téllez, L. "Carta Abierta." *Revista de Sanidad Militar* 14, no. 303 (1 February 1900): 56.

Tubino, Francisco María. "De la unidad nativa del género humano o del parentesco por consanguinidad universal entre todas las razas de la especie humana, diseminadas por todas las regiones de la Tierra." *Revista de Antropología* 1 (1874): 51–52.

Unsigned editorial. *Revista de Antropología* 1 (1874): 75.

Contemporary Monographs

Antón y Ferrándiz, Manuel. *Antropología o la historia natural del hombre.* 1903. 2nd ed. Madrid: Sucesores de Rivadeneyra, 1927.

————. *Doctorado de Medicina: Conferencias de antropología dadas por el Catedrático de esta asignatura y tomadas taquigráficamente por el alumno E.F.* Madrid: Sánchez Covisa, 1892.

————. "Fernando Póo y el Golfo de Guinea, por Osorio." *Antropología* 15 (1891).

————. *Programa razonado de antropología.* Madrid: Imprenta de la Viuda de M. Minuesa de los Ríos, 1897. Association Culturelle Orientale Israélite de Paris. *Compte rendu de la fête en l'honneur de M. le Dr. Angel Pulido.* Paris: Imprimiere H. Elias, 1920.

————. *Razas y naciones de Europa: Discurso leído en la Universidad Central en la solemne inauguración del curso académico de 1895–1896. Catedrático de Antropología en la Facultad de Ciencias.* Madrid: Imprenta Colonial, 1895.

————. *Razas y tribus de Marruecos.* Madrid: Sucesores de Rivadeneyra, 1903.

Aranzadi, Telésforo de. *Etnografía: Razas negras, amarillas, y blanca: Lecciones de antropología.* Vol. 4 of *Lecciones de antropología.* 2nd ed. Madrid: Romo y Füssel, 1900.

————. *Etnología: Antropología filosófica y psicología y sociología comparadas.* Vol. 2 of *Lecciones de antropología.* 1893. 2nd ed. Madrid: Romo y Füssel, 1899.

————. *Problemas de etnografía de los vascos.* Paris: Paul Geuthner, 1907.

————. *El pueblo Euskaldun.* San Sebastián: Dipt. Gral. de Guipúzcoa, 1889.

————, and Luís de Hoyos Sáinz. *Un avance a la antropología de España.* Madrid: Est. Tipográfico de Fortanet, 1892.

————. *Etnografía: Sus bases, sus métodos y aplicaciones a España.* Madrid: Biblioteca Corona, 1917.

————. *Lecciones de antropología: Ajustada al programa del Catedrático Don Manuel Antón por los doctores Ara. y Hoyos: Antropología General.* Madrid: Imprenta y litografia de Los Huérfanos, 1894.Bernaldo de Quirós, Constancio. *Figuras delincuentes.* Madrid: n.p., 1907.

————. *Modern Theories of Criminality.* Translated by Alfonso de Salvio. Boston: Little, Brown, 1912.

Carpena, Fructuosa. *Archivos criminológicos.* Madrid: Impr. de V. Rico, [1914?].

————. *El hombre criminal: Asociación Española para el Progreso de las Ciencias, Congreso de Zaragoza.* Madrid: Imprenta Enrique Arias, 1909.

Castelar, Emilio. "Breve historia de la democracia española." In *Cuestiones políticas y sociales,* vol. 3. Madrid: A. De San Martín y Agustín Jubera, 1870.

Castro, Américo. *España en su historia: Cristianos, moros y judíos.* Buenos Aires: Editorial Losada, 1948.

El Conde de Gobineau [Arthur Comte d'Gobineau]. *Ensayo sobre las desigualdad de las razas humanas.* Translated by Francisco Susanna. Barcelona: Editorial Apolo, 1937.

Congreso de Zaragoza: Asociación Española para el Progreso de las Ciencias. Vol. 1, pt. 2. Madrid: Enrique Arias, [1909].

Costa, Joaquín. *Oligarquía y caciquismo.* 1902. Madrid: Ediciones de la Revista de Trabajo, 1975.

Esquerdo, [José María]. *Locos que no lo parecen.* Madrid: Ateneo de Internos, 1880.

Hoyos Sáinz, Luís de. *Una hoja para el estudio de la herencia en el hombre: Grupos sanguíneos y carácteres antropológicos.* Madrid: Laboratorio de Antropología Fisiológica, 1929.

————. *La raza vasca: Discurso inaugural de la Asociación Española para el Progreso de las Ciencias, San Sebastian.* n.p.: [1949].

————. *Técnica antropológica y antropología física.* 1893. 2nd ed. Madrid: Imp. del Asilo de Huérfanos del S.C. de Jesus, 1899.

————, and Telésforo de Aranzadi. *Unidades y constantes de la crania hispánica: Discurso presentado a la Asociación Española para el Progreso de la Ciencias, Congreso de Granada, 1911.* Madrid: Eduardo Arias, 1913.

Juarros, César. *Atalaya sobre el fascismo.* Madrid: M.a. Yagüe, 1934.

Letamendi, José de. *Discurso sobre la naturaleza y el origen del hombre.* Barcelona: Ramirez y Cía, 1867.

Maetzu, Ramiro de. *Defensa de la hispanidad.* Buenos Aires: Editorial Poblet, 1942.

Mariscal y García, Nicasio, and Joaquín Decref y Ruíz. *Discursos leídos en la Solemne Sesión Inaugural Celebrada el día 22 de enero de 1933 en la Academia Nacional de Medicina.* Madrid: Julio Cosano, 1933.

Menéndez y Pelayo, Marcelino. *Historia de los heterodoxos españoles.* 2nd ed. Madrid: Librería General de Victoriano Suárez, 1911.

———. *Historia de los heterodoxos españoles.* 1948. 4th ed. Madrid: Editorial Católica, 1986.

Olóriz y Aguilera, Federico. *Diario de la expedición antropológica a la Alpujarra en 1894.* Granada: Caja General de Ahorros de Granada, 1995.

———. *Distribución geográfica del índice cefálico en España deducida del examen de 8.368 varones adultos: Memoria presentada al Congreso Geográfico Hispano-Portugués-Americano, en sesion de 19 de Octubre de 1892.* Madrid: Imprenta del Memorial de Ingenieros, 1894.

———. *Manual técnica de anatomía.* Madrid: Editorial Cosmos, 1890.

———. *Morfología socialística: Morfología exterior del hombre aplicado a ciencias sociales.* Madrid: Enrique Teodoro, 1911.

———. *Recolección de cráneos para estudios antropológicos, Trabajo publicado en la Gaceta Médica de Granada.* Granada: Librería de Paulino Ventura Sabatel, 1884.

———. "Recolección de craneos para estudios antropológicos." *El Siglo Médico* 31, no. 1594 (13 July 1884): 444–46.

———. *La talla humana en España: Discursos leídos en la Real Academia de Medicina para la recepción pública del Académico Electo Ilmo. Sr. Dr. D. Federico Olóriz y Aguilera el día 24 de mayo de 1896.* Madrid: Nicolás Moya, 1896.

Ortega y Gasset, José. *El tema de nuestro tiempo.* 3rd ed. Madrid: Revista de Occidente, 1934.

Ovilo y Canales, Felipe. *La decadencia del ejército: Estudio de higiene militar.* Madrid: Imprenta del Hospicio, 1899.

———. *Discurso leído en la Sociedad Española de Higiene en la sesión inaugural del Curso Académico de 1898–1899: Consideraciones acerca de la higiene militar en España.* Madrid: Imprenta del Hospicio, 1899.

Pulido y Fernández, Ángel. *Actas y memorias de Sociedad Española de Antropología, Etnografía y Prehistoria* 1 (6 February 1922): 36.

———. *El cáncer comunista o la degeneración del socio-sindicalismo: Necesidad de su regeneración higiénica y moral.* Madrid: Casa Editorial de M. Núñez Samper, [1921].

———. *El Doctor Velasco.* Madrid: E. Teodoro, 1894.

———. *Españoles sin patria y la raza sefardí.* 1905. Facsimile ed. Granada: Universidad de Granada, 1993.

———. *Intereses nacionales: Los Israelitas Españoles y el idioma Castellano.* Madrid: Imp. Sucesores de Rivadeneyra, 1904.

———. *La medicina y los médicos (Mosáico de discursos, articulos, correspondencias, semblanzas, pensamientos . . .).* Prologue by Dr. José de Letamendi. Valencia: Librería de P. Aguilar, Caballeros, 1883.

————. *Mica: Homenaje a la mujer hebrea*. Madrid: Ibero-Africano-Americana, 1923.

————. *Relación de las clases médicas con las asociaciones cooperativas e industriales benéfico-sanitarias*. Madrid: Imprenta y Librería de Nicolás Moya, 1903.

————, and Pedro González Velasco. *Discurso leído en la apertura del Museo Antropológico y Escuela Libre del Dr. Velasco*. Madrid: Imp. Juan Aguado, 1875.

————, and Manuel Tolosa. *De carabanchel al paraíso: Recuerdos de un manicomio*. Madrid: Imprenta de Enrique Teodoro, 1882.

Real Academia Española. *Diccionario de la lengua castellana*. 12th ed. Madrid: Imprenta de los Sres. Hernando y Compañía, 1884.

Salillas y Panzano, Rafael. *La antropología en el derecho penal: Tema de discusion en la Sección de Ciencias Exactas, Físicas y Naturales del Ateneo de Madrid*. Madrid: Imprenta de la Revista de Legislación y Jurisprudencia, 1888.

————. *Hampa: El delincuente español o la antropología picaresca*. Madrid: Librería de Victoriano Suarez, 1898.

————. *Orígenes de una tragedia: Morral el anarquista*. Madrid: Librería de los Sucesores de Hernando, 1914.Sánchez de Toca, Joaquín. "Introducción." *AMSEAEP* 1, no. 1 (18 May 1921): 5–6.

Sánchez y Fernández, Luís. *El hombre español útil para el servicio de las armas y para el trabajo: Sus características antropológicas a los 20 años de edad*. Madrid: Imprenta Eduardo Arias, 1913.

Sergi, Giussepe. *Origine e diffusione della stirpe mediterranea*. Rome: Soc. Ed. Dante Alighieri, 1895.

Vallejo Nágera, Antonio. *La política racial del nuevo estado*. San Sebastián: Editorial Española, 1938.

SECONDARY SOURCES

Abellán, José Luís. "Una manifestación del modernismo: La acepción española de 'raza.'" *Cuadernos Hispanoamericanos* 553–54 (July–August 1996): 203–14.

Aguilar Fernández, Paloma. *Memory and Amnesia: The Role of the Spanish Civil War in the Transition to Democracy*. Translated by by Mark Oakley. New York: Berghahn Books, 2002.

Alonso Baquer, Miguel. *El ejército en la sociedad española*. Madrid: Ediciones del Movimiento, 1971.

Álvarez Chillida, Gonzalo. *El antisemitismo en España: La imagen del judío (1812–2002)*. Madrid: Marcial Pons, 2002.

Álvarez Junco, José. *Mater Dolorosa: La idea de España en el siglo XIX*. Madrid: Taurus, 2001.

Álvarez Peláez, Raquel. "Eugenesia y fascismo en la España de los años treinta." In *Ciencia y fascismo*, edited by Rafael Huertas and Carmen Ortiz. Madrid: Doce Calles, 1998.

Álvarez-Uría, Fernando. *Miserables y locos: Medicina mental y orden social en la España del siglo XIX*. Barcelona: Tusquets, 1983.

Álvarez-Uría, Fernando, and Julia Varela. *El Cura Galeote, Asesino del Obispo de Madrid-Alcalá*. Madrid: Ediciones La Piqueta, 1979.

Anderson, Benedict. *Imagined Communities*. 1983. London: Verso, 1991.

Andrade, Jaime de [Francisco Franco]. *Raza*. Madrid: Ediciones Numancia, 1942.

de Areilza, Enrique. *Epistolario*. Bilbao: Epistolario El Tilo, 1999.

Armegou, Monste, and Ricard Belis. *Las fosas del silencio: ¿Hay un Holocausto español?* Barcelona: Plaza y Janés/Televisió de Catalunya, 2004.

Aronsfeld, Caesar C. *The Ghosts of 1492*. Jewish Social Studies Series. New York: Columbia University Press, 1979.

Arquiola, Elvira. "Anatomía y antropología física en el positivismo español." *Asclepio* 33 (1981): 3–22.

———. "Broca y el positivismo en la antropología francesa." *Asclepio* 28 (1976): 51–92.

———. "Paul Topinard: Médico y antropólogo físico." *Asclepio* 30–31(1978–79): 41–44.

———. "Anatomía y antropología en la obra de Olóriz." *Dynamis: Acta Hispánica ad Medicinae Scientiarumque Historiam Illustrandam* 1 (1981): 165.

Ausejo Martínez, Elena. *Por la ciencia y por la patria: La institucionalización científica en España en el primer tercio del siglo XX*. Madrid: Siglo XXI de España Editores, 1993.

Avni, Haim. *Spain, the Jews and Franco*. Translated by Emanuel Shimoni. Philadelphia: Jewish Publication Society of America, 1982.

Balfour, Sebastian. *Deadly Embrace: Morocco and the Road to the Spanish Civil War*. Oxford: Oxford University Press, 2002.

———. *The End of the Spanish Empire*. Oxford: Oxford University Press, 1997.

———. "Spain and the Great Powers in the Aftermath of the Disaster of 1898." In *Spain and the Great Powers in the Twentieth Century*, edited by Balfour and Paul Preston. London: Routledge, 1999.

Balibar, Etienne, and Immanuel Wallerstein. *Race, Class and Nation: Ambiguous Identities*. London: Verso, 1991.

Ballbé, Manuel. *Orden público y militarismo y la España constitucional (1812–1983)*. Madrid: Alianza, 1983.

Banton, Michael. *Racial Theories*. Cambridge: Cambridge University Press, 1987.

Barkan, Elazar. *Retreat of Scientific Racism*. Cambridge: Cambridge University Press, 1991.

Baroja, Pío. *Obras completas*. Vol. 7. Madrid: Biblioteca Nueva, 1949.

Basabe Pardo, José María. *La población vasca en perspectiva biológica*. Lecture presented in honor of the retirement of the Catedrático of Anthropology. Servicio Editorial de la Universidad del País Vasco, 1984.

Bastos Ansart, Manuel. *De las Guerras Coloniales a la Guerra Civil*. Barcelona: Ediciones Ariel, 1969.

Bauman, Zygmunt. *Modernity and the Holocaust*. Ithaca: Cornell University Press, 1989.

Biagioli, Mario. "Science, Modernity and the 'Final Solution.'" In *Probing the Limits of Representation*, edited by Saul Friedländer. Cambridge: Harvard University Press, 1992.

Botrel, Jean-Francois, and Jean-Michel Desvois. "Las condiciones de la producción cultural." In *1900 en España*, edited by Serge Salaün and Carlos Serrano. Madrid: Espasa-Calpe, 1991.

Botti, Alfonso. *Cielo y dinero: El nacionalcatolicismo en España, 1881–1975*. Translated by Botti. Madrid: Alianza Editorial, 1992.

Boyd, Carolyn. *Historia Patria: Politics, History and National Identity in Spain 1875–1975.* Princeton: Princeton University Press, 1997.

———. *La política praetoriana en el reinado de Alfonso XIII.* Madrid: Alianza, 1990.

———. *Praetorian Politics in Liberal Spain.* Chapel Hill: University of North Carolina Press, 1979.

Bronfman, Alejandra. *Measures of Equality: Social Science, Citizenship and Race in Cuba, 1902–1940.* Chapel Hill: University of North Carolina Press, 2004.

Bunzl, Matti. "Franz Boas and the Humboldtian Tradition." In *Volksgeist as Method and Ethic,* edited by George Stocking. Madison: University of Wisconsin Press, 1996.

Burdiel, Isabel. "Myths of Failure, Myths of Success: New Perspectives on Nineteenth-Century Spanish Liberalism." *Journal of Modern History* 70, no. 4 (December 1998): 892–912.

Cacho Viu, Vicente. *La Institución Libre de Enseñanza.* 2 vols. Madrid: Ediciones Rialp, 1962.

Cañizares Esquerra, Jorge. *How to Write the History of the New World: Histories, Epistemologies, and Identities in the Eighteenth-Century Atlantic World.* Stanford: Stanford University Press, 2001.

———. "New World, New Stars: Patriotic Astrology and the Invention of Indian and Creole Bodies in Colonial Spanish America, 1600–1650." *American Historical Review* 104, no. 1(February 1999): 33–68.

Cardona, Gabriel. *El poder militar en la España en la España hasta la Guerra Civil.* Madrid: El Siglo Veintiuno, 1983.

Caro Baroja, Julio. *Los Judíos en la España moderna y contemporánea,* Vol. 3, pt 5. Madrid: Ediciones Arion, 1961.

———. *Razas, gentes y linajes.* Madrid: Revista de Occidente, 1957.

Carr, Raymond. *Spain: 1808–1975.* 2nd ed. Oxford: Clarendon Press, 1982.

Casanova, Julián, ed. *Morir, matar, sobrevivir: La violencia en la dictadura de Franco.* Barcelona: Critica, 2002.

Cirillo, Vincent J. *Bullets and Bacilli: The Spanish American War and Military Medicine.* New Brunswick, N.J.: Rutgers University Press, 2004.

Cleminson, Richard. *Anarchism, Science and Sex: Eugenics in Eastern Spain, 1900–1937.* Bern: Peter Lang, 2000.

Contreras, Jaime. "Aldermen and Judaizers, Criptojudaism, Counter-Reformation and Local Power." In *Culture and Control in Counter-Reformation Spain,* edited by Anne J. Cruz and Mary Elizabeth Perry. Minneapolis: University of Minnesota Press, 1992.

Conversi, Daniele. *The Basques, the Catalans and Spain.* Reno: University of Nevada Press, 1997.

Corominas, Joan, and José A. Pascual. *Diccionario crítico etimológico Castellano e Hispánico.* Madrid: Editorial Gredos, 1981.

Count, Earl W., ed. *This Is Race.* New York: Henry Schuman, 1950.

Dardé, Carlos. "La larga noche de la Restauración." In *El republicanismo en España, 1830–1975,* edited by Nigel Townsend. Madrid: Alianza Universidad, 1994.

Davies, Rhian. *La España moderna and Regeneración: A Cultural Review in Restoration Spain,* *1889–1914.* Cañada Blanch Monographs 5. Manchester: Manchester Spanish and Portuguese Studies, 2000.

Degler, Carl N. *Neither Black nor White: Slavery and Race Relations in Brazil and the United States.* Madison: University of Wisconsin Press, 1971.

Díez Medrano, Juan. *Divided Nations: Class, Politics, and Nationalism in the Basque Country and Catalonia.* Ithaca: Cornell University Press, 1995.

Díez Torre, Alejando R., et al., eds. *La ciencia española en Ultramar: Actas de las I Jornadas sobre "España y las expediciones científicas en América y Filipinas."* Aranjuez: Doces Calles, 1997.

Dikötter, Frank. "Race Culture: Recent Perspectives on the History of Eugenics." *American History Review* 103, no. 2 (April 1998): 467–78.

Doaks, Kevin. "What Is a Nation and Who Belongs? National Narratives and the Ethnic Imagination in Twentieth-Century Japan." *American Historical Review* 109, no. 2 (April 1997): 283–309.

Escudero, Maria A. "The Image of Latin America Disseminated in Spain by the Franco Regime." Ph.D. diss., University of California, San Diego, 1994.

Esteban Navarro, Miguel Angel. "De la esperanza a la frustracion, 1868–1873." In *El republicanismo en España, 1830–1977,* edited by Nigel Townsend. Madrid: Alianza Universidad, 1994.

Esteva Fabregat, Claudio. *El mestizaje en Iberoamérica.* Madrid: Editorial Alhambra, 1988.

Fernandez Rodríguez, María Dolores. *El pensamiento penitenciario y criminológico de Rafael Salillas.* Santiago de Compostela: Universidad de Compostela, 1976.

Ferrer, Ada. *Insurgent Cuba: Race, Nation and Revolution, 1868–1898.* Chapel Hill: University of North Carolina Press, 1999.

Fogarty, Richard, and Michaela Osborne. "Constructions and Functions of Race in French Military Medicine, 1830–1920." In *The Color of Liberty : Histories of Race in France,* edited by Sue Peabody and Tyler Stovall. Durham: Duke University Press, 2003.

Foster, George. *Culture and Conquest.* Chicago: Quadrangle Books, 1960.

Fox, E. Inman. *Ideología y política en las letras de fin de siglo.* Madrid: Espasa Calpe, 1988.

Foucault, Michel. *The Birth of the Clinic.* New York: Vintage, 1994.

Fraser, Ronald. *The Blood of Spain: An Oral History of the Spanish Civil War.* New York: Pantheon, 1986.

Frederickson, George. *Racism: A Short History.* Princeton: Princeton University Press, 2003.

Friedländer, Saul. *Nazi Germany and the Jews.* Vol. 1. New York: HarperPerennial, 1998.

Frye Jacobsen, Matthew. *Whiteness of a Different Color: European Immigration and the Alchemy of Race.* Cambridge: Harvard University Press, 1998.

Gasman, Daniel. *Haeckel's Monism and the Birth of Fascist Ideology.* New York: Peter Lang, 1998.

———. *The Scientific Origins of National Socialism.* New Brunswick, N.J.: Transaction, 2004.

Gibson, Mary. "Biology or Environment? Race and Southern "Deviancy" in the Writings of Italian Criminologists." In *Italy's "Southern" Question: Orientalism in One Country*, edited by Jane Schneider. Oxford and New York: Berg, 1998.

———. "The 'Female Offender' and the Italian School of Criminal Anthropology." *Journal of European Studies* 12 (1982): 155–65.

Gillette, Aaron. *Racial Theories in Fascist Italy*. London: Routledge, 2002.

Glick, Thomas. F. *Einstein in Spain: Relativity and the Recovery of Science*. Princeton: Princeton University Press, 1988.

———. *Islamic and Christian Spain in the Early Middle Ages: Comparative Perspectives on Social and Cultural Formation*. Princeton: Princeton University Press, 1979.

———. "Spain." In *The Comparative Reception of Darwinism*, edited by Glick. Chicago: University of Chicago Press, 1988.

Glick, Thomas F., and Oriol Pi-Sunyer. "Acculturation as an Explanatory Concept in Spanish History." *Comparative Studies in Society and History* 11, no. 2 (April 1969): 136–54.

de Gobineau, Arthur. *The Inequality of Human Races*. New York: Howard Fertig, 1999. Originally translated in 1915.

Goicoetxea Marcaida, Ángel. *Vida y obra de Telésforo de Aranzadi*. Salamanca: Ediciones de Salamanca, 1985.

Goldstein, Jan. *Console and Classify: The French Psychiatric Profession in the Nineteenth Century*. Cambridge: Cambridge University Press, 1987.

———. "Foucault among the Sociologists: The 'Disciplines' and the History of the Professions." *History and Theory* 23 (June 1984): 170–92.

González Calleja, Eduardo, and Fredes Limon Nevado. *La hispanidad como un instrumento de combate*. Madrid: CSIC, 1988.

González, Isidro. *El retorno de los Judíos*. Madrid: Nerea, 1991.

Goode, Joshua. "La contradicción como arma: Ortega y Gasset y el concepto español de la modernidad." *Foro Hispánico* 18, no. 18 (September 2000).

Gould, Stephen Jay. *Mismeasure of Man*. New York: Norton, 1981.

Grace Miller, Marilyn. *Rise and Fall of the Cosmic Race: The Cult of Mestizaje in Latin America*. Austin: University of Texas Press, 2004.

Granda Juesas, Juan Manuel. *Don Misael Bañuelos, Medicina, Antropología y Sociedad*. Valladolid: Universidad de Valladolid, 1987.

Granjel, Luis S. *La frenología en España*. Salamanca: Instituto de Historia de la Medicina, 1973.

Granjel, Luis S., and Gerardo Sánchez-Granjel Santander. *Cartas a Dorado Montero*. Salamanca: Europa, 1985.

Gray, Rockwell. *The Imperative of Modernity*. Berkeley and Los Angeles: University of California Press, 1989.

Greer, Margaret R., Walter D. Mignolo, and Maureen Quilligan, eds. *Rereading the Black Legend: the Discourses of Religious and Racial Difference in the Renaissance Empires*. Chicago: University of Chicago Press, 2007.

Gurr, Ted Robert, Peter N. Grabosky, and Richard C. Hula. *The Politics of Crime and Conflict: A Comparative History of Four Cities*. London: Sage, 1977.

Haller, John S. *Outcasts from Evolution: Scientific Attitudes of Racial Inferiority, 1859–1900.* Carbondale: Southern Illinois University Press, 1971.

Hannaford, Ivan. *Race: The History of an Idea in the West.* Washington, D.C.: Woodrow Wilson Center Press, 1996.

Harvey, Joy Dorothy. "Races Specified: Evolution Transformed: The Social Context of Scientific Debates Originating in the Société d'Anthropologie de Paris, 1859–1902." Ph.D. diss., Harvard University, 1983.

Headrick, Daniel R. *Ejército y política en España (1868–1898).* Madrid: Editorial Tecnos, 1981.

Heiberg, Marianne. *The Making of the Basque Nation.* Cambridge: Cambridge University Press, 1989.

Helg, Aline. "Race in Argentina and Cuba, 1880–1930: Theory, Policies and Popular Reaction." In *The Idea of Race in Latin America, 1870–1940,* edited by Richard Graham. Austin: University of Texas Press, 1990.

Herf, Jeffrey. *Reactionary Modernism: Technology, Culture and Politics in Weimar and the Third Reich.* Cambridge: Cambridge University Press, 1984.

Historia de un olvido: La expedición científica del Pacífico (1862–1865): Museo de América, diciembre 2003–mayo 2004. Madrid: Ministerio de Educación Cultura y Deporte, 2003.

Holguín, Sandie. *Creating Spaniards.* Madison: University of Wisconsin Press, 2002.

Hughes, H. Stuart. *Consciousness and Society.* Rev. ed. New York: Vintage Press, 1977.

Jacobson, Stephen. "A Mixture of Spaniards." *Times Literary Supplement,* 3 October 2005.

———. "Professionalism, Corporatism, and Catalanism: The Legal Profession in Nineteenth-Century Barcelona." Ph.D. diss., Tufts University, 1998.

Jensen, Geoffrey. *Irrational Triumph: Cultural Despair, Military Nationalism, and the Ideological Origins of Franco's Spain.* Reno: University of Nevada Press, 2002.

———. "The Peculiarities of 'Spanish Morocco': Imperial Ideology and Economic Development." *Mediterranean Historical Review* 20, no. 1 (June 2005): 81–102.

Jiménez Lucena, Isabel. "Medicina social, racismo y discuro de la desigualdad en el primer franquismo." In *Ciencia y fascismo,* edited by Rafael Huerta and Carmen Ortiz. Madrid: Doce Calles, 1998.

Jover Zamora, José María. *Realidad y mito de La Primera República.* Madrid: Espasa Calpe, 1991.

Juaristi, Jon. *El bucle melancólico: Historias de nacionalistas vascos.* Madrid: Espasa, 1997.

———. *El chimbo expiatorio.* Madrid: Espasa Calpe, 1999.

———. *El linaje de aitor.* 1987. Madrid: Taurus, 1998.

———. *Vestigios de Babel: Para una arqueología de los nacionalismos españoles.* Madrid: Siglo Veintiuno de España Editores, 1992.

Juliá, Santos. *Historias de las dos Españas.* Madrid: Taurus, 2004.

———, ed. *Víctimas de la Guerra Civil.* Madrid: Temas de Hoy, 1999.

Kaplan, Temma. "Luís Simarro and the Development of Science and Politics in Spain, 1868–1917." Ph.D. diss., Harvard University, 1969.

———. "Spanish Positivism." *Cuadernos Hispánicos de la Medicina y de la Ciencia,* no. 12 (1974).

Keene, Judith. "Review Article: Turning Memories into History in the Spanish Year of Historical Memory." *Journal of Contemporary History* 42, no. 4 (2007): 661–73.

Koepping, Klaus-Peter. *Adolf Bastian and the Psychic Unity of Mankind*. St. Lucia: University of Queensland Press, 1983.

Kolchin, Peter. *Unfree Labor: American Slavery and Russian Serfdom*. Cambridge: Harvard University Press, 1987.

Laín Entralgo, Pedro. *España como problema*. 2nd ed. Madrid: Aguilar, 1957.

Lemon, Alaina. "Without a Concept? Race as Discursive Practice." *Slavic Review* 60, no. 1 (Spring 2002): 54–61.

Lisbona, José Antonio. *El retorno a Sefarad*. Barcelona: Riopiedras Ediciones, 1993.

Lisón Tolosana, Carmelo. *Antropología social en España*. Madrid: Siglo XXI de España, 1971.

Litvak, Lily. *Latinos y Anglosajones: Orígenes de una polémica*. Barcelona: Puvill Editor, n.d.

López Morillas, Juan. *Hacia el '98*. Barcelona: Ediciones Ariel, 1972.

———. *The Krausist Movement in Spain*. Cambridge: Cambridge University Press, 1981.

López Piñero, José María, Luis García Ballester, and Pilar Faus Sevilla. "Las ciencias médicas en la España del siglo XIX." In *La ciencia en la España del siglo XIX*, edited by López Piñero. Madrid: Marcial Pons, 1992.

———. Introduction to *La ciencia en la España del Siglo XIX*, edited by López Piñero. Madrid: Marcial Pons, 1992.

———. *La introducción de la ciencia moderna en España*. Barcelona: Ediciones Ariel, 1979.

López Piñero, José María, et al. *Medicina y sociedad en la España del siglo XIX*. Madrid: Ediciones Rialp, 1964.

López Piñero, José María, Thomas F. Glick, Victor Navarro Brotóns, and Eugenio Portela Marco., eds. *Diccionario histórico de la ciencia moderna en España*. 2 vols. Barcelona: Ediciones Peninsula, 1983.

Lorcin, Patricia M. E. *Imperial Identities: Stereotyping, Prejudice and Race in Colonial Algeria*. London: I. B. Tauris, 1999.

———. "Imperialism, Colonial Identity, and Race in Algeria, 1830–1870: The Role of the French Medical Corps." *Isis* 90 (1999): 653–79.

Macmaster, Neil. *Racism in Europe*. London: Palgrave, 2001.

Maiocchi, Roberto. *Scienza italiana e razzismo fascista*. Scandicci: La Nuova Italia, 1999.

Marchand, Suzanne. *Down from Olympus: Archaeology and Philhellenism in Germany, 1750–1970*. Princeton: Princeton University Press, 1996.

Maristany, Luis. *El gabinete del Dr. Lombroso: Delincuencia y fin de siglo España*. Barcelona: Editoriales Anagrama, 1973.

Massin, Benoit. "From Virchow to Fischer: Physical Anthropology and 'Modern Race Theories' in Wilhelmine Germany." In *Volksgeist as Method and Ethic*, edited by George Stocking. Madison: University of Wisconsin Press, 1996.

Massons, José Ma. *Historia de la Sanidad Militar Española*. Vols. 1–4. Barcelona: Ediciones Pomares-Corredor, 1994.

Matilla, Valentín. "Cuatro secretarios perpetuos ejemplares de la Real Academia Academia Nacional de Medicina." *Anales de la Real Academia Nacional de Medicina* 98 (1981): 58.

Maurice, Jacques, and Carlos Serrano. *J. Costa: Crisis de la Restauración y populismo, 1875–1911*. Madrid: Siglo XXI Editores, 1977.

McGovern, William Montgomery. *From Luther to Hitler: The History of Fascist-Nazi Political Philosophy*. Boston: Houghton Mifflin, 1941.

Molina Aparicio, Fernando. *La tierra del martirio español*. Madrid: Centro de Estudios Políticos y Constitucionales, 2005.

Moritz Schwarcz, Lilia. *The Spectacle of the Races: Scientists, Institutions, and the Race Question in Brazil, 1870–1930*. Translated by Leland Guyer. New York: Hill and Wang, 1999.

Mörner, Magnus. *Race Mixture in the History of Latin America*. New York: Little, Brown, 1967.

Mosse, George. *Toward the Final Solution*. 1978. Madison: University of Wisconsin Press, 1985.

Nash, Mary. "Social Eugenics and Nationalist Race Hygiene in Early 20th Century Spain." *Journal of the History of European Ideas* 15, nos. 4–5 (August 1992): 741–48.

Netanyahu, Benzion. *The Origins of the Inquisition in Fifteenth Century Spain*. New York: Random House, 1995.

Nirenberg, David. *Communities of Violence: Persecution of Minorities in the Middle Ages*. Princeton: Princeton University Press, 1996.

Nordau, Anna, and Maxa Nordau. *Max Nordau: A Biography*. New York: Nordau Committee, 1943.

Núñez Escabó, Manuel. *Manuel Sales y Ferré: Los orígenes de la sociología en España*. Madrid: Edicusa, 1976.

Núñez Ruíz, Diego. *La mentalidad positiva en España*. Barcelona: Tucar Ediciones, 1975.

Nye, Robert. *Crime, Madness and Politics in Modern France: The Medical Concept of National Decline*. Princeton: Princeton University Press, 1984.

Órtiz García, Carmen. *Luís de Hoyos Sáinz y la antropología Española*. Madrid: CSIC, 1987.

Otis, Laura. *Organic Memory: History and the Body in the Late Nineteenth and Early Twentieth Centuries*. Lincoln: University of Nebraska Press, 1994.

Pagden, Anthony. *The Fall of Natural Man*. Cambridge: Cambridge University Press, 1982.

Pan-Montojo, Juan. Introduction to *Más se perdió en Cuba*, edited by Pan-Montojo. Madrid: Alianza Editorial, 1998.

Pardo Bazán, Emilia. *The White Horse and Other Stories*. Lewisburg: Bucknell University Press, 1993.

París, Carlos. "El pensamiento de Unamuno y la ciencia positiva." *Arbor* 22, no. 77 (May 1952): 11–23.

Pascoe, Peggy. "Miscegenation Law and Ideologies of 'Race' in Twentieth-Century America." *Journal of American History* (June 1996): 44–69.

Payne, Stanely. *Falange: A History of Spanish Fascism*. Stanford: Stanford University Press, 1961.

———. *Fascism: Comparison and Definitions*. Madison: University of Wisconsin Press, 1981.

———. *The Franco Regime: 1936–1975*. Madison: University of Wisconsin Press, 1987.

———. *History of Fascism, 1914–1945*. Madison: University of Wisconsin Press, 1995.

———. *Politics and the Military in Modern Spain*. Stanford: Stanford University Press, 1967.

Pick, Daniel. *Faces of Degeneration: A European Disorder*. Cambridge: Cambridge University Press, 1989.

Piedra, José. "Literary Whiteness and the Afro-Hispanic Difference." In *The Bounds of Race*, edited by Dominick LaCapra. Ithaca: Cornell University Press, 1991.

Pike, Frederick B. *Hispanismo, 1898–1936: Spanish Conservatives and Liberals and Their Relations with Spanish America*. Notre Dame: University of Notre Dame Press, 1971.

Preston, Paul. "The Answer Lies in the Sewers: Captain Aguilera and the Mentality of the Francoist Officer Corps." *Science and Society* 68, no. 3 (Fall 2004): 277–312.

———. *Franco*. New York: Basic Books, 1994.

———. *The Politics of Revenge*. London: Unwin Hyman, 1990.

———. *The Spanish Civil War*. London: Grove Press, 1986.

Primo de Rivera, José Antonio. *The Spanish Answer*. Madrid: Artes Gráficas Ibarra, 1964.

Proctor, Robert. "From *Anthropologie* to *Rassenkunde* in the German Anthropological Tradition." In *Bones, Bodies, Behavior: Essays on Biological Anthropology*, edited by George Stocking. History of Anthropology Series no. 5. Madison: University of Wisconsin Press, 1988.

———. *Racial Hygiene: Medicine under the Nazis*. Cambridge: Harvard University Press, 1988.

Puig-Samper, Miguel. *Crónica de una expedición romántica al Nuevo Mundo*. Madrid: CSIC, 1988.

Puig-Samper, Miguel Ángel, and Andrés Galera. *La antropología española del siglo XIX*. Madrid: Instituto Arnau de Vilanova, CSIC, 1983.

Puig-Samper, Miguel Ángel, and Consuelo Naranjo Orovio. "Ciencia, racismo, y sociedad." *Asclepio* 15, no. 2 (1988): 21.

Pulido Martín, Ángel. *El Doctor Pulido y su época*. Madrid: F. Domenech, 1945.

Radcliff, Pamela. *From Mobilization to Civil War*. Cambridge: Cambridge University Press, 1996.

Ramsden, H. *The 1898 Movement in Spain*. Manchester: Manchester University Press, 1974.

Rein, Raanan. *In the Shadow of the Holocaust and the Inquisition*. Portland, Ore.: Frank Cass, 1997.

Richards, Michael. "Spanish Psychiatry c. 1900–1945: Constitutional Theory, Eugenics, and the Nation." *Bulletin of Spanish Studies*, 81, no. 6 (September 2004): 823–48.

———. *A Time of Silence: Civil War and the Culture of Repression in Franco's Spain, 1936–1945*. Cambridge: Cambridge University Press, 1998.

Riera, Juan. "Letamendi y Turró: Romanticismo y positivismo en la medicina catalana del siglo XIX." *Asclepio* 17 (1965): 117–53.

Ringrose, David. *Spain, Europe and the "Spanish Miracle," 1700–1900*. Cambridge: Cambridge University Press, 1996.

Rodrigue, Aron. *French Jews, Turkish Jews: The Alliance Israélite Universelle and the Politics of Jewish Schooling in Turkey, 1860–1925*. Bloomington: University Press of Indiana, 1990.

Romero de Tejada, Pilar. *Un templo a la ciencia*. Madrid: Ministerio de Cultura, 1992.

Romero Maura, Joaquín. *La rosa del fuego*. Madrid: Alianza Universidad, 1989.

Ross, Dorothy, ed. *Modernist Impulses in the Human Sciences 1870–1930*. Baltimore: Johns Hopkins University Press, 1994.

Ruse, Michael. *The Darwinian Revolution: Science Red in Tooth and Claw*. Chicago: University of Chicago Press, 1979.

Russell, P.E. "The Nessus-Shirt of Spanish History." *Bulletin of Spanish Studies* 36 (1959): 219–25.

Sánchez Gómez, Luis Ángel. "Contextos y práctica de la antropología 'oficial' en los fascismos ibéricos." In *Ciencia y fascismo*, edited by Rafael Huertas y Carmen Ortiz. Madrid: Doce Calles, 1997.

Sánchez Martín, Rafael. "El epistolario (1886–1912) de Federico Olóriz (1855–1912)." Ph.D. diss., Universidad de Granada, 1979.

Scott, Joan Wallach. *Gender and the Politics of History*. New York: Columbia University Press, 1988.

Seco Serrano, Carlos. *Militarismo y civilismo en la España contemporánea*. Madrid: Instituto de Estudios Económicos, 1984.

Serrano, Carlos. "Conciencia de la crisis." In *Más se perdió en Cuba*, edited by Juan Pan-Montojo. Madrid: Alianza Editorial, 1998.

Serrano, Rafael. "En busca del Gen Rojo." *El Pais* (Madrid), 7 January 1996.

Sicroff, Albert A. *Les controverses des statuts de "pureté de sang" en Espagne du XVe au XVIIe siècle*. Paris: Didier, 1960.

Silverman, Deborah. *Art Nouveau in Fin de Siècle France*. Berkeley and Los Angeles: University of California Press, 1989.

Smith, Anthony. *The Ethnic Origins of Nations*. Oxford: Blackwell, 1986.

Stallaert, Christiane. *Ni una gota de sangre impura*. Barcelona: Circulo de Lectores, 2006.

Stepan, Nancy. *The Hour of Eugenics: Race, Gender and Nation in Latin America*. Ithaca: Cornell University Press, 1992.

———. *The Idea of Race in Science: Great Britain, 1800–1960*. Hamden, Ct.: Archon Books, 1982.

Sternhell, Ze'ev. *Neither Right nor Left*. Translated by David Maisel. Berkeley and Los Angeles: University of California Press, 1987.

Stocking, George. "The Idea of Race in the American Social Sciences." Ph.D. diss., University of Pennsylvania, 1960.

———. *Race, Culture, and Evolution*. 1968, Chicago: University of Chicago Press, 1982.

———. *Victorian Anthropology*. New York: Free Press, 1987.

Sweet, James. "The Iberian Roots of American Racist Thought." *William and Mary Quarterly* 54, no. 1 (January 1997): 143–66.

Tannenbaum, Frank. *Slave and Citizen*. New York: Knopf, 1947.

Taylor, Paul C. "Appiah's Uncomplete Argument: W.E.B. Du Bois and the Reality of Race." *Social Theory and Practice* 26, no. 1 (Spring 2000): 103–28.

Tone, John Lawrence. *War and Genocide in Cuba, 1895–1898*. Chapel Hill: University of North Carolina Press, 2006.

"Trouble: Spain and Race." *Economist*, 24 July 1999, 27.

Túñon de Lara, Manuel. "Grandes corrientes culturales." In *Los orígenes culturales de la II República*, edited by José Luis García Delgado. Madrid: Siglo XXI de España, Editores, 1993.

Turrado Vidal, Martín. *Estudios sobre historia de la policía*. Vols. 1–2. Madrid: Ministerio del Interior, 1991.

Ucelay da Cal, Enric. "The Hispanic Studies Ghetto." *Bulletin of the Society for Spanish and Portuguese Historical Studies* 19, no. 3 (Fall 1994): 11–15.

———. *El imperialismo Catalan*. Barcelona: Edhasa, 2003.

Ullman, Joan. *The Tragic Week: A Study of Anti-Clericalism in Spain.* Cambridge: Harvard University Press, 1968.

Unamuno, Miguel de. *Obras completas,* Vol. 4. Madrid: Escelicer, 1968.

———. *Recuerdos de Niñez y de Mocedad.* 5th ed. Madrid: Espasa-Calpe, 1958.

Urry, James. "Englishmen, Celts and Iberians: The Ethnographic Survey of the United Kingdom." In *Functionalism Historicized: Essays on British Social Anthropology,* edited by George W. Stocking. Madison: University of Wisconsin Press, 1984.

Varela Ortega, José. *Los amigos políticos: Partidos, elecciones y caciquismo en la Restauración (1875–1900).* Madrid: Alianza, 1977.

Villacorta Baños, Francisco. *El Ateneo Científico, Literario y Artística de Madrid (1885–1912).* Madrid: CSIC, 1985.

———. *Burguesía y cultura: Los intelectuales españoles en la sociedad liberal, 1808–1931.* Madrid: Siglo Veintiuno de España, editores, 1980.

Vinyes, Ricard, Montse Amengou, and Ricard Belis. *Los niños perdidos del franquismo.* Barcelona: Plaza y Janés, 2002.

Wade, Peter. *Race and Ethnicity in Latin America.* London: Pluto Press, 1997.

Weber, Eugen. *Peasants into Frenchmen.* Stanford: Stanford University Press, 1976.

Weindling, Paul. *Health, Race and German Politics between National Unification and Nazism, 1870–1945.* Cambridge: Cambridge University Press, 1989.

Weitz, Eric D. "Racial Politics without the Concept of Race: Reevaluating Soviet Ethnic and National Purges." *Slavic Review* 60, no. 1 (Spring 2002): 1–29.

Winant, Howard. "Race and Racism: Overview." In *New Dictionary of the History of Ideas,* edited by Maryanne Horowitz, vol. 5. Detroit: Scribner's, 2005.

Wohl, Robert. *The Generation of 1914.* Cambridge: Harvard University Press, 1979.

Yerushalmi, Yosef. *Assimilation and Racial Anti-Semitism: The Iberian and the German Models.* Leo Baeck Memorial Lecture no. 26. New York: Leo Baeck Institute, 1982.

Young, Robert J. C. *Colonial Desire: Hybridity in Theory, Culture and Race.* London: Routledge, 1995.

Zimmermann, Andrew. *Anthropology and Anti-Humanism in Imperial Germany.* Chicago: University of Chicago Press, 2001.

Index